TO
Claire
lots of love
Nan Doll
xxx

GU01019470

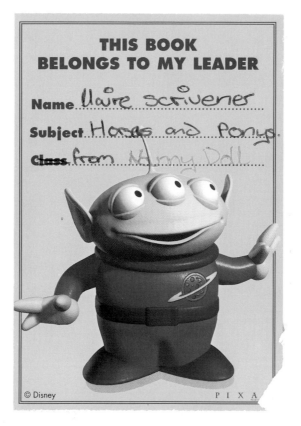

**THIS BOOK
BELONGS TO MY LEADER**

**Name** Claire Scrivener

**Subject** Horses and Ponys.

**Class** from Nanny Doll

© Disney                    P I X A

# YOU AND YOUR PONY

# YOU
# AND YOUR PONY

**Pepper Mainwaring Healey**

**SOUTH BRUNSWICK AND NEW YORK: A.S. BARNES AND COMPANY**
**LONDON: THOMAS YOSELOFF LTD**

© 1977 by Elsie (Pepper) Mainwaring Healey

A. S. Barnes and Co., Inc.
Cranbury, New Jersey 08512

Thomas Yoseloff Ltd
Magdalen House
136-148 Tooley Street
London SE1 2TT, England

**Library of Congress Cataloging in Publication Data**

Healey, Pepper Mainwaring, 1923-
 You and your pony.

 Bibliography: p.
 Includes index.
 1. Ponies. 2. Horse-training. I. Title.
SF315.H38    1976    636.1'6    75-5173
ISBN 0-498-01671-4

PRINTED IN THE UNITED STATES OF AMERICA

TO MY MOTHER AND FATHER

# CONTENTS

# PREFACE

This book is for everyone interested in ponies, whether from the riding or the schooling point of view. Since ponies, like people, come in all sizes, it is for adult as well as junior riders.

It is written not only for beginners who have a pony and don't know what to do next, but also for riders with some experience in riding a schooled horse but little or no experience in starting and training a young "green" pony.

It is a book for both parents and children. Ponies are ideal for a family, and you'll get more fun out of your pony—and even your family!—if you all share in working him.

To those parents who don't know the first thing about riding and suddenly find themselves responsible for helping and supervising young riders: be of good cheer! You don't have to be a horseman to help your children train their pony. You do have to be interested, patient, willing to spend some time regularly, and, if you want them to have fun with safety, prepared to keep an eagle eye on what goes on.

This book is also for the boy or girl who rides a little and longs for a pony of his own but sees no hope of his dream coming true. If you live in the city, or your yard is too small, or if your parents cannot afford a pony, don't give up. I was one of you, but eventually my dream came true. Until your dream comes true, do what I did: ride all you can, read all you can, learn all you can about the world of ponies and horses; if the opportunity arises to have a pony of your own or to help with someone else's pony, you will be ready. The training suggestions in this book can be put to practical use even in occasional riding.

*You and Your Pony* is not theoretical. It is based on years of practical day-to-day experience in teaching children to ride ponies and training ponies to be ridden.

High Hickory, where this riding and training goes on, is our "backyard." It is a wooded hilltop in a western suburb of Boston, five minutes' drive from Longfellow's Wayside Inn. Despite encroaching developments, there is still good riding cross-country through woods and fields, but roads and traffic are an increasing problem. As a family we have cleared heavily wooded land for pasture and paddocks and struggled with rocks to put up fencing for the ponies and sheep. (We're far from being farmers; the sheep are there so that we can work our Border Collies.)

There are four of us: Dave, a sea-captain, master of a tanker; Eric, twenty-one and a senior in college; Robin, now fifteen; and me, Pepper. As the two children grew, so did our collection of ponies: Nina, Tuffy, Top Rail Stardust, her filly High Hickory Galaxy, Farnley Ogwen, Peggy, Lutine Bell. . . . More and bigger ponies and acquisition of a Thoroughbred filly and a Quarter Horse meant more and bigger stalls. We started with a simple shed built entirely by our own labor from reclaimed lumber and now have several stalls.

Every week four or five youngsters—they call themselves "Pony Pals"—come here for lessons. We try to give each one the sort of experience and knowledge he would have if he had a pony of his own.

Our goal at High Hickory is "day-to-day fun with safety and a little bit of glory too"—at occasional shows and Pony Club rallies, dressage competitions and horse trials.

If not theories, we do have one cardinal rule: Never ask a pony to do anything you cannot make him do. All riding is based on control of a horse's superior strength by man's superior brain. If it comes to a tug-of-war, your pony can always win.

Remember, a pony has a one-track mind, and we take advantage of this to train him. We create a painful or unpleasant sensation; we stop when the pony responds. The pain may be as mild as the pressure of your hand on the pony's flank to push his rear away from you or it may be as severe as a jerk with a lead chain over a sensitive nose, or a jab with the spurs.

Ideally, you never have to resort to severity with your pony. Ideally, through a process of association he soon responds to the slightest signal.

We feel strongly that kindness pays off. In the fifteen years of schooling children and ponies covered by this book a good many ribbons and championships were obtained. Neither a crop nor spurs were ever used. Too many children are plopped aboard ponies and handed a crop, as if that were the secret of riding and the only way of making a horse obey. I suggest that if a crop is necessary as a regular aid to get a pony to do what is wanted, something is missing in his schooling. (If this is your case, those of you with schooled ponies may find the book helpful as well as those of you with green ones. It is often more difficult to reschool or break a pony of bad habits from poor training than to start from scratch with an untrained one.) Just remember, every time you ride your pony, green or "finished", you are schooling him: giving him a good or a bad education.

Twenty-three hundred years ago an ancient Greek who knew a lot about horses wrote: "See to it that the colt be kind, used to the hand, and fond of man." Xenophon's advice still holds true today, and it is what I shall stress in this book on working with a pony.

# ACKNOWLEDGMENTS

Several chapters of *You and Your Pony* have appeared, in considerably different form, in *Horsemen's Yankee Pedlar; Northeast Horseman, The Welsh News* (now *The Welsh Pony World*); *Green Mountain Horse Association Magazine;* and *The Chronicle of the Horse;* and I thank the editors of those magazines. Quotation from the poem, "The Centaur" by May Swenson is printed by permission of the author as originally appearing in *To Mix with Time*, New and Selected Poems, copyright © by May Swenson and Charles Scribner's Sons, 1963. Lines from ME AND MY BIKE by Dylan Thomas (first read at High Hickory in *Esquire Magazine*) are quoted through the kindness of Sydney Box of Australia. Mr. Box graciously penned his permission on his gift of a rare first edition of the poet's work (A Triton Book, © copyright by Triton Publishing Co., Ltd.) charmingly illustrated by Leonara Box. I thank them all.

Photographs are by the author, by Captain Dave Healey, or by Dr. Marion Mainwaring with these exceptions: p. 74 top, Kenny Alden; p. 219, Betty Bassett; p. 224, Thom Chesser; p. 33 bottom, p. 176, p. 220, Stacy Holmes; p. 27, Warren Patriquin; p. 109 top, p. 114, p. 234, Barrie Schwartz; p. 35 top, Elmer Stimets; p. 222, Margo Ward; and p. 26, p. 198 top, Ulrike Welsch. Several by Ms. Welsch and Mr. Patriquin appeared originally in feature articles by Virginia Bohlin and Betty Curtis in *The Boston Sunday Herald Traveler*. Kenny Alden has given photographic assistance. Drawings are by Robin Healey.

I thank H.P. Gill, D.V.M., for reading the chapter on "Your Pony and His Health" and Mrs. Alexander F. Turner and others of the Framingham Library for their friendly cooperation. I am grateful to my sister Marion Mainwaring, who read the manuscript from its earliest stages, and to Professor Raymond F. Bosworth, whose creative writing course has been a lasting inspiration to me and to so many other Simmons College students.

I should like to express my appreciation to Mr. and Mrs. James Dennison, Mr. and Mrs. Edward Dow, Mrs. Gardiner H. Fiske, Dr. Robert E. Gross, Mr. and Mrs. Henry Hall, Mr. and Mrs. George Harrington, the staff of Don Jackson and Sons, Mr. and Mrs. Alvin Levin and their daughters Kathy, Bara, and Jennifer, Messrs John and Tom Markinac, Peter Nelson, D.V.M., Mr. and Mrs. Eugene O'Donnell, Mrs. Frank Paine, Joseph Seremeth, D.V.M., Dr. and Mrs. William Temby, the indispensable Eric Healey and Captain Dave; the Robert Carney's, the Robert Montgomery's, the James McCracken's, Mr. Billy Begg, Mr. Benjamin Pike, Miss Hannah Weir, and Mrs. Martin H. Wittenborg, M. Jean-Pierre Berthélemy du Bucq, Président of La Fédération Française des Éleveurs de Poneys, and M. J-H. Turgis, Président of Le Poney Club de France.

Very important to the book are the children and young people who have shared Pony Pal fun and lessons, the Clinics for Young Horsemen, and the Pony Camp at High Hickory: Julie and Andrew Arvedon, Alicia Carroll, Susan Chandler, Eric Healey, Betsey Hilborn, Meri-Jo Kahn, Tracy Levenson, Barbara Levitor, Andy McArthur, Amy and Julie MacDonald, Scott and Alan Mainwaring, Shirley Maxwell, Susie Ocher, Cecily and Monica O'Donnell, Donna, Karen, and Krista Reed, Jane Schelong, Cathy, Regina, Anne, and Mary Silver, Diane Stacie, Kathy Sutton, Lisa Tennebaum, our special Kate Temby, Jim and Mary Tolland, Bailey

Van Hook, Debby Van Vleck, and Sue Varisco, Alice Levy, Dana Ricciardelli, Wheet twins Diane and Denise, Marlaine Carr, and Leslie Bartlett. I thank them, as well as the groups who come for Visits with a Pony from the Learning Centre for Deaf Children in Framingham (Libbie Bake, Joseph Baril, Paul Bratica, Jeannette Brennan, Jeannette Britto, Thomas Brown, Arsenio Chaves, Susan Collins, Jacqueline Correa, Sue Cotton, Lynn Cummings, William DeCosta, Lisa Flaherty, Mark Glynn, Harry Greenlaw, Bruce Harrington, Darlene Hilliard, Christopher Huggins, Dermot Keohane, James Kisiday, Alice Kopas, Joseph Kopas, Sean Krasinski, Mark Laspesa, Steven Manuel, Mary McCaffrey, Ann Meehan, Kenneth Osborne, Annette Posell, Janet Pruett, Brian Quinlan, John Raimondi, Stephen Regan, Theresa Robinson, Jill Shulman, Jill Syper, Mark Vose, Gordon White, Linda Yenkin) and the many visitors who have come for Pony Parties in support of public television (WGBH, Boston).

Special mention must be made of Robin Healey, who, starting at the age of four, has trained four green ponies and a green Quarter Horse to ribbons and championships: Garrison House Lane's Tuffy (four to eight), Top Rail Stardust (eight to ten), High Hickory Galaxy (nine to eleven), Lutine Bell (ten on), and now Baldy Suprise (fourteen on). Robin has schooled along the lines advocated in this book and her work is used throughout as illustration.

# YOU AND YOUR PONY

# 1

# ADVANTAGES OF A PONY

## PONY VERSUS HORSE

WHY A PONY? WHY NOT A HORSE?

Perhaps this is not too soon to touch boldly on this old but persistent controversy—the pony versus horse issue.

Pro-horse often equates with professional horseman. It did in my case. When I was an active professional no one could have been surer that horses, even for the small rider, were the answer. But no one can be more pro-pony than I am now, as the result of my "mother of young riders" teaching years.

Admittedly, for the summer camp, school, or local stables that have to fit hundreds of riders of all sizes, shapes, ages, and abilities to a limited string of schooled mounts, a horse is the necessary choice. Individual "backyard" owners are not handicapped by such considerations. They should reflect on the following points.

Why do people argue that a youngster should begin on a horse rather than a pony? Because they do not know today's ponies!

What are their arguments?

The first is: "Any pony is too much pony (i.e., too spirited) for anyone small enough to ride him, and too small for anyone experienced enough to ride him."

With a miniature breed of pony this may be so. (Exceptions like our sweet thirty-nine-inch Shetland Tuffy exist), but then not many tiny youngsters are capable, in terms of physical, mental, or emotional maturity, of independent riding off the lead line. Even for the tiny child starting out on the lead line the smaller ponies of many breeds—Welsh, New Forest, Dartmoor—are narrow enough to be in proportion to the child rider but big enough, sturdy enough, and "horse-gaited" enough for the older child or adult rider to mount for schooling or pleasure.

For the wee beginner, nothing is so good as a gentle, aged[1] pony. I'd like to see the lead-rein classes in horse shows filled with ponies. I don't like the spectacle of a tiny child, legs spread beyond any possible comfort or safety, being taken around the ring on a horse. One stumble for the child-fly on that rocking elephantine back could result in a spill that would forever end any desire to ride.

As a parent who has spent hours on "the other end" of a lead-line, I can vouch for the advantages of a pony to the leader, also, in terms of speed, smoothness, and the pleasure of having the child's head close to mine. Many's the pause we have made in the woods, with one arm around a youngster's waist, the other on the lead-rein pony's neck—the whole world of sharing is much closer. Branches overhead and flowers underfoot are equally near for rider and leader. Trusty lead-line ponies have made it possible for us to include a two-year-old or a four-year-old on rides with older children or on otherwise too-long hikes with adults—and have most happily solved the baby-sitter problem on those occasions!

If a child is beyond the lead-rein stage, it is all the more important for him to be mounted on a gentle, reliable pony of suitable proportions, rather than on

1. This does not mean antiquated. See the section on Age in Chapter 2.

**15**

Pony or horse? The child's-eye view. David gravitates towards something closer to his own size.

Tiny Tuffy easily keeps pace with large pony Peggy. A leadline affords safety with a feeling of independence for a small rider.

16

a horse, so that his legs can grip something besides saddle skirts. Furthermore, many a horse is too much horse for a small rider. The issue here boils down to schooling, disposition, and temperament—and the importance of putting a child on a mount suitable to that particular child, to that child's size, age, temperament, ability, or lack of ability. Here a pony with an affectionate disposition, intelligence, and willing response to its young owner wins out hands down.

Let's face it: the best of ponies may get a bad reputation because too many "unschooled" parents turn an unschooled child loose with an unschooled animal. Perhaps the most difficult silence I ever maintained was when I watched a neighbor taunt his timid nine-year-old son (who had never been on anything livelier than a bicycle!) into being put on an unbroken and unhandled two-year-old colt. Needless to say, this partnership did not work out. On the other hand, my daughter Robin—aggressive, athletic, already a beginning rider—moved on from thirty-year-old Nina and the lead line to her second pony, Tuffy, at four. While not broken to riding, Tuffy had been handled since birth and having a child on her back was just one more schooling progression that she accepted with trust and confidence. When we chose Top Rail Stardust, a three-year-old filly who never had anyone on her back, she had a sweet disposition and wise handling from her Welsh breeders. Her reaction to Robin's being on her back was one of interest and curiosity, utterly free of alarm. In this case, a child with riding experience was handling a pony under knowledgeable supervision, and the partnership of child and pony worked out very happily.

Quite aside from the riding/horsemanship aspect of the pony versus horse controversy is another consideration that "sells" the pony for a child to me (a critical horseman-parent). In a day when we buy tricycles by size, two-wheel training bikes, child-size kitchen sets, junior bows for archery, children's skis, and junior tennis rackets, all in proportion to our youngsters' height and weight, we can hardly fail to recognize how much more suitable and in proportion a well-schooled pony is for a child.

There is an affection, a rapport, possible only with a pony. Perhaps this loving child and pony relationship can exist only under a certain size or age, but the rapport between the pony and his young owner certainly does exist.

A pony opens up a whole world of casual fun to the

child that the horse cannot. Barn chores and grooming are within a child's strength and reach, and the magnitude of the job to be done (currying, for instance, or cleaning out a stall) is in proportion to his physical endurance and his interest span. Saddles and bridles can be put on easily and, often being smaller, are easier to handle.

**A world of casual fun: a four-year-old's backyard picnic with Border Collie Fling and Shetland Tuffy.**

One vital consideration: mounting and dismounting aren't major undertakings. Once aboard, the pony rider is reassuringly close to *terra firma* not only physically but psychologically. The child who goes for a ride on his pony is more likely to hop off and on along the way and return with his knapsack full of devil's paint brush, pine cones for a Christmas wreath, or an odd prized stone from the brook, than

**17**

a child who feels that dismounting and mounting his horse is more effort than any other part of his ride.

A pony is safer. For example, the child can easily slide to the ground. He can easily dismount at a walk or a trot, at a canter if need be, and many a spill can be avoided by a deliberate "action dismount." Such a worthwhile skill as riding without stirrups is more readily mastered if dismounting is a casual affair. Many times "falling off" is prevented by "slipping off"; and what would be painful results with a horse are avoided with a pony.

Parents tend to forget what the world was like from a child's "adult's-elbow-level" point of view, or perhaps were fully grown when they learned to ride. At eight, Robin, who had ridden on smaller ponies since she was two, was very conscious that her 12.2 Welsh pony was "big." Yet before we chose this little pony we faced constant urging to buy her a horse. (One Hunt Club instructor had "the ideal mount": a 15.3 horse.) However, at High Hickory we apply the same theory in picking a mount for a child that we do in buying skates or ski boots: we want them to fit now. We don't want them outgrown immediately, but we are not going to select something too big for present use just for a child to "grow into." Until a child is grown, shoe sizes "last" a year; ponies seem to last three or four—but we expect—and hope—that a youngster will outgrow a pony in terms of riding ability as well as in physical size.

Perhaps the pony versus horse controversey betrays a certain provinciality on the part of the American pro-horse contingent. In any country other than the United States, the accepted mount for a child (even for adults in pony-trekking regions) is a pony—ça va sans dire. Perhaps the urge to put a small child on a big horse ties in with our delight in big cars and double outboard motors. Even among pony devotees, the pressure is felt to move a child "up" before a pony is really outgrown.

Much of the prejudice against ponies comes, I believe, from people of my vintage who have not kept abreast of the improvement in the situation. With the fine work being done by many Pony Clubs, by many 4-H riding groups, and with the raising of riding standards in general, we have today many more well-schooled ponies than in my childhood. Furthermore, with the tremendous upsurge in pony ownership and the increased number of young riders keen to move up in ability (again as encouraged by Pony Club tests), there are more well-trained ponies available. The child who had to start on a horse can now start on a suitable schooled pony. Thus for every full-grown experienced rider there are probably one or two "passed on" ponies available to starting and progressing youngsters.

With pony breeders maintaining high standards so that good disposition and temperament combine with conformation and beauty, a wider world of fine registered purebreds and crossbreds[2] is open to discerning parents. The versatility of a pony such as the Welsh—its intelligent tractability as a backyard pony, its beauty and flash in the show ring, its joy as a driving pony, its surefootedness and innate "mountain pony sense" when hunting or riding cross-country, its native ruggedness that makes possible the simplest of stabling even in New England winters, its friendly reliability in a crowd of admiring children in the pony paddock—all these attributes enable a good pony to put finis to the controversy once and for all.

## TO BUY OR NOT TO BUY

Is owning a pony worth the time and effort and money involved? Does "a pony of your own" provide more than regular riding lessons at the local stable do?

Usually the decision to buy or not to buy is not made merely on the basis of practical possibility. True, there's that empty, fenced-in field, that extra stall, or that unused garden shed that would convert to a perfect pony barn. True, there's the Christmas bonus—not to mention the contents of the children's piggy bank, counted and recounted eagerly, almost as endlessly as the wish for "a pony of our own" is expressed. True, you would be no more tied down with a pony than you already are with a dog, a cat, three hamsters, a parakeet, six goldfish, and two children in school, but . . . does owning and riding a pony pay dividends?

My answer is an enthusiastic Yes! Your children as children and your family as a whole will benefit in countless tangible and intangible ways.

The point is not that riding is one of the most popular sports (though it is: its popularity is zooming), or that it is healthy fun for all ages. Riding is more than an "in" accomplishment or a passing amusement. Merely taking riding lessons at a stable

2. See Chapter 18, Pony Breeds.

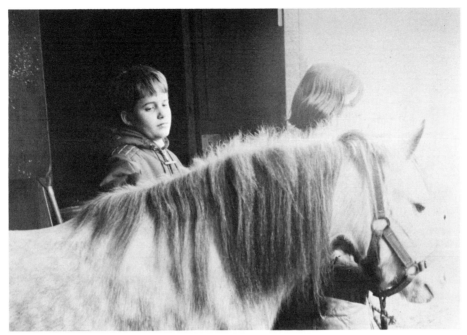

**So many children long for a pony of their own.**

is like studying piano without having an instrument at home.

Caring for a pony is as important as the actual riding of him. Personal responsibility for the care will develop self-confidence, self-discipline, and a sense of responsibility, in a child, and with a pony all requirements—stabling, tack, paddock, and upkeep—are in pony proportions. Work is at minimum when the child's free time is at maximum.

The self-confidence the child develops is sound self-confidence, for it is based on day-to-day development. A little experience with a pony shows the overeager, impetuous child that calmness and steadiness pay off, and helps the unsure child to a fairer evaluation of his own abilities. Many a youngster who is awkward with a tennis racket or a baseball bat, clumsy in ballet lessons, or tongue-tied in reading class, quickly masters the fundamentals of caring for a pony—and learns self-mastery. He may be able to lose his temper with playmates and to bully a cat or dog, but he soon learns that impatience or anger gets him no place with a pony. To get the desired results he must be calm and controlled. He soon learns that eventually (and usually sooner!) he gets what he wants by being patient and kind, while he may never accomplish his aim if he blows up.

Today all too many children lack the opportunity to develop the sense of responsibility that most

**Ponies are ideal for a family.**

children once had. The biggest responsibility some boys and girls have today is to empty the wastebaskets regularly. For many families, owning a pony provides the first chance for the children to be responsible for a living creature. It gives a youngster the opportunity to learn what it is like to have someone dependent on him for basic needs and well-being.

Probably none of us would make a child go without water for as many hours as he had forgotten to water his pony, as an old White Russian riding

**19**

master of mine once made his son. However, the child who is forbidden to ride or play with his pony because he has not proved dependable soon begs for another chance.

The fun of doing barn chores (among thousands of children with a passion for ponies these chores are actually regarded as a privilege!) is so great that every job is done to the best of the youngster's ability.

With the acceptance of responsibility comes self-reliance. Since he is dealing not with an inanimate object like a lacrosse stick or a canoe but with a live animal with a mind of its own, a child soon learns that he has to be ahead of his pony. He develops a sense of timing and rhythm and a physical coordination which many children (boys especially) find it hard to acquire in a dancing class or on a diving board.

Self-confidence, sportsmanship, self-reliance, responsibility—such lasting, far-reaching contributions make owning a pony "worth it." In buying a pony you are not paying a set price for a specified object. Rather you are making an investment in happiness, one that will pay dividends to you and your children.

# 2

# CHOOSING YOUR PONY

NOW TO FIND THE IDEAL PONY—IDEAL IN TERMS of you, your child, your riding aims. On these variables your choice will depend.

Do not expect to find the right pony immediately. Perhaps you will. More likely not. The more time given to your search the more satisfied you will be with your final selection. Allow six months to a year to find the right pony.

## THE SEARCH

If in the joy of the newly made decision to buy this sounds too much to bear, remember that the search itself will be exciting and rewarding, especially since your time will be spent on other pony-connected activities besides the search itself.

If you are a nonrider or a novice, the period of the search should certainly be spent in regular riding lessons from a competent instructor on a variety of schooled mounts. Before and after lessons, glean as much information on stable management as you can.

If you are moving up to a bigger mount, you will want a final period of pleasure from the pony you now have. If you must part with your present pony, you will need this time to find a suitable new owner.

Use these months of looking for your ideal pony to visit local Pony Club meetings and rallies, 4-H horse-project affairs, children's events in shows offering pony classes, and various breed shows or classes. Talk to horsemen, to riding instructors, to trainers, to children who already have ponies, to pony parents—they love to "talk ponies."

Spend these months boning up on pony lore. Go to the library; read everything you can on different breeds, on conformation and soundness, on stable care and on horsemanship, on both riding and training (see the lists at the end of this book for suggested material).

Very often children's fiction provides dense factual information and emphasizes points of pony-oriented sportsmanship and responsibility. The whole family can learn while enjoying these stories. For instance, a rapid adult reading of such juvenile fiction as *The Auction Pony* or *A Pony in the Kitchen* will make for more knowledgeable pony parents! Some favorite "horse and pony" stories are listed in Chapter 21, Reading and Riding.

Visit families who have ponies; go during barn chores, not just during riding time, so that you can see some of the work involved as well as the fun. Perhaps you will get a chance to curry or feed—or help clean tack.

Spend part of the period of the search preparing for your pony's arrival: shelter and fencing. Nothing elaborate; but don't wait till the pony is coming up your driveway to decide where he's going to live.

The more you look and read and talk, the more your ideal pony will crystalize in your mind and the more successful your search will be.

## ESTABLISHING YOUR CRITERIA

First of all: For whom is the pony intended? For one child? For several children of different ages, sizes, and ability levels? Is it a first pony, or a second, or a third? A green pony for an experienced rider to school? Do you want a show pony, a hunter, an all-round fun pony? Are you interested in riding, or driving, or jumping, or a combination of all three? Is the pony going to be handled by a beginning rider with horseman parents, by a beginning rider with nonhorseman parents, by an experienced rider with nonhorseman parents, or by an experienced rider with horseman parents? All these factors will affect your search for the ideal pony.

Here two important points should be raised. One: Is your estimate of your child's riding ability a valid one? Possibly your own riding experience is so slight that you mistake Pandora's "skill" as a passenger on a well-schooled riding hack for horsemanship. Perhaps you are so ardent a horseman that your idea of what less enthusiastic Tommy ought to have achieved is colored by your desire rather than by the realities. Time and again we see children of good riders start riding very young—and then not continue, because they were overmounted, expected to meet impossible standards, and pushed into an activity they really weren't ready for or didn't care about.

Far wiser to be casual about it when the tiny child's age limits the type of riding he can do, so that when he is mature enough to ride on his own with his peers he will still be interested. The four- or five-year-old who is a fine little horseman is still too young to ride without close adult supervision.

It may be worth obtaining an impartial evaluation of your child's riding ability—from another horseman, a 4-H leader, or a professional instructor. In the beginning at least, the seller of a pony cannot form an estimate of your youngster, but must take your word for his ability. If he shows his ponies mounted, it will be with his own rider up, one who is used to the pony and will show it to the seller's advantage. The pony that acts meek and mild under such an experienced rider may behave quite differently under a novice—your novice.

Is your evaluation of Tommy's or Pandora's enthusiasm, knowledge of horses, and pony-dreams accurate? While undoubtedly you as a parent will have the final say as to the choice of a pony, it goes without saying that you and your child should have similar aims so that the child will like the pony you choose.

Often a parent's choice is not the child's. For over a year, my husband and I had our hearts set on buying a Welsh gelding as Robin's next pony. The owner, Helda, would be outgrowing Tecwyn just when Robin was outgrowing Tuffy. We admired Tecwyn's versatility in neighborhood gymkhanas and "talked Tecwyn" at home. Finally, when Helda's new bigger pony was due to arrive, we went to try Tecwyn out. With Robin actually on Tecwyn for the first time, all went well at a walk, trot, and canter. They looked a perfect pair. Dave and I were more enthusiastic about Tecwyn than ever. Robin dismounted in an uncharacteristic silence that lasted till she was home. Then she said emphatically, "I don't want Tecwyn. I thought I did, but I don't. He's just too broad for me."

Had Robin been a few years and a few inches older Tecwyn would have been ideal for her. As it worked out, there was a happy ending for both Robin and Helda—and parents. Helda decided she couldn't bear to have Tecwyn sold out of state and passed her on to a neighboring child; we continued our search for a Welsh pony and ended up with Top Rail Stardust. Reaction to a pony by the child should be given fair consideration.

On the other hand, and perhaps more common, there is the case of the child who falls madly in love with an utterly inappropriate pony. Because of this danger, it is frequently wiser to do some of the preliminary looking at ponies without your child along—or (since one hates to deprive youngsters of all the thrill of the search) to emphasize strongly that no decision will be made until many, many ponies have been looked at.

Don't choose a pony for his looks. There are more important criteria.

The pony should be such that the child rider is neither over- nor undermounted. This is essential. For purposes of simplification, let's assume that you are looking for a pony for one child. If your pony is to be shared by several children of different sizes and abilities, you will have to add these differences to either end of the scale of values forthcoming. In every such case of multiple consideration, the smaller, weaker rider must have priority. (Far better to undermount your experienced rider than to overmount your beginner.)

The beginning rider faces two major challenges at once: He must control a strange animal with a mind and motion of its own. (Unlike a bicycle, a pony may keep on going even though the rider is no longer pedalling.) He must also control his own hands and legs and body (independently and together) and attain an entirely new equilibrium on his animal. Therefore he should be mounted on a pony that will go evenly—and stop willingly—no matter how incorrectly the basic signals are given.

Frequently a pony is described as "suitable for D rider," or, more rarely, the advertisement will read: "carried rider through Pony Club A"—the first description identifying the pony as a beginner's mount and the second as an advanced rider's.

The first pony would be of a steady, placid disposition, responding to elementary aids and undisturbed by a child's mistakes as he learned to post or sit to a canter. Such a mount would carry novice over a series of low jumps and not be disturbed if a beginner was occasionally "left behind" or jabbed him in the mouth.

The second pony would be livelier, responding more quickly to subtle signals—a shift of the rider's weight, a closing of the fingers on the reins, a squeeze of the legs. This more challenging mount would carry his more experienced rider through a more difficult round of higher, wider jumps in a ring or cross-country or in the faster company of the hunt field and would be schooled through lower levels of dressage.

A pony that "never does anything wrong" with a good rider in the saddle might do a lot wrong with a beginner—who would indeed be "overmounted."

**12.2 Stardust is a more suitable mount for Robin (who did all her growing early) than for neighbor twins, Denise and Diane, although all three were born only minutes apart.**

### SIZE

"What size?" is the next question. Size is so important that when ponies are described it is the one point always specified. Measuring in hands at the height of the withers, with four inches to a hand, we speak of a pony's being 12.2 (50 inches) or 12 hands 3½ (51½ inches). (Don't make the mistake of referring to a pony as "12 hands 4 inches"; obviously, he is 13 hands.)

There is an old rule of thumb for fitting child to pony:

Child under seven years—Pony up to 11 hands
    7 to 9 years—10 to 12 hands
    11 to 13 years—12 to 13 hands
    13 to 15 years—13 to 14.2 hands

The rub, of course, comes in the fact that there is such variety of size in a given age group. One eight-year-old child may be a full foot taller than another.

Since a short-legged child on a broad pony or a long-legged child on a narrow pony can be poorly mounted, the size and shape of your child must be taken into consideration along with the size and shape of the pony. Perhaps the following guide is more helpful than the traditional one:

When the rider's leg is in proper position, the heel should be above the line of the pony's belly but below the saddle skirt. If your child's foot is below the belly or against the skirt, he cannot use his aids properly. In the first case he tends to hook himself on with his heels (pulling his knees out) and in the second he is forced to use the leg aids against the saddle instead of the pony's sides.

One trifling but helpful thing we did at High Hickory during our search for our Welsh pony was to add several marks to the wall where we keep a record of the youngsters' growth. On this wall is Tuffy's height—marked on one of this pony's frequent visits into the kitchen for a carrot. Above it, but below the line for the top of Robin's head, is the mark for Top Rail Stardust's height (not the result of a social call). During our search, several other pony measurements were penciled in. The ponies we most keenly considered all measured about six inches under Robin's head. This differential promotes ease of grooming, tacking up, and mounting.

### AGE

Along with height, age is usually stated when

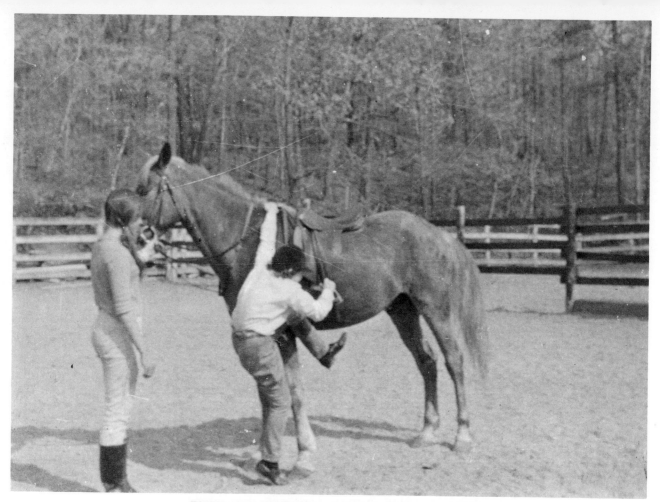

Eight-year-old Robin, already a rider over fences and used to mounting unaided, tries to mount horse conventionally, using stirrup;

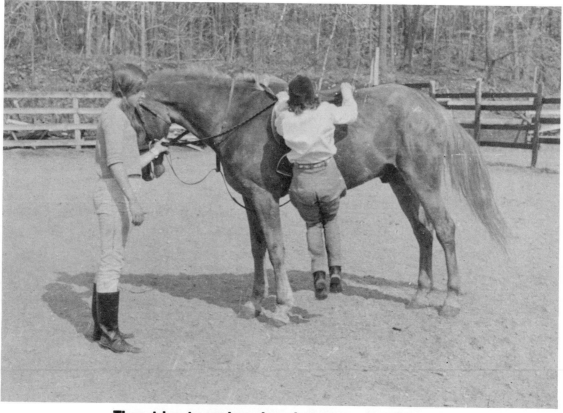

Then tries to spring aboard as one can when mount is a suitable size;

**And finally accepts a poorly executed leg-up. Ears, tail, hind leg indicate horse's attitude; if an assistant hadn't held him, he'd have moved off long ago.**

**Mounting a pony is no problem. The stirrup is in easy reach for this same child with 12.2 Star.**

**With the right size pony, even a small child can scramble aboard by herself.**

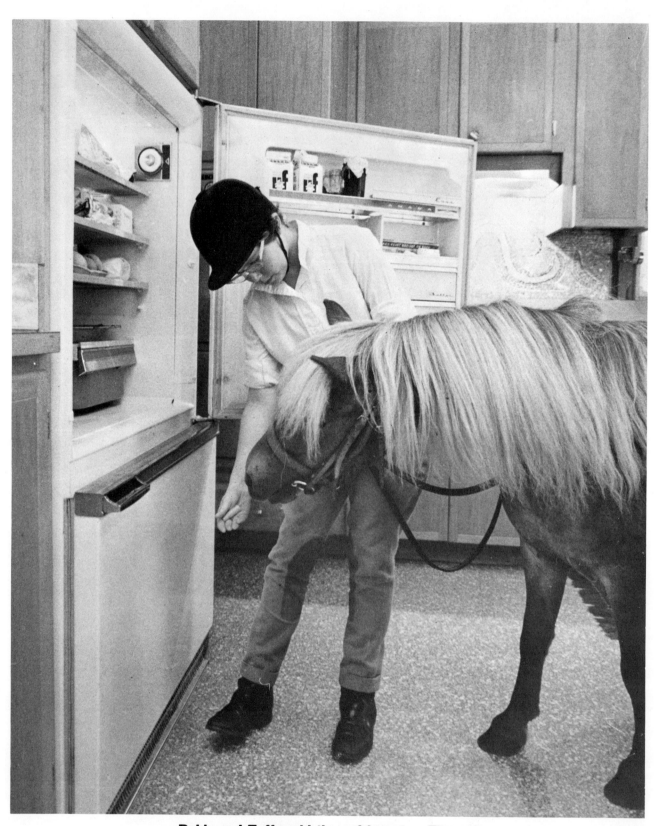

**Robin and Tuffy raid the refrigerator. The only restriction: No children or ponies in the kitchen with muddy feet.**

basic information about a pony is given. If you're not familiar with the jargon, an explanation of the terms used by horsemen may help:

A foal is a baby colt (boy) or filly (girl) still nursing its mother. Weanlings are foals that are no longer nursing or are weaned (usually at about six months). Yearlings are colts or fillies in their first year after weaning.

From then on, we speak of two-year-olds, three-year-olds, and state their ages up to eight. (The terms colt and filly are used up to four, when the colt is either a stallion or has been gelded (castrated) and is a gelding, and the filly is a mare.) After eight, we describe a pony as aged. A pony past fourteen is referred to as overaged, although he may be good for many more years—for example Robin's first pony,

still with an occasional buck at thirty-plus, was ideal for a lead-rein pony in daily use for a tiny child, up to all the walking and trotting a mother leading the pair was up to!

Three-year-olds and four-year-olds might be considered adolescents. As with children, their disposition as well as their physical appearance may change with maturity. Adolescent ponies are not up to the strenuous life a mature pony can thrive on. In fact, their schooling should still be in its early stages and should take up only a small portion of their day, most of which should be spent in "just plain growing." This is not the age pony to select for a hard-riding youngster who wants a mount for daylong hacking or hunting.

A pony is generally considered finished in its

**Thirty-year-old Nina proved a fine leadline pony for her two-year-old rider.**

27

schooling by five and in its prime between five and eight. The aged pony (remember the meaning of aged; don't be misled) may be the perfect pony to provide several childhoods with wonder and delight.

In cases where you have no proof of a pony's age (certificate of registration or other reliable record of birth date), it may be important to judge age by teeth (see Chapter 6).

You will not mistake the yearling with his still-short fluffy tail; and the two-year-old is obviously a youngster. The mature three-year-old could be passed off as a four- or five-year-old ready for work, and the less well developed five-year-old passed off as younger. You might be unwilling to pay as much for an eleven-year-old as for a nine-year-old if you want years of future use or are thinking of eventual resale. You might be willing to consider a fourteen-year-old, but feel that a seventeen-year-old is out of the question. You might decide to breed a ten-year-old (not knowing whether she'd ever been bred before) but would be reluctant to breed a twenty-year-old for the first time. These are extremes, but they suggest how important a factor in choice age can be.

Age plays such a role in pricing that dishonest sellers have stooped to bishoping. In this fraud named, according to Webster, "after the scoundrel who first practised it," the bishoper shortens the teeth, scoops out cavities, and blackens them so as to reproduce marks present in the teeth of younger ponies. It's hard to understand how there can be enough increased profit to justify the time, effort, and loss of honor involved in this, and yet unfortunately bishoping is not altogether a lost art!

From five to eight are considered the best "selling" or "buying" years: nevertheless, as I've suggested above, for a pony owner eight to twelve are often the best "using" years. With this information you can tell which category a pony falls into. However, age alone should not be a criterion for rejecting a pony you like if he meets your other standards.

### COLOR

Color is the first thing you notice about a pony. To horsemen and laymen alike it's his most conspicuous feature. In a "Pony for Sale" notice it's one of the first points listed.

Colors may be solid (whole) or broken. The solid "hard" colors are bay, brown, chestnut, black, gray, and roan. Bays are browns with black "points" (the lower legs, the tips of the ears, the mane, and tail). Chestnuts are browns with matching manes and tails (or lighter, as in the case of sorrels). True blacks are rare, but very dark seal-browns are often miscalled black. (When in doubt whether a pony is a black or a brown, look at his muzzle, eyelids, and flanks. If the hairs there are brown he is not a black, regardless of whether his body looks so.) Both bays and chestnuts come in every shade of brown, so that we further describe them as blood bays, mahogany bays, golden chestnuts, liver chestnuts, and so on.

It's interesting that grays and roans are considered solid in color, since both appear a tweedy mixture of a basic color with white. Gray, however, is caused by a failure of pigment in the hair. Some grays are born black and, as this pigment continues to disappear, turn white with age. Some grays turn white with the colder season—our Welsh ponies, for instance. When white patches appeared on Ogwen's rump and Galaxy's gray lightened the Pony Pals would bemoan the end of summer. (Was this changing of coat for protective coloring, like rabbits and ermine, they wondered? Did it have something to do with the Welsh being such an ancient breed?)

Grays, like bays, may have black points. Some have white legs. The old saw has it that this betokens weakness. Grays are classified further as steel or iron, black gray, roan gray, dappled, or fleabitten. (A six-year-old rider's indignant reaction on hearing a pony of the last category referred to: "With flea collars and all the things they can do for dogs that have fleas, you'd think they'd do something for ponies!")

Roans have coats with white hairs evenly interspersed in the solid colors: black (giving a blue roan), bay, or chestnut (giving a strawberry roan), or gray (giving a gray roan). As with the whole colors, you can tell whether a roan is a bay or chestnut by the presence or absence of black points. A roan may have legs of its body color, but unless it has black points it is a chestnut, not a bay, roan. Roans may vary from near white to deep tweedy shades of the whole color. Lutine Bell, with a light rose gray to white shades depending on the season, is often mistaken for a gray roan until the chestnut dapples on her hindquarters are pointed out. "She's a pine-needle roan," the Pony Pals insist. Roans may have manes and tails of their body color or have black points or, as with Lutine, have white mane and tail and markings.

Other solid colors, ones which are considered "soft" or "odd," are any wishy-washy shades of the above whole colors and the more seldom seen cream, mouse, or dun colors. Buckskins are duns with black points, frequently with a black dorsal stripe. While white is not truly a color but rather a complete absence of color (of the pigmentation for color in the hair), white seen in white ponies with pink skin is considered soft. "White" ponies (and horses), by the way, unless albinos, are never called white, but light gray.

Two solid colorings not traditionally listed are palomino and albino. Palominos are golden with white manes and tails and their coats, on a dark-skinned body, range from light yellows to the ideal "newly minted gold." Albinos are pure white with pink skin and eyes and white manes and tails.

Broken colors include solid-colored ponies with markings (usually white) of any sort and ponies with patches of contrasting colors. Under broken colors are included paints or pintos or spotted ponies. Ponies with black and white in clearly defined splotches are piebalds; those with white and any other color than black are skewbalds. Most skewbalds are brown and white; but Taffy, a pony in my past, was a tri-color of white, taffy-brown, and black. Special categories of broken colors cover the unique Appaloosa spotting of the P.O.A.'s.[1]

Since there are few ponies of broken color, they stand out in a group of more "conventional" colors. Not only their performance but their conformation attracts more attention. Where conformation is equally good, the advantage is with the solid color pony, if only because his body (and therefore his conformation) seems more of a piece, less broken up. Similarly, the success or failure of one pony of unusual coloring in a jumping class with nine bays will make more of a splash than the success or failure of a tenth bay.

Markings, unless specified, are white. Black spots on a white sock are called ermine. Black stockings on a bay, gray, or buckskin come under points. Markings are usually on the head or legs. Even a few white hairs remove a pony or horse from the "solid color" category; no matter how tiny, such markings are an important element in any identifying description (for insurance, registration, show purposes).

Markings on the face include star, stripe or race, blaze, snip. On the legs they are stockings or socks,

or white on the fetlock, pastern, heel, or coronet. White areas on the body may be "scars" (areas of injury where hair pigmentation was destroyed) rather than congenital markings. Wall-eyes and other oddities are also listed as markings.

Leg color often carries down into the foot. Some horsemen prefer dark hooves to light; others dispute whether or not blue horn is denser or tougher than white. The not uncommon striped hoof must disconcert adherents of both schools of thought. (And certainly if a pony has three dark hooves and one white, or vice versa, he is no more liable to go lame on the leg with the odd color.)

Over the centuries, prejudice has shifted pro and con certain colors, varying from place to place. Grays were long unpopular but are now much in demand. They may be thought hard to clean and a nuisance when shedding; they may be thought to show sweat or body dirt less than a black or dark color. ("Are grays less bothered by heat?" asked Scott, with his scientific approach. "You know, light colors reflect heat and dark ones absorb it. Look how Jet sweats up.") The way sweat grays a true black like Jet might give grounds for prejudice against blacks, but the sweeping statement "Blacks are bad-tempered" is as worthless a generalization as "Buckskins are common and coarse but good jumpers" or "Brown horses with no white are prone to swellings from saddle and girth pressure." You will hear that "soft" colors are bad, that washy colors mean weak ponies with no stamina. There is no evidence to back up such notions.

Other points being equal, solid colors are often favored over broken colors in the show ring. Personal preference, or prejudice?

The best-known pseudo-scientific formulation of color prejudice comes in the oft-quoted doggerel:

One white leg, buy him.
Two white legs, try him.
Three white legs, sell him to your foes.
Four white legs, feed him to the crows.
(Or: Four white legs, he's sure to cause you woes.)

Or:

Four white legs, keep him not a day.
Three white legs, send him far away.
Two white legs, give him to a friend.
One white leg, keep him to the end.

And so on through a dozen different versions. Fortunately, where true horsemen cast a vote,

---

1. As the Pony of the Americas is commonly called. See Chapter 18 on breeds.

prejudice is discarded. Since they realize that Pony One is not Pony Two, their final verdict has always been that a good pony is never a bad color.

## BREEDS

Youngsters throng around the little gray pony. His young rider, still flushed from the pole-bending contest, pats him proudly.

"What's his name, kid?"

"Is he yours?"

"What kind of pony is he?"

With the superiority that horsemen have always instinctively felt over men on foot, the young rider looks down. He smiles, happily.

"His name's Smoke Bomb. And he's mine." He reaches forward to untangle a lock of the black mane. "And he's—he's just a pony."

Many of the ponies you look at in your search will be "just ponies." For ponies are like people. Sometimes we know what country a person comes from, we know about his ancestors and his family tree. With a pony this would mean we know what breed he is, what his "bloodlines" are, what his pony parentage or pedigree is.

More often, of hundreds of acquaintances, we know nothing beyond what we see as "outward appearance," nothing of their background. With a pony this lack of information can't be supplied by asking him questions and he is put down as "breeding unknown." (This may mean history—previous owners, training and show experience, if any—unknown as well.) We class him as "just a pony."

"Just ponies" give as much pleasure as ponies "with papers." We may say that a certain pony "looks part Shetland" or that he "must have a little Connemara in him" or that he "moves like a Welsh." But lacking other credentials, "just ponies" are judged strictly on their individual merit and individual personality. Chapter 18 deals with various breeds and with reasons why you might want a purebred pony rather than just a pony. Whatever your choice, if all other criteria for selection are met, be assured that many "just ponies" hold their own against ponies of identifiable breeds.

## OTHER POINTS TO CONSIDER

So far we have not discussed whether we are looking for a mare or a gelding or a stallion.

While it is not unheard of for a stallion to be tractable, almost without exception stallions do not come under the heading of child's mount. Many horsemen believe that a gelding is the best choice for children or adults. At High Hickory we are partial to mares and have had no trouble with the occasional temperamental fussiness that some people say mares are prone to. Disposition seems to be more a matter of the individual pony than of the sex as such. Either a mare or a gelding can be steady, easygoing, and affectionate. It may be tempting to opt for a mare because "it would be fun to have a foal" or "we can always breed her some day." Don't let the sex matter on that basis. It is more important to consider what you want now to fill your present needs.

To add to our list of essential points: the pony must, of course, have good manners in the stall and paddock—no kicking, biting, or nipping. It should come willingly to the handler, so that a child will not have to spend riding hours trying to catch it. It should be happy living alone, if need be, and not repeatedly jump fences if confined to a small paddock. It should be safe in traffic, since today's riding country is so cut up by roads. It should be free of such outright vices as bolting, balking, rearing, and shying. It should load easily. It should pick up its feet willingly for cleaning and shoeing. It should of course be sound.

Actual soundness is something best left to your veterinarian's certification. You can spot the narrow chest which may result in interference with the forelegs, or recognize that cowhocks look ugly even if you don't know what they're called or that they may indicate weak hindquarters. You may suspect

**Taking off a halter and bridling are easy when pony and child are of a size.**

**Disposition counts. A child's pony should stand quietly while his rider mounts from a fence rail or a rock.**

*Horse* are particularly useful and have a horse or pony directory listing farms and dealers. Information as to addresses can be obtained through your library, your state agricultural college or extension service, or the American Horse Shows Association.

These are the most satisfactory sources, but "Buyer beware," goes the old phrase; and this holds true no matter where you buy your pony.

One advantage of buying from a breeding farm is that you have a chance to see not only the pony you are considering but quite likely his sire, dam, and related offspring too. A breeder keeps track of other ponies he has sold and will proudly give you "progress reports" on their accomplishments. He can put you in touch with other people who have purchased ponies from him, so that you have them as references not only as to the type of pony he produces but as to the reliability of his dealings, if you wish to check.

lack of shoulders from the use of a crupper to keep a saddle from slipping, even if you have to ask what "that thing around the tail" is called. You can feel the sharp withers that may require special saddling or see the too-heavy neck that will make unpleasant riding for a child's small arms, although you may not know just what's wrong. For many points you must take the seller's word—hence the value of buying your pony from a reputable dealer.

Another essential to check is the pony's willingness to walk away from other ponies or to stay when other ponies are ridden away from it. The pony should also be easy to saddle and bridle. Of prime importance, it should have a good disposition.

Finally, even though looks aren't everything, you do want a pretty pony. Your ideal will become clearer as you look and look.

**Registered Welsh yearlings, in their rough spring coats, at Crossroads Farm (Lyme, New Hampshire) suggest a promise of things to come.**

### WHERE TO LOOK

Where do you start looking?

Your search may already have been simplified by your recognition of one particular breed as what you want. In that case, through its registry or national association (see Chapter 18), you can obtain a list of breeders and members throughout the country. Usually their official publication (such as *The Welsh Pony World*) carries a breeders' directory and monthly advertisements of ponies currently on the market. All-breed monthlies like *The Horsemen's Yankee Pedlar* or weeklies like *The Chronicle of the*

General horse magazines, Hunt Club and riding stable bulletin boards, sales yards, auctions, 4-H and Pony Club leaders and members—all these are sources of "ponies for sale" and offer places where you can post: "Pony Wanted." Horse shows, too, are selling arenas; but be prepared to pay more for the pony that comes out of the ring wearing the blue ribbon! Two years ago I would have been skeptical about a tiny classified ad in the "Pets and Livestock" column of a big-city newspaper; but it was such an ad with its "Large gentle Welsh ponies for sale" that led us to the farm where we found Top Rail Stardust.

Robin, who learned to ride at two on Nina, the thirty-year-old pony that had been on loan to neighborhood youngsters over the years, located her second pony in a unique way. Eric, then nine, made her a sandwich-board sign boldly lettered "I Want a Pony." In smaller lettering was "My Mother Is Willing," and our telephone number. Robin wore this over her riding togs at a Millwood Hunt schooling show at which I was taking entries, and besides providing a merry afternoon it brought pony results. More orthodox approaches in the search are telephone calls, letter-writing, and visits.

Occasionally a telephone call about an advertised pony may save you a trip, for price, age, and hands may be wrong for you. The call may extend the range of possibilities, for often a breeder will have several more ponies than those specifically advertised, even if the one you rang about is out of the question. Horsemen frequently know one another's stock and you may be referred to another pony farm or individual owner who has something more suitable for you.

If you are answering an ad by mail, snaphots and complete descriptions can be obtained before you decide on a first-hand inspection. Usually if the distance is so great that inquiries are made by mail eventual trucking may be a major expense for you to take into consideration.

At last, with all these ideas put into action, you have located a possible pony. This is a schooled pony, at a nearby farm, and you have decided to take the children along, to try it out. Will it be your pony?

HOW TO TRY A PONY OUT

We always go for a tryout equipped with lunge-line, hunt cap, saddle and bridle, and notebook. The lunge-line is a wise precaution when your youngster tests an unknown pony. You can use it to watch the pony's gaits as he is lunged without a rider and also as an "emergency check" with your youngster in the saddle. As was pointed out earlier, the pony that behaves nicely under the seller's familiar rider may be quite a different mount under your child. We have tried out schooled and green ponies with foals galloping alongside, with dogs running underfoot, with other ponies and foals free in the same field. Of course you will certainly test out the pony without the lunge-line as well.

If you don't have a hunt cap, borrow one to use for the tryout. You'll want your own once you get your pony. (See Chapter 7, Basic Safety Rules.)

If the pony you are trying is schooled, chances are that the seller will have a saddle and bridle. Do not buy either until you have your own pony or you may end up with a bad fit. Often the seller will pass both on with the pony. However, if you have tack already, take it along; you may find a Western saddle whereas you're used to a forward seat, or vice versa.

The more ponies you look at, the more your notebook will come in handy to keep information straight and to evaluate it at home. List ahead of time points that you want covered: height; color; age; sex; degree of schooling; experience in jumping, driving, show; in foal or not; shots; breeding; reason for selling; price; whether or not trucking is included in the price. In our search we found this charting a great help, as we often looked at five or six "possible ponies" on the same farm.

**Good-natured Peggy accepts a carrot when Robin leads Tuffy out of the pasture for grooming.**

When you arrive at the farm, start "scoring" right from the start—from first sight. See how the pony behaves when approached in pasture. (A pony that is extremely hard to catch is a time-waster and a great frustration to its would-be rider.)

Notice how the pony behaves when one or two children are in the box stall with him. Does he swing his hind end towards them, with his ears back? If in a straight stall, does he move over willingly? How is he about having both front and hind feet picked up? About being tied to a fence rail? About going through puddles, if there are any?

Have the pony tacked up in your presence. If he's tacked up on your arrival, ask to have him untacked and let your child saddle and bridle him himself. The pony may behave one way for an expert, another way for a child. If the child is inexperienced, it is all the more important to have a pony that tacks up easily—without flinging his head up to avoid the bit or nipping back when being girthed. Here again the size of the pony in relation to your youngster's height is important. Tacking-up can be discouragingly difficult with a too-big pony.

Ideally, after a lunging, your Pandora and Tommy will have a chance to try out the pony first in an enclosed field or paddock. Let Tommy lead the pony out. Watch him mount. Does the pony stand, or does he have to be held while Tommy mounts and adjusts his stirrups? Does he move away willingly from other ponies? Will he stand quietly while other ponies move away from him, or does he insist on following? Is he bothered if other ponies pass him?

**Tacking up can be child's work if pony and child are truly a pair. Four-year-old Robin checks Tuffy's girth.**

**Mane and tail freshly shampooed, Tuffy moves on quietly for her young rider in their first walk-trot class.**

Test his reaction to such things as a jacket being removed by the child on his back or to your handing the child a sweater. Sometimes a pony is so crop-shy that it is hard for even an empty-handed person to approach his rider.

See what the pony's reaction is to cars passing on the road or to the sound of your car motor starting up in the stable yard. How does he react to a toot on your car horn?

If you are buying a pony for jumping, you will want to try him out over a variety of fences, possibly cross-country as well as in the ring. If you are interested in showing, arrange to enter the pony in a nearby show—or to see his past show record.

If interested in driving, have the pony harnessed and try him out to a cart. Some neighbors of ours had a lovely grade pony that was everything the seller claimed under saddle. They never questioned his claims about her driving. Months later they hitched her for the first time—and there wasn't much left of the little cart after she took off! Much more typical is the seller who tells you that a pony is broken to drive but needs more work done on backing, or some other special aspect.

Looking back through our battered notebook, its pages separated by snapshots of ponies we particularly considered, I find comments like: "Right size; well schooled; R. could concentrate on her riding, not on breaking another green pony." "Yearling; will be right size eventually but not up to R.'s strenuous riding for two years." "Good with dogs underfoot" (a

serious matter for us, since we raise Border Collies, and also for any family with dogs in the neighborhood). "Completely people-broken but no schooling beyond being halter-broken." "In foal; this would limit schooling and riding some." To glance through these notes is to recall vividly the pleasure of visiting different breeding farms, seeing the beautiful ponies, and being welcomed by fellow horse-lovers.

If you are considering bloodlines, your notebook will prove even handier. In our first search, we were not concerned with any particular breeding or bloodlines. We wanted a registered purebred Welsh and felt that by going to member breeders of the Welsh Pony Society of America we were protected by the Society's high standards. Usually when looking at young stock we had the opportunity of seeing dam, sire, grandsire, other related offspring, and all this helped in evaluating whatever individual pony we were considering. We did enjoy looking through Stud Books and listening to breeders discuss the background of their Welsh stock. When, long after our final choice of Top Rail Stardust, we realized that we had fallen in love with a filly with top breeding, this was merely an added bonus.

FINAL ARRANGEMENTS

At last you and your children find a pony you like when you try him out. He passes every test satisfactorily. At home that night the entire family agrees that this is it.

Now is the time to have the pony checked for soundness by a veterinarian. You can accept the seller's veterinarian's certificate (not wise), have a veterinarian of your own choosing examine the pony at the place of sale, or have your veterinarian do so after the pony is delivered to you. Now is also the final opportunity to have a professional opinion, if you need one, of the pony as a mount. (Possible experts to consult: a riding instructor, a Pony Club D. C., or a 4-H leader). Naturally, you should expect to pay for such services. Now is also the time to check on shots, Coggins Test, shoeing, accustomed feeding, delivery arrangements; and perhaps schedule lessons on your new pony.

Occasionally you can arrange to have a pony on trial for a limited time. In such a case, you the buyer pay the trucking both ways, and if the pony goes back it is usually in exchange for another pony from the same dealer, not for a refund of money. Such a

**A young pony's growth may not keep pace with a child's. In this case, the crossbred pony bought as a two-year-old kept on growing and the youngster stopped, so there was no "sadly outgrown."**

New owner Kate gets a lesson on Galaxy at High Hickory while her mother observes.

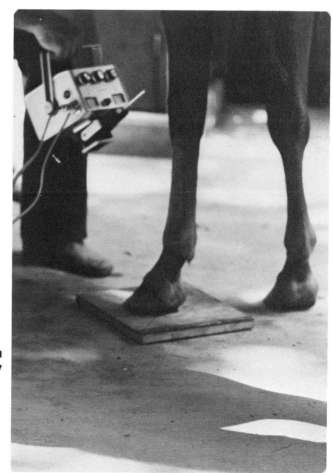

A portable X-ray machine makes possible a thorough on-the-spot examination of a pony under consideration for purchase.

35

trial period is seldom necessary if your search and tryouts have been thorough.

At last, with your family's preference backed by your veterinarian's okay, you can go ahead with the deal. Occasionally you can buy an animal "on time," but the age-old tradition is that all money and pony change ownership at the same time.

## YOUR PONY'S ARRIVAL

### FINAL ARRANGEMENTS AND INSTALLATION

When your pony arrives—happiness in a horse van!—give him a few minutes to look around after he steps out. Undoubtedly he'll be surrounded by a circle of eager admirers; but try to keep his first hours in his new home quiet ones. Let him adjust to his new surroundings. Pleased as you may be with your carpentry, he may at first be reluctant to go into his new stall. Let him take his time. Provide hay or grazing and water, a welcoming carrot or two, and leave him alone except for quiet casual company.

**Conformation chart: Good conformation.**

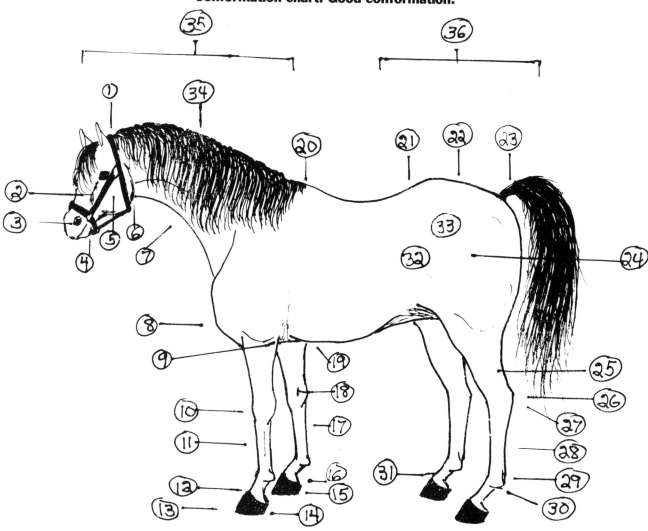

1. Poll
2. Cheek bone
3. Nostril
4. Chin or curb groove
5. Cheek or jowl
6. Throat latch
7. Throat, or wind pipe
8. Point of shoulder
8/20. Line of shoulder
9. Elbow
10. Knee
11. Cannon
12. Coronet
13. Hoof
14. Near foreleg
15. Off fore
16. Heel
17. Back tendon
18. Chestnut

19. Girth groove
19/20. "Depth through the heart"
20. Withers
21. Loins
22. Croup
23. Dock of tail
24. Quarters
25. Gaskin or second thigh
26. Hock
27. Seat of curb
28. Cannon or shank
29. Fetlock
30. Ergot
31. Pastern
32. Flank
33. Hip
34. Crest
35. Forehand, or forequarters
36. Hindquarters

**Conformation chart: Faulty conformation.**

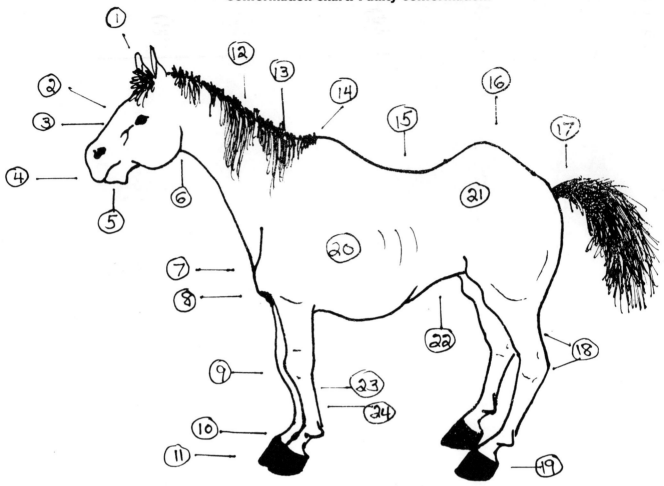

13. Ratty mane
14. Prominent withers
15. Sway back
16. Goose rump
17. Scrawny tail, set too low
18. Sickle hocked, or, cowhocked
19. Huge clumsy feet
20. Slab sided
21. Prominent hips
22. Herring gutted
23. Bowed tendon
24. Light boned

1. Donkey or lop ears
2. Roman nose
3. Pig eye
4. Parrot mouth
5. Coarse muzzle
6. Thick throat latch
7. Too straight shoulder
8. Narrow chest
9. Over-at-the-knees
10. Too long pasterns; or, too short and straight
11. Pigeon toes
12. Ewe neck

# 3

# FACILITIES FOR YOUR PONY

DURING THE MONTHS OF THE SEARCH, YOU WILL make all the necessary preparations for your pony.

One of the great advantages of having a pony is its ease of upkeep. Its inherent stamina, toughness, and adaptability mean that it can be kept in good condition with the simplest of stabling facilities. Indeed, if your pony is used to the simple life he may prefer it to a more elaborate, less natural existence. Just as a pampered pony may at first find it difficult to fend for himself if suddenly thrown out to live on pasture only, so the pony used to living out may find it hard to be confined in a stall, restricted to a small paddock, fed and exercised only on his owner's prerogative. Any change towards either extreme should be made gradually.

## FENCING AND PADDOCKS

A large field is fine but not necessary. Even if you have one for grazing you will still need a small paddock (with access both to field and to barn) for the days when you want your pony to be out of doors but restricted. If there is no other shelter, be sure to leave the stall open to provide escape from the wind, the rain, or the summer sun and flies. Ponies love to roll, and a pile of sand in the paddock corner will give yours a place to roll in without becoming grass-stained or muddy.

Besides the water pail carefully hooked in each stall, there should be water outside (in a second pail or a boxed-in old bathtub if you can find a place where it won't be an eyesore). Automatic waterers

are available now that connect to an ordinary garden hose, instead of the involved piping once required. Convenient in many ways, they may tempt a playful pony to flood a stall—and make it difficult for you to gauge his water consumption for purposes of good animal husbandry.

Fencing can be of wood (post-and-rail is ideal, or sheep-hurdle, or plank) or metal (electric or pipe is

**Eric, without a halter or lead rope, holds Peggy by the nose at the sheep field gate. Stock fencing is not safe for ponies.**

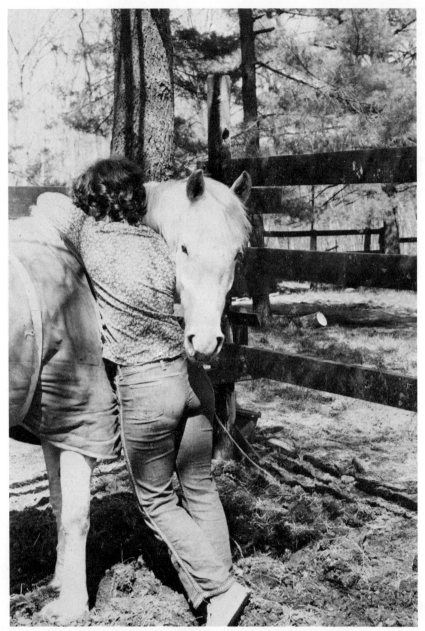

**Wood planks make a sturdy fence, with rails high enough for 14.1 Lutine Bell, low enough for 39-inch Tuffy. Some equine escape artists squeeze under or through openings "no pony could get through."**

hazardous, and do not risk barbed wire. Stock fencing catches between hoof and shoe). If you are putting in new fencing, use eight-inch spacing for the rails so heads can't go through. Make it high— horse height, not pony. Top Rail Stardust can jump casually over our three-foot-six-inch sheep barricades, and at two months her filly thought nothing of jumping a two-foot bar to leave her dam and be with her friend Tuffy. Wood fencing must be treated repeatedly with creosote or some kind of "no-chew" nonpoisonous paint to prevent chewing.

An extra line of fencing can help you extend your grazing also. If possible, divide your pasture into at least two sections so that you can rotate their use several weeks at a time. If you do not have a separate area for a lunging circle or riding ring, you can use the perimeter of your pasture without ruining the turf and can perhaps set up a few jumps as well.

## STABLING

Your pony barn (to use an informal term: strictly speaking, horses and ponies are kept in stables) should be conveniently sited for feed delivery, for doing daily chores, and for supervising activities in the barn and paddock if necessary. Not only is it a joy to see ponies peeking over stall doors and moving about their paddocks from the windows of the house at High Hickory, but many steps are saved because the pony barn is within hailing distance.

If you are going to have running water and electricity, their source may be a deciding factor in siting your stables. Both are nice to have; neither is an absolute necessity. A lantern-type flashlight that allows for two free hands can be used for evening feeding during the all-too-early dark of winter months. Since we use a long hose and from frost-in to frost-free lug water by the pailsful, I wouldn't

Helping with barn chores at Needham, Alan drags a bag of feed out of the way while Scott manhandles a heavy bag of shavings past the wheelbarrow used for cleaning stalls.

want our stalls any farther from the house. Your stables must, however, be far enough away from your house and your neighbors' so that any temporary accumulation of manure or flies is not a nuisance. (Good stable care eliminates most of this problem.) You will of course check the regulations of your local Zoning Board and Health Department.

### DESIGN AND MATERIALS

A simple three-sided shed facing south that provides shelter from wind and weather may be sufficient for your pony. For the worst days of winter you may add a partial fourth side and a dutch door (a wide one). Our barn started out as a simple shed with a cant roof; one third of it a "hayloft" with a board floor all of one foot off the ground, and the remainder one large stall with a natural dirt floor, a dutch door, and three removable windows that are in place about three months of the year. We have since added other box stalls and electricity.

Building materials for your pony barn exterior, whatever its scope, can be as simple or as fancy as your budget permits—roofing and siding to match your house, or temporary plastic sheeting tied over a board roof and a siding of creosoted second-hand planks. Avoid board and batten: unlike smooth surfaces the strips give ponies something to grip with their teeth and so require frequent repair.

A standard horse stall is twelve by twelve feet. Pony stalls can be proportionately smaller, down to four by eight feet for a straight stall. For ease of cleaning and economy of bedding, a stall not-too-big for your own pony is best. Some ponies are tidier than others, soiling only one portion of their stalls; most are quite indiscriminate. Many ponies are housebroken: no matter how long they've been out, they relieve themselves the moment they enter a clean stall.

Since many rainy days at High Hickory are spent with Pony Pals grooming and playing with ponies under cover, I am glad that we have at least one big stall. There several children can work in a group while others work separately in other stalls but can talk back and forth over the slatted partitions.

### Height

While it is possible with a tiny pony to have something like a big dog kennel, most stalls should, regardless of size, be high enough for an adult to work in without stooping. Best is to allow sufficient height so that a pony who jerks his head up in fright or good spirits cannot bang it on the ceiling.

Besides the pony's stall, you will need a place for tack (see next chapter) and storage space for hay, grain, and bedding. If you have ample, easily accessible overhead storage, with sufficient ventilation to avoid fire hazards, you can buy supplies in quantity conveniently, if not more economically. (Perhaps you can plan a loft so that you feed from above through openings over each pony stall.)

You must be able to close your feedroom securely and be most conscientious about the closing. Ponies are extraordinarily dexterous at opening hooks, locks, and latches, even at untying knots (a clever pony loose on an orgy in the grain may soon be a very sick one).

Whatever your feed room, you will need rodent-proof storage for your grain. A wooden box can be rat-proofed by covering the outside with fine-meshed wire or lining the inside with zinc, but it is simpler to use metal containers. (Plastic cans or barrels are not satisfactory, as rodents do gnaw through them.) With metal ash cans, lids must be put on carefully or you may be startled to find a plump feasting field mouse inside. Pelleted feeds may be left in their plasticized bags.

Access to the pony's manger and water pail can be through a small opening in the wall dividing the stall from the feed room—which will have its own outside door. Even gentle ponies may seem cross and impatient at mealtime. Children may find feeding simpler if they do not have to go into the stall—but even so they may want to "sit and just talk to Stardust while she eats."

The traditional and best material for all partitions inside the barn is oak—2 inch oak with metal covering any exposed edges that might tempt a pony to chew.

### INSIDE THE STALL

Stall furniture is of the simplest and is "functional" in that it depends on your method of feeding your pony. You can use a ring for hanging a water bucket with a double-ended snap hook. If you use a hay net you'll want a ring high on one wall for that. (Hay nets sag as they empty; because pawing ponies get their forelegs trapped in them, we think them too dangerous to use unsupervised.) For ponies like Tuffy that get only hay on the ground, you need nothing more. For ponies on short feed, you need a box or tub for grain. Except for Tuffy's, our stalls have built-in wooden mangers with space at one end

**Fresh hay tossed out on clean snow may be ruined by ponies rolling and trampling it into the mud.**

to hold removable plastic feed tubs. (We like mangers where ponies can look out while eating, near a door if not a window, and we have a tie ring at each.) Shaped plastic feed tubs are easily cleaned and can be bolted into a corner or hooked to rings, again with double-ended snaps. Combination hay rack and feed tubs are now available in plastic also.

No one, child or adult, should ever lock himself into a stall with a pony with the exterior latch: it is impossible to get out in a hurry if you have to reach over the lower half of your dutch door. For the times when you want the door shut while you work inside, a small hook and eye on the inside are sufficient. For other times, a web-guard, a rubber-covered chain, or a rope—all with snaps on both ends—can be put across the doorway, attached to rings on the sides of the frame.

Close to the stall you will want hooks to hang your pony's halter and lead ropes. Wherever you keep the rest of your tack, these two items should be in a conspicuous place in the stable. They are not only regular equipment, they may be emergency equipment—and a spare lead rope at least should always be kept handy, along with a fire extinguisher.

Hooks, like door latches, should be blunt and should not protrude in such a way that a pony can hit or tear himself on them. If they must be low enough for youngsters to reach, recess them between a couple of two-by-two's. If your stall door has a decorative wooden X reinforcing its halves, you can put your halter hook there. (Check that no points go through to the pony's side.)

All electric fixtures must be out of reach and lights sturdily caged. (One night Lutine Bell chewed loose a wire cover and broke the bulb of a light mounted ten feet high and "well out of reach" on the other side of a partition.) It is a good idea to shut off all current when people are not in the barn by a master switch (one in the barn and another with an "in use" indicator at the house). This practice, along with strict adherence to the No Smoking rule (in barn and woods) helps lessen danger of the horseman's bugaboo: fire in the stables.

Your pony may have a long reach like Lutine's, so put manure forks, rakes, (plastic rather than metal, remember), and other tools away where he cannot pull them into his stall. Plan a place to store wheelbarrows and cleaning gear where he won't knock them over when you take him out of his stall.

FLOORING

Your stall flooring can have various surfaces: dirt, clay, wood, cobblestone or brick, cement, asphalt. I shall deal with them in inverse order of desirability:

Cement and asphalt are popular in stables (breeding, boarding, livery) where turnover (transient horses) makes sanitary procedures like hosing with disinfectant a prime consideration. A decided pitch, hard on a four-legged occupant, is required to drain off wetness into a gutter or drain, which frequently clogs. Cobblestones and brick, seen in older buildings, are slippery underfoot for a pony getting up and down and uncomfortable for a pony resting. All these surfaces are hard on a pony's legs and should be covered with maximum bedding.

Heavy planks are a better and general choice, but wood becomes slippery and smelly from urine, holds germs, rots, and become splintery. However, one step better than a cement floor is heavy planking put down over such an existing surface.

Where the comfort and well-being of the animal is put first, horsemen prefer a natural surface. Clay, or some form of it such as stone dust, ground slag, or commercial concoctions with various trade names, put down over a good base of crushed rock and gravel (natural dirt drains well for us) offers superior absorption. Other advantages: unlike wood or asphalt, which can become damaged by pawing, clay floors can easily be patched by the addition of another wheelbarrowful. With no drains or pitching towards a gutter, floors can be level. Underhoof, clay gives a nonslip surface and the most comfortable one for a pony standing or lying down.

Clay or stone dust, delivered mostly by truckload, is shoveled about six inches deep into the stalls and then packed down by lightly walking over it. The clay, gray green when fresh, gradually blackens, an indication that it needs to be replaced—perhaps annually. Each spring the Pony Pals dig out and discard the old floor, now only about two inches thick, much as one would clean a stall. They sprinkle lime on the exposed base, that is left to dry for a day or more if it's sleeping-out weather for the ponies. (Lime can be sprinkled on any stall floor to freshen it—once a week on hard-surfaced ones.)

Such a natural surface can also be used for your main aisle floor if you're making a new barn. It is a little harder to keep tidy than wood, but economical, and safe footing for your pony.

BEDDING

Whatever your flooring, in your stall you will want on top of it a deep layer of bedding. Bedding is the pony's mattress: of shavings, wood chips, sawdust, peat moss, and straw. (One autumn we even utilized endless rakings of hickory and oak leaves, and pine needles: but beware of wilted lawn clippings, moldy hay, anything bad that your pony might eat.) The curious pony will sometimes nibble a mouthful or two of fresh sawdust or shavings when he first enters a freshly bedded stall, and will be eager to roll; hay providently waiting in his manger may prove more tempting.

You can buy bedding by the bag or bale or, in the case of sawdust and shavings, by the truckload as well, if you have storage. (Once the show season is over, Pony Pal Virginia's family fill their horse trailer with shavings at a local lumber mill. By the time spring comes the trailer is empty and ready for their little pinto again.) We used to buy shavings and store the paper bags inside; now we store sawdust outside under a huge tarpaulin or plastic cover, screened by pines.

Clean bedding can be put down in various ways: the main thing is to have enough of it to provide dry footing and clean sleeping. To skimp on it is a false economy. Inadequate bedding means a dirtier pony since his coat and feet, not his mattress, absorb dirty wastes. It will mean you have to spend

**43**

**Shirley fills a wheelbarrow with sawdust for bedding during Pony Camp at High Hickory. Pulled-back plastic protects the diminishing pile.**

more time grooming him. It results in thrush or capped elbows or sore legs, not to mention a malodorous fly-filled barn.

The more your pony can be outside, of course, the less replacement (and stall cleaning) will be needed.

Start with a clean stall and put down as much bedding as you can—six to eight inches over the floor and deeper around the sides. Pick up manure and wet bedding daily and fork extra from sides to center. Once a week, clean out to the bare floor and start over with fresh.

That is the method we used for many years; but two winters ago we started "deep bedding"—with sawdust—and will continue to use it! With deep bedding (or deep litter) you initially put down twice as much bedding as usual (absorptive sawdust works better than shavings). Each day (several times a day

if possible) pick up your stall: remove any droppings and wet spots, perhaps a wheelbarrowful a day. Then add fresh bedding: two or three wheelbarrowfuls a day. Since you always add more than you take out, your stall remains dry and the depth of bedding increases slightly. Gradually the bedding darkens till it resembles peat moss. It also generates a certain amount of heat, advantageous on cold winter nights but necessitating open windows and doors in Indian summer or mild spells in early spring if you shut your pony in at night.

How often you completely remove this deep bedding and start over depends largely on how many hours your pony is confined and on his size in relation to the size of his stall and the original depth of bedding. If you keep a good ratio of what goes in to what goes out this method can provide dry fresh-

Kate helps with Pony Camp chores. Two-man jobs to handle when full, manure baskets may be more convenient than wheelbarrows in some stall work.

smelling stalls for three to four months without need for a major stall-cleaning—and this means stalls from which even our gray ponies walk out clean and unstained in the morning. During the school year—and in anyone's life!—the saving in time, the elimination of a weekly chore that can take several hours, gives this method my vote.

### CLEANING

Stall cleaning is commonly referred to as "mucking out." Mucking out sounds unpleasant—and if you let your stall get so dirty that it needs to be mucked out, it can be unpleasant. (The classical example of the bad stable manager was of course King Augeas—and you'll remember that to clean his stables Hercules had to divert the course of a river and let it rush through, mucking out!) If you keep your stall clean, mucking out is all right.

Whatever your bedding, stall cleaning is more easily accomplished with proper utensils: a manure basket or a wheelbarrow and a manure fork (not a hay fork). Twelve-tined forks were designed for Paul Bunyanesque workers, so you may want to shorten the handle to lessen the weight; but the close-together tines speed the work of picking up droppings without taking too much bedding as well.

To clean your stall, put your pony out in his paddock or cross-tie him so that you can work in an empty stall. If you work around him you're more cramped and you run the risk of pricking him. Of course, you'd never take a wheelbarrow into the stall with him. Remove or cover buckets so that dirt won't contaminate drinking water. For quick pick-ups during the day, you can use a small manure basket and a small scoop or flat piece of wood without shifting your pony.

Some arrangement for disposal of manure is essential. On a "farm" like High Hickory, in a rural area like our part of Middlesex County, this is not the problem it is for many pony owners. With deep bedding, the manure pile is more sawdust than manure, so it is not smelly. It can be dumped by the wheelbarrowful on a midden to age and be used months later in gardening. It can even be scattered in a field or meadow which the ponies will not be grazing for some weeks.

Increasingly stricter requirements are being laid down in suburban areas; check with your local authorities. Disposal must be handled in such a way that manure does not attract flies or become an eyesore. So, when you clean out your stalls or pick up droppings from your paddocks, where do you put your gleanings?

One solution is the compost heap. Aged manure, peat moss especially or "wood" bedding with any excess acidity balanced by the addition of lime, is welcome in the garden. Tidily contained by cinder-block wall or snow fencing, a manure pile can be inconspicuous. It should be convenient to your barn (consider muddy footing when it's hard to push a wheelbarrow) but as far as possible from your house or anyone else's.

Manure pile or midden, dunghill or compost heap, call it what you will—the Pony Pals yell "I'm the king of the midden" as they dump their barrows on the top of the pile—it must eventually be removed.

**45**

Like the dairy farms, the larger stables and riding centers around us remove theirs by the truckload, manure spreaders clacking, as they scatter the contents around the hayfields each spring. One-pony owners have sought different solutions. "Yours for the Taking" signs appear around the neighborhood, and strangers appear with baskets or small trailers to get free fertilizer. Organic gardeners, especially appreciative of this nonchemical soil enricher, telephone their willingness to recycle. Enterprising Pony Pals one year held a road-side sale of bagged manure. Posters advertising it nearly caused a traffic jam, as motorists who habitually ignored "Lemonade for Sale" signs queued up for these choice packages and asked to be put on the mailing list for next year. The Pony Pals made over $32 in one day—the proceeds going to rescue an old mare from the knackers.

However you dispose of your manure, one thing is certain: as long as you have a pony you will always have a fresh and continuous supply. But with proper bedding and careful disposal visitors to your barn will say what visitors to ours say: "Your barn always smells so good!"

**"Fun for the whole family. . . ." mutter Josephine's parents.**

# 4
# TACK AND ITS CARE

TACK OF COURSE IS HORSEMAN'S JARGON FOR saddle and bridle, dating from the days when harness and such were referred to as tackle. We speak of tacking up and untacking as often as we do of saddling and unsaddling or bridling and unbridling; it's quicker.

## TACKROOM

You will need a handy place to keep your tack. The old injunction "a place for everything and everything in its place" should be obeyed, if only because it means more time for riding.

If your stable is unheated, you may want to keep your tack in the house during the coldest months. Like all leather, it suffers from extremes of heat, cold, and moisture, a point to consider before storing unused tack in a basement or attic.

If your plans run to a special tack room, running water is convenient for cleaning tack as well as for watering the pony, but it's not necessary.

Whether you keep your equipment in a tackroom in your pony barn or in the house, you will need a support for your saddle and a bracket for your bridle. The saddle rack can be a wooden upside-down V or a metal rack at a convenient height on the wall, or it can be a sawhorse. The bridle support, whether a commercial metal bracket or an old saddle-soap can or section of wood nailed high on the wall, should allow the headpiece to hang in a broad curve, not in a sharp bend as it would on a hook.

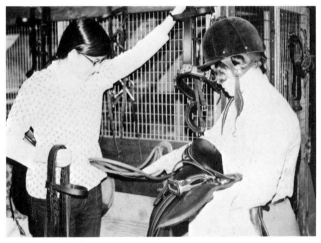

**Meri-Jo lifts a lunging cavesson from a bridle rack while Robin dusts the saddle rack. On the saddle, stirrups are run up with leathers put through to hold them in place.**

## TACK

With a pony of your own you will need tack of your own. Both saddle and bridle should fit the pony; the saddle should fit you, the rider, as well.

If you have never bought tack before or had to decide whether it fits or is properly adjusted, get the help of an expert: your instructor, your 4-H leader, a horseman friend, a local saddlery dealer. You can look over and choose from a wide assortment of styles and prices at a tack shop. The proprietor may let you take several items to try on your pony for fit (*you* can test the saddles on a wooden horse in the shop), and our tack shop people even go to the customer's barn on occasion. You can order through a catalogue—more of a gamble and more of a wait, but you can learn a lot from tack catalogues.

Good used tack is in many ways preferable to new. It is already broken in, less stiff, and therefore more comfortable. It may also be harder to find, whether at a tack shop, a Pony Club or 4-H sale, an auction, or from an individual. If you locate used tack, check leather for cracks, stitching for breaks, metal for cracks or chipping. With a used saddle, be certain before you even check for fit that girth billets are still well stitched, buckles secure, safety clasps operable, the panel well stuffed, and the saddle tree in perfect condition. Have it checked and overhauled

by your local saddle repair man (you'll want to get to know him eventually). Fittings (stirrup leathers and irons and girth) must be checked too, but can be bought more easily. Your saddle is your big investment.

## SADDLES

The type of tack you choose depends on your school of riding, your "seat." Even if you "ride English" as opposed to "riding Western," you have hunt seat, saddle seat, dressage seat, balanced seat, etc. I was once asked to set up a Riding Department at Purdue University; not till spending that year in Indiana did I realize what a false impression the bald terms "Western" and "English" give. Each type has a wide variety of subtypes, a whole array of designs; and every rider has his favorite.

Basically a saddle is a seat tied on to your pony around his middle. All the leather parts that make up the saddle as we see it cover or are attached to a foundation consisting of a seat framework attached at its front to an arch that straddles the pony's back. This entire unit makes up the tree. To this skeleton are attached the girth billets, the stirrup bars, the underskirts and flaps, while webbing and padding for the seat are added before the final skin of leather goes on.

Saddles are made with hard- or soft-wooden trees, spring trees, flexible trees, laminated plywood trees, fiberglass trees, even all-leather trees. Under normal circumstances a tree is strong and holds its shape, but the best of trees can break, and for this reason a saddle must be handled correctly.

On the finished saddle, flaps may be padded by sponge or foam rubber, covered with smooth or rough (suede) leather and may have knee rolls and thigh rolls, concealed or exposed. Saddles may be waterproofed, sweat and mildew resistant, "require no soaping or care of any kind." They come in all kinds and combinations of kinds of leather—water-buffalo skin, calfskin, pigskin, doeskin, cowskin, even horsehide (not pony skin). The country of origin gives some indication of the quality of the leather and the caliber of craftsmanship. Generally saddlery from England, France, Germany, and Italy is highly rated, while that from India, Japan, and South America is questionable. Knowing the "selling points" of top saddlery will help in your selection.

**Ben Pike, saddlemaker of Arlington, puts a Dee on a saddle. Padded underseat with its dividing gullet shows under his left hand.**

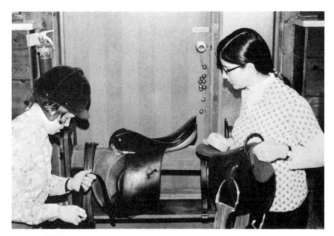

A saddle stripped of fittings rests on a portable rack. Suede skirts contrast with the smooth leather of the seat, as do felt parts of the saddle Meri-Jo holds. Robin slides irons off leathers in preparation for tack cleaning.

when a heavier rider used it on bigger, broader Lutine Bell.)

The smaller your pony the harder it may be to find just the saddle you want. Small ponies, especially tiny ones, fat ones, ones with no withers, are notoriously hard to fit. An inexpensive saddle can be had in felt or in felt and leather, with or without a partial tree. It is like an exercise pad and, unlike the all-leather, conforms to the pony's shape. One hazard is that it has no safety clasp; the leathers often go through a closed ring and cannot come free without being unbuckled. The girth is often webbing stitched on to the saddle on the off side. Some have a handle or leather loop on the pommel so a tiny child can hang on. These features and their small size indicate that they are basically for the lead-line rider, but they are very durable and, like the suede on other saddles, give the riding youngster a bit of grip.

Whatever the style and whether new or used, invest in the very best saddle you can afford. Look on it as an investment, not only in money-back but in safety. If you can't locate or afford safe tack that fits it is better to do without and ride bareback or school unmounted until you can.

Poorly fitted tack in bad repair is dangerous to rider and mount alike. Don't risk getting hurt because old rotten equipment gives way. Don't lose out on riding fun because broken, improperly fitted tack gives your pony a saddle or girth sore. (Saddles have caused sore backs ever since the Romans first thought them up back in the fourth century!)

Saddles, like shoes, come not only in styles but in sizes. They are measured straight across from the pommel nailhead to the center of the cantle. Common sizes are 14½ inches, 16 inches, and 17 inches through 19 inches; but a given size that fits one pony may not fit another same-size pony.

(Often saddles are known by the manufacturer's name or by style: a Keiffer Bavaria, a Crosby jump saddle, a Passier All-Purpose. In our barn our Passier fits Lutine Bell while our Keiffer does not—while both saddles fit Baldy. Eric's old hunt saddle, purchased for his pony Peggy, "fit" Stardust, but the forward flare of the saddle flaps hid her shoulders, making her forehand appear shorter than it was; and the entire saddle was too big for Robin. Eventually we got a pony saddle of suitable proportions for both; this saddle was later broken at the tree

Tuffy's bridle is a halter with reins and lead line snapped to its rings. Felt-seated saddle provides more "stick" than leather. Tuffy's rider wears washable jods and vital hunt cap.

With roly-poly witherless ponies, a crupper helps keep the saddle in place and prevents its tipping forward. This adjustable strap goes from a padded loop around the tail to a metal ring (known as a D or dee) on the back of the cantle. A breastplate keeps a saddle from slipping back but is seldom needed unless you're doing a lot of work over fences.

The extent of flare in a saddle and the amount of padding in the knee roll again are matters of personal preference. Beginning riders or those schooling over jumps or those with slab-sided ponies may like the added security and "bulk" knee rolls and/or knee suedes can give. I've found that as the Pony Pals improve in riding ability and sensitivity to their mounts, the less padding there is, the closer they are to their ponies and the better they "feel" them. The chief thing is that the rider should be able to sit comfortably as deeply as possible in the center of the saddle over the pony's center of gravity. He should feel that he's *in* the saddle, not *on* it, and not be tipped to the front or back of the seat.

Several very fine saddles are designed especially for the small-division pony. While unlike the saddle for a large pony, which may fit the rider for much of his adult life, these saddles are a money-back investment as they are much in demand and can be sold when outgrown. Properly cared for, a saddle should last ten to twenty years.

In choosing and fitting your saddle, consider these points: You're more likely to need a broad arch, as ponies are more often broad and low-withered and round through the ribs, than a cutback pommel, which is for high-withered animals. Remember that a saddle will often fit better when a pony is firmly muscled up than when he is flappy fat. When you put the saddle on your pony, there should be space under the pommel so that it does not press on the withers. When you look from the rear, the center line or gullet should clear the pony's backbone.

If the saddle seems to fit down over the pony and not just perch on his back, check it again with a rider in it. Another pressure point is directly under the back panels; the rider's weight should not cause the saddle to bear down on the loins. Move your pony forward so that you can make sure his shoulders do not rub against the under skirts. Pressure at any of these points will give him discomfort and may develop rubs or sores which will put an end to your riding for some time.

If possible try your saddle out at a trot and canter as well as a walk, to see whether it fits you in action.

When we speak of a saddle we visualize it complete with stirrups (irons, leathers) and girth, but when you buy a saddle you may buy it with these fittings or "bare." Never compromise with quality as far as these are concerned; if you purchase them individually, get the best. If buying the leathers used, see that there are not cracks in the fold where the irons hang or at the top where the buckle is stitched in place, and that stitching is secure.

Stirrup leathers come in different widths and lengths (don't get them too long for a small saddle; have them shortened at the buckle end if need be). Beveled edges and numbered holes make for easy adjustment. If you're sharing tack and pony, you can shorten stirrups for a little rider by wrapping the leathers (always wrap them away from your pony, not towards his sides, so the irons will hang properly); but a leather-punch can do a onetime job that makes shortening them in the usual way possible. Cheap leathers stretch, and you may have to move up a hole after use. If you normally ride in the last hole, punch a few extras above it to allow for this or for shortening for cross-country work or jumping.

Don't settle for just any stirrup irons. They come not only in various styles (off-set, break-away,

**A lead line rider may be excused for using her hand to adjust her stirrup—one that is the correct size for a little foot.**

safety, and regular, to name a few) but in various metals (stainless steel the best). They should be heavy so that they will swing back on your foot if you "lose" one. Judge size by allowing space for your finger on either side of your foot at its widest point: any narrower, and your foot might become wedged; any wider, and your foot might slip through.

The footrest of a stirrup has a slot to prevent dirt from your boot sole from piling up. If the tiny points or pricks seen on new irons are worn down, ridgy rubber pads may be inserted in the slot for added resistance (security) and for (to a debatable degree) warmth in winter. The sheepskin foot warmers that resemble the toes of shoes can also be used to keep a beginner's foot from sliding through.

Meri-Jo holds a stitched leather girth while Robin, a Balding girth slung over her shoulder, slides a clean mohair girth through stirrup irons.

The girth—that all-important "belt" that holds your saddle on your pony—comes in different materials and different lengths. There are various styles in leather, canvas or webbing, "string" (cord, nylon, mohair), even in vinyl, and with elastic or "stretch" inserts. Mohair remains a favorite among the many (Balding, stretch, tubular linen, Fitzwilliam, folded) that we've accumulated over the years. Mohair has some give to it, so it's comfortable, particularly for a green and growing pony or one that's being jumped; it does not chafe, and it keeps a saddle in place. It is not hurt by mud or water and is easily dried and brushed off or completely washed and dried.

Girths end in buckles attached, with the exception of the self-bound string girths, by leather tabs. Both leather and stitching must be checked regularly (along with the girth billets on your saddle to which they fasten). You don't want to pop a girth!

To figure for a girth, measure from two holes down on your girth billets. You want to do up your girth evenly, and to go higher than that under your saddle flaps is awkward. Of course, girth billets themselves vary in length, and you can get girth extenders to buckle on to them as well as a buckle guard to slip over them to protect the underside of your saddle flaps.

One extra piece of tack could be a third stirrup leather to use as a neck strap. You could also use the neck strap of a martingale, but the martingale itself (a device to restrict the upward movement of a horse's head) has no place in our pony schooling.

Tubular girth covers of washable fleece can be slipped over a girth to prevent chafing or for added protection if your pony has recently had a girth sore. For daily riding, you will want a pad under your saddle to protect it from sweat and your pony from friction. (You may omit it during a brief show appearance if you decide your pony looks trimmer without it.) Pads can be of quilting, felt (hair felt or wool felt), sheepskin (the wool goes next to your pony's back), or artificial fleece (single or double faced). Sheepskin remains the tops in terms of absorbency, ventilation, and length of life—and of cost and care. Artificial fleece ones and quilts can be washed; felt must be brushed. Use only clean, dry pads.

This saddle pad has been left hanging so that it can dry and the underside of the saddle air.

Be certain the pad fits the contour of your saddle and allow for about an inch around the edge. Loops on the pad go around your billets before you attach your girth and keep the pad in place. A pad should of course be carefully put forward on the withers and then slid back into position so as not to rough the pony's hair the wrong way, with care taken that the pad is pulled high under the pommel. The rider's weight exerts great pressure on a pad stretched taut under the arch, so it undoes the benefit of well-adjusted tack to put a pad on sloppily.

## BRIDLES

Your other major piece of tack besides your saddle is a bridle. This, simply put, is a fine leather fitted headstall (or fancy halter) to which a bit and reins are fastened. The bit goes into the pony's mouth, and by manipulating the bit with the reins you direct the pony. ("Your bridle's there for *navigation*," Captain Dave told the Pony Pals.)

Like saddles, bridles come in sizes: pony, cob, full or horse, oversize. Because the cheekstraps, the cavesson or noseband, and the crown piece with throat latch that make up the bridle head are adjustable, a given size affords a lot of leeway. A tiny pony like Tuffy may need adjustments made by a saddlemaker in the smallest pony size available, while top-limit ponies like Lutine Bell may require a horse one, adjusted to its minimum size.

There are three basic types of bridle: snaffle, pelham, full or double bridle, with one or two reins and a wide variety of bits of varying severity. Your

**A double bridle (borrowed and completely unsuitable) makes a mouthful of metal for a green pony, a handful of reins for an eleven-year-old rider without the finesse such tack requires. Simple snaffles are normally used on our ponies.**

52

pony should be ridden in the simplest bit possible—the snaffle, which is pleasant for him and easy for you to put on and use. However, you'll want to recognize other bridles and their purposes.

A full or double bridle requires riding finesse and a pony beyond the level of schooling discussed in this book. It has two separate bits—a thin snaffle called a bradoon and a curb with a shank and a curb chain, and two reins—the snaffle, and the curb. It is a mouthful for any horse, and its misuse in uneducated hands is sheer cruelty.

A pelham bridle has one bit with a shank that provides rings for both a snaffle and a curb rein as well as for a curb chain.

The pelham and the full bridle are sometimes seen in use with the curb rein knotted and lying idle; this is to help the horse on the theory that the rider is "just using the snaffle." To only a slight degree is this true, for the bradoon and pelham bits do not work in the same manner as a true snaffle. With the pelham, the design of the port still acts on the tongue, even on the roof of the mouth, while the curb chain still presses against the chin groove of the jaw.

Both these bridles (or any version that combines a shanked bit and a curb chain) trap both the pony's tongue and his lower jaw in a severe vise; even a light touch on the reins causes a disproportionate pressure. The Pony Pals are given a lesson to show how the pony is affected:

One youngster holds a pelham bridle by the headpiece and by the curb shank with the curb chain hooked short. Another puts his hand on edge between the bit and the chain and pulls the reins with his other hand. With even a light touch on the reins there is a painful pinching and squeezing of the imprisoned hand. On the pony, the movement of the bottom of the shank slightly backwards and up also pulls the top of the shanks forward and down; and since the shanks attach to the cheekstraps, and these to the crownpiece, they in turn cause added pressure on the top of the pony's head.

Such pressure caused by tack at that point, the sensitive poll, is often overlooked in handling a pony not only in a bridle but in a halter. With a device called a war bridle we can take deliberate advantage of it; with our ordinary tack we must not be unaware of its existence or of its effect when we are the cause.

Besides the pelham, hybrid bridles include the Kimberwick with its curb mouthpiece and chain but single rings for one rein only and the Tom Thumb pelham with its snaffle mouthpiece, curb chain, and short shanks with double rings for both snaffle and curb reins. (If you wish to avoid the complication of double reins, a bit converter can be used, providing small straps that buckle from top to bottom ring, the snaffle rein then attaching to the strap.) In each case pressure on the rein applies not only to the bit but to the curb chain with that viselike action.

The solution with a pony that pulls or has a "hard" mouth is seldom a more severe bit: it is corrective schooling—often of rider as well as of pony. A change to a less severe bit that no longer causes pain and allows the pony to concentrate on your requests, not his discomfort, may be the answer. (As has often been said, very few ponies spoil their own mouths.)

Our choice, the simplest and mildest of bridles, is the snaffle with its one bit and single reins.

Here the bit rests on the pony's tongue and his "bars" (see Chapter 6, Your Pony and His Health). This is the one spot in his mouth where we can safely put our hand (to open his mouth, as for bridling). Supersensitive, it is a bony ridge only thinly covered with delicate gum tissue. It is on these bars and on the corners of the mouth that the snaffle acts.

Even within the simplicity of the snaffle there is a variety of bits: a jointed snaffle , for instance, puts less pressure on the tongue than a straight mouthpiece but may have a more nutcracker effect or may bump the roof of the mouth.

Whatever the bridle—full, pelham, or snaffle—its severity is determined by: the thickness or thinness of the bits (the thinner and lighter the more severe); the extent of twist and the roughness of the metal; the material the bit is made of (soft rubber, hard rubber, metal, string, wire); whether it is in one piece or jointed; whether it is with or without dangles; whether it is fixed or sliding on the cheeks; the degree of and abruptness of curvature in the port; the length of the shanks or cheeks which influences not only the leverage exerted on the viselike effect of bit and curb chain but the pressure of the crownpiece on the poll; whether the curb chain is thick or thin, chain or leather; whether the links are twisted or lie smoothly; whether it's hooked correctly or too tightly; whether the crown and nosepiece are plain leather or (yes!) lined with wire; and—what sort of hands, knowledge, ability, and consideration the rider has.

Whatever your choice, your bit is your means of communication with your pony. If your communication is not successful, don't turn to a more severe bit: turn back a step or two in training your pony and stick to your mild snaffle.

From this explanation of bridles, you can see why

a green pony should start out with the mildest snaffle possible. A Dee Bit with a one-piece soft rubber mouthpiece is ideal, or a thick jointed snaffle with large rings such as "egg-butt" or Dee. Full cheeks keep the bit from pulling through to either side and being less effective with a beginning rider. Robin schooled Galaxy in a ring snaffle but novice rider Kate went better in a full-cheek. Tuffy started out in a half-cheek bit because that was the only one we could find tiny enough.

How your snaffle bit acts depends partly on correct adjustment of your bridle head. The brow band is the only part that does not adjust, since both ends have sewn loops through which the headpiece and cavesson straps slide; it must be wide enough to rest on the forehead above the eyes without pinching or without surplus bulge and without rubbing the base of your pony's ears. The noseband should fit an inch below his cheekbones with room for only two fingers between it and the nasal bone. Often cavessons hang too loosely and too long (notice Tuffy's in many pictures). The throat latch, on the other hand, is often adjusted too tightly. Test yours after buckling by inserting your clenched fist or four fingers on edge between it and your pony's jaw. Your throat latch and cavesson should of course be buckled and unbuckled each time you use the bridle.

Cheekstraps, however, are fixed once—when you fit the bridle and bit to your pony. Adjust them evenly on each side so that the bit lies in your pony's mouth just barely wrinkling the corners of his mouth without pinching them. A bit that hangs too low may bang his teeth and it offers little control. A bit that is pulled too high will pinch the corners of his mouth and through the cheekstraps cause pressure on his poll by the headpiece. The cannon or mouthpiece of the bit should not extend out beyond his mouth, nor should the rings be pulled inside; the rings or Dees should rest against the side of his muzzle at the curve of his lips. The right size—4½ inches, 5 inches, and so on—is important so that the joint will not bump the palate and the bit not slide through to one side before the opposite ring or cheek comes into place as a "stop."

Once your bridle and bit are fitted to your pony, you'll unbuckle the cheekstraps only for cleaning. Nevertheless, each time you tack up, face your pony to see that the bit hangs evenly and that a cheekstrap has not been pulled up through the crownpiece so that it is off center. With cheekstraps adjusted, slide the keepers in place, as you will each

time when you do up your throat latch and cavesson. These leather loops, some fixed, some sliding, keep ends in place and prevent a "mare's tails" impression of sloppy tack.

Of the metals bits are made of, stainless steel is the best. Cheaper metals may pit, flake, or rust. When you think that your pony is going to have his bit in his mouth for hours on end, you'll see why the smoothest, most durable, most easily kept-clean metal should be chosen.

## REINS

Reins come plain (smooth), laced, plaited or braided, rubber-covered. Some are made of webbing or cord. They, like the ends of the cheekstraps, may be secured after they fold around the bit rings (this fold is called the mount), permanently by hand-sewn stitches or by hook studs or buckles. Sewn ones are the most elegant and costly; buckles the cheapest and least desirable; hook studs the most common.

The single rein of a snaffle is usually buckled at the end and may come in any of the materials and styles described. (Your pelham and full bridles require two reins, both usually smooth, the curb narrower and sewn at the end.)

Reins can be purchased separately, or a preferred type or length substituted for the ones that come with a bridle. For a small pony or a pony with a short neck or forehand it may be necessary for a saddlemaker to shorten your reins so that the bight (that dangle of rein ends after your hands) is not so dangerously long that your foot could get caught or such a nuisance that it catches under your saddle flap. Since you hold the reins in your hands all the time you're riding, it's nice to have them of a length, width, and texture that you like.

## HALTERS

Your pony's halter and lead rope might be compared with your dog's collar and leash. In fact, a halter is sometimes called a head collar. Workaday halters of sturdy construction have a simple noseband with a ring underneath for your lead to snap to, short side straps or cheeks, and a connecting strap that goes under the jaw and around the poll and buckles the halter into place.

Like the saddle and bridle, the halter should fit. The noseband should lie below the cheekbones but above the sensitive cartilege with room for a finger or two (but no more). The cheekstraps or sides should be long enough for the head strap to buckle and leave ample room under the pony's throat.

Halters are made in sizes—foal, weanling, pony, large pony, and full, to name some—and the size should be checked frequently where young animals are concerned. They come in rope, nylon, webbing, and leather. They may be riveted, or stitched with hardware of brass-trimmed metals, solid brass, or nickel. They can be strictly utilitarian or quite elegant, complete with name plates. Halter nosebands may be fixed or adjustable, throat latches may be fixed or snap or buckle, head straps may buckle at both side or, more commonly, on the near side only.

Eventually you may want not only a work halter—for teaching to tie up, for hosing and shampooing, and so on—but also a show halter for special occasions. You can buy sets of sheepskin or fleece tubing to slip over any halter to prevent rubbing.

If you follow the safety rule of never leaving a halter on an unattended pony, a halter and lead rope should be kept handy to his stall or paddock, no matter where you keep the rest of your tack.

Your safety and your pony's well-being depend on your tack. If you have any qualms as to your ability to choose and fit your saddle and bridle, get help. Tack shop dealers will gladly advise.

If your pony comes "with tack," don't take it for granted that his tack fits. It's surprising how many people who put a high price tag on a pony for sale will bring that pony out for trial with dirty, ill-adjusted tack, even with broken reins knotted on to encrusted bits and dirty saddles with cracked fittings. (Need I add, never use such equipment in trying out a pony.)

Once you've bought good tack, remember to check its fit periodically, for as your pony's condition changes with growth or athletic schooling so may his muscles; minor adjustments may be needed.

While tack has not changed very drastically over the decades, fads have their moments. Saddle pads appear in synthetic fibers in violent colors better associated with carousel horses; so do halters and lead ropes. Polka dots and checkerboard squares ornament brow bands, pompoms of all shades adorn braided manes. Currently popular saddle pads flaunt fluffy edges where the traditional sheepskin

allows one discreet inch. Over-girths, breastplates, Chambon or draw reins, martingale rein-sets have their craze. Suddenly "everyone" has round cavessons or rolled reins. Recessed stirrup bars and thigh rolls become "a must." Figure eight or dropped nosebands spring into vogue, but plain traditional saddlery is always in good taste.

Fads in fashion can be amusing and innocuous. Fads in schooling devices can be harmful. Train your pony so that he moves with correct head carriage *without* a martingale; train him so that he mouths his bit correctly and doesn't *need* to have his jaws kept shut by a dropped noseband.

## CARE OF TACK

Now that you have your own tack, take care of it. A saddle and bridle, like a favorite tennis racket or a particular copy of a favorite book, become unique and have a certain feel as you use them.

The proper ways of handling tack are also the easiest. Your youngster can carry a saddle when its heaviest part is balanced correctly on one arm with the pommel and flaps towards the bend of his elbow. You can also carry a saddle "straddling" your thigh with the underpart against your side, cantle up, and your hand supporting the pommel. With both methods of carrying the saddle you can at the same time carry your bridle with your shoulder, your arm, or your hand just as you take it off your bridle rack (or your pony), through the crownpieces and the rein ends. Small Pony Pals often put their hands around the folded reins and cheekstraps and carry the bridle doubled over to keep the reins from dragging on the ground.

If you must put a saddle down temporarily, stand it pommel down with the seat tilted forward so that the cantle rests against the wall or some other support, such as a tree trunk, with the arch or knee rolls taking its weight. Protect the leather with your saddle pad or girth—or a grain bag. Never put a saddle down on the ground "right side up" with its skirts spread, as this may stretch or break the tree; it would be better to put it down completely upside down.

Your saddle should be put on its rack without the pad so that its underside can air. Although it's correct to put your stirrups up when untacking, let them dangle if gritty and keep your girth, if muddy, off your saddle seat. Leather scratches easily. Later, clean irons can be run up on the leathers and the girth be hung in such a way that it dries without twisting.

Let your reins hang full length or double them back with the buckle end resting over the crownpiece.

Ideally, tack should be cleaned each time you use it. Dirty tack is disagreeable not only to your pony but to you, and salty sweat and mud disintegrate leather. However, when riding time is at a premium (during the school year or if you're working) it's better to ride than to clean tack. By doing a thoroughgoing job every few weeks you can maintain good condition with daily "survival housekeeping." If you wipe your bit clean and get mud off your stirrups and girth as promptly as possible, take-apart cleaning can be left for after dark or for a rainy day.

Survival cleaning is simplified by keeping a cloth and soft brush where your tack goes. Of course bits will stay much cleaner if you never let your pony eat hay or grass with one in his mouth. The longer such gunk stays on the harder it gets, so remove it promptly with a wet cloth, or dunk the bit briefly in a bowl of water, being careful to keep the rings out so that the cheekstrap and rein leather does not get wet. Water is bad for leather; use as little as possible during any cleaning process.

You may choose between washing mud off a leather girth and saddle flaps or letting it dry and then gently brushing it off before wiping the leather clean. Either way, when the leather is clean and dry go over it with a saddle-soapy sponge squeezed almost dry. This "lick and a promise" makes a real difference.

Thorough tack cleaning requires a little more space, since you take everything apart, and a little more equipment.

You can work on a tack horse designed to support

**A three-year-old gives her saddle "a lick and a promise" cleaning, without removing the fittings.**

**Pony Pals prepare to clean tack out of doors. Such work takes longer when you're giggling over Thelwell!**

your saddle upside down as well as right side up, or on a saw horse or a chair. The Pony Pals like to clean tack in company—on the long studio table or on the floor, or out of doors in summer, with old plasticized grain bags spread out to protect the working surface from soapy wetness and oil and the saddle leather from scratches. You may have a tack-cleaning hook (what the Pony Pals call the anchor) hung from the ceiling and suspend bridles from it, or you may spread bridle parts out on a flat surface. Allow enough room so that the parts don't get mixed up.

Your cleaning kit should include:

At least two sponges (one for washing, one for soaping); keep them separate
Saddle soap (paste or glycerine bar)
Neatsfoot oil and brush
Soft rags for drying and polishing (or a chamois if you prefer)
A very stiff brush for cleaning pad, string girth
Metal polish and burnishing rags
Toothbrushes for cleaning crevices and bit joints
Wooden skewers to slip into the mounts of reins and cheekpieces and make it easier to slide the leather forward off the hook studs
A pail (even if you have a sink and running water where you clean)
A work apron
Elbow grease (make your own!)

You can store your kit in a pail or box, left uncovered so the sponges won't mould. The Pony Pals like string or net bags for both tack-cleaning and pony-cleaning sponges, as they can easily be hung

up wet and not tempt playful Border Collies by being spread out to dry.

The neatsfoot oil may be the material you use the least often, but the times when you do use it are important for your tack. Neatsfoot oil (not the more drying neatsfoot compound) or any unsalted vegetable oil softens and helps to waterproof your leather.

While some new leather comes pre-stained, most comes in "natural"—the so-called saddle-leather shades. You can let new leather darken gradually, but water and dirt may spot it before it does; you can buy liquid stains; or you can darken it in one oiling. (This is useful to know if you have to replace a part of 'an old bridle and want to avoid a patchy look.)

Nothing looks more "johnny come lately" than brand-new tack. Just as (in accordance with the old joke) you wear your new riding togs around the barnyard a few times before you appear with them in public, so you will feel that light-colored fresh-from-the-store tack stands out like a sore thumb. Old tack, or freshly darkened tack, does look better on most ponies. And, aside from this, oiling gives added protection.

If your tack is used, oiling supples the leather and makes reins and leathers as well as skirts and flaps more flexible. Remember that once leather is cracked and old there is no way of restoring it; you can only maintain the status quo. If you have any doubt about there being enough life in the leather to stand up to the work expected, throw it out.

To oil, prepare tack as for a thorough cleaning, but just apply neatsfoot once over lightly. Use a rag or brush to oil every bit of your saddle or bridle inside and out (except for any suede parts), let it sit overnight to permeate, and then wipe off any excess.

Too much neatsfoot oil, like too much water, will do no good; it will damage stitches, swim on the surface and not be absorbed, be slippery and messy to handle, and stain anything it touches—your shirt, your gloves, the seat of your pants. Use it only rarely: for example when you've been caught in a downpour or had to swim your pony.

Thorough tack-cleaning is done with fittings stripped from the saddle, buckle guards pulled off the billets, irons pulled off the leathers. If you use a saddle pad, the underside of the saddle will be quite clean; if not, the panels may be gray and waxy with sweaty scurf and the gullets and skirts may have splashes of dried mud.

The bridle, with the bit removed, should be taken completely apart so that you can get at every fold of leather and wherever buckles fasten.

For the first few times, undo only one part of the bridle at a time, clean that part, and redo it before going on to another. You'll soon become familiar with how it goes. In putting it back, be certain that your bit hangs properly. (With a jointed snaffle, be certain that the bit is put back on the cheekstraps properly. Pony Pal Jill was puzzled by Timbertot's unusual head tossing. Investigation revealed that the joints of the snaffle, instead of moving in concave flexibility, were pointing rigidly up into the roof of the pony's mouth. The bit had been put back in reverse. There is a right side up to even a straight snaffle.)

If straps seem hard to undo, on or off your pony—halter, bridle, or girth billets—the trick is: don't pull the buckle. Hold on to the leather strap with a slight downward pressure and *push* the buckle up. As soon as the buckle tongue is clear of the hole you can slide the buckle down the strap and off.

Thorough cleaning means that every bit of leather should be cleaned and saddle soaped on both sides and that all metals (except the cannons of your bit) should be polished and buffed.

Clean your tack first with a moist sponge. Dry with a soft cloth. Then apply saddle soap—sparingly. Perhaps saddle soap is a misnomer. Saddle soap is not for cleaning; it's for protection, to keep your tack soft, flexible, and water-repellent. It ought not to be applied to dirty tack, as it's more likely to rub dirt in than to lift it off.

To avoid excessive suds, before you pick up saddle soap with your sponge (either by dipping into the paste type or by rubbing the bar type), wet your sponge and squeeze it as dry as possible. Never have your sponge so wet that the saddle soap lathers into suds. Work the soap well into all leather (the rougher under parts of skirts and flaps, the bend of stirrup leathers, bridle and rein mounts seem more absorbent) and then finish off rubbing in one direction. If your soapy sponge was sufficiently dry, none will remain filming the surface. If any does, wipe off in a final polishing with a dry cloth.

If the holes in your leathers or the braids of your reins hold excess saddle soap, remove it lightly with your blunt skewer. While you have your tack apart, check billets, keepers, and buckle leathers for broken stitches or cracking and inspect bits, irons, and metal pieces for cracks or pitting.

If your pony saddle is a felt one, saddle soap only the leather parts and brush the rest. Occasionally

leather saddles have panels of linen or other cloth; this part, of course, should never be wetted but be cleaned by brushing.

Folded leather girths should be soaped inside as well as out, and you can insert a strip of oily flannel to keep the leather flexible. Avoid wetting the elastic sections of stretch girths, and soap all buckle leathers on other types. Mohair or other string girths can be washed by hand or machine. (Be prepared for a temporary fractional shrinkage when you next tack up.)

Like these girths, saddle pads, brushed and aired daily, should be washed whenever necessary. Meticulously clean pads protect your pony's back from minor irritations and potential sores.

If you have driving harness, it can be cleaned and soaped in like manner and its metal parts polished. The set should be hung or stored in such a way that traces and lines are folded as few times as possible.

You may also want to do head bumpers, halters, leather lead shanks, and any other leather pieces when you do your thorough tack cleaning.

Your clean tack can be put up in several ways. To put it away for next day's use, you can hang your bridle with the reins over the headpiece and with the cavesson and throat latch undone. Your saddle can be put away, leathers on and irons run up, with the girth placed over the seat and buckle ends through the irons on each side—or just resting on the seat.

Both bridle and tack can be protected with shaped covers or plain cloth or left uncovered so you can admire your handiwork. Clean tack looks great—well worth the elbow grease!

To be stored, tack should be well soaped or coated with vaseline. Fittings should be left off the saddle and ends of straps left unbuckled and free of keepers on reins and bridle. Moth balls can be put in among the papers stuffed around the saddle to support it in its storage box or chest. Store in a not too dry, not too hot, not too cold place.

To put tack away for a few weeks, hang your bridle in the usual manner but cross the throat latch in a figure eight around the cheekstraps, sliding its end through the keeper without buckling. Another way is to fasten the throat latch and then buckle the ends of the reins so they hang from it rather than resting on the headpiece as usual. Your saddle can be stored on your saddle rack with the fittings removed. Girth and leathers can hang straight on the wall from right-angle hooks. Irons can be hung from wall hooks or on the hook found under some saddle racks.

# 5

# CARE AND FEEDING

*Despondently Terry scuffed along the shore. Would he ever have a pony? Quarters from his paper-route piled up all too slowly in his coffee-can bank. He'd be an old man by the time he had the price of a broken-down merry-go-round horse, let alone the brave pinto that filled his every dream.*

*Waves curled against his bare toes. Spray soaked his rolled-up jeans. Gulls shrieked; but, head down, Terry ignored them.*

*Suddenly he whirled, alert–A whinny! . . . surely that was a whinny? Shading his eyes against the coastal sun, he searched the little cove. The sound came again. There–Terry broke into a run. There where the dunes curved to block the ocean view a pony struggled in the surf.*

*Terry plunged waist deep to its rescue. Exhausted, mane wet, forelock plastered over frightened eyes, the pony raised its piebald head and surged through the retreating waves.*

*"Here, boy, here." The spotted neck slipped seal-wet under Terry's hand. He grabbed the mane and pulled. Safe on the sands, the pony nuzzled against him. "You're mine, boy, mine," Terry declared. "Flotsam, that's what I'll call you. A pony of my own. Mine by right of salvage!"*

Everyone who's ever longed for a pony of his own dreams such fantasies—but, alas for storybook luck, it isn't so much the acquiring of a pony that is the problem, it's the upkeep. Even if you have a pony given to you, even if you have a place to keep him, daily expenses must be met.

What is involved in feeding and caring for a pony? What does "upkeep" mean? How much does it cost to keep a pony?

Upkeep includes supplying food and "clothing" and routine veterinary and blacksmith services.

Upkeep varies, depending on the pony (age, size, health, individual constitution, and activity) and on your facilities (climate, shelter, availability of grazing, and type of footing). In certain regions, a small mature pony, an "easy keeper," can live "for nothing" all year round on grass. You may never have to buy feed. If the footing is good (not rocky) you may never have to buy shoes, but you'll need a blacksmith regularly to trim his bare feet. If your pony is healthy and has no accidents or ailments you'll need a veterinarian only for routine health care several times a year.

Supplementing such an "easy keeper's" diet with hay only several months of the year, you could probably still keep expenses low.

At the other extreme, a large pony kept in top condition for strenuous daily riding and occasional hunting or showing, fed "bought feed" all year round, and being shod with new shoes or re-sets every six or seven weeks, but still getting only routine veterinary care, could cost hundreds of dollars for maintenance. (This does not include entry fees, capping fees, trailering, or other expenses for pony-related activities.)

But with any pony you must be prepared for the odd expense: a broken halter or lead rope; a lost shoe; an epidemic of VEE where ponies are protected only against EEE and WEE in their annual shots program; a cut leg from tangling with a strand of wire; an unexplainable cough; a bout of colic. Veterinarians charge for house calls (we pay fifteen dollars) and add more for emergency calls. Shots, worming, antibiotics, special salves, powders, bandages, all are extra. As with most things nowadays, the price of hay or grain fluctuates, upwards!

Usually, the bigger the pony the more upkeep costs. Regardless of size, however, growing active ponies, like growing active kids, cost more to feed than grown ones. The food your pony eats provides for growth and/or body maintenance, plus bloom, energy, and heat. (It may also provide fat and surplus energy!) The pony that is unprotected against winter wind or rain, that must expend more energy moving to find sufficient grazing, that is ridden hard several hours a day, will require more feed than a blanketed pony standing idle in a stall. A mare in foal, a nursing dam, foals and young stock have special dietary needs. Even within given ages and sizes, ponies like people vary in how they utilize their feed.

In your search for a pony, remember that what the seller calls an "easy keeper" may not be the buyer's "easy keeper." The seller need not be deliberately misrepresenting, but his grazing or his can of oats may be different from yours. (More on this later.)

Some ponies are easy keepers. Some, like Tuffy, get fat on the scent of hay, and the problem is to keep them healthily slim. Others, like Lutine Bell as a filly, belie their ample diet by adolescent gauntness. (It took a winter's confinement at Pine Hill Riding Center to fatten Lutine. At High Hickory she self-exercised constantly by galloping free on what became known as Lute's Race Track, an oval she wore in the Field Beyond. Like some two-legged teenagers, she was always on the move—perhaps because of her New Forest bloodline, expressed now in her love of going cross-country.)

Confinement to a stall is not however the sole answer to keeping a pony well fed. To have a healthy appetite your pony must get exercise. Without exercise, he may not eat much—or he may eat a lot out of boredom—but the resulting fat melts away when work is done. Specialists in showing a pony "in hand" are aware of this need for exercise if even an unridden pony is to be in condition and radiate beauty, fitness, and bloom. A vital rule for any pony owner is that feeding and exercise go hand in hand. For this reason, no matter how much help they have with other chores, the best horsemen prefer to feed their mounts themselves, or closely supervise the feeding.

Just as your pony must exercise to eat well and to make the most of what he eats, so if he exercises he must eat well not to drain body reserves and go

down in condition. Often ponies are underfed—through their owners' neglect or laziness or deliberate and cruel economy or plain ignorance. The pony boom is a fairly new thing, and so it is not surprising that ignorance of proper feeding requirements and of the necessity for internal-parasite control is all too prevalent. Owners (particularly, alas, parents who pay the bills but don't supervise the pony or child firsthand) sometime allot a fixed amount for the pony's budget, and fail to increase it when the pony's needs change or feed costs rise.

How can you plan a realistic pony budget? What expenses should you expect? What must you know so as to make the most of what you spend on upkeep? All horsemen, no matter how unlimited their funds, strive to keep food costs low by following a stringent worming program for parasite control, by providing ample water, and by using grazing and bought feeds knowledgeably.

You must first understand certain basic facts about your pony. A pony, herbivorous like other equines, lives in his wild state on grass and water, grazing almost constantly, with regular rest periods. When we deprive him of the freedom to graze, we must provide substitutes for grass—hay and/or "short feed," *i.e.* grain. In proportion to his size a pony's stomach is very small, and his metabolism is geared to a continuous digestive process. Because of this, he cannot benefit from huge amounts of food given at any one time. We must consider this when we take over his feeding and arbitrarily put him on three or four meals a day. Long foodless intervals between feedings which shut down his digestive motor and necessitate its being started up again at mealtimes may be more costly to you (as well as harmful to him) than providing him with a continuous supply of food for free-choice eating so that his body mechanism never "shuts off."

With this elementary knowledge of your pony's insides, you can understand the importance of following the basic rule of:

Order of Feeding: Water first, then hay, then
grain or short feed.

The wrong order means waste of feed and, worse, discomfort—even to the point of death—for the pony. Feeding grain on an empty stomach and then feeding hay may cause the roughage (hay) to push the grain through the pony's system before proper digestion can take place. Feeding grain and then water to a pony that has had no water for some time,

**Pony Pals Alicia and Shirley discuss feed with
Robin during Pony Camp at High Hickory.**

who eats and then drinks thirstily, may result in colic
and death.

Having this basic knowledge, and following these
basic rules, you can choose from several methods of
feeding the individual pony, your pony.

## KEEPING A PONY AT GRASS, OR
## ON GRAZING ONLY

To keep a pony at grass, so that he gets all his food
by grazing, is certainly the cheapest method; but it
involves more than merely having a front lawn or an
overgrown spare lot. The rule of thumb is a half to
one acre of grazing per pony, but the less the acreage
the more the nutritional value is adversely affected
by various factors: The grazing may be poor in the
first place. Grazing may become nonexistent as

hoofed traffic destroys grass in muddy or dusty
weather. Pawing and digging for food in frost or
snow may break roots and destroy normal spring
growth. Seasonal growths of different grasses may
make pastures too lush and watery at one time and
too rank to be eaten at another. At all seasons the
stage of growth affects the nutritional value (protein
content, and so on) of the grass.

Poisonous weeds—ragwort, deadly nightshade—
may be present, and pests—dandelions, plaintain,
goldenrod, steeplebush—may crowd out and eventually eliminate edible grasses. Privet, yew, laurel
or sheep-kill, rhododendron, rhubarb, choke-
cherry, even fallen acorns prove poisonous if eaten
copiously by a pony desperately foraging for food in
an overgrazed field.

New pony owners express puzzlement at seeing certain areas grazed to the bare roots and even

to the dirt while other areas, waist high with "beautiful" grass, are ignored. Such tall grasses with their maturing seed-heads, pretty to us, are unattractive to your pony. Preferring his grass fetlock-high and sprouting, he will ignore even early growth contaminated by his own droppings, stable runoff, acidity from nearby pines, or unknown causes. Cut and fed fresh to a pony confined in a dry paddock, such tall grasses may seem delectable. (Anything green and juicy would: a pony must never be hand-fed weeds, for he might even relish what he would wisely ignore if he had free choice of grazing.)

The more limited your grazing facilities are the more they require proper pasture management if they are to provide sole upkeep for your pony. You must practice division and rotation so that one section is rested while another is grazed. Fencing for such division need not be so sturdy as perimeter fencing. Electrified wire or portable panels like sheep hurdles are sufficient. Riding and schooling should be done elsewhere so as not to destroy the turf. Small areas must be picked up as regularly as a stall; larger ones can have droppings spread by dragging or harrowing. Both, ideally, should be mowed every month to keep grass fetlock high and therefore palatable to your pony.

Never feed a pony lawn mowings: such short "hot" clippings mould too rapidly and may cause indigestion or colic. It is safe to feed by hand long grass, freshly picked, in only the amount your pony consumes before your eyes, but remove whatever he doesn't eat promptly. Mowed *pasture* grass can safely be left where it falls, however, for your pony will probably ignore it to eat the growing shoots and will return to it only when it has been cured in the sun.

To establish and maintain proper grazing may mean a little work. Many pony owners today have no background in farming or pasture management; but reference books and pamphlets are available, and farm bureau and extension service personnel will give first-hand advice and assistance as to seed selection, liming, fertilizing, and maintenance.

## GRAZING WITH SUPPLEMENTARY FEEDING

Next to keeping a pony at grass, the cheapest upkeep is grazing with supplementary feeding. With this system you provide hay (which, after all, is

**Shavings litter Galaxy's coat. Other ponies prefer to roll in the snow, but if shavings were not put out, this yearling would roll in the hay and ruin it for eating.**

grass cut, dried, and packaged) or short feed at certain times of the year either to make up for insufficient grazing or because your pony is working hard.

The best time to put out supplementary feed for a pony at grass is in the early evening or in both the early evening and early morning. Place hay where it won't be trampled on, or in a rack. Put grain in a tub rather than directly on the ground so that your pony will not pick up dirt or parasites as he eats. Since his digestive mechanism sets its own clock, he will expect this extra food at regular hours.

Taper on and off with any supplements. Any change in feeding, especially if it coincides with a drastic increase or decrease in exercise, should be gradual. For instance, a pony suddenly thrown out full time on rich pasture in the spring will get grass diarrhea or may even founder. When first turning out to grass, work your pony up to a full day by starting with a ten-minute period once, then twice, a day for several days (on a stomach already filled with hay), then half an hour, and so on, until you eliminate the hay and leave him grazing full time. In the fall, slowly compensate for inadequate grazing with increased amounts of hay.

## WATER

With either grazing arrangement, as with all feeding, water will be of prime importance. Your pony will need a supply kept clean and plentiful.

**Tuffy and in-foal Stardust ignore their own feed to investigate hay intended for sheep waiting in the meadow. With an abundance of fresh snow, the animals often ignore water in pails and nibble first snow, then hay.**

Natural water—brook, pond, spring—must be checked out for pollution at any point along the way and rechecked to make sure that the supply is not lessened by a dry spell or freezing. A pony's normal intake is from five to fifteen gallons or more per day. Filling a pail once or twice a day is not enough.

Buckets should be tied securely to a fence post or tree so that their contents will not spill or their handles become a trap to pony legs. Large containers like farm tubs or old bathtubs must have sharp corners boxed and projecting faucets removed to prevent injury. Though such tubs (often kept full by a carefully dripping hose) may hold several days' supply, the water must be kept free of debris (leaves and occasional drowning victims—squirrels, toads, even field mice).

**Your pony will never get his daily water requirements this way, but Lutine enjoys drinking from a hose. Here she is at a Pony Club Clinic at Green Mountain Horse Association in Vermont.**

## IN THE PASTURE

Before you turn your pony out, you must check the pasture for holes, sharp broken roots or stumps, wire or tin cans, and other booby traps. While he is out at pasture you will want to pick up or scatter his droppings—otherwise the best of pastures will be spoiled—and while you are taking care of this you can check again to be sure that no litter has been tossed over your fence.

The pony on pasture needs his full mane and tail (and whiskers) for fly protection. If he's show-trim, protect him periodically with fly wipe or spray.

In hot weather or fly season he'll graze at night, so expect to find him loafing in his shelter or in the shade of trees during the day. Much of the time he will rest standing up; if he does lie down during the day, you will seldom see him flat out unless he's a foal, exhausted, or ill.

Ponies in a herd are better off barefoot—as even a playful kick hurts more with a shod hoof. (Often hind shoes only are removed.) Whether or not your pony has shoes, when he is first turned out in company watch to see that no serious bullying goes on. Ponies quickly establish a pecking order that permits peace when observed, but occasionally one pony will be a perpetual bully or a perpetual scapegoat, and in that case separation is the only solution.

Tiny Tuffy, sweetest of all ponies with people, got her inappropriate name because she was boss of her herd till we bought her as a three-year-old. She staked out her status at High Hickory, too. Despite our careful and gradual preparation for group grazing—acquaintanceship across the stall doors, over the fence of separate paddocks, on the lead line—a frightening set-to occurred the first time new Stardust and Tuffy were turned out together. Ears back, they squealed and feinted, then wheeled and turned their hind ends to each other. Each dug in her forefeet and let fly with her hind. Hooves cracked loudly on bone—and when they finally stopped, it was twice-as-big Star who hobbled away. Fortunately she was not hurt, and there was never any more unpleasantness. But ponies have their likes and dislikes. Watch them as they're turned out: one of them will let two or three go by as he waits for a friend, or will hassle one and ignore the rest.

Your pony should be checked daily while at grass, especially if you do not go out with supplementary feed or to pick him up to ride. Not only do you need to make sure that cuts and scratches do not go

Tuffy and Peggy are fed in separate fields so tiny Tuffy won't assert her rank and eat more than her share. Robin waits to retrieve the pail with its potentially dangerous handle.

The contrast in size of two ponies, one for four-year-old Robin and one for ten-year-old Eric, stands out as Peggy watches Robin give Tuffy a little "T.L.C." Sheep, companions in grazing, unwittingly aid in surprise-proofing.

untended, but you need to give him a bit of attention. Ponies are gregarious, and a solitary pony needs some tender loving care (better known as T.L.C.) at least once a day. You have only to hear a left-behind whinnying for a stablemate or to witness the attachment formed by a pony for another animal. Before Top Rail Stardust came to High Hickory, Tuffy's constant companion in grazing—and in games—was our ram Bluebeard. When Bluebeard paid his annual visit to the Levins' flock in Lincoln, he was adopted by their Connemara pony Ballin, who had the same penchant for playmates. Part of the satisfaction of pony ownership is the pony's response to your attention even when his stomach is full and he has other animals around him. His welcoming nicker when you're the attachment in his life is most flattering.

## BAG OR BOUGHT FEEDS

More and more ponies across the country are "backyard" ponies and cannot be kept on grass, even on grass with supplements. More and more of them are kept year-round on bag or "bought" feeds, with grass the doled-out and rare supplement. What does this involve as to upkeep?

First, your pony becomes dependent on you for his every need. You are responsible for him twenty-four hours a day, day in and day out, all year long. You must supply all his water, either a constant supply through a waterer or a perpetually full bucket or a regulated supply offered an hour before meals and an hour after. You must provide all his food—some form of a substitute for grass. The traditional substitute is of course hay; a more modern one is "complete" feed in pelleted form. To these base staples (water and hay or pellets) you can—but may not need to—add from a variety of short feed: oats, corn, barley, bran, and sweet feeds that have these ingredients plus molasses and other additives. Each has its own characteristics and its own effect on your pony and each will be discussed individually.

## HAY

First, our substitute for growing grass: hay. Since hay is now your pony's staff of life, you want good hay. To be able to recognize good hay, beyond whether it smells good and is free of dust or mould, requires agricultural training or background. Until you acquire such skill by questioning your hay man, by examining thousands of bales, by investigating many stands of growing, cut, and curing hay, by

looking at the hay you use (not just tossing it out to your pony), the best test of the hay you buy is whether or not your pony eats it all up.

What is good hay for a horse (or a cow or a sheep) is not necessarily good for a pony. Our ponies prefer second cutting hay to "better" hay. We use fresh second cutting hay for our sheep and top protein alfalfa or timothy for our Thoroughbred; but, given free choice, the only hay the ponies clean up—blades, stems, and all—is the lower-priced second cutting. General rules always have their exceptions; but generally speaking the smaller, closer-to-the-native-breed pony does better on coarser, less rich food (pasture, hay) while the larger, more refined pony (refined by man's crossbreeding) may require concentrates as well. As with all feeds, change in quantity and quality of hay must be controlled. A sudden switchover from brackeny roadside gleanings (hardly to be rated as but often sold as hay, complete with flattened beer cans and brambles) to rich alfalfa would have the same hazards as a sudden switch to lush pasture or rich grains.

What are the characteristics of good hay? It smells sweet, it feels crisp. If there are seed heads, you can roll them between your fingers without their crumbling. Second cutting hay usually has no heads or only tiny ones, but the grasses lie flat and leafy. Besides smell and feel, color is one of the best tests to go by. "We go ninety per cent by color," my hay expert tells me; and, pooh-poohing an old wives' tale, he adds: "and don't be afraid of greenness."

Another old adage is discounted: that hay should not be used until six months after baling but must be used before eighteen months. Hay can be used right away, although some animals may prefer it cured longer, even "bone dry and clean"; and, unlike certain short feeds, it does not decrease in nutritional value with age.

In our part of the country, as in many regions today where smaller acreage must produce maximum yield, fields are limed and fertilized. Seeding may be done with timothy or with mixes including timothy, orchard grass, red top, clover and other grasses. Alfalfa is seldom grown because it is hard to cure locally.

Curing is the drying-by-the-sun that turns cut grass into hay, a process which takes several days. Hay that is rained on during this period loses in nutrients. From time immemorial men have struggled to make hay while the sun shines—and yet not bale so soon that dangerous mould develops within

**Massachusetts hay men take pride in their crop; here Bob Jackson of Marlboro delivers stringtied bales and checks quality with Dave.**

the compressed hay, imperiling livestock with its poisonous qualities and buildings with its heat to the point of spontaneous combustion and fire. This battle with nature has finally turned in the farmer's favor. When weather conditions offer a threat to curing, he can, with each stroke of the baler, add a chemical to the partially cured hay as it is machine baled in the fields. Green in color, salty to the taste, this dry absorptive material cures and preserves the hay and even adds vitamins. A whitish dust rises almost unnoticeably if you toss up a flake, but it is clean and beneficial, unlike the sour-smelling dust that indicates dirt or mould. (Never feed that type of dusty hay.)

Hay, even when you buy it always from the same source, differs from season to season, from field to field, from cutting to cutting, even from bale to bale. (In this, it is just like wine!) A reputable dealer will suggest that you try different hay, a bale or two at a time, rather than put pressure on you to buy one or two tons. Such a dealer will want to replace the odd bale that may be poor, for he will be proud of his crop. He will tell you that good hay totally consumed at any price is a better buy for your pony than poor hay fifty per cent wasted at half the price—and if your pony's tastes are like ours, the dealer will be recommending the lower-priced hay. Even when you can recognize quality, your best bet is to deal with a supplier whom you can trust.

Hay can be purchased by the bale or by the ton—tons of bales, that is; for loose hay is seldom seen today by the one-pony owner. You may find it more convenient to pick up or have delivered only a few bales at a time. To store the number of tons necessary to effect any savings for quantity would require tremendous space. As with any feed, if you buy in quantity you may perhaps achieve some almost negligible reduction in price, but it will be your loss if the hay gets wet, if it moulds, or if dirt of any sort makes it inedible.

Bales range from fifty-or-so-pound string-tied bales to two-hundred-and-fifty-pound-plus wire-bound ones; the size of course governs the number of bales to the ton. A bale breaks naturally into flakes or sections when opened, the folded grasses that the baling machine compressed into rectangles (or less commonly circular drums) springing apart into blocks. String-tied þales are lighter to handle and safer. Wires, harder to cut, pop apart when opened and endanger the eyes; if carelessly discarded, they wreak havoc. Recyclable hay twines, single or braided in threes, secure doors, mend fences, bundle empty grain sacks, tie pails to fence posts, substitute as lead ropes, and are generally indispensable!

Both indoors and outdoors, hay can be served on the ground, in a manger or hay rack, or in a hay net. The first method is natural (to your pony) but wasteful; once walked on or soiled the hay will not be eaten. As with any food on the ground, it may give parasites a direct entrée to your pony's insides. In stalls, mangers may be against a wall with a separate compartment for grain, racks high on the wall near or over a feed box. Outdoor mangers or racks are ideally covered with a pony-head-high roof and, if serving more than one pony, should be long enough to prevent crowding and fighting.

Hay nets come in several sizes and materials (nylon, tarred rope, etc.), but, indoors and out, even when secured at the proper eye-level height when stuffed, they sag as they empty. Ponies, perhaps more than horses, tend to paw at the last wisps, and there is such a risk of a leg's catching that at High Hickory we use nets only when trailering.

Wherever you place the hay, reduce wastage by measuring judiciously so that your pony cleans up everything. In these days of shortages "Waste not, want not" applies to hay, grain, bedding, and even water.

How to measure hay so that you waste not, but your pony wants not? It is possible to dole it out by the flake, but careful pony husbandry calls for measurement of *all* feed, including hay, by weight. A rule of thumb is one and a half pounds (of good hay: possibly up to three if the hay is poor) for every one hundred pounds of pony. Since it's harder to estimate a pony's weight than his height, you can figure roughly this way:

| Pony | Hay Only |
|---|---|
| Tiny pony (39″ Tuffy) | 1 to 2 pounds per day |
| 300 pound small pony (under 11.2) | 4 to 7 pounds per day |
| 400 to 500 pound medium pony (under 13.2) | 7 to 10 pounds per day |
| 500 to 800 pound large pony (under 14.2) | 10 to 16 pounds per day |

(In spot checking, we find that our average "flake" weighs about three pounds, but the checking emphasizes how much flakes vary even when tossed out from the same bale. Weighing results in more consistent feeding.)

Adapt such basic measurements to your pony's individual needs. Never consider your feed schedule "set." The amounts will (and should) increase or decrease according to the quality of the hay, the amount if any of short feed given, and your pony's appetite as determined by exercise, age, and metabolism. Soon, figuring by weight or by flake and by consumption, you can judge how many days a bale (and thus a ton) will last, so as to reorder before you run out, and know how much you will need to carry you through a year.

Hay, providing not only roughage but bulk, prevents weediness. On the other hand a "hay belly" is no laughing matter. A too-fat pony is in as much danger (from founder or laminitis, from heart strain, etc.) as an undernourished one (from exhaustion, anemia, disease). In a culture where affection (for people and pets alike) is often expressed by edible offerings, it may require strength on your part not to overfeed. "I feel so mean," my nephew

Alan moaned, "always going past Tuffy with grain that's for someone else!" It takes a disciplined heart not to feed a hopefully nickering pony, but fortunately for us two-legged softies, ponies are quick to accept their own routine. Except at time when her hopes have been raised by a surreptitious handout the day before, Tuffy, who stays fat on the smell of food, does not beg, but quietly enjoys her restricted diet.

## COMPLETE FEEDS

Instead of hay, you can use the modern substitute for grass: the so-called complete feeds commercially produced in pelleted forms. These rations—pellets, horse checkers, pony cubes, however they're named—are more than hay alone; they combine chopped hay, various grains, plant proteins, salt, phosphate, oxides, vitamins, minerals, and molasses, all mashed and pressed and shaped into tiny cylinders similar to deer or rabbit or guinea pig or hamster pellets. From a nutritional standpoint, a pony requires no other feed stuff.

From a convenience standpoint, these complete feeds are great. Unlike other short feeds, they do not attract rodents of any sort. They are of consistent quality. They eliminate some of the waste (estimated at up to twenty-five per cent of what you feed loose), so they are economical. With limited storage space, the fifty-pound paper sacks are easy to handle if you bother to empty them into an ash can, while the hundred-pound sacks are plasticized, providing their own dry storage.

The best thing about pellets, from our experience, is that you can feed a pony all you want and keep him in top form without his getting "high."

However—one big however—despite their being a complete food nutritionally, pellets have one lack: they are not a complete feed psychologically. If you offer them as your complete feed, you had still better supply some minimum hay for roughage to satisfy your pony's instinctive need to chew. If you don't, he will chew something else—his stall, fencing, barn walls, tree trunks, anything woody, dry or growing. While such wood chewing is not the same as cribbing, it is an annoyance that will keep you constantly busy with creosote or anticrib paints.

Hay serves not only to prevent such destructive chewing but to diminish boredom. Its role in this case can be compared with that of a pacifier, or of

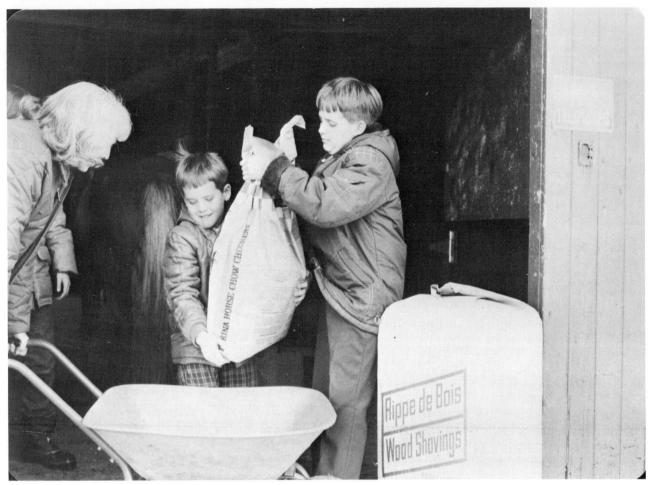

**Alan and Scott help Pepper and Kate with bags of pellets at McCrackens' barn.**

chewing gum. With hay as a tranquillizer, instead of pacing or chewing, your pellet-fed pony will relax and be better dispositioned. (Hay can also serve as a safety control: a pony who gets high on short feed can be brought back to good behavior on hay only, or a pony who is sick and confined to his stall can be kept from stocking up by being taken off pellets and other shorts and fed on hay only.)

When hay is served for these emotional fringe benefits, we've found that, contrary to some suggestions, it is just as important to use the best hay as it is when hay is the only food left. The pony who gets his nutritional requirements from tasty pellets may scornfully reject poor hay and chew tastier materials.

Pellets, too, are best measured by weight. When you measure by volume bulk varies according to moisture. The rule of thumb is one and a half pounds of pellets per one hundred pounds of pony. Our table reads:

| Pony | Complete feed |
|---|---|
| Tiny pony (39″ Tuffy) | 1 to 2 pounds per day |
| Small pony (under 11.2) | 2 to 4 pounds per day |
| Medium pony (under 13.2) | 4 to 6 pounds per day |
| Large pony (under 14.2) | 6 to 8 or more pounds per day |

In any feeding, the importance of watering first must be remembered. With short feeds, and particularly with pellets, water, if not present at all times, *must* be provided first, and time must be allowed for the pony to drink it before there are sounds of preparation (rattling of the grain bin, for instance) that will make him ignore it because he's anticipating his feed. With pellets special care must be taken not to turn a pony out on to wet grass directly after eating. If either water or wet grass follows dry pellets into his stomach and intestines, there may result a glutinous ball of compacted material that can cause blockage and death.

## SHORT FEEDS

For most ponies the twelve per cent protein content of the average pellets is sufficient, but we may turn to regular short feeds to increase the content for growing stock, nursing dams, in-foal pony mares, working or performance ponies, whose normal feed may be pellets, pellets and hay, or simply hay. Each of these short feeds—oats, barley, corn, bran, or sweet feed—has its special effect upon your pony.

"He's feeling his oats" is part of our common speech, but the full force of the expression can only be understood by people who have actually observed the effect *oats* have on a horse or a pony. They are a source of (often excess) energy.

When we talk about ponies being overfresh from overfeeding, we must differentiate between a pony bucking and acting up (on the lunge line only, we hope!) when first taken out and then settling down to work energetically, and a pony playing up but quickly flagging after a short period of work. The latter is not feeling his oats but feeling his confinement; you must recognize this release for cooped-up feelings and feed to provide staying power. Such flagging after momentary exuberance is most often seen when a pony is not ridden regularly.

When used, oats may be fed whole, crimped, rolled, or crushed. A pony may benefit more from ones that have been mangled in some way, but in his free state what seeds or grains he might find are most likely whole. An older pony may find treated oats easier to masticate and salivate, thus starting the digestive juices that promote utilization of feed farther in his digestive tract, but any kernel, once cracked open, loses nutrients with time. The important thing, again, is to get good quality oats—plump, heavy ones, more expensive initially but not in the long run, as you can feed fewer with better results.

Most ponies are better off (and the rider is better on!) without oats. Generally they have a heady effect on a pony, and unless yours is doing several hard hours' work a day—hunting, doing cross-country or endurance work—leave them out of his diet.

*Barley*, less commonly used, is best served rolled or crushed. It is slightly higher in protein than oats but is less heating. It should be used with the same precautions.

*Corn (maize)* may be fed whole (on the cob or ear), full kernel, or cracked. Corn is highly regarded for fattening purposes and for putting a shine on a pony's coat. Considered "heating," it is often fed for warmth in winter; its value (served in smaller quantity) for energy in summer is often overlooked. Because corn is heavier than oats, problems occur when it is substituted for them by volume rather than by weight. Feeding less corn than oats by weight could cut down on feed costs; but usually it is fed not separately but as part of a sweet feed mix.

*Sweet feeds* contain oats, corn, soy bean and/or linseed meal, alfalfa meal, rolled barley, and the various minerals and vitamins added to the complete feeds. The molasses which serves as a binder, making the feed fragrant and slightly moist to the touch, makes sweet feeds (sold under various trade names) as pleasant for children to measure out as for the ponies to eat.

*Wheat bran*, light and fluffy, may be fed dry or wet. You can use it partly for the bulk which it, like hay, provides, for its laxative quality when served as a wet mash or gruel or for the opposite when served dry, and for its high phosphorous and protein properties. Like any crushed grain, its flakes lose some of these properties with age. Mixed with grain, it slows down a greedy eater. It is light in weight, great in volume, and illustrates the problem of how to measure short feeds.

Just as with hay you have to decide whether to feed by the flake or by the pound, so with short feeds you have to decide whether to feed by the measure or by the scales. Old-timers used special feed tins or wooden measures, but, as mentioned above, today's scoop is the coffee can. If you use this container, you must remember that can A is not can B. A can of oats may equal half a can of corn, but three cans of bran, by weight. If one day "a can" is a full can, carefully filled and levelled off like a chef's spoonful of baking powder, while the next day "a can" is feed minus the space your hand takes gripping it over the edge, the amount your pony really gets varies with your degree of precision in measuring.

Even with accurately measured or weighed feedings where you control the quality and quantity of the feed your pony is getting, it is possible to be misled as to his condition. Just as the pony thrown out on grass for the summer must be checked regularly, so in winter the horseman must handle his pony to see what the furry coat hides. One check is to run your hands over your pony's rib cage. He should not feel like a xylophone, and neither should he feel like foam rubber. You should be able to feel his ribs as you lightly stroke his sides without pressing through a layer of blubbery fat. He should not have a sunken hollow just in front of his hip bones, should not have a weedy, tucked-up, whippetlike look. Neither should he be too fat, with a hay belly or an in-foal look. Ideally good condition means that his eyes are bright, that his skin moves over his ribs, that his quarters are rounded. His top line should be level without a sudden bump for bony angular hips, his underline be roughly parallel with the ground. His neck should be filled out with well-muscled flesh so that its line feels firm and hard, not hollow under the crest. Whether your outdoor pony is summer-sleek or shifting his coat in the autumn or furry-bear in the winter, you must not judge his condition by looks alone. If he's too fat or too thin, make the necessary adjustments in feeding gradually.

Basic feeds should be given in three, or preferably four, rations a day, with the largest proportion at night.

## SOME FEEDING SUGGESTIONS

Any pony dependent upon his owner will benefit most from a fixed feed schedule, but you'll find that the routinely well-fed pony is flexible. Only an abnormally hungry pony "tears the barn down" because a meal is late. There'll be mornings when any faithful pony-owner oversleeps or just delays getting up because of a snowstorm or a holiday, there'll be school days when you are late getting home from the library or a club meeting. Of course if you expect to miss a feeding you can put out extra hay to extend the pony's supply.

While it is important to consider your pony's well-being when you work out his feed schedule, your main purpose in having him is to use and enjoy him—to school and to ride him. His schedule can be made to fit yours (i.e. the school year, vacations, full- or part-time work day). Since the pony needs at least an hour to digest his meal before being worked, and since it is better to leave him alone rather than be grooming him while he is eating, you may have to advance or delay a meal when you don't have an entire day to devote to pony matters.

This hour's rest that your pony needs after eating is so important that, with exercise, it might almost be listed as an "ingredient" along with water, hay, and grain. Rest is important because if you ride your pony immediately after feeding you do so at a time when his digestive tract is most distended with food. Obviously your weight in the saddle presses on his organs and adds strain. Moreover, the inner muscles of the tract must compete against the outer muscles of the body (back, legs, neck, and so on) at a time when the greatest demands are made of each.

The more strenuous your riding, the more you should replace bulk food with concentrates or short feeds and the more rest you should allow after feeding. If you cannot allow your pony an absolute minimum of an hour's rest (two hours are better), then you had better omit the meal.

On the other hand, regardless of your pony's schedule, if for any reason he is going to be confined to his stall or is not going to get his usual exercise for several days—or if he is overfresh, mounted or unmounted—cut back on his short feed. Eliminate all grains (sweet feed, oats, corn) and reduce the amount of pellets and bran. If in doubt, serve only hay.

It goes without saying that clean food should be served in clean utensils to a clean pony. Hay must not be climbed on or played on or dirtied by grooming scruff, floor debris, or leg-lifting dogs. Short feeds must be kept covered to keep out mouse droppings. The tidiest eater slobbers, whether dry or moist feed is on the menu, leaving damp chaff in mangers and a messy coating on the sides of feed tubs. Mangers must be cleaned so that mould does not develop, and tubs must be scrubbed free of hardened film to prevent formation of bacteria. Your pony must be clean inside and out—as worm-free as possible so that his feed benefits him and not various internal parasites.

I have pointed out the vital importance of water in your pony's diet and the times when you should or should not give him water. One more word of warning: Never give him water when he is hot. Of course you try to bring your pony home from a ride at a walk so that he will be cool enough to put up; otherwise you walk him until he is. You may offer a hot pony about ten swallows of water (watch his throat and count them), pull the pail away, cool him some more, then offer another ten or twenty swallows. Only when he is cool should he have his fill. By then his thirst may be less acute.

Don't turn a hot pony loose in a field or paddock with a water supply in it. (If you are schooling or riding cross-country you may let your pony drink when hot provided you are going to move on again directly.) Some ponies are too canny to drink when hot, but others will drain buckets if given a chance, at the risk of founder or colic.

Since you always water and hay before graining, if

you heed this warning you are not likely to grain a warm pony—which is definitely a "don't." It is wiser also not to grain a very tired pony: let him recover a bit, then settle him with a few swallows of water and a flake of hay. If he's really exhausted—from a long day's hunting or a strenuous trail ride—after you've settled him in and left him alone for a while with some hay you can later substitute a hot bran mash for his usual short feed.

Occasionally a pony will be in dire need of staling (that is, urinating) but, in odd contrast to his nonchalance about dropping his "calling cards" or faeces wherever he may be, will not do so when under saddle, on the lunge, or in the trailer. (For one thing, he has to be standing still in order to stale.) Often you must give your pony a chance to relieve himself before you decide he doesn't want any water and go ahead and grain him. He may simply want the space and privacy of his stall before he urinates and will then head for his water bucket.

To fatten a young, sick, or run-down pony, hand-feed him. Every time you are near, give him a handful of pellets or sweet feed—beyond his usual rations. (You may prefer to present the handful in a small feed tub or pan.) By feeding frequently in small amounts you avoid over-loading that small pony stomach, but keep food going in and reap full nutritional benefits.

To get more out of a given amount of feed, delay graining until your pony has cleaned up his hay ration. (As explained earlier, hay provides essential roughage but this fibrous material tends to push the more concentrated feeds on and out before they are properly digested.) This may ease barn chores during the school year, for a youngster can water and hay and leave feed measured out ready to be fed by an adult after the school bus has gone.

To improve a stringy dry mane or tail, add an ounce of vegetable oil (ordinary cooking or salad oil) to his feed once or twice a day. To keep a shine on his coat and help him shed out in the spring, add a handful of linseed meal.

To the basic foods you can add vitamins and minerals and various supplements (wheat-germ oil, kelp, or seaweed, for example). Add them in pellet, powder, or liquid form to your short feed. If you're vitamin-minded where people are concerned, you may be with your pony. If you're on a tight budget, money may be better spent in obtaining the finest quality feeds available.

Old ponies and young ponies may need such additives as much as working ponies, but all too often they are the ones whose feed is given the least attention; in old age and in childhood many ponies must fend for themselves. With young ponies this is unfortunate, for if ever it is important to feed animals well it is in their growing, formative years. The best of feeding after maturity will not make up for faulty nutrition in the first few years as far as skeletal structure and development are concerned. (This is one reason why the first two or three years of raising a colt or filly, plus the prenatal and nursing period when the dam's protein requirements are high, can be the most costly, and why one should expect to pay a fair price for a well-developed three-year-old even if it is completely green.)

With old ponies, negligence is even more deplorable. What a dismal reflection on a person to see a once-fine pony who has served usefully throughout his middle years left with a matted mane, broken or curling hooves, and staring coat. The outgrown pony should be "passed on" to spend his day loved and babied by some novice pony-owner, or maintained in top condition and shared with many young would-be pony owners, as our tiny Tuffy is . If this is not possible, it is the owner's responsibility—if hardship and sorrow—to see that his old friend is mercifully put down. The pony that is well cared for may (like Nina) live to be thirty or older.

Besides the basic feeds and the supplements which the ponies routinely get at High Hickory, the Pony Pals love to add variety to the bill of fare. Occasional hot bran mashes (bran mixed with boiling water, stirred, and covered till cool enough to serve) may be spiked with grated apple or carrot, a handful of oats or sweet feed, a scoop of sugar or molasses. Molasses may be added to drinking water if a newcomer to the pony barn turns up his nose at the local $H_2O$; for the taste of strange water sometimes discourages a pony from drinking sufficiently. If a pony is going to be away for several days, we put molasses in his water at High Hickory his last few meals, and then in his water while traveling, to disguise the taste of unfamiliar water. Again, at home, if your pony is not drinking enough you can wet his hay with slightly salted water—be sure that his water bucket is kept full.

Visitors to High Hickory sometimes bring sugar lumps (long relegated to second place behind carrots and apples, since the Pony Pals claim their share as well as the non-cavity-prone ponies) or commercial "horse treats." When on green grass, the ponies take no interest in parings, but during the winter months they relish lettuce cores and celery butts. Cabbage leaves or potato peels may be refused by one but eaten by another. Tuffy vies with our Border Collies for pieces of stale bread, but Lutine Bell turns up her lip as well as her nose at them.

As long as your pony is on a well-planned basic diet, such minor tidbits do no harm; but varying amounts of varying fodder fed hit or miss as his only food will certainly affect his digestive system and ultimately his health.

Whatever his diet, a quick check of your pony's droppings (faeces, manure, pony chips) can be revealing. Are the oats going through whole? Perhaps his teeth need "floating," or perhaps he needs more time on his hay before graining. Droppings tight and hard? Beware of constipation. Is he getting enough water? He needs saliva to masticate his food properly; he must produce eight to ten gallons of it daily. To do this he must have plenty of drinking water and time to drink it. Even though you water first, if he is grain-greedy or very hungry he may ignore his water to go to his food, and therefore not drink enough to have normal firm-but-not-hard manure balls. Is he getting enough roughage? Some fibre—hay or grass—is essential, no matter how "complete" a food pellet may be. Perhaps he needs more bran daily, or, right now, a bran mash. Are his droppings greenish yellow and cowflap loose? They will be the first few times he is turned out on grass; but this is no cause for concern provided it does not continue or turn to scouring (diarrhea).

The old saying "The eye of the master fattens the pony" applies to what goes in and to what comes out if the pony in between is to be healthy and a joy to look at as well as happy and a pleasure to ride.

## GROOMING

Grooming is an important part of pony care, and a pleasurable one. With the Pony Pals it's a time to make friends with their mounts or to lavish affection on a favorite. It can be efficient brisk routine or a leisurely way of spending a whole rainy afternoon. Work will be cut down if you do it regularly and keep the pony's bedding clean.

You can groom your pony in his stall or on the cross ties of your barn or out of doors—tie rings can be put on trees. If you work in his stall, see that body dirt doesn't get into his food or water.

Once you have your work coat or apron on, your pony tied or cross tied where you want him, and

your grooming kit at hand, begin by checking his feet.

**Properly tied with a halter hitch, Tuffy looks back and starts to pick up her foot on request.**

Before you ask your pony to pick up his foot, be sure he knows that you are there and be sure that he is standing square. If he's standing on three legs, he can't lift up one of those three. Teach him to lift each foot at a mere touch and the word "Up." Facing his rear, run your hand firmly down his leg from below the knee or hock and pinch in slightly as you approach the fetlock joint, saying "Up." (Leaning your weight against him may help.) He will lift his foot slightly, and you can grasp his hoof, supporting it in your cupped hand while you clean it out. (If your pony is touchy and you don't want to get kicked, you can stand on one side and reach across to pick up a foot on the opposite side.) Clean each foot out with a hoof pick, working from heel to toe so as not to bang the sensitive fetlock with the metal point. When you have finished all body work you may come back to the hooves and paint them with hoof oil or dressing. In snowy or icy weather you may protect the pasterns with a coating of vaseline or put grease on the bottom of the hooves to prevent snow balling up. (Snow can pack up in a pony's feet so that he is walking several inches off the ground on what seem like marble balls—destructive to his balance and grip, and often hard to remove without a tap of a hammer and intensive work with a hoof pick.) If your pony wears shoes, now is the time to see that none is loose and that clenches have not risen.

Sheets or blankets, if worn, should be removed, aired, and brushed on both sides. In cold weather, or outside on windy days, turn your pony's blanket back first over the rump, then back over the withers, each time grooming the half of his body thus exposed. Be certain to undo buckles and surcingle and to drop the straps carefully so that the metal parts do not bang his sensitive legs. If you neglect to undo them your pony's coat may be ruffed up when you put his blanket back in place. If possible, replace a night blanket with a day sheet or New Zealand rug or rain sheet.

Your rubber curry comb and your dandy brush are your basic cleaning tools, the ones you use for removing surface dirt like sweat, mud, and dried manure. (A metal curry has no place in our grooming kit, and even a rubber one must be used carefully on

sensitive areas; lower legs, for instance, are better cleaned with your dandy brush.) Rub with your curry with a circular, against-the-hair motion, with a little elbow grease! and follow with your brush. You can work with one tool in each hand, banging your curry clean against your brush, or you can curry first, then brush. Old-time grooms had a rhythmical left-hand right-hand motion—curry, brush, curry, brush, clean—that' went well with their silent hissing whistle. If your pony is roughing it in a winter coat, never curry and groom down to the skin or you will destroy protective body oils; stroke only in the direction of hair growth.

Start with the top of your pony and work back and down. Begin at the poll and do his neck (under the mane, too), then his back and sides. Put your hand on his back while you reach under to do his belly; and remember, if he's ticklish, a light firm stroke is better than a jabbing feathery one. Talk to him while you work, not just "Ho" or "Stand" but "Easy boy, steady Gal—." Professional horse establishments may require silent grooms: at High Hickory we don't mind "quiet noise" so long as it's happy—we even encourage singing.

Dirt and scurf removed, use your body brush with its shorter bristles to smooth your pony's coat and stimulate his skin. Use this brush to do his head (and cover his eye with one hand if vigorous brushing is necessary).

Your body brush can also be used on a Thoroughbred-fine mane and tail, but with many ponies a mane-and-tail brush, oval with stiffer bristles, is more effective. (Mane-and-tail combs break the hairs.) As with any long hair, yours or the pony's, you must start at the ends to remove any tangles; starting at the roots will just cause more snarling. If your pony has a very thick mane like Tuffy's you'll want to flip it over on his neck to brush the underside as well.

To do your pony's tail, first let him know that you are behind him by your voice and your hand on his rump. Then slide your hand down his tail to the end of his dock, grasp the tail there, and brush out a lock at a time until the entire fall of hair is done. Then brush from the top down.

These are the "clean your teeth, wash your face and hands, brush your hair" things that must be done every day, even if you don't ride your pony, but just put his blanket back on or turn him out. Do them regularly and he can quickly be ready for a spur-of-the-moment ride.

**Kate leads Galaxy from a muddy pasture to the barn for cleaning. Scott carries a rubber grooming mitt, Alan a curry and brush.**

**The height of luxury (and good luck!)—a horse vacuum with grooming attachments won by Robin from Farmers' Exchange in Framingham.**

**Kate holds Galaxy in a work halter, while Scott and Alan groom. Note Gal's winter coat and long eyelashes. Plastic curries like Alan's make good mane combs when ponies roll during spring thaws.**

The "right size" pony makes grooming easy—no stretching to reach an invisible top line. In-foal Stardust got more grooming than riding when footing was icy; during this sociable procedure she was allowed to eat hay.

If not needed for protection, manes can be trimmed and thinned. "Pull" it with your fingers, or,

"Pull" with a mane comb. Never hack a mane short with scissors.

Your heavier cleaning should be done after you ride, not before, for it is then that your pony is sweaty, dirty, and itchy. Never put him away dirty. At least sponge off saddle marks and when he is dry give him a quick brushing. Ideally, do this, let him have a roll and freedom for a half hour or so, and then groom thoroughly.

Other grooming steps that should be part of daily routine if time permits include: cleaning your pony's eyes and nostrils with a wet sponge; cleaning the dock area and teats or the sheath with another sponge; going over the entire body with your polishing cloth or rubbers; laying the mane by taking a wet brush to the roots so it all lies flat on one side; washing and oiling the hooves. But like a girl's makeup these extras can be omitted if time is short.

Just as you fuss more with your own grooming for special occasions, there are times when you fuss more with your pony's grooming. You may want to shampoo his mane and tail or wash his entire body. (We often hose ponies off, when the weather permits, just as we frequently "pipe" or hose their legs.)

For horse shows or rallies you may want to pull, then braid your pony's mane and tail. Since this takes practice, try it ahead of time. Divide the mane into even sections, braid, fold under, and secure with thread or an elastic band close to the crest. A thick neck looks longer with many small braids, while a thin one benefits from fewer thick ones. Don't forget a single braid of the forelock.

Tails (is it partly because ponies can swish them right at a critical moment?) are harder to do. You start with three sections at the very top and braid down. Using only under hairs, you bring these up and over until the bulk of the tail is neatly self-bound with a central plait. When you reach the dock or slightly below it you no longer pick up hairs but continue to braid the plait independently to the end of the hairs. Finish off with thread or elastic, coil, and secure. Brush out the loose hair below your braid, stand back, and admire. (Bandage overnight or for traveling.)

Whiskers, "cat hairs" that stand out on jaws and neck as winter coats are shed, hair sticking out of ears (never the fine inner hairs), fetlocks, chestnuts or ergots, all need to be trimmed. If not kept long and full, manes are hand trimmed to the desired length and thickness—the hairs are not pulled out at the roots, but are snapped off at the desired length, a few at a time. Tails can be cut about four inches below the hock, but they are better left unpulled at the roots as these hairs protect the dock. Forelocks, if they must be altered, are better pulled than banged (as an abrupt shearing is called). With all trimming, remember that the hairs we remove for beautification are there for protection, as radar or raincoat.

Full manes that won't stand over on one side can be wet down and held in place with an elastic for a day or two. Thick coats can be shed more rapidly in spring by using a shedding blade (at the risk of broken hairs); blanketing in warm weather and sweat-creating exercise seem to speed the process also.

Stains from pine pitch, creosote, paint, which always seem to pop up the day before a show, can be removed by rubbing a little peanut butter or lard into the pony's coat. Hooves can be shined with a little scrub brush and polished with a cut onion.

In principle, you groom three times a day. A first quick grooming when you go out to your pony first thing in the morning is called quartering, for quartering or partially turning back the blankets—a term borrowed from the British. The Pony Pals call such Morning Stables "giving a lick and a promise."

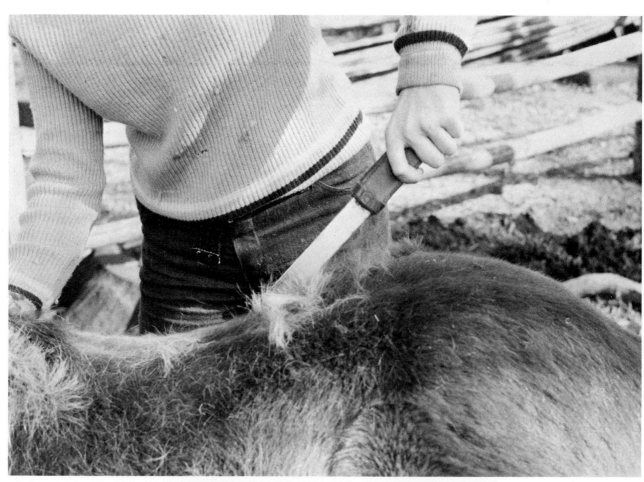

**Used open with two hands, the shedding blade with its serrated edge pulls winter hairs out by the strokeful.**

**Meri-Jo uses the shedding blade in a loop with one hand. Tuffy indicates her pleasure at such scratching by wriggling her lips.**

The promise is the thorough grooming later in the day, after riding: for this the British term strapping is formally used. The quick going over and tucking in at the end of your pony's day is called (again a British term) brush-over, set fair, Evening Stables, or—simply barn chores.

Whatever terms you use, during all your grooming let your pony know where you are, by voice and touch. Work in close. The closer you are the less likely you are to get kicked. (If by chance you should somehow get stepped on, move the pony off your foot. Don't pull your foot out from under his hoof, or you may lose a toe nail.)

Grooming can be a schooling experience. Train your pony to stand still. Don't allow him to nose you or to nip. "Move over," "Ho," "Back," "Behave," "No!"—grooming can be a vocabulary lesson, too!

When you're through grooming and have put your pony up, clean up your work area. (Put tangles of mane and tail hairs where birds and mice can find them for nests.) Check to see that brushes are clean before putting them in your tack tray, and wash them occasionally in disinfectant.

The object of all this? Grooming serves more than the superficial end of better looks and a mount that is clean and therefore more pleasant to ride: it improves your pony's condition. Cleaning his coat prevents skin problems caused by scurf or parasites; the massaging effect stimulates his skin and even helps the muscle tone.

Your can share the fun of grooming with a nonriding friend—and your friend, even if not up to riding in a show, may enter the pony in a "Fitting and Showing" class in which the pony that looks as if he'd just stepped out of a bandbox wins the blue ribbon.

# SHOEING

For want of a nail, the shoe was lost.
For want of a shoe, the horse was lost.
For want of a horse, the battle was lost.
For want of the battle, the kingdom was lost.

For want of a pony you may lose, if not a battle, at least a lot of fun; so arrange to have a blacksmith see yours regularly, about every six weeks. A pony in need of a blacksmith may stumble and fall—and your safety in the saddle depends on his surefootedness.

The purpose of a shoe is to protect the pony's hoof. The hoof itself is nature's shoe, a protective boot that encases the hidden moving parts of the sensitive inner foot. It consists of the hard horny wall that we see at the end of each leg, and the under part which is visible only when the pony picks up his feet.

The wall starts from the coronet and grows downward. It curves in at the back of the heel and turns back in two bars with a cleft between. The front, sides, and back of this wall are called the toe, quarters, and heel.

When you pick up your pony's foot you see a rather round surface with:

The wall, forming a thick somewhat heart-shaped frame.

The bars, coming back at the heel in two ridges.

The white line, a narrow line following the curve of the wall and separating the hard outer horn from the softer sole. This is more conspicuous when the hoof is freshly trimmed.

The sole, the bottom of your pony's foot: slightly concave, of softer horn than the outer wall, and not very thick for the protection it must afford.

The frog, a darker wedge with a cleft at the heel coming well into the concavity of the sole. An odd rubbery consistency allows for expansion and contraction; this elasticity is vital to its role as shock absorber as it cushions the impact of your pony's (and your) weight at each step. Since the frog serves as a pump, pressure on it being the only means of maintaining circulation in the vascular system of the foot, it must maintain contact with the ground.

Special care must be given by your smith and by you in your daily grooming to the space between the frog and the bars and the "seat of the corn" or reverse V where the bars bend back—all indentations where dirt and waste may lodge, thrush or other infection develop.

The parts of the hoof stand out as blacksmith Tom Markinac checks a shoe for fit. Clearly visible are the frog and the concavity of the sole.

Because of the grip and texture of the foot with its domed sole, a barefoot pony is more surefooted than one with metal shoes. (Often ponies shod most of the year have their shoes pulled and go bare for the winter.) If you can avoid the expense of shoeing, by all means do so. A trim costs less than shoes, a reset less than new shoes.

Whether your pony goes barefoot or wears shoes, his hooves, like your fingernails, grow constantly, about half an inch a month. Unshod feet wear down somewhat but need trimming and rasping so that edges do not crack, split, or break. Shod feet do not wear down. They just grow long, setting the pony back on his heels and causing strain on tendons and pasterns; they may also grow over the sides of the shoe.

Your smith will know whether shoes, and possibly pads, are necessary. Nina, Tuffy, Ogwen, and

Tom kneels to trim Tuffy's hoof. The Shetland's
bare feet must be trimmed as regularly as other
ponies are shod.

Galaxy never had shoes at High Hickory. Stardust
started out bare but added front shoes when Robin
began jumping at home and hind shoes when they
began going cross-country. Lutine Bell got shoes
from the start, and with a full program of cross-
country riding, eventing, and hunting in our rocky
part of New England wears pads as well. Even if
your pony has "good feet," shoes may be needed to
keep them that way if you live in rocky trappy
country, do a lot of jumping, or drive on hard roads.
The smith will spot incipient troubles (corns,
thrush, contracted heels, quarter cracks) and do
corrective shoeing. In winter he will see that your
pony is "sharp shod" with special caulks or borium
points.

You may need your blacksmith in between his
scheduled visits. You'll need him in a hurry if a shoe
is twisted or loose or lost (cast). If the clenches have
risen you have a few days' warning. Shoes that are
still tight and unworn can be pulled off, the feet

trimmed and the same shoes (removes) reset. More
often shoes have worn thin, shiny, and scraped
round at the toe and must be replaced by new ones.

Your blacksmith may shoe by one of two methods.
If hot shoeing, he will shape and fit a shoe while it is
red-hot, creating it for the individual hoof. This
conjures up the classic picture "Under the spreading
chestnut tree/ The village smithy stands—" though
today there are portable forges. Under the spreading High Hickory trees, our smith does cold shoeing, the more common method for traveling farriers.
He carries a large selection of ready-made shoes in
many sizes, and shapes the appropriate one to an
individual fit on his anvil.

During his visits, the Pony Pals have learned:
That front shoes may have a toe clip, hind shoes
quarter clips, one on each side towards the front.
That shoes for front feet are rounder, wider, and
shorter, hind ones longer and more oval. That
ready-made shoes have pre-stamped nail holes,

**79**

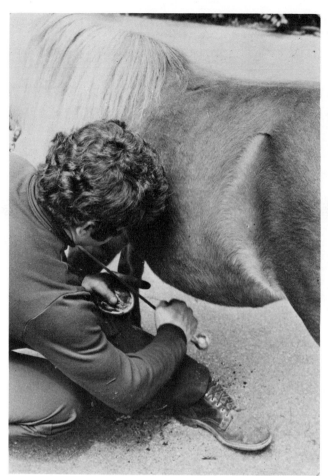

Doing a 39 inch Shetland's feet is more strenuous than doing a 17 hand Thoroughbred's! Here Tom rasps Tuffy's hoof after trimming it.

Torch and acetylene tanks replace the old-fashioned forge as John Markinac, Tom's father, works on a shoe.

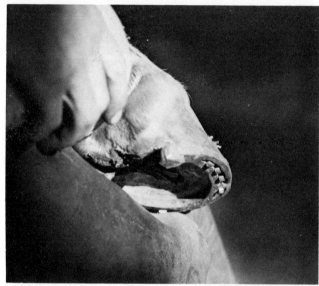

During shoeing nails protrude through the hoof wall. "No," little visitors are told, "it doesn't hurt."

Shoe and pad on, clinches set, hoof lightly filed, Tom Markinac applies the finishing touch of hoof dressing.

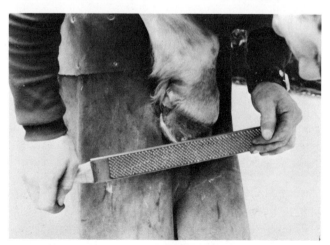

A final light filing with the rasp. The protective leather pad shows as a light band between shoe and hoof.

usually four on the outside and three on the inside. That horse shoe nails, with their flat sides and rectangular heads, come in sizes to fit those holes. That a pony's feet may be smaller behind than in front, or the same size, but almost never larger behind. That the answer to "But doesn't it hurt?" is No, not when the nails are put precisely into the hoof wall so as not to injure the sensitive "quick." That the sharp ends of the driven nails are twisted off into a sharp downward bend that, embedded in the wall, is called a clench. That these clenches, smooth and flush with the wall when new, work up as the hoof grows and the shoe wears. That when clenches have risen, a light tap may keep one tight temporarily, but it's time to call the smith. That the reason it's so hard for us to remove a loose or twisted shoe is that these fish-hook clenches must be snipped off before the shoe can be pulled off without damage to the hoof.

The Pony Pals watch with fascination as the smith puts on his leather apron and lifts out his tripod ("A footstool for a pony!") and sets up his anvil and vise. They try to name the contents of his tool box: hammer, tongs, knife, rasp, pinchers, hardy, pritchel and buffer, horn cutter—blue chalk for testing the fit of a shoe, a magnet on a string to dangle over sweepings till it's covered with silvery nail points.

The smith's procedure is always the same, but each pony is treated (and greeted) as an individual. Shod many times before or not, each pony is "walked" before and after shoeing for a careful check. Old shoes are removed, the hoof is cleaned and trimed ("Do it in one piece, Mr. Markinac, so we can have a shoe!"), new shoes are fitted and nailed on, clenches are set, the joining of hoof and shoe is lightly filed smooth, and a dab of dressing is rubbed on. *Voilà!* New shoes.

Old shoes are saved for pony projects (see Chapter 19) or to give to youngsters from the Learning Center for Deaf children who come for a Visit with a Pony. Smithing gear is packed in the van, and the smith drives off in a chorus of "Thank you's" and "See you in six weeks!"

## BLANKETING AND CLIPPING

With the approach of cold weather, your pony begins to grow a furry winter coat. You must decide whether to let it grow thick or to clip it and keep it down. To blanket or not to blanket—that is really the question.

You can blanket without clipping (for warmth and to try to keep a coat down, that is, less thick). You must not clip without blanketing. Clipping is the equivalent of a close shave and deprives the pony of protection.

Ponies with thick coats can weather cold and rain and snow with little attention from you. Given free choice, they'll be out in the elements. If you shut them in on extremely stormy nights all you need do is brush off loose snow. Once clipped, your pony will need a blanket, possibly two, even three if your 'weather drops well below zero. Blanketing a clipped pony is something like clothing a baby; you have to decide for someone else how warmly he must be dressed not to be cold.

Your decision about blanketing may depend on a number of factors. Is your pony out free choice or is he shut up at night? If shut up, is he alone or with other ponies, so that their body heat will help keep them all warm? How cold do your winters get? (Some people blanket only when nights drop below zero.) Is it windy? (Wind and the chill factor may mean more than absolute temperature.) Do you ride a lot during the winter? Do you plan to blanket night or day? (Some people blanket only at night, thinking a restricted pony feels the cold more even though in a stall; others think a pony needs a blanket more when exposed to the elements out of doors.)

The easiest thing is to let nature take its course. Blanketing means spending time putting on, taking off, brushing, cleaning, drying, airing, folding away. It may mean not just one indoor blanket but some kind of outdoor waterproof like a New Zealand rug or rain-resistant canvas-topped rug. These should not double as indoor blankets; they are not porous and may cause sweating. Furry ponies sweat up more than clipped ones when worked and take longer to cool off, but if they are cool under the wetness they can be put up without discomfort, whereas if you blanket your clipped pony after a ride he must be dry as well as cool. A wet blanket may be worse than none; it holds the dampness close to the pony, while a wet natural coat traps body heat in a protective airy layer. A blanket that does not stay in place may be worse than none: if a clipped pony is turned out in a blanket that twists and slips under his belly the "blanketing" does not protect. (Do use a separate body roller as well as the sewn-on blanket surcingles.) Ideally, you'll use a day sheet and a

In any season a sheet helps keep a pony clean. Lutine, mane winter-long, shares a moment of relaxation with her trusted friend.

Blankets must be aired and brushed inside and out . . . and a pony must still be groomed.

Introduce your pony to the electric clippers before you turn on the motor. Lute, winter whiskers and all, looks inquisitively before clipping begins.

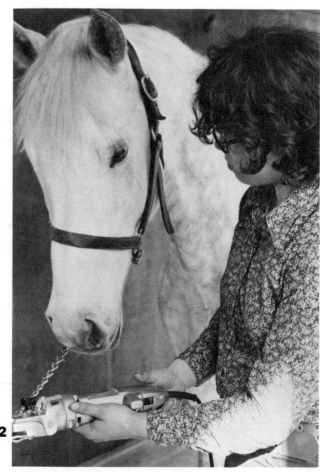

night sheet; and if you clip you'll find that at times you want two or three blankets on the pony—his wardrobe tends to grow, and with it your expenses.

The sheer cost of professional clipping may rule it out. If you buy clippers (you might want to pool either purchase or rental with friends), remember that clipping takes practice, even with a surprise-proofed pony, and don't clip the day before your pony is to look his best at a show!

Fall clipping is usually done before the winter coat sets in (figure the end of October as the last date). Clipping to get rid of a winter coat should be done by the last of February so as not to damage the incoming summer coat. Whenever you clip, never do the insides of ears or the roots of tail or mane (even along the withers). Never use body clippers on the backs of lower legs. Feathers there and fetlocks

are best done with small trimming clippers or curved hand clippers, working upwards.

You can clip certain areas only, and in various "styles", perhaps full, hunter, blanket, or trace high. We do a full clip on "active" ponies in early fall and late spring and in between leave legs and neck protected if we clip the "blanketed" areas.

After clipping your pony may seem a different, lighter color. He not only looks naked, he is; and it is now your responsibility to clothe him.

Clearly the easiest, most economical course is to take advantage of a pony's natural protection. Why then do so many pony owners go to all the trouble and expense of clipping and blanketing?

At High Hickory, we have based our decisions on the pony's natural coat and on the use he is going to get during the winter months. Tuffy, Stardust, and

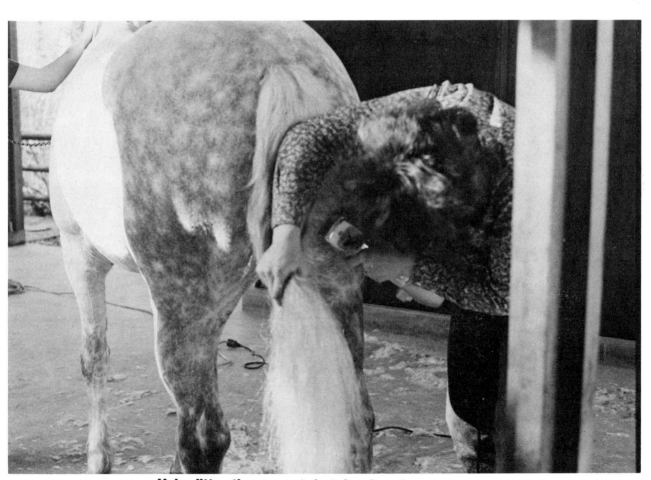

Hairs litter the carport, but dapples show areas still to clip. Lutine will be another color (white) when done. Feathers on back tendons will be trimmed with small clippers. Her hind legs show "The Tetrach lines."

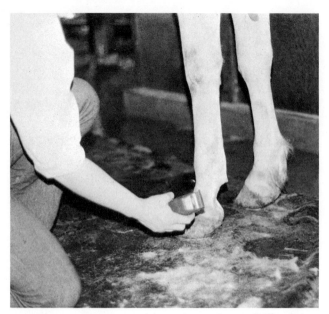

**Fetlocks and legs are gently and carefully done with special trimmers. Note the chestnut on the inside of the upper off foreleg.**

**Only when cleanup is complete do the Pony Pals realize just how much coat was removed. No wonder Lutine Bell will now need a blanket.**

Galaxy stayed home at High Hickory and use was sporadic and casual. Looking like Teddy Bears, they roughed it happily in their winter coats. At the other extreme, our Thoroughbred filly Visite hardly grew a winter coat and had to be well-blanketed at all times. Now, with larger ponies and more advanced riding, with a "real" ring of our own usable much of the year, with more indoor facilities nearby, and with a horse trailer for getting to them, riding activities go on all year round. In order to have daily riding on a serious level with less sweating up and faster cooling off during our short hours of daylight, we clip and blanket.

At times I long for the simple life!

If you favor the simple life where your pony is concerned, if you do little riding through the winter, *don't* get into clipping. If your pony grows a thick coat (you'll know early enough to get a blanket for occasional use if he doesn't), if he's generally a robust animal, don't blanket. Don't judge his comfort by yours. Shelter from wind and draughts with dry bedding underfoot and room to move around is all a pony needs, with the odd drop in temperature compensated for by extra hay and a handful of heat-producing feed during a cold spell.

## BASIC DAILY WORK SCHEDULES

### IDEAL AND WEEKEND

| | |
|---|---|
| 6:00 A.M. | In barn: Clean buckets, fill with fresh water. Morning hay ration. Quick grooming while hay is being munched. Quick pickup of stall. Ration of pellets or grain, to be eaten undisturbed. |
| By 9:00 A.M. | Complete grooming (thorough). Tacking up. |
| 9:30 to 11:30 A.M. | Schooling and/or riding. |
| 11:30 A.M. to 12:00 P.M. | Untack, brush off, water and feed (hay or grain or pellets). |
| 12:00 to 2:30 P.M. | Pony's siesta, in paddock or grazing. |
| 3:00 to 5:00 P.M. | Schooling, or riding, or driving. |
| 5:00 to 6:00 P.M. | Untack, brush off. Clean stall thoroughly and set fair for night. Pick up paddock or loafing shed (pony in paddock or grazing). Feed, water, and hay. Grain (in stall) and leave for evening. |
| 6:00 to 6:30 P.M. | Tidy barn and tack room, leaving tack ready for morning. |
| 8:30 or 9:00 P.M. | Final barn check. Perhaps shut pony in for night, or let him out for the night if he was kept in during fly season. Shut doors and windows according to weather. Additional hay or grain if on four feeds, or in very cold weather. |

REALISTIC (WEEKDAYS, FOR CHILD GETTING 7:00 A.M.
SCHOOL BUS, RETURNING AT 3:00 P.M.)

| | | | |
|---|---|---|---|
| 6:00 to 6:30 A.M. | Turn out into paddock or pasture. Water and hay. Grain if no helper to do it later. | 12:00 P.M. | The same. |
| | | 3:30 P.M. | Groom. Tack up. Ride as late as daylight and homework permit. |
| 7:30 or 8:00 A.M. | Mother or assistant grains, checks hay and water—may do stall pickup if horsey. | 4:30 or 5:00 P.M. | Do stall as thoroughly as possible. Put pony up for the night. Water, hay, grain. |
| | | 8:00 or 8:30 P.M. | Final barn check if possible. |

**85**

# 6

# YOUR PONY AND HIS HEALTH

DESPITE THEIR SIZE, PONIES ARE PRETTY RUGGED individuals, not prone to illnesses and bouncing back quickly from minor injuries. While a pony owner must be aware of the various possible problems outlined below, trouble can usually be prevented by reasonable care—daily care—and good sense.

## ROUTINE HEALTH CARE

Before your pony arrives, make arrangements with a veterinarian. Not all veterinarans treat ponies and horses; some are strictly small-animal doctors. You will need a large-animal doctor, not only for

**Ponies are generally rugged creatures who, given free choice, would rather be out than in. Note winter coat.**

possible emergencies but for routine shots and worming.

If your new pony is going to join others already on hand, keep him isolated for about three weeks before he shares grazing, water, and stabling. No matter how admirable a place he comes from, or with how clean a bill of health, observe quarantine. No nose-touching another pony, no sniffing over the fence rail. During this isolation period you can chart his temperature, pulse, and respiration as well as get to know the newcomer as an animal (not as a mount).

Most Ponies for Sale advertisements say that the animal has already had "all shots and negative Coggins"; and few ponies and horses change hands today unless a "negative Coggins certificate" changes hands also, stating that blood has been tested for equine infectious anemia and found negative. If you have other ponies on your place or are stabling with other animals on somebody else's property, you certainly should not buy or accept delivery without this certificate.

E.I.A. (also known as swamp fever, slow fever, malarial fever, and mountain fever) is spread by biting insects. While it does not spread directly from horse to horse, it can be spread from an infected animal to a sound one by biting insects (mosquitoes, horse or stable flies) or by a contaminated hypodermic needle previously used on an unidentified carrier of the disease. Victims suffer anemia, fever, weight loss, swellings, marked depression, weakness, and in acute cases death. They may suffer lighter but repeated attacks. Infected animals must be isolated immediately; and since complete con-

**Even a stay-at-home pony gets routine shots. Tuffy eyes Dr. Seremeth with apprehension but stands quietly.**

tinuous (lifelong) isolation is a practical impossibility they must more often be "put down" or killed humanely.

The obviously sick infected equine whose illness will be diagnosed is less hazardous than the unidentified carrier of E.I.A., the horse or pony who has the virus in his blood but has an immunity that makes him appear healthy outwardly. He is a menace to every other animal in his vicinity. While more research is needed, riding groups and state governments are more and more requiring proof of current negative testing before they allow horses or ponies to enter their riding areas or cross borders. (As with your other pony papers—breed registration, shots, etc.—keep the original in a safe place and use photocopies when mailing entries or traveling.)

"All shots" should mean shots against tetanus, equine influenza, and three types of encephalomyelitis. If your new pony has not already

had these shots he must have them now with disposable one-use hypodermic needles. It is best to work out an overall shot program with your veterinarian, for the series must be worked out not only so as to be medically correct but so that the pony will not be out of action on the day of some special event like a Pony Club show.

Encephalomyelitis has been called sleeping sickness, staggers, and brain fever. In the past thousands of horses and ponies have died from three forms of this highly contagious virus (Eastern, Western, Venezuelan), believed to be spread by mosquitoes and other biting insects. Your pony should be protected against EEE, WEE, and VEE by vaccine.

He should be protected against tetanus, which is also known by the frightening name of lockjaw, because victims experience a stiffening or freezing of muscles, especially those of the head and neck. Unable to eat or swallow, the animal dies of starvation plus other complications. The bacterial organisms that cause tetanus thrive wherever there is manure, so tetanus shots should be kept up to date both for ponies and for people. (See "Some Basic Safety Rules.") Once your pony has had his shot he will be better able to fight off infection should he get hurt (an unprotected animal must be given anti-toxin); he will then need only a booster and whatever antibiotics the veterinarian recommends.

Another shot that is particularly desirable if your pony is going to travel (or be exposed to ponies who travel and come back home to him) is the one for equine influenza, another contagious virus-caused illness with all the symptoms human beings have when they have the "flu." It causes abortions in pregnant mares and may be fatal to any animal. Highly infectious, it necessitates extreme sanitary precautions, including isolation of the sick pony and disinfection of the entire stable and equipment.

It is possible to own a pony and not have all these shots given. You can follow a "wait and see" policy or can protect only traveling ponies and let stay-at-homes take their chances, but a truly responsible pony-owner follows a policy of preventive medicine. The possible loss of time for working and riding the pony, the expense of medical care for a sick pony, the hours of home "vetting" under the doctor's orders, the avoidable suffering your pony endures—these far outweigh the cost of routine protection.

To a great degree the health and well-being of your pony and of other animals and people around him depend on something you can't buy: they depend on your working hard every day to maintain high sanitary standards. You must arrange for collection and disposal of manure so as not to harbor parasites and attract germ-spreading flies, mosquitoes, and other insects, especially blood-biting ones. You must drain or spray any stagnant ditches or puddles and see that discarded tires or barrels used for jumps do not hold just enough stagnant water to host larvae; you must spread discarded hay or straw about so that it does not become a damp, mouldy mosquito factory. You must work with your neighborhood or county insect control agency to eliminate mosquito larvae everywhere.

Perhaps some day mosquitoes will be eliminated. Till that time comes, protect your pony against them and the viruses they spread by stable and animal sprays, screening, bug-lighting ("bug zapping"), pasturing in dry high windy areas rather than swampy low ones, and regular preventive shots.

All this sounds alarming, but with the ever-increasing awareness of the need for vaccines, and their ready availability, far fewer ponies suffer even occasionally from such diseases (except in rare epidemic situations) than suffer constantly from internal parasites. Many ponies suffer from "verminous infestation." In spite of easy access to worming medicines in grain stores and tack shops as well as in the veterinarian's kit, even in our day and age many ponies still die from it.

The three most common types of internal parasites are round worms, botworms, and bloodworms, but pinworms, tapeworms, and hundreds of other species also infest ponies. If your pony is to be strong and healthy you must fight them all—incessantly—not only by the worming procedures recommended here but by proper pony, stable, and pasture management.

Start with a clean pony in a clean stall in a clean stable in a clean paddock in a clean yard—and keep everything clean. Almost all internal parasites at one time or another in their life cycle leave a pony's body through his faeces in one form and enter it again in another form through his mouth while he grazes or scratches himself. Therefore it's obvious that a pony's portable plumbing system works against him in that it continually spreads his enemy over his own eating and living quarters. An astonishing number of people who maintain clean stalls and tidy barns seldom or never pick up droppings in the barnyard or pasture; others casually dump or carefully spread fresh manure over present grazing.

Never turn an infested pony into a clean field. Worm him; then keep him confined where you can pick up and dispose of his infested manure in such a way that it will not continue the parasite's life cycle. (Manure stored in pits for several weeks generates enough heat to destroy parasites; freezing temperatures also kill them.)

Avoid overstocking pastures. Practice rotation grazing. If possible, share grazing with other livestock (sheep, cattle) who are not vulnerable to the same parasites. Pick up droppings inside and out as often as possible during the day. Keep the barn and surrounding areas free of flies. Do all this; and dose the parasites present under a worming program worked out by your veterinarian.

Obvious signs of internal parasites include scouring, or very loose droppings; malnutrition shown by an overall undernourished gauntness or by a bloated belly but sunken hips, patchy coat, lack-lustre eyes, and weary manner; rubbing of the rear end in an attempt to scratch the tail and dock area; anemia; and even partial paralysis. Some symptoms may be hidden by a rough winter coat: feel the body under the coat, and don't be misled by a "fat" belly.

Whether or not they exhibit such extreme symptoms, all ponies have worms. No part of a pony's body is safe from these destructive hordes: mucous linings of gums, pharynx, stomach, intestines (bots); bloodstream to liver, heart, lungs, windpipe, pharynx, intestine (ascarids); caecum and colon, all vital organs, liver, lungs, large intestine (bloodworms). These parasites can cause coughing, fever, general debility, anemia. You can never completely free your pony of them, but you can keep them under control.

Drug and animal-supply companies are constantly improving worming materials; your veterinarian will be up to date on the best ones to use. Remember: they are poisons—potent and lethal; they must be kept in a locked cupboard and used only as directed for one particular pony (for weight, age, and height are considered in figuring dosage).

Worming can be done in various ways. The medicine may be a capsule or bolus administered by a "gun" placed in your pony's mouth; it may be a liquid or "drench" poured through a tube inserted in his nose and eased down into the stomach. These methods of treatment are considered the most thorough, but they should be applied only by an expert. Or the medicine may come in crumble or powder form and be administered either by your veterinarian or by you. Until recently worming powders were very unappetizing; ponies had to be "starved" before they would eat feed that was mixed with such powders. Now some are so tasty that ponies will eat them out of hand as well as nonchalantly with their regular feed.

At High Hickory we have our ponies "done" by our veterinarian twice a year and between visits we give them worming powders in their feed every two months. This program is so successful that the only time the Pony Pals have seen worms was when a new pony arrived here for training. Fortunately, though healthy-looking, he was restricted to the meadow "isolation" stall for routine quarantine, and worming, which in his case had been skipped because of gelding, was done immediately and thoroughly by our veterinarian. The parasitic worms, a few of which had been visible in the rectum area, were

Dr. Gill tube-worms newcomer Baldy Suprise. Liquid medication, poured into the funnel, enters the stomach via tube inserted through the nostril. Funnel must be held high when this gravity method is used.

Here worming is part of a routine health schedule. This time medication is injected into the tube by syringe.

conspicuous among his droppings for several days after the treatment.

The pharmaceutical companies put out descriptive booklets (free of charge at your tack shop, grain store, or through the mail) with up-to-date information on treatment. Their diagrams and pictures of the life cycles of these internal parasites are unpleasant. ("Oh, gross!" say the Pony Pals.) But the real things are more so—and anyone who has seen them will be prompt to set up a strict program against them. Contagion from parasites is not a problem; but the Pony Pals needed no reminder to "wash up" after barn chores once they had seen the things.

Treating against these internal parasites is "strong medicine," so your veterinarian may prefer not to worm at the same time that he gives shots. It will depend on what medications he uses and on your pony's physical condition.

It is important to take conditioning and schooling into consideration in planning the shots and worming schedule. Your pony will have to rest for several days after WEE and EEE shots, longer after the VEE and the flu vac; otherwise he may have a serious reaction. This means a tapering off as well as a building up in your conditioning program.

Generally, a healthy pony will have only a slight reaction, if any: but even among healthy ponies reactions vary. Lutine Bell's neck was sore from her flu shot—the Pony Pals say "She's a bleeder," as even a tiny spot from an injection bleeds and is sore for days—while other ponies are indifferent. Tuffy's slight swelling was sensitive to the touch for several days; K.V. had a hand-size swelling very sore for days. As among persons, difference in reaction is to be expected.

"HAVE D.V.M.; WILL TRAVEL"

Your veterinarian charges a base fee for his "house call" (emergency calls cost more), then so much per shot or per worming per pony. He will charge extra for bandages, salves, and other medications used by him or left for your use. Telephone his office in time for him to fit you into his schedule on the day he routinely visits your part of the country.

Have your pony ready, in his stall or in a small paddock with a halter and lead rope near by (and you should be near if he's difficult to catch). Neither the veterinarian nor the blacksmith should have to go looking for a pony to catch him, or be expected to wait a long time while you go after him. The pony should be there, clean and well-groomed if possible. (For one thing, should the time ever come when you want to sell him, you want these two discreet members of the horsemen's grapevine to remember him at his best!)

On routine visits for worming and shots, your vet with his trained eye can spot incipient health problems that may escape yours. Between visits keep a list of questions that come up—about those bumps on Bilbo's back, that rash in Popover's ears, the waxy secretion in Sweet Thing's teats, the skin peeling off Brownie's nose.

You can learn a lot from your veterinarian and your blacksmith. They may not have time for a cup of coffee, but they always have time (make time!) to answer your questions. Days when "the vet's due" or "the blacksmith's coming" are special ones at High Hickory, and all the Pony Pals try to be here to see these valued friends.

Pony Clubs, 4-H groups, and other riding organizations often organize clinics so that members can ride or trailer to a central location for annual shots and wormings. With such clinics, a veterinarian can charge a minimum fee. If you have several ponies, the saving may not be worth the time and effort involved in trucking, but you might be able to work out a "mini-clinic" at home with neighboring pony owners. In areas where large-animal doctors are at a premium, your veterinarian will gladly cooperate, to shorten his long hours on the road.

Every pony barn should have a simple medicine cabinet (chest, cupboard, box); but any medicating you do should be under supervision. Anything done before your veterinarian advises you should be merely "first aid," anything done afterwards "post aid." For the few times when you may need them, keep the following in your pony barn medicine cupboard:

| | |
|---|---|
| Scissors | A flashlight |
| Rubbing alcohol | A small pail and sponge |
| A medicated salve such as | Absorbine or similar |
| Furacin (ask your | linament |
| veterinarian) | Epsom salts |
| A medicated powder | Boric acid |
| Leg cottons | A four-cup measure |
| Leg bandages or 3M self- | A measuring spoon |
| adhering bandage rolls | A long-handled spoon for |
| A set of paper cups | stirring |
| Cotton batton | |
| A horse thermometer | Vaseline |

These items should be kept clean and dust-free, for medical use only. Purchase in small sizes so that items like cotton batton remain sterile and medicine does not pass its "shelf life." Poisons such as worming powder left with you by the veterinarian—and even boric acid—should be kept separate so that their being locked up does not prevent access to other aids in an emergency.

Have your veterinarian's telephone number on the outside of this cabinet, on your regular emergency list beside your telephone, and also on several tear sheets in the barn. In a recent emergency at High Hickory we tragically lost a lovely Thoroughbred filly who had to be put down because of spinal lesions. This freak accident made me aware of the need to have the vet's number where anyone, not just you, can find it quickly. In a crisis any adults present may be too busy to do the phoning. Have a pad prepared in triplicate in the barn so that the smallest youngster can rip a sheet off rather than have to repeat a strange number frantically over and over as he races to the phone, or hunt for it on your inside list.

When should you call the veterinarian? As with family health, common sense is usually a good guide, and there is usually no doubt in a case when accident or illness requires expert attention. If it is a real emergency, there is seldom any question. The next section sets forth some ways of knowing whether your pony is in good health or not.

But first, there is something you can do that will help in the event that medical care and nursing are ever needed: you can teach your pony how to be a "good patient."

Begin with your earliest handling of him. When you work around his head, touch his ears. (A sick pony may have cold ears, and you will want to warm them by "stripping" or pulling gently from base to tip.) Most ponies love this. Let your pony get used to the sound of scissors close to his ears, even before you trim them. Handle the inside lining of his outer ear.

When you groom, be careful in working about his eyes, but accustom him to your putting your hand over them, wiping them with a clean cotton or sponge. If he's used to water dripping from the sponge, that will help if you ever need to bathe his eye with a boric acid solution. Sometimes it helps a veterinarian to work on a frightened pony if you cover one eye or blindfold both, but "surprise-proofing" is even better.

This grip demonstrates where to squeeze to control your pony. As lack of tension in the fingers and in the pony shows, no pressure is being exerted here, but the area is so soft that indentation occurs nonetheless.

Of course you're teaching the pony to let you pick up his feet for cleaning hooves or putting on bell boots. By holding up a foot you can prevent his moving about when the veterinarian is working on him. He will then think about balancing on three legs and not about being medicated.

You can also prevent his moving about by placing him in a corner or against a wall. You can hold him still by placing your hand on his nose and squeezing. (Gripping his ear, another method, is far less desirable as it may make him head-shy.) Often it's enough restraint to have him on a lead rope and to put your hand on his withers: this steadies him and discourages his moving back. Better to start out with a loose lead rope and a relaxed manner than get a death grip on the halter or a chain that will make the pony tense up and struggle as he otherwise might not have done.

Let your pony see and hear—and smell—when you open jars of salve or cans of vitamins, so that he will not associate such things only with medication of a painful sore or with the veterinarian.

If you accustom him to bandaging of all his legs (even if you never trailer him or use stable bandages) he will be less liable to rip off a medical bandage. Teach him to let you put his foot in a bucket of water (or poultice mash) and keep it there, eventually with his weight on it. This will simplify vetting if you ever need to soak a foot because of a puncture wound on the sole of a hoof or an injury to a pastern. Teach him to let you open his mouth, hold back his lips to examine his teeth and gums, pull his tongue to the side.

**Lutine patiently keeps her hoof immersed in water during one of many daily soakings required in vetting a punctured sole.**

Most of all, instill confidence in your pony—confidence in you. If he knows that you are kind but consistent in expecting obedience from him, he will obey your "Ho" and "Stand"; in this way you can assist your veterinarian. In other words, surprise-proof your pony in a hundred little ways so as to make him a good patient, should he ever need to be one, *before* the veterinarian comes.

HOW TO KNOW IF YOUR PONY IS HEALTHY

The best veterinary safeguard is to know your pony. No program of health care, preventive or remedial, can work unless you know what a *healthy* pony is. To be able to recognize sickness in its earliest, preventable stages you must know what your particular pony looks like when he is normal: you must know how he walks, how he stands, how he holds his head when idle, how much he eats, how he eats, when he lies down to rest. Only in this way can you tell when he is not walking sound or when he is "off his feed."

You must know your pony's normal temperature, pulse, and respiration.

Your veterinarian will show you how to find these things better than printed words can, but it will help if you have some idea of the procedures.

Temperature is usually taken rectally with a thermometer inserted under the pony's tail. Horse thermometers end with a glass loop to which you can fasten a piece of string. You are not likely to insert it so far into the rectum that it disappears; even partially inserted, it is more likely, unless held, to be evacuated into the bedding. Should you insert it too far, do not attempt to "go in after it" with your hand. Wait, and the pony's eliminatory system will push it out very shortly. Keep a small jar of vaseline with your thermometer to lubricate it before insertion. You can omit this in an emergency; but it slips in more readily with clean grease. You can wipe it off and rinse in alcohol, but, again, this is not strictly necessary. Thermometers are commonly used from pony to pony, though we prefer each pony to have his own.

Your pony's temperature ought to be about one hundred degrees Fahrenheit (37.5 Centigrade) or close to it—ninety-nine to 101.3 degrees. It may be low in the morning and high in the afternoon; you should take temperatures routinely often enough to know what it is when. If it goes to 103 you have cause for concern; if it goes to 105 you should call the veterinarian.

Your pony's normal pulse is strong and steady and can range widely in animals of different sizes, ages, and sex, from twenty-eight to forty-eight beats per minute. It is of course a reflection of the heart throb, which you can count more directly by putting your ear on the side of his chest just above his elbow. Pulse is usually checked by counting the throbs or beats of the artery located right under a pony's jawbone. Try this yourself, then ask your vet to let you practice a few times under his supervision.

Your pony's respiration varies with his activity or inactivity. To take his respiration, look at his flanks. Even at rest, they rise and fall with his breathing. After strenuous exercise they heave in proportion to his exertion. The easiest time to check respiration is after exercise, when movement is conspicuous. Then compare this obvious movement with the slight rise and fall after an hour's rest. Even normal respiration may vary from eight to twenty-one per minute, so you can see it is important to know your pony's normal rpm. In certain events such as endurance riding or combined training, the time it takes your pony to regain his normal rpm after strenuous work is of prime importance in determining whether he is fit to continue.

Have a chart or notebook where you note statistics of temperature, pulse, and respiration. Check frequently enough, at the same hour each time, to make this a valid record of what is normal for your pony. Then if you have reason to think he is not well, you can check these three points against your record. It is a good idea to put these statistics on a sheet or card that gives your pony's name, his age, and use, his regular feeds and quantities, and any special requirements (such as "no hay" or "dampen feed").

If you know these points and your pony's normal condition you will be aware of and can describe any abnormal symptoms to your vet over the phone. He will advise you what to do until he arrives and can judge just how urgently he is needed. It may be reassuring to know that most health and accident problems with ponies occur not through ignorance on the owner's part but simply through lack of looking, through "not noticing" until things were bad: not looking around the barn and yard to see that no hazards existed, not looking at the pony when he was well so that the least bit of "off" could be promptly remedied.

Sometimes, of course, we have the reverse: new pony owners worry about perfectly normal things! Occasionally one will see his pony resting half-asleep standing on three legs, with the fourth akimbo, and will phone to ask: "Is he lame?" Invariably we're surprised at realizing afresh how few people see a pony at rest. Most are used to seeing ponies moving under saddle, coming to meet them in a field, or standing "square" in hand.

Your pony's resting a hind foot is not cause for alarm, but his "resting" a forefoot is cause for concern. First-time pony owners may not be aware of this. Some other points:

Unless he is eating, a pony normally holds his head high, so a low heavy head may be an indication of sickness. Until you wonder whether your pony is ill, you may never have noticed that the lining of his eyes and nose, mouth and gums is normally salmon-pink; that the usually hidden white of his eye is normally white, not yellowy or bloodshot; that his urine is normally thick and light yellow; that his droppings normally break as they hit the ground and have no slime or mucus or bad odor; that he normally passes faeces eight to sixteen times a day and urinates four or five times a day (and if traveling or being worked must be given time to do so); that even when ungroomed his coat normally lies flat and doesn't stand up dry and staring as if brushed the wrong way; that normally his ears are warm and his lower limbs cool to the touch; that faint rumblings can normally be heard in his stomach, and that, with other symptoms, "silence" could be a sign of trouble.

Some signs of good health or sickness in a pony are charted for quick comparison.

**Hanging head, drooping quarters, unusual swelling on neck—all indicate a sick pony. Galaxy with new owner Kate in Needham was back to normal after several days of misery.**

# PONY HEALTH CHART

| HEALTHY | | SICK |
|---|---|---|
| Normal for individual | Pulse, temperature, respiration | Too high, too low, too fast, too slow—off recorded "norms" |
| Warm, pricked, alert, clean inside | Ears | Cold, lopped, droopy, scabby, flaky, sore to touch |
| Nose free of discharge | Nose and Mouth | Nose full of mucus or phlegmy, "running" |
| No coughing or sneezing, or only occasional sneezing or deep blowing | | Coughing from deep down, frequent sneezing |
| Gums pink | | Gums pale to whitish; even a bluish tinge |
| Bright, lively, whites clear | Eyes | Dull, lacklustre; whites bloodshot or yellowy |
| Up, alert | Head | Down, indifferent; if colicky, the pony looks back at its own body |
| Well filled out | Body | Emaciated; belly bloated, hips sunken |
| Lively even if winterthick; glossy if groomed | Coat | Staring, on-end as if brushed wrong way; dull, dry, doesn't respond to grooming |
| Flexible and lively, full of nerve-endings and muscles, so pony moves freely; loose and elastic, not hidebound: pony flicks or twitches to rid himself of flies; free of bumps or rash | Skin | Flaccid or hidebound; pony doesn't twitch off bugs or flies; hot or cold sweat without activity to cause it; lumps, bumps, rash, or irritation |
| No heat in legs or hooves; pony stands square or rests a hind leg; normal gaits | Legs | Pony rests a foreleg, points a toe; gaits irregular, or lame; heat in legs and/or hooves |
| Moving, swishing flies; well-carried | Tail | Drooping as if no muscle |
| Good; pony consumes usual feed; normal thirst | Appetite | Off feed and water; not tempted by grain; may or may not eat hay; hay may hang from corners of mouth |
| Normal interior sounds of digestion and peristaltic motion going on | Digestion | No sounds of digestion; flanks sunken or moving in unusual way; or bloated |
| Regular. Urine thick and light yellow; droppings firm, no bad odor | Elimination | Too frequent or too infrequent; urine unusually dark; pony strains when staling; droppings too loose or too hard; mucous or green slime; foul odor |
| Impression of contained energy: "ready to go" | General appearance and behavior | Lackadaisical; hang-dog, run-down look |
| Pony moves about paddock or pasture; if standing, looks around | | Stands in one place, doesn't care what is going on; lies down when normally up; may not get up when approached, even when coaxed |
| Lies down at usual periods of day; may not get up if he trusts you, but pays attention to your presence; may stretch with pleasure and even grunt or groan | | May seem to make a tremendous effort if he does get up; if cast, cannot get up; if colicky, rolls violently, getting up and down; if foundered, may get up part way and sit on haunches, front legs still, delaying putting weight on them |
| Greets you with a whinny, nicker, or by approaching; comes when called (or runs away) | | Usually suffers in silence; ignores you |

## ILLNESSES, ACHES AND PAINS, AND ACCIDENTS

What, specifically, are the things that may go wrong with a pony? What are the pony equivalents of measles, mumps, and chicken pox, skinned knees, or sprained ankles?

One ailment many ponies fall victim to is colic. The most prevalent cause is strongyl migration, and such bloodworm damage to the intestines and to the arteries supplying the intestines is the greatest cause of death from colic. Other common causes are nervousness, overworking, and eating new feeds. Colic has been defined half-jokingly as the price a pony pays for gluttony.

You can prevent colic from these causes by (most important) proper worming under veterinarian supervision, considerate informed handling, and proper stable management. It is of course your responsibility to do so.

But what if there is a slip? What if you find Billy Blue bolting grain and the feed bin contents half gone (obviously into his ballooning stomach) what may you expect, and what should you do?

Colic is a stomach-ache, and like human indigestion it varies in intensity. It may start with mild twinges which the pony, turning his head back towards his flanks, regards with bewilderment. He may cowkick at his belly. He may lie down and get up repeatedly, may roll wildly in an effort to relieve sharp attacks of pain; he may groan. In severe seizures he may even rear and throw himself over, thrash, and not get to his feet. He may break out in patchy wet sweat.

If you suspect colic, the first thing to do is to alert your veterinarian. Even if the attack is mild and over by the time he arrives he may want to give some medication. While you wait for him, keep your pony moving quietly. (If he is in a stall, it is important that he not get cast if he rolls.)

A danger in colic of any sort is that, in his throes, a pony may twist an intestine or cause other internal damage. As a youngster I watched a friend's mare die of colic; but I have since seen another come through with no after-effects (and with no lesson about overeating learned).

A pony cannot relieve an overloaded stomach by vomiting; thus pains of indigestion are compounded if impaction sets in. Such overeating can be followed by diarrhea and/or followed by founder if the pony lives or can be fatal from a ruptured stomach. You can see why the best advice is: Do not treat overeating by putting more of anything in your pony's stomach. Keep a colicy pony away from all food and all water and contact your veterinarian.

The best "medicine" is prevention. Keep feed locked up at all times. Carefully follow the rules stressed throughout this book on feeding, watering, turning out to grass—on all phases of pony management.

Founder (or laminitus) may also be caused by overeating, by too much lush grass too soon or too much feed—not only feed eaten in one fell swoop resulting in colic, but feed doled out regularly in too great quantity for the pony's size, activity, and age. Another cause is too much work, or no work; hence it's often seen in idle, outgrown, overweight, put-out-to-pasture ponies.

Whereas colic affects the digestive system, founder affects the vascular system, specifically that within the pony's hooves. The ensuing congestion results in painfully sore feet and lameness. It may be so severe that infection sets in. Most often it affects

**One symptom of founder is this "sit like a dog" position as its victim delays putting weight on his feet.**

the front feet, and the pony, reluctant to put weight on them, may lie down. When he does stand, he may spend some time sitting dog-like on his haunches before unwillingly surging up, avoiding till the last moment putting his weight on his front feet.

If you press or tap on the sole of his hoof, a foundered pony will react by trying to pull his foot away. There may be heat—hence the name "fever in the feet." In extreme cases, ridges develop and deform the hoof wall, while a "dropped" sole gives permanent proof that the pony has once been foundered and may have trouble always.

Founder is one of the most serious problems affecting ponies (a problem, ironically, usually generated by overfeeding by too kind and too ignorant owners). Founder is considered an emergency and should be treated by your veterinarian. His prompt initial treatment will markedly determine a pony's chances for eventual soundness.

Besides any medical treatment, your veterinarian will undoubtedly recommend a strict weight-loss diet. For immediate easing of pain, old timers used to suggest hosing your pony's legs with cold water (this is no longer a favored treatment), then careful exercise eventually to stimulate circulation, and possible farrier work.

Again, the best medicine is prevention. Feed properly in relation to sensible exercise on a regular schedule without abrupt intervals of inactivity. Prevent both people-generosity and pony-gluttony in the feed room or lush pasture. With a small old outgrown pet pony especially you must hard-heartedly resist the temptation to overfeed; it is better to have him slightly thin than to have him so fat that children ask: "Is *he* in foal?"

*Coughs, sneezes, colds*

A perfectly healthy pony will cough or sneeze once in a while, like a healthy person. If a pony bolts his feed, particularly dry feed, without enough salivary mastication he may choke and mucoussy food come out of his nostrils. Usually this soon ends. If it does not, take away all his food, leaving water. In case of prolonged choking call the vet. Prevent greedy eating by feeding sufficiently at regular times, by placing salt bricks or large stones in the feed tub, or by moistening feed slightly. Slice carrots diagonally or grate them into the feed.

"*Gesundheit!*" takes care of the stray cough or sneeze, even if the pony doesn't answer "*Danke schön!*" But repeated coughing, deep and from the chest, often with a reach-for-the-paper-hanky discharge from the nostrils, is cause for concern. Accompanied by a rise in temperature, a cough calls for a "day in bed" and possibly the veterinarian. Often a virus or cough is making the rounds, and the vet will supply you with medicine. This may be a powder to add to your pony's feed. Coughs may be contagious, so isolate as much as possible and follow the rules about not sharing blankets, feed tubs, water buckets, and so on.

Any cough requires a rest from work, since it involves the lungs among other things. In a run-down pony persistent, neglected coughs and colds can develop into pneumonia. Your invalid may appreciate a tasty bran mash and, if not too sick, regular grooming. Rest will speed his recovery; put him back to work too soon and too hard and he will have a relapse. Resume use gradually, to develop his wind and muscle tone till he is back to normal.

Coughs and colds are not caused by cold. Healthy ponies don't mind cold or wet so long as they have shelter free of draughts, with freedom to move about. Put up hot and wet in draughty confinement or not blanketed when clipped and accustomed to such protection, or stabled in an overinsulated barn made damp from body heat, they do sicken.

Ponies may get something referred to as *Tying Up Syndrome*, a disease less severe than azoturia but of similar origin. Azoturia or Monday morning sickness attacked heavy horses with sudden crippling when, having labored hard six days and stood idle on the seventh, they were again led out to work. In like manner, "tying up" occurs when an active pony in the peak of fitness is abruptly rested a few days. When the pony is first put back into use, he gets tied up, usually within the first half hour: stiffness and soreness in the hindquarters becomes so acute the pony may pivot on his hind feet rather than walk.

He will not "walk out of" this! Immediate rest and an immediate call to the veterinarian are in order. The pony may be rubbed, blanketed, and put into a comfortable stall without food until the veterinarian arrives.

Like many pony problems, "tying up" can be avoided by following the suggestions for exercise and diet and general good care stressed throughout this book. But it should perhaps be pointed out that even the pony that is worked regularly *but only lightly* may be struck by similar almost paralytic stiffness if he is suddenly subjected to long extremely hard work.

What are some of the aches and pains we strive to prevent? Knowing what they are and what to do about them helps lessen the probability of their occurring.

*Ears*

Scaling and itching may occur inside the outer ear. Your pony will show this by shaking his head in irritation and by objecting to his ears' being handled. Dandruff-like flakes crust the lining of his ear, which in severe cases may be raw and reddened. The most common cause of inflammation is black flies.

Prevent this by gentle daily cleaning of his ears. Do not trim the fine hairs inside that protect him against mites and other bugs as well as rain and snow. (If he is on grass, leave his mane and forelock long for protection.)

Fight bugs! Attacks by fleas, ticks, lice, and mange mites, as well as by black flies and horse flies, can be prevented by thorough grooming and routine spraying of all pony quarters. During the bug season use a liquid or powder on your pony's coat to make bugs and other insects keep their distance.

Treat irritated ears with medicated salve, not a liquid (always avoid getting any liquid in the inner ear), until the crusty rawness is gone.

The tips of a pony's ears may get hurt. In olden days, people used deliberately to nick or cut the ears of ponies or horses turned out on common grazing; it was a form of branding. (Other means of branding are still practiced—on gums, hoof, neck, rump, or saddle area.) Today the nicks one sees are much more likely to have been caused by a barb in wire fencing, a dog bite, or a fleck from a hunting thong or lashing branch. They may bleed profusely but heal rapidly if kept clean and flexible with a simple salve.

Cold ears may indicate a temporary chill or the onset of illness. If your pony is wet, cold, and shivering, rub him briskly with a hay wisp or rough burlap. Quarter his blanket so that while you rub as much of his body as possible is covered. When he's rubbed down, blanket him with a fluffy layer of straw or hay stuffed under his rug. You'll remove this hay when the pony's coat is dried out and put on a dry blanket—or if you have only one blanket you can throw a couple of burlap grain bags or any old cloth over the hay stuffing and under his blanket. This lining, like the hay, will soak up moisture and can later be removed. (But if you have no extra, even a damp blanket will hold in body warmth.) Once you have him blanketed, strip those cold ears, to restore circulation and warmth.

Just because your pony was chilled, do not from overreaction now stable him in too warm a place. He is better blanketed and left with his door open than shut up in a confined area that may become overdamp from body heat. Remember that he needs shelter free from draughts and freedom to move around: cold quarters do no harm, draughty ones do.

*Eyes*

Your pony's ear and eye muscles seem closely connected. (Notice how he pricks his ears as he looks about at different things.) And like his ears his eyes play an important part in the general impression he makes. When we look for a pony, we hope to find one with a large clear eye, dark, alert, and inquisitive. In a good eye the iris appears almost black or like bittersweet chocolate, with the center (or egg-shaped pupil) rather purpley, free of specks or milky opacities, and the whole eye looks moist. This dark "liquid" eye is surrounded by the sclera or white, but you don't usually see this part of the eyeball in a pony, and it is generally considered undesirable to do so.[1] When the white shows a pony has a slightly wild, unreliable, "sclerotic" look. However, the white is there, and if we hold the eyelids open to observe it, it should be opaquely white, not yellowish or bloodshot.

Occasionally a pony (most frequently one that is parti-colored, with a lot of white) will lack pigment in the iris, usually in one eye only, so that that eye appears blue or grayish blue or bluish white. This comes about when (rarely) a particular combination of recessive genes combine in a dominant condition. Like most oddities, the blue eye coloring has a number of old wives' tales associated with it: known as watcheye, blue eye, and China eye, it has erroneously been considered a sign of weakness. Also erroneously, it has been called wall-eye, though it does not involve the muscular imbalance of that condition. It is not the pink eye of the albino. (In breeds where bloodlines and breeding are controlled it is seldom seen, and most breed registries consider this eye coloring "undesirable.")

Whatever the color of his eye a pony, unlike us, seldom sees simultaneously with both eyes. His eyes are set wide on the sides of his head. This enables him to see not only both sides at once (separately! with a different picture or view) and also to the rear. Only if concentrating and looking directly in front of him does he have our type of binocular vision, as indicated by the pricking of his ears as he focuses forward on a very limited field. Most of the time he uses duo-monocular vision (the seeing to each side and to the rear, and therefore seeing different things at the same time). Since his left eye may not see what his right eye sees, it's small wonder that a pony sometimes shies.

Despite the wide range of vision this arrangement gives him, a pony has two "blind" spots—directly behind him and directly (about four feet) in front of him. To see what is under his very nose he must put his head down. (While it's down, he can see behind him through his own legs while grazing—one reason why it's hard to "sneak up" on your pony.) To see what's above the level of his eyes he must put his nose up. That faraway "look of eagles" is necessary: if your pony is to see far away he must raise his head to create different focal lengths for his eyes, rather like a Zoom camera. This is partly because his retina has a flattened arc. It is generally believed that a pony cannot see details of distant views.

A good space between large dark eyes has always been regarded as desirable in a pony, but some claim has been made that less space between the eyes means greater binocular vision and (according to this theory) therefore greater intelligence. The theory has not been substantiated, nor has the theory that watcheyes are not susceptible to moon blindness.

1. See exceptions in chapter on Breeds: *i.e.*, the visible sclera normal in Appaloosas and P.O.A.'s.

Wherever set, the large prominent eye we all like in a pony seems very vulnerable to injury. A pony is extremely eye-conscious, quick in reflex movements of his flexible neck, and with an uncanny ability to assess space, so that he can gallop under a tree branch but never bang his head. He has special eyelids, two outer lids, the upper with eyelashes, and a third inner one. You may have noticed the bony socket over each eye without knowing that this provides a protective cavity into which the eyeball can retreat under pressure while at the same time the lid closes as a protective covering. While what he sees—such as a wave of your hand—will cause your pony's eye to shut, some of the protective action of the eyelids depends on the "warning system" of long hairs about the eye itself. When we trim these, and the whiskers on his muzzle, we deprive a pony of some vital radar; and for this reason hairs and whiskers are best left untouched on the pastured pony.

The extreme vulnerability of the eye (both equine and human) is one reason why a rider should never hold branches for someone following behind: the increased whipping when a branch is released may cause injury whereas just riding carefully through might not. A free pony is unlikely to hurt himself no matter how wildly he gallops through woods and underbrush, but a pony whose head movement is restricted by a rider's use of the reins cannot make instinctive adjustments on his own behalf.

Only recently we visited a family whose mare was blinded by a "soft" pine branch during a trail ride. Her eyelids were sutured together by the veterinarian surgeon and she is back in use. Over the years I've seen other blind ponies—one with no eyeball but exposed pink muscles, one with an opaque eye, both with eyelids functioning and both providing safe pleasant rides for their experienced riders. How they were blinded no one knows. But the Pony Pals, alas, once witnessed the blinding of a horse by its livery-stable rider's brutal use of a crop. With our emphasis on "no crop, no spurs," it is hardly necessary to say: *Never* hit a pony about the head.

Eye injury is often revealed by a puffed and closed eyelid or by tears streaming from an eye. A weak boric acid solution, or even plain water, will comfort and lessen the swelling; you can hold the wet cotton batton in place for a brief cold compress. Your vet-proofing will come in handy here, for with one eye sore and "blind" your pony will be doubly quick in reacting to any movement about his head.

Often the swelling indicates that the blow or bump was sustained only by the protective eyelids closing over the eye rather than by the eye itself. Such swellings often subside within twenty-four hours. If there is the slightest indication of a cut or tear, or bleeding, or of continued weeping from between the lids, your veterinarian should be summoned at once. (More often in the case of an injury to the eyeball the eyelid is open, not closed.) An injured eye or lid must be kept free of infection and annoying flies.

Periodic ophthalmia and cataract can cause blindness in ponies. The former, fortunately rare, is called moon blindness, and at present no cure is known. If you suspect poor vision, have your veterinarian examine your pony's eyes—even if the pony can't explain his problem for himself as in *Doctor Doolittle:*

'You know, Doctor,' said the horse, 'that vet over the hill knows nothing at all. He has been treating me for six weeks now—for spavins. What I need is *spectacles*. There's no reason why horses shouldn't wear glasses, the same as people. But that stupid man over the hill never even looked at my eyes. He kept on giving me big pills.'

### Mouth

Your pony may have a sore mouth, tongue, or gums because of poor bitting, poor fit or pressure on the bit rings from a dropped noseband, roughened or sharp edges of a bit or cheeks, a wrong-sized or extremely severe bit or from his own teeth. When a lead chain is used for control under the lip such severity may break the gum tissue.

Apply a mild saline solution (about two teaspoonfuls of table salt to a pint of water) with a little syringe or cotton batton, or apply vaseline to outside areas. Do not use a bit while the sore persists. Have his teeth checked and make sure that the reason for the sore is corrected.

### Head

Your pony may nick or rub hair or skin off his head—face, cheek, poll—ducking under fence bars for grass in another field. Change the bar spacing or add another rail—or throw out more hay. If such rubs are caused by a halter or by rivets on a halter, leave the halter on less often (only while grooming) or cover it with sheepskin or artificial fleece. Rope burns cause similar sores. For all such superficial rubs a mildly medicated salve or vaseline, applied daily, will be sufficient.

The Pony Pals nicknamed a foal "Easter Bonnet" because of the sheepskin headpiece we attached to his halter after he had repeatedly banged his poll sticking his head through fence rails. Your pony may not need a bonnet except for travel, but make sure that you have enough overhead in any building (stall, barn, carport, garage) where you take your pony. Put a padded shipping helmet on him when trailering.

*Teeth*

Ponies need dentists, too! They sometimes have trouble with their teeth. This may be indicated by difficulty in chewing, by food dribbling or hay hanging from the corners of the mouth, or by food left uneaten. Dental problems may lead to general debility, or to grouchiness and under-saddle-and-bridle difficulties. (When Stardust was teething, she made alarming grinding sounds whenever she was ridden in a bridle. This gnashing of teeth had the children singing "Fee, fi, fo, fum . . . I'll grind your bones"; but it never affected her agreeable disposition. For a while she was ridden with a halter only.) Occasionally a pony will have a tooth broken by a kick from another pony, by mishandling, or quite mysteriously.

Teeth are one determining factor in judging a pony's age. Like us, a pony has baby teeth and permanent teeth (don't be alarmed to see the baby ones being shed and dangling, or lying in the manger), and the stages they go through reveal his age to the horseman.

**Galaxy shows a six-year-old's full mouth. "Why, she has more teeth than I have," seven-year-old Alan exclaimed with a grin that proved his point.**

To be able to judge age by teeth you must examine hundreds of "mouths" belonging to ponies of all ages (ages verified by registration papers or veterinarian expertise). Pictures and texts on dentition can only provide a beginning on which to build eventual firsthand knowledge.

Except when he wriggles his lips at some strange taste or draws them back in a horse laugh, your pony's teeth are hidden. To examine them you must open his lips and/or his mouth. Have your pony held on a lead rope or cross ties, grasp his upper lip firmly with one hand and his lower lip with the other, and pull them apart. To look inside his mouth, put one hand on the upper and lower jaws (in the gap known as the bars where there are no teeth) and pull down gently. If necessary to see better, you can grasp the tongue and pull it to one side.

Your pony's front teeth are incisors or biting teeth, six on the front of the upper and the lower jaw. Farther back beyond his bars, hidden by his cheeks, are his molars or grinding teeth, twelve on a jaw, six to each side.

You can't tell a pony's sex by his teeth, but if there are two pairs of tusklike teeth separate from (but close to) the incisors he is almost certainly a horse; mares only rarely have these tushes. Don't confuse tushes with wolf teeth, rudimentary eruptions in front of the upper molars. Wolf teeth are remnants of the first premolar but may be in the way during bitting and become painful. Like our wisdom teeth, they can be removed by dental surgery.

Born with two central incisors (little nippers!) and three cheek teeth, by his first year a pony has all his baby teeth and his first permanent molars. Baby teeth are whiter and much smaller than permanent teeth. When he is shedding them, the pony does not go round with gaps like the child who's just put a baby tooth under his pillow for the Tooth Fairy, but you may find the irregularly shaped caps in his manger or feed tub. They resemble convoluted ivory or bone with yellowy markings; Lutine's are bigger than Galaxy's, and collections of both sit on a shelf along with sharks' teeth, puppy teeth, and one huge whale tooth.

Most easily identifiable stages occur at the erruption dates for:

First incisors at two and a half years.

Second incisors at three and a half years.

Third incisors at four and a half years.

Cusps between six and eight years.

and also when:

First incisor cusps disappear at six years.

Second incisor cusps disappear at seven years.

Third incisor cusps disappear at eight years.

Less simple points of identification are "the Mark" (a dark depression in the center of the top grinding surface or "table" of each tooth, by six years); "the Hook" or "the Seven Year Hook" (a hook to the back outer corner of the top outside incisor, by seven); and, "the Dental Star" or "the Star" (a brownish line between the Mark and the outer edge of the tooth, by eight). Both the Hook and the Star disappear after about a year; both reappear at around eleven or thirteen years of age.

From eight, when a pony becomes "aged" (see Chapter 2), age is ascertained partly by a brown mark known as Galvayne's Groove. This line appears at eight years at the top or gum edge of the upper corner incisor and gradually grows downward. It is not a reliable identification of age.

A quick look at your pony's teeth in profile will give you an approximate age. The angle of occlusion (or the bite of the teeth) changes considerably, even with a pony that has a good mouth. A pony with a "bad" mouth may have problems of malocclusion which an orthodontist would work to correct in a human being. In a pony, such things as parrot mouth, its opposite undershot mouth, and shear mouth, where incisors and molars don't meet, are obvious unsoundnesses.

Up to age four or five, the angle is slight; it's a matter of what teeth are present. After five, it's a matter of wear and tear. At eight the angle is greater, the teeth seem more oblique; this slant continues conspicuously from ten on. By twelve, as Eric once observed, the teeth themselves "look as if they've been around a long time." At sixteen, both teeth and the jaws themselves are very long and sloping. At twenty the angle is so extreme that the teeth seem to protrude horizontally from the jaws. From this age on you see in old ponies the disproportionate prominence that caricatures of old horses seem to exaggerate.

At different ages the tables also change in shape: from oval (up to about seven) to triangular (from nine to thirteen) to round (after thirteen), until in extreme old age they again become triangular. In order to see the tables and such things as the Mark and the Star, you must of course open your pony's mouth, whereas to see the profile you merely open his lips.

"I'm tired of being told to take care of my teeth, they're the only ones I'll have," declared Pony Pal Susan: "I wish I were a pony, then my teeth would just keep on growing." But the continuous growth of a pony's teeth can cause problems. If normal grinding of food does not wear down the teeth, sharp edges may make eating a misery, or so impossible that starvation results. A broken tooth in one jaw may result in puncture by the still-growing opposite tooth in the other jaw.

Your pony's teeth should be checked annually. If the molars have sharp edges, your veterinarian can float or file them with a rasp. Floating is (to the human ear) unpleasantly noisy, but it doesn't hurt. You can also help the pony by adapting his diet to his age, for instance by giving an older pony crimped or crushed feed rather than whole, for easier mastication and digestion.

*Body*

Most problems on your pony's body will be minor ones. The skin under his coat is his complexion, and like ours it is affected by diet, nerves, allergies, infection. Unlike ours, it is extremely "lively"; sensitive, it can twitch and wiggle all over, a great help in getting rid of bugs and insects. Except when hidebound it is loose over the rib cage, so that you can "pinch" an inch or so. Some body waste is eliminated through the skin, hence the importance of proper grooming and of avoiding contact with infected animals directly or through handlers or dirty equipment that serve as carriers. Ponies vary in skin-sensitivity to wipes and sprays used not only on them but around their stalls and barns; use chemicals only as directed, and realize that some household insect sprays can cause burns or allergic reactions when used on a pony.

Much "exterior" skin trouble can be prevented by thorough grooming and by routine washing—simply hosing off with plain water—of your pony's entire body. In winter, keeping blankets and sheets clean on the next-to-the-pony side helps. You can use a washable inner sheet, one for day and another for night, adding warmth as needed by heavier outer rugs or blankets. If you have only one, it should be removed and brushed inside and out to remove accumulated scurf. Your pony's daily cleaning must not be skipped. (After years of greater expense and inconvenience in having all blankets dry-cleaned, we now wash them in cold water in the heavy-duty machines at a local coin-operated laundry, then dry

**Newly arrived colt stands relaxed during his first hosing. Slack in lead rope shows there was no need for the chain put over his nose by his young handler "just in case."**

them at High Hickory on an outside clothes line. As it is hot water or dryer heat that causes damage, blankets can be done without risk of shrinking.)

Grooming equipment must be kept clean, as must tack. All too often dirty pads are put on clean backs or dirty girths around clean bellies. Today fast-drying washable pads and girths can be had and should be washed often (even daily) to prevent bumps and minor swellings or irritations.

Open sores are another story. Girth and saddle sores are best prevented not only by strict cleanliness but by properly fitted, clean, supple equipment properly adjusted to the pony and carefully put on and taken off each time. If a rub appears, do something about it before it becomes an open sore: use a better-shaped pad, a thicker one; see that the saddle fits and has no projections underneath or a broken tree; put a fleece or sheepskin liner over your girth.

Once he has an open sore, your pony should be "out of commission" until it heals or it will just get worse. Often swelling accompanies the beginnings of such sores, so hosing or applications of cold water can lessen their development. To keep skin flexible and avoid a crusty scab that will be repeatedly rubbed off, use a salve on the raw areas. Use fly wipe or spray around them to keep them free of fly or maggot infestation.

A pony just brought in from grass is particularly susceptible to girth and saddle sores, as is the blanketed pony standing idle in a stall. Old-timers toughtened the up-from-grass pony by washing the appropriate areas with a salt water solution to harden the skin, and the stabled pony by keeping a surcingle on over his blanket.

Some skin trouble must be cured from the inside: tiny bumps or a hives-type itch may be caused by allergic reaction to something in the diet. These bumps, not too unsightly in themselves, may so irritate your pony that he will rub mane, tail, and body against trees and fences and damage the hairs. They may be caused by overfeeding the hot feeds or by sensitivity to weeds or chemicals in pastures. Pine resin or even sunshine may trouble some ponies. To identify the cause, you may have to try different "cures": avoid turning out near pines; take off corn or sweet feed; give a laxative bran mash; stable during the day and turn out at night; pull up weeds and eliminate spraying near grazing fields.

Let us hope that your pony will never suffer from ringworm. Like mange (now so rare that some fear a flare-up, as all the old-timers who could recognize its early stages are gone) ringworm is one of the few equine afflictions which we can get. A fungus (not a worm, hence not discussed under parasites), ringworm causes loss of hair and round scaly areas the size of a quarter or bigger on your pony's body, head, or neck. Since it is contagious to humans as well as to other ponies, get a prompt diagnosis from your veterinarian if you suspect any itchy hairless patches or infected-looking lesions.

Not only should you isolate the victim, but you should disinfect his stall by liming and/or spraying. Carefully discard bedding and any leftover feed and sterilize his utensils. Of course the strictest of rules about not interchanging equipment apply here (as always), and you must thoroughly disinfect anything used on your infected pony.

Realize that you could be a carrier to other people and to other ponies; the fungus may be on your clothing, hands, arms, hair, feet. Wear a coverall and boots that you keep only for working on your patient and wash up before doing anything else.

Since good diet and proper husbandry prevent ringworm, it speaks well for the general level of stable management in this part of the country that none of us at High Hickory (none of the Pony Pals, nor I) has ever seen a case of ringworm. Since one way the disease can be spread is through rat excrement of infected rats in feed bins and mangers, it may speak well for all the stable cats, too. . .

You will sometimes see a pony with warts on the

lips and muzzle. More offensive aesthetically to the owner than painful to the pony, warts (the result of viruses) can be contagious. For that reason you should check out any warts with your veterinarian, who will control them with injections or leave them alone depending on the type. Until you get a diagnosis, your treatment should be isolation and disinfection. Some warts seem to come and go as the pony is stabled or at grass.

Perhaps the most painful "bumps" your pony ever suffers will be bee stings. One or two may not be a problem, but if, as happened to little Tuffy when inadvertently tied directly over a ground bees' nest, your pony is attacked by a whole swarm, he may have an allergic reaction. If washing the swollen areas with witch hazel (rubbing alcohol, absorbine, listerine would have worked, or even just cold water) had not relieved Tuffy's discomfort, our veterinarian (quickly alerted by phone) would have come out to give an antihistamine injection.

Two possible afflictions of the lower extremities are cracked heels and thrush. Cracked heels cause much discomfort, rather like chapped hands with us. They involve a reddening, scaling, and itching in the pastern area; the cause is wetness—too much hosing and washing off of mud without proper drying afterwards, or standing in soggy footing. Once sore, cracked heels are particularly sensitive to uriney mud or wet bedding. You may see your pony kick out behind in short irritated jerks at a standstill, as if to shake off, not kick at, something. Rawness may cause swelling, infection, and even lameness.

Cracked heels (along with mud belly or mud fever, a similar inflammation of the skin, this of the inner forelegs and hind legs and even up under the belly, wherever caked with mud) can be prevented by providing dry pasturing or stabling and by allowing mud picked up during a ride to dry so that it can be brushed rather than washed off. If you hose your pony's legs regularly, protect the sensitive pastern area with vaseline first. In very muddy weather or when there is crusty snow do the same. (In some of the more refined ponies, this heel area is quite hair-free and vulnerable; in native breeds it is less so. At High Hickory we let fetlock hair grow long from late fall through spring to give protection, but in days past even heavily feathered draft horses had oil or grease applied to protect them against mud and the salt brine used on roads in winter.) Daily care should mean quick spotting of any

reddening. Should cracks develop your veterinarian may recommend a medicated ointment such as zinc or furacin and may give a tetanus booster, since the pony's heels are particularly exposed to barnyard germs.

Thrush, another undesirable, can also be caused by neglect or dirty stabling. Admitting to thrush in your barn is like admitting to bad breath or body odor. However, it is an infection of the frog of the hoof, and therefore it can appear in freak fashion in properly maintained stables. Thrush results from dirt and moisture being in prolonged contact with the sole of the hoof, usually in the area of the frog. A pony's constant standing in wet bedding or swampy pasture often results in thrush. Neglected hooves, with deep sulci that trap damp matter, further increase the risk. Thrush could also develop in a faulty frog that, because of a poor foot or poor shoeing, does not come in contact with the ground and so does not get the pressure necessary to stimulate and prevent such deterioration of the frog.

You will recognize thrush by its foul odor as you clean out the cleft of an infected hoof and (at a later stage) by the softening and rotting of the surrounding frog. Thrush is most often found in hind feet—and if for any reason you think a child is not picking out his pony's hind feet properly, for fear of being kicked, or out of basic timidity, do help out, or do the job yourself.

If thrush exists, the hoof must be washed out with a stiff brush and disinfectant or strong soap and water. The diseased part must be pared away and a medicine such as Thrush-X or Kopertox or the old-time Stockholm tar or even a dry antiseptic powder be applied daily. If you are taking care of your pony's feet you can clear up early thrush without the more extreme measures a severe (advanced) case requires, measures which must be taken in cooperation with your blacksmith as well as your veterinarian. Correcting shoeing and exercise are both important to proper use and stimulation of the frog. Here, as with other foot problems, proper diet (especially green grass in season) helps with good hoof growth necessary to replace the thrush-destroyed horny parts.

Once you have taken the above steps, you can use your pony normally. Only in the most severe cases will there be lameness, and your medication will have removed the risk of infecting other ponies.

Prevention of thrush is through regular blacksmith care, daily cleaning of all four feet, sanitary stable management, and routine hoof disinfection after a visit away from home.

Injuries where there is bleeding are particularly upsetting to young pony-lovers, so it's reassuring to know that a pony can lose what seems like a lot of blood without being in danger of "bleeding to death." If there is copious bleeding, apply pressure or bandage to stop the bleeding until the veterinarian comes. Never attempt to apply a tourniquet unless he so orders.

Often the amount of bleeding is far in excess of the severity of the injury. Once it has stopped and the injured area is gently cleaned the wound itself will not seem so bad. Washing with clear water or mildly soapy water may be done, but if you think a veterinarian should see the injury, keep it free of salve or powder till he comes.

Minimum first aid is always best. Put on one bandage and leave it alone even though it soon becomes blood soaked; don't keep replacing it. If any sort of first aid seems to excite your pony, thus causing more bleeding, leave him alone.

One of the most serious wounds I have seen occurred when one of our ponies stepped on a rake while away at a riding camp. Lutine Bell was out of commission for several months because of a groom's carelessness in leaving a rake in a stall. However, this mishap taught a lesson: put work tools away and, where possible, use sturdy plastic rakes, not iron ones. (The camp now enforces that rule.)

Such puncture wounds on the sole of a foot can be caused by the pony's stepping on a broken bottle or a nail. If still embedded, the object causing the puncture must be removed and the hole washed with soapy water or iodine. If the veterinarian is not there, after sealing the hole by wadding cotton batton into it you can protect the hoof with a sock made of an old grain-bag or sheet. (Cut it as you'd cut paper to make a child's pinwheel, put the solid center under the hoof, bring the cut strips up, and secure around the pastern.) Since the hoof of all parts of your pony's body is in contact with manure, he will certainly require a tetanus booster or antitoxin. For a deep slow-healing wound he will probably need a series of antibiotic injections.

If daily injections are prescribed, your veterinarian may leave the task—and the one-dose disposable syrettes (hypodermic-and-antibiotics)—to you. If you have never given a shot, ask him to explain and demonstrate as often as necessary, to be certain exactly what to do.

To heal properly, puncture wounds (which are usually deep and narrow rather than broad or long like lacerations or incisions) must heal from the inside out. Puncture wounds that drain downward heal more easily and rapidly than ones that open upwards—underneath on the belly as opposed to on top of the withers, for example.

Sometimes the object causing the puncture is so deeply embedded that you don't even know it's still there. Lutine Bell arrived with a "small puncture wound" in her chest but no sign of what had caused it. After several weeks of daily vetting and increasing sensitivity a piece of wood an inch and a half long and three-quarters of an inch wide at the penetrating end worked itself down—and projected enough to be pulled out. Had a scab formed over the top of the wound this would have caused severe infection. Your veterinarian will give you directions for keeping such deep wounds open and for preventing the development of "proud flesh," possibly by applying caustic powder.

In shallow wounds where a flap of skin is dangling, try to clean this and put it gently in place (under a bandage if one is applied). Your vet may cut it off or take a few stitches to make it heal in its proper position. Such wounds may heal by themselves, but not always neatly. Little Miss Marzipan, a top model pony, has a permanent bump on her nose (hidden by her show halter) because when she was a foal a tiny triangular cut was not discovered in time for stitching.

Scarring from wounds, especially minor nicks and scrapes, can be kept at a minimum by keeping a mild ointment like Bag Balm or vaseline on them until the hair grows back in. Often without this treatment the new hair grows in white, leaving a permanent record of injury on the pony's coat. Scarring can also be caused by too lavish use of caustic powder. Too frequent and too heavy application can destroy the hair follicles so that, even though the wound heals, the area remains a pink and hairless blemish.

Fortunately, with an "accident prevention" attitude towards everything in your pony's world—with awareness that broken glass or rusty nails may be hidden in deep grass on a soft shoulder, that flimsy jumps and makeshift fences can break and splinter, that projecting door latches or improperly opened gates can break a hip or stifle, that hooks or bolts can rip skin and muscle—injuries will be few or nonexistent, and the only bleeding you may see will be a nosebleed!

Ponies do have nosebleeds once in a while—not prolonged, and apparently caused by a twig or hard weed puncturing the sensitive membrane during grazing. Coming in little dribbles from one nostril, they usually stop without medication. Blood streaming from both nostrils would be a "Call the vet immediately" situation indicating lung or other internal damage (seldom seen in ponies). With a nosebleed as with many other minor "Band-aid" injuries, leave it alone, but keep an eye on it—.

### LAMENESS AND OTHER POSSIBLE PONY PLIGHTS

The "leg at each corner" is all-important; but a discussion of splints, ring bone, bog spavins, navicular, etc., etc., will be left to more scientific tomes. See the reading list at the end of this book if you wish to read about these, but pray that you have no occasion to learn about them first hand.

If you have chosen a sound pony with good working conformation (that is, no conformation defects that lead to unsoundness when worked, such as excessively long and low-jointed pasterns), most of these leg problems will be avoided by proper riding and schooling.

Any pony may go lame, however, and here again it is essential to know your pony. Many mounts are ridden by insensitive unobservant riders beyond the point of beginning lameness into severe crippling. The first rule with lameness is: "Get off your pony!" To detect unsoundness in its earlier stage you must know by feel, by sound, and by sight how your sound pony moves.

*By feel,* you suspect or recognize lameness because of an irregularity in the step or an unusual dipping or stiffness under you, if not an outright hobbling, as you ride. By feel, you detect lameness by heat or swelling when you run your hand down the leg or foot in question.

*By sound,* you suspect or recognize lameness if you hear stress on one beat—rather than an even beat (one, two, three, four at the walk, for instance).

*By sight,* you detect lameness in the pony at rest pointing a foreleg or resting a hind, and in the pony under saddle moving abnormally. To recognize acute lameness is not difficult—the hobbling pony or the pony who can barely put weight on a leg at a standstill, let alone move. To recognize incipient or slight lameness can be quite difficult.

You may have seen horsemen watching a pony being led in hand at a walk and at a trot, seen them

To decide whether your pony is lame, it's helpful to have someone lead him on hard ground with a long enough rein if he is bridled or lead rope if he is haltered (better, so that he can move his head freely). While you may see unevenness, even when lameness is agreed upon it may still be strangely difficult to decide which side or which leg.

When a pony is lame behind, from the rear you will see him lean towards the sound side. Since he favors the bad leg by avoiding putting his weight on it, he will have a much higher and more decided hock action and a much higher hip movement on the bad side. From the side you may notice him drop his head as the *lame* hind leg is on the ground.

If a pony is lame in front, he will shorten his stride and move with his head bobbing noticeably up and down. Unlike action in lameness behind, his head drops as the *sound* foreleg is on the ground. From the rear you may notice his tail swish towards the lame side, but this is a less reliable test. "An old wives' *tail*?" one Pony Pal punned.

He may appear lame on the diagonal hind at the trot and take a shorter stride with the lame fore. Catching a toe or swinging a foreleg out may also suggest lameness.

At the very first suspicion of lameness, stop work. If lunging, stop. If driving, get out of the cart. If riding, get off.

As Jorrocks said, "No foot, no 'oss"—and the first thing you check is your pony's feet. See if there's a pebble or an acorn or a thorn or a nail in his hoof. Removing an object wedged in the cleft will often solve the problem. Sometimes nothing is stuck there but something has bruised the sole, laming the pony briefly.

A loose or twisted shoe can cause lameness, or merely make walking difficult and uncomfortable as well as unsafe. Even a shoe that is almost completely off can be hard to remove without farrier tools, so the only procedure, if you're not at home, may be to walk slowly with your pony in hand. Twisting and looking from the side, the front, the rear before deciding that the pony is lame, let alone where. You may hear someone say "He'll work out of it"; for occasionally a pony is lame only at the trot, and if warmed up more carefully at a walk does "work out of it." If he's lame at a walk, he's really lame!

(Supposedly, you can also look at hoofprints and detect a difference in depth; but I've never had the necessary unmarked footing when lameness was suspected to put this visual proof to the test.)

yanking to get the shoe off may be futile or break his hoof and cause more trouble. Prevention for this "lameness" is regular blacksmith care and daily checking before you tack up to see that clenches have not risen nor a shoe loosened. Since Jorrocks's phrase could be lengthened to: "No foot, no 'oss, no rider," for safety of child riders an adult should regularly check the condition of a pony's feet.

Improper shoeing can cause lameness (from pricks, from corns, from trimming too close), but with an experienced blacksmith this is not likely to be the case.

Lameness can be anywhere from the sole of the foot on up the leg into the shoulder or the hip, but ancient odds still hold that "lame behind, it's the hocks; lame in front, it's the feet."

Lameness can be caused by the wrenching of a joint or tendon, by a strain, by slipping or falling (on ice or hardtop, or on wet grass or into a jump). It can result from too much jumping or from overwork on the flat when the pony is out of condition or overtired. It can be caused by overeating and overweight (see founder). It can be caused by your not taking proper care of a pony after a ride. It can be caused by a pony's catching his hind foot in his halter when, while grazing or loose in a stall, he scratches himself or strikes forward at a fly on his jaw. Most lamenesses can be avoided by proper care and consideration for your pony.

Check your pony's feet not only before a ride, but after; and also check his legs for heat. Heat at night may predict lameness in the morning; a little time spent massaging (dry or with a linament like Absorbine) or hosing down could nip it in the bud. During such a check you might also spot thorns or brambles in the pasterns or lower leg which, if they are not removed, could cause swelling, infection, and lameness.

Lameness detected in the early stages may disappear after a day or two of rest. Rest may mean no work, being confined to a box stall, no exercise, or being walked in hand only or grazed on a lead rope. Lameness does not always immobilize a pony, and a lame pony may injure himself further if turned out free to buck or gallop.

If lameness persists, you should certainly check with your veterinarian. He may simply have you continue hosing or cold-water applications and massaging with or without linament. He may recommend use of stable bandages or he may give an injection of cortisone. Again, he may recommend a consultation with your smith. Aside from this, time may be the only cure.

One way you can avoid injuries to the "leg at each corner" is by the use of overreach or bell boots, exercise bandages, or front and hind galloping boots; but proper shoeing and proper riding will help also, and will keep pony procedures simple. The work you are doing with your pony—backyard play or serious combined training—will determine the need for such protective gear.

As mentioned in "Fun beyond Your Own Backyard," trailering injuries (cuts caused by a pony's stepping on himself, banged hocks or knees) can be avoided by careful hauling and protective travel wear. In the event of a trailering accident, safe removal of the pony from the trailer (before attempting to right the vehicle, for instance) is of vital importance. Here, as in any accident where the pony is down, emphasis should be placed on keeping him quiet to prevent more injury from his thrashing around. This can usually be accomplished by reassuring with familiar voice commands, kneeling or sitting on his head to keep him from raising it (a first move in his attempting to regain his feet), pulling his muzzle back towards his own shoulder, or covering his eyes with a blindfold (jacket, blanket, or towel), being careful not to block his nostrils and mouth.

Ponies can get into some pretty impossible predicaments without getting hurt. Getting cast is one of them. This happens when a pony rolls and is unable to get to his feet. This may happen because he ends up too close to the side of his stall or because he is downhill or in a ditch. One young colt at High Hickory rolled in his paddock in such a way that he was cast under a gate, with his hind legs wedged one on top of the other between the gate post and a tree less than a foot away. In Smiley's case, good pony sense and trust prevented even a hint of panic. He lay quietly with Robin ready to keep his head down while I lifted first one hind leg, then the other, and pulled them clear of tree and post. He then got up alone.

Often when a pony is in difficulties there is a question of priorities. Here, had we opened the gate first, Smiley might have tried to regain his feet before his hind legs were free, with consequent panic or broken bones. As it was, the colt's only injuries were scrapes on his bony cheek and eyebrow and slight muscular stiffness next day.

A pony cast in a stall needs help to get up. One

way is to loop a lunge line over both forelegs and another over both hind legs so that two people can pull the legs away from the wall. Thus rolled over, the pony lies on his opposite side, with room to get to his feet. While helping him you must of course watch out for flailing hooves and keep clear when he scrambles up.

Once rescue operations are over, you try to figure why he rolled: Was it because, put away dirty, he was itchy and rolled for relief? Because there was fresh bedding and he rolled just for the pleasure? Or because he was having stomach pains and rolled in an attack of colic? Once he's back on his feet, watch him for a while.

Some ponies roll in "impossibly" tight quarters and never get cast, others roll and get cast even in a palatial stall. . . . We theorize that the pony that gets cast is cast-prone and is going to do it again and again. However, ample stalls and level floors and bedding all help prevent casting. Give your pony a chance to roll outside: spread a wheelbarrowfull of bedding or provide a pile of sand in a paddock, to encourage him. Having rolled once or twice (or three times over, to meet the old test of a "good" horse), your pony will be unlikely to roll again in his stall.

One pony predicament is associated with the luxury and comfort we provide. We take electricity so for granted that, like people who have no toddlers about, we forget the hazard it presents. Today's pony barn may have many electric appliances: not only for lights, but vacuum cleaners, horse clippers, units for heating water pails, tack room heaters, radios, power tools such as drills and saws, devices for killing flies. All are potentially dangerous—lethal, in fact. We know of a Morgan mare who chewed through the cord of a water-heating unit and electrocuted herself. An extension cord run by a paddock may prove an object of interest to a pony whose stall lighting is carefully caged and inaccessible to him. A pony investigates things that pique his curiosity with his nose and lips, and he may bite through a cord.

If a pony bites an electric wire and the current surges through him, his shocked, electrified body becomes a danger to those who try to help him. The first thing to do is to cut off the current, at the main switch or circuit breaker if possible. Your pony may be dizzy with shock, knocked stiff, or even dead—but still in contact. Do not touch him. Impress this rule on your children. Explain to them about conductivity. Never touch a pony if he is still touching an electric cord or a fallen power line or fencing which has been electrified by fallen power lines.

If he is clear, artificial respiration can be applied. Kneel down forcefully and heavily, get up, thump down again, and again, and again, on the pony's side. Or pull a foreleg back and forth in a pumping motion. You can also massage his rib-cage area. Of course, telephone your veterinarian.

(Lightning takes its toll with similar effect, but more often than with man-harnessed electricity the pony is dead when found, or paralysed and blind.)

Again, prevention is the best cure: lights properly caged, cords detoured out of pony reach, heating elements not left in pails when in use. In other words, be a Worry-wart rather than a Woe-wart!

Should the calamity befall that your pony is so desperately ill or so badly injured that it is necessary to put him out of his misery, have the courage to do so promptly. The instinct to prolong life is deep within us, and admirable; but alas, with ponies and horses we must sometimes act against it. If "saving" an injured animal means not only the labor and expense of a year's daily vetting but also continuing agony for the pony with no certain improvement at the year's end, it is kinder to have him put down.

Let me give two instances, one of a decision to work for months to save, the other of a decision to put down.

Discard, a small buckskin, was skin and bones when my friend Jerry discovered her starving to death. The badly cut pastern that had caused her owner to "throw her out" made it impossible for her to forage for food, and lack of water had added to her debilitation. Under matted skin her belly had a parasitic bulge. The threat of the S.P.C.A. and a dollar bill made her legally Jerry's. The vet's appraisal of her age, her size, and her condition determined Jerry to gamble on her recuperative powers for a week or two. The progress she made indicated that the months of work that would be required for real recovery would pay off—and pay off Jerry's decision did, with the "Surprise Bonus" of a foal, named just that!

There was no happy ending in the case of our 16.2 Thoroughbred's accident. Efforts to save her were hours of anguish for all concerned. Continued efforts would have required mechanical equipment—horse ambulance, block and tackle, slings and overhead trolley. Such equipment was simply not available even if money to pay for it had been. Decisive, also, was the knowledge that even after many months (a year at the least) of the best of medical care permanent crippling or, worse, brain damage would still be a strong probability. We spent almost two hundred dollars in the eight hours we endeavored to save her: and even putting her down cost money. Not begrudged, indeed! but clearly only the "Swaps Syndicates" can afford to save an animal in such a case. Where ponies are part of a family and their expenses part of funds that must also cover college, orthodonture, and Unicef donations, and where time must be given to some other activities besides ponies, saving may be an impossibility.

Don't let a misplaced sense of values persuade you to defer your decision. The head of a girls' camp (not a riding camp, but one with a riding program) refused to let the camp mount, Timothy, be put down when his leg was broken by a kick from another horse: in three days more camp would be over and the campers would all be gone; why make them sad? As a result, though all the children wept over his audible pain, poor Timothy stood three-legged in agony until the camp was empty. Every camper later heard through the grapevine of Timothy's delayed demise, and indignation super-seded sorrow.

But ponies, sturdy little creatures, typically live a long and useful life. The important thing is to treat your pony well while he is with you.

# 7
# BASIC SAFETY RULES

IN ALL PONY ACTIVITIES, FUN WITH SAFETY IS THE goal. Set up basic rules for safety—and stick to them.

## SAFE RIDING CLOTHES

Wear safe riding clothes. Unless you are competing in shows it's not necessary to have a formal outfit or even a first-hand one, but you do need something practical and safe. Check with your local 4-H and Pony Club both for buying and selling. (New items will not be a bad investment, as there is always a demand for used riding togs.)

• Wear a hunt cap or safety helmet. Don't say "They never stay on." The hat must of course be the correct size, with an elastic band or chin strap; but they do stay on even an acrobatic child. They are a safety investment comparable to seatbelts in a car. (And as with seatbelts, the parent should set an example and wear a hunt cap himself.)

• From head to toes, or—safe boots next. I suggest jodhpur boots rather than knee boots. They can be worn with jods, stretch jeans, or suede schooling chaps, are more comfortable for running around in (young horsemen spend a lot of time on foot), and are less expensive. Note the spelling, and the pronunciation: jod-PUR. To say jod*fur* is a terrible gaffe.

Knee boots come in all price ranges. Good-looking copies are available in rubber for less than leather ones and, like the traditional Newmarket boot, are most sensible for stable work or bad weather. (Riding boots are intended for riding.)

Whatever your choice, do not work around your pony barefoot. Do not ride in soft-soled shoes such as sneakers (your foot could slip through the stirrup) or loose-at-the-heel loafers. Be sure that your hard shoe has a heel to it and a sole that is one piece from toe to heel (not a half-sole with a ridge that could catch on your stirrup bar).

• Both riding jackets and riding pants (either breeches that stop below the knee and require high boots, or jodhpurs that have legs ending at the ankles and are worn with jodhpur boots) are designed for action and comfort as well as style. Riding pants prevent knee sores and rubbing by fitting closely at the knee, yet provide room for action (such as mounting) by their cut (pegs or flares above the knee) or their material (modern stretch fabrics which allow for close-fitting style). Suedes on the inside of the knee provide a bit of grip and reinforcement.

In length and cut the traditional jacket, also, provides protection with freedom of action and comfort—with a tail split for safety. Available in all weights and seasonal materials, a well-made jacket will "last forever," but is *de rigueur* only for formal riding. Tweed jackets stand up under hard use and bad weather with a minimum of care, so if you want to keep ski jackets or other clothing from smelling horsey consider getting a medium-weight one, roomy enough for a sweater underneath. Whatever sort of jacket you wear should be cut so that its tail does not catch on the cantle of your saddle.

"My turn—I'm wearing the hunt cap!" Always-wear-a-hunt-cap rule applies to any youngster who gets on a pony at High Hickory. Visitors (here Learning Center for Deaf children) are fitted from an assortment of outgrown ones.

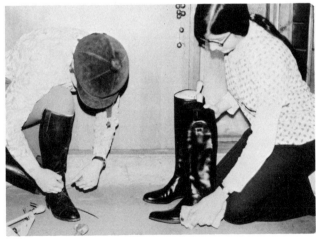

Riding boots not only feel special; they serve special purposes—protection, durability, style. Robin ties brown cross-country boots that lace over the instep. Meri-Jo polishes more formal black dress boots.

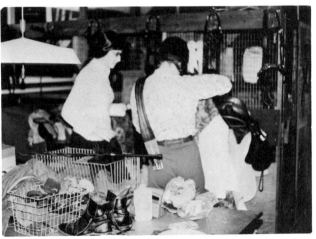

Low jodhpur boots (foreground) are fine for everyday, even suitable for showing.

Ordinary oxfords with a hard whole sole and a heel make safe riding shoes. Boots for tiny riders like Tuffy's are hard to find, rapidly outgrown.

A tweed riding jacket, part of a "ratcatcher" outfit worn here by Robin with Farnley Ogwen, provides serviceable daily wear and can double for informal show apparel.

Storm or snowmobile boots with cleated soles such as the Pony Pals wear here are ideal for unmounted work but not safe for riding with stirrups.

Not for backyard play, the more formal riding clothes (complete to white stock and tie pin) shown here. "This is one horse that never needs grooming," Robin says of the model at the Equestrian Shop in North Andover.

## SAFE RELATIONS WITH YOUR PONY

• Ride a pony suitable to your size and your riding ability.

• As in skiing and swimming—never ride alone or without supervision.

At High Hickory, no child rides or works with the ponies unsupervised. With better riders, supervision may mean only periodic checks, and from a distance.

• When riding with others, keep in mind the ability of the rider with the least experience. For instance, don't gallop your pony if one of your campanions can hardly post to a trot.

**Supervision can mean help or just encouragement and interest, but no one (child or adult) should ride alone. Here Robin, used to scrambling on bareback, learns to mount conventionally.**

**Suitability of pony to child is apparent as Tuffy halts on voice command and a gentle touch. For a child this age a pony is very much a pet; rapport is closer if the two see eye-to-eye.**

• Never mount your pony in the stall or in a low-roofed barn. Doors, like branches of trees, may seem high when you're on foot but be dangerously low when you're mounted. When riding your pony through an opening or under or by anything, remember that the pony will never allow for your head or your knees. He will not bump himself by trotting close to a tree trunk or under a bough, but he may hurt you.

• When you take your pony into the stall or paddock to turn him loose, take time to do so properly. Go into the paddock or stall and turn him; stop, close the gate or door, and remove his halter. Pat him and walk quietly away. Do not release him with his rear towards the exit. Do not send him off

**111**

Supervision of a young rider on a green pony can be "free" but take advantage of the fact that the pony associates proximity of the adult with voice commands and the controlled freedom of the lunge line.

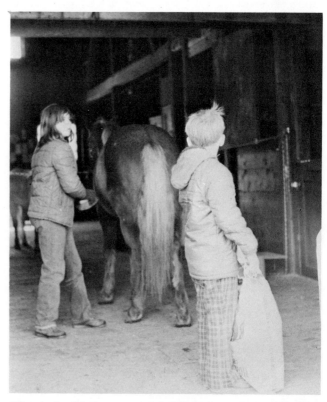

The rule "Let your pony know where you are" applies when working in the barn. Alan waits for Dana to say "Come on by" her pony on the crossties at McCrackens'.

This relaxed little rider is allowing her pony to eat but such grazing under saddle could become a bad habit: the pony might suddenly put his head down at a walk or a trot.

Youngsters showing kitten Emma Peale to Galaxy are guilty of breaking the safety rule "No bare feet around ponies", but couldn't resist joining the foal on the lawn.

**Safety rules must be explained to all visitors. Learning Center for Deaf children "listen" as their teachers interpret what Pepper is saying about Tuffy.**

with a slap on the rump or a flap of the halter—that's a great way to develop a kicker. (Even the sweetest of ponies may injure you with an exuberant though unmalicious kick of the heels as he gallops off free.)

• Whenever you're around a pony, let him know you're there. When possible, approach from the front so he can see you. If you must come up from behind, speak to him—make certain he hears you and knows you're coming by. A startled pony may kick.

If he is loose in a field or a box stall, go up to him calmly—and stop just before you reach him. Let him come up to you. A playful or tricky pony may suddenly turn his rump to you or kick his heels as he gallops off. Do not chase him. If you coax him with a pail of feed, give him some: he will remember if you cheat him. If he associates you with food and if he finds grooming and riding time pleasant, he will come willingly. It pays to be friends with your pony.

If when grooming you want to go from one side to another around his rear, keep a hand on his rump and stay in close as you pass. If you want him to move over, push with your hand against his side where your heel would be if you were mounted. Press and press again and say "Over" as he steps away with his hind end; eventually he will move over on voice command alone.

Whenever you touch him, to pat or brush, do so firmly. A gingerly touch may feel like a fly, to him. When you pick up his feet, run your hand down his leg; don't suddenly stoop and grab his hoof.

Suppose he turns his rear to you when you enter his stall? Stop in the doorway and wait for him to turn. Just as the pony in the field will return to you out of curiosity if you simply sit and jiggle a bunch of keys, so the pony in his box will come if you ignore him and pretend to look out the door. (For the first few days our new two-year-old Thoroughbred was at

High Hickory, she could be haltered only by someone who backed into her stall: if you faced her, the filly put her ears back and swung her rear menacingly. As soon as she developed confidence, and realized she wasn't going to succeed in creating a fuss, she required no special handling.)

• This next matter is discussed more fully under training but is mentioned here to stress that safety in the saddle depends on a well-schooled, well-exercised pony.

Even the lazy-on-a-hot-day pony will feel peppy if he's been cooped up all day, just as he's bound to be livelier when the wind gets under his tail on a cold snappy morning. Exercise your pony regularly. If he has a field or paddock to move around in, he will exercise himself some. Otherwise, take time to lunge him before you mount. With a beginning rider or in cold weather this is an especially worthwhile rule. Lunging will give the pony a chance to act up, will take the edge off him and help him settle down before you start your ride, rather than bucking or playing under you. Spend some time with him every day to keep him obedient and "worked down."

• Another point discussed under training: Remember that every time you ride your pony you're schooling him. If you let him get away with bad behavior once he will try it again and it will become a bad habit. (Remember, that one-track mind and take advantage of it.) If you let him graze when you're in the saddle once because just then you don't happen to mind his doing it, he may suddenly decide to stop short and duck his head down when you're trotting across the field—and you may land hard in the grass in front of him. If you turn him towards home at a gallop, he may tear home when you don't want him to—with or without you on his back.

• Gentle though he may be, never lock yourself in the stall with your pony. A small hook and eye on the inside of the lower door and jamb will keep the door shut in cold or wet weather while you groom or talk to him. It would not be sufficient to keep him in if he leaned on the door, but you can open it more quickly, should you have to get out in a hurry, than if you had to reach for the outside lock. In good weather, a bar, a chain, or a web gate may be used.

If you have a tie ring in the stall, you can simply leave the door open.

## SAFETY FOR YOUR PONY

Having a pony in the back yard is like having a small child in the house: your definition of what's "dangerous" changes. Just as a bachelor may be astonished that steep stairs, unlocked medicine cabinets, and cleaning materials stored under the kitchen sink constitute hazards for a toddler, so the new pony owner may be amazed at how many things can hurt a pony. Holes in the paddock, nails protruding through a board, unprotected light bulbs or glass windows, projecting latches on a barn door, screws not properly recessed in hinge holes, carelessly disposed of hay wire, electric cords—all are hazards for a four-footed charge who can't be told "Look out" or "Don't touch."

• Equipment must be put where your pony cannot get into it. Never leave cleaning tools such as a manure fork or rake where a pony can knock it down or pull it off a hook. (Better not use one while your pony is in his stall; cross tie him outside first, or use just a small basket and handscoop if manure pickup must be done while he is in place.)

Equipment must be put away safely for reasons other than the pony's safety, too. The curry comb left in the manger, the blanket left over the stall door may have been trodden in the dirt by the time you want them next. The saddle pad you dry on the fence rail may have been dunked playfully in the water trough. Since ponies are playful and curious, you may want to leave a paper shavings bag or a plastic gallon jug in the paddock for your pony to shake and toss about. But take care of things you don't intend him to use as toys.

• As mentioned in the chapter on "Facilities," doors must be high enough and wide enough so that a pony will not crack his head or whack a hip. Open doors and gates wide and lead the pony through straight, not on a diagonal, to avoid bumping that vulnerable stifle. Not only do you of course want to avoid causing pain to your pony, but every nick or blemish detracts from his value both financially and in show ring standing.

• Do not have any electrical fixtures where a pony can chew them. When using extension cords or power equipment, keep an eye on inquisitive ponies who investigate by nibbling. Switches and light bulbs should be recessed and glass—bulbs or windows—protected with strong wire.

• Projections inside a stall or out may seem beyond reach, yet be dangerous to a pony who's acting up. Feed or water pails should not be hung on open hooks but secured with double-end snaps to a tie ring. Pails with handles simply set down on the ground are potential traps, as are hay nets—the pony may get his pawing hoof snagged in them.

• Hay is best put in a wooden manger or outdoor crib. Avoid slats or corners under which the pony may catch a leg if he lies down or rolls in his stall. (See *cast* in Chapter 6). Remember to clean out the manger bottom occasionally to prevent soured feed being eaten. (Feeding on ground level may be closest to nature's ideal, but you increase the risk of your pony's picking up parasites and you waste hay.)

• Keep supply rooms containing grain or medicines securely locked. If your barn is used for other supplies, such as gardening sprays and fertilizers, see that they are properly stored. Don't assume that because such things are unappetizing to *you* your pony will not eat them. Often a chain and snap will be necessary to guard them from him, for ponies are adept at opening latches.

• Not only poisons but the pony's own feed can be deadly if eaten in too great quantity. (See *colic*, *founder*, in Chapter 6.)

• If the barn has a scuttle or trap door for manure disposal, never allow a pony on the barn floor while it is open.

• Tie your pony properly.

You may tie him with a lead rope attached to the center ring of his halter, under his nose, or you may cross tie him with ropes snapped to the side rings. Cross ties prevent a pony from moving his head or hind end so freely. Cross ties are usually permanently fastened to rings on opposite walls of the barn corridor, but you can either use lead ropes with snaps on both ends or tie regular lead ropes with a halter hitch. You can make your own by putting rings in two trees about six feet apart.

The halter hitch is the horseman's safety knot—one that can be untied in a hurry if need be. (See any good book on knots.) Tighten the knot so it won't slip, especially if your lead rope is nylon rather than cotton or manila hemp. If your pony is clever enough to undo the knot by pulling on the end, the way you do yourself to untie it, then slip the loose end through the loop: he'll only tie himself tighter. Adjust the rope so that his nose can reach the ground (if you wish him to) but not so that his legs can get tangled in it. Tie "high and short" with a single lead rope.

• Never go away and leave your pony tied unattended.

• Never tie your pony to anything that may give way or drag if he pulls back—for instance a wheelbarrow, a flimsy garden fence, a child's swing set. Don't even tie him to your horse trailer: I once saw a small frightened Shetland yank a big trailer out of place. Tie to the post, not the rail, of your paddock fence; to a sturdy tree, not a whippy sapling. If you have frequent mounted visitors, or if you tie up your own pony a lot, consider some outside tie rings, perhaps near the kitchen door or your favorite picnic spot.

• Never hitch your pony by the reins or fasten a tie rope to the bit: a broken bridle may result. For long rides, leave the halter under the bridle (make sure cheekstraps and cavesson are adjusted for the extra bulk) and wrap the attached lead rope around the pony's neck Mountie-style. Or carry equipment with you. When tying up, you can remove the bridle or you can just secure the reins so that the pony can stretch his neck but not step in them.

• Should your pony get caught in his rope, don't rush to his head. Circle and approach him quietly from the rear so that he will not pull back farther. If the rope and halter are pulled taut, do not try to unsnap the hook. Pull the end of the rope and release the safety knot. (In a real emergency cut the rope—near the knot, not near the pony.)

• Always use a lead rope when you take your pony anywhere. Never lead by the halter alone. Clip the snap on your lead rope to the center ring under the nose band, slide your right hand down a few inches so that you're holding it at a comfortable height, and carry the free end of the rope in a loose coil with your left. To give the pony slack (going over a bar, because he is acting up, etc.), slide your right hand farther down, or even let go—you still have hold of the rope with your left hand. A pony led by the halter only can give your arm and shoulder a painful jerk which might force you to let go.

• Occasionally a pony on a lead rope may be fractious or unmanageable. Good behavior "in hand" (on the halter and lead) comes from schooling, not from the handler's strength. Not even a grown-up can control a headstrong pony by halter alone. The pony that has once gone where he wills with a child hauling vainly on the lead rope may try it again—with the child being stepped on, bumped, or dragged till he lets go.

If there's any possibility of disobedience in a strange situation or with other ponies, don't wait for trouble. You have an emergency brake: use it. Instead of putting the lead rope on the usual halter ring, snap it to the off side ring, run it over the pony's nose, and then through the usual ring. Now when you yank on the rope you no longer simply pull the broad nose band against the nose. Instead, you pull the sharper ridge of rope against a more sensitive part of it. For still more control, a lead rope or leather shank with about twelve inches of chain at the snap end can be used in the same manner. (More severe methods, discussed later, such as putting the chain between the pony's lip and gum are hardly to be recommended for children's usage.) If you do use a chain lead, remember to handle it carefully so that unintended pressure is not created; and then work on schooling your pony at home so that such a device will not be necessary again.

• Never leave a halter on your pony in his stall or in the paddock. Ponies have caught their feet in halters kicking at a fly while grazing, have hooked a hind foot in them while lying down, or have caught the halter on some projection . . . with consequent serious injury or death. (A broken halter is the least of all possible damage.)

• However, do keep a halter and lead rope always ready in a handy spot for emergency use—in case of fire, for instance.

• Of course, No Smoking is the rule for every barn.

• In any emergency situation, keep calm—so your pony won't panic. The well trained, trusting pony will respond to your voice. Even in situations where one might expect justifiable panic, some instinct of self-preservation seems to take over even the green or problem pony. A once mistreated pony that "no one could get near"—let alone be allowed to pick up her foot—stood quietly by while rescuers freed her from entangling barbed wire.

• When turning out, leading, or doing anything with several ponies together, remember "It's the hind end that kicks." Keep the ponies' heads together rather than turning them away, as that swings their hind ends towards one another. Ponies do nip or bite or even strike out at each other with their forefeet, but since you lead near their shoulder you can see this and prevent it more easily than misbehavior at the rear.

• If you see a loose pony, always sing out loud and clear: " 'Ware horse!" in hunt field jargon, or: "Loose pony!" If the owner is nearby, better to let him "pick it up" than for strangers to try to catch it.

## ACCIDENT PREVENTION AND FIRST AID

As in any other active sport, despite precautions bumps and bruises may occur.

• Even minor cuts or scrapes around the stable yard must be taken care of immediately. Where there is manure there is always the possibility of tetanus. Preventive shots of tetanus toxoid and boosters should be kept up to date. (If you are uncertain about your record, check with your doctor; antitoxin shots for emergency use on unvaccinated patients are not pleasant.) Tetanus is a reason for outlawing bare feet in the barnyard, besides the risk of being stepped on.

Keep a first aid box for riders alongside the one for ponies—best in an unlocked cupboard and not along with such other medications as poisonous sprays or worming powders. Wash and medicate any cuts that happen around your ponies. Bandage and protect from stable dirt any that happen elsewhere (in the "safety" of the kitchen, for instance).

• If you follow all the suggestions in this book, most spills will be avoided—certainly serious ones will. But it's wise to give some advance thought to procedures in case one should occur.

The age-old practice when someone goes off is to get him back into the saddle as soon as possible, willy-nilly.

Obviously someone who is injured or dazed should not be moved or straightened until he can do so himself—and if he cannot, qualified help is needed.

What about the child who falls off but gets up on his feet and "is all right"? Should he get back in the saddle? Usually he'll want to, if he was properly mounted in the first place and wasn't being made to do something beyond his capabilities. Even if he wants to get on, he may want to go at a walk for a while—even want to be led. And if he is afraid of the pony, or if he was overmounted, then he should not be just "popped aboard" again. It is better to wait and put him on a pony he can control and work with him at slow gaits to build up his confidence—and his ability.

Remember, our goal in teaching children to ride ponies is not to develop child prodigies for the show ring, but to give them day-to-day fun with safety—so that they'll want to continue riding as adults.

• In this day and age no section on safety would be complete without mention of riding on the road. Rare is the situation where a rider does not have at least to cross a road—even a highway; more commonly, you need to ride along one or more roads to reach fields and trails. Today's pony rider must face the hazards of a slippery surface underfoot—hardtop of some kind, often decorated with a disconcerting white or yellow line which a pony may try to avoid or to jump—as well as the hazards of motor vehicles on-coming, overtaking, and passing, at all speeds.

Never trot on hardtop, if you must ride along the road; but look out for broken glass or rusty cans and keep out of deep grass along the soft shoulder, to avoid cuts to the pastern.

Technically, the same rules of the road that apply to automobiles apply to ponies and riders. (Youngsters used to pedestrian rules of facing traffic need to be informed of this.) Riders should observe the precautions of looking behind and giving hand signals before making turns or crossing.

By law, vehicles are required to stop if a horseman so indicates—but *Don't Count On It*. All too often the sight of a horse or pony seems to trigger a honk of the horn or revving of motor as a car zooms by with wanton inconsideration. Your best protection for even the once that you must be exposed to the dangers of the road is to "surprise-proof" your pony. An entire chapter (Chapter 10) is devoted to this important part of training.

• No one ever plans to be out after dark on his pony; but it may sometimes happen. Be prepared, especially during the winter months. At High Hickory the Pony Pals carry an "emergency kit." Hooked to saddle billets (like the sandwich box or wire cutters carried in the hunt field), this contains a small flashlight, a jack knife, a pinny or safety vest similar to those worn by traffic policemen or newsboys, and a roll of reflecting tape. Strips of this red tape can quickly be stuck on the back of boot heels, around a hunt cap, on the back of the cantle, on the outside edge of stirrups, even on bridle cheekstraps and browband; they can easily be removed when the need for them is over. (It is alarming to realize how hard it is for a fast-moving driver to see something as big as a pony at dusk.)

## RULES FOR VISITORS

Like so many Pied Pipers, ponies have an irresistible attraction for children. You may never have realized the enormous size of the juvenile population until the word gets round that you have a pony.

And grown-ups are not immune to the charm. It is a good idea to supplement your basic safety rules with a special set for the benefit of visitors (invited and otherwise). Here are some suggestions:

• Visitors are welcome, but must "check in"—*i.e.*, come to the house and say hello if there is no one about outside. This should be normal courtesy on a visitor's part, but for some reason the child who would not go into a strange yard to play on a swing will climb a fence to play with a pony—adults who would not go into a stranger's garage will stroll into his barn. If your field is near the road you may need to put up a sign with some such notice as: "Ask before feeding—Please call at the house."

This checking in gives you a chance to explain your regular rules.

• No one should go into a paddock or the barn without permission, and then usually only when accompanied.

• What gates or doors are left open or shut is of course up to you. But on your property or anyone else's the age-old horseman's rule is: Leave things as you find them. If a gate is open, leave it open. If it is closed, close it after you. Visitors may need to have this impressed upon them.

• What about letting visitors ride?

Many parents share my strong feeling that, unlike dolls or other inanimate possessions, a pony is one thing a youngster should not share. Accidents can occur all too easily if a child pony owner lets a little friend "have a ride." Children who have never been closer to a horse than a television Western "know how to ride"—till they're actually on a pony. Once in a while a pony parent may be willing to spend time supervising so that his child can share, but to avoid becoming a regular neighborhood baby-sitter the pool-owner's rule of "If your mother or father is with you—" works very well.

The serious rider who is training or showing his pony may not want to let his friends ride, even if they are competent enough. Considering the work and expense involved, and so long as the child does not expect to ride someone else's animal, I would respect his refusal and back him up without making him feel that explanations or apologies were necessary.

A lawyer friend flatly refuses to let his daughter allow anyone else on her pony; and such legal aspects of this problem as liability and insurance coverage might be a factor for other families with ponies to consider also.

As you practice the rules outlined in this chapter, and often reiterated throughout the book, you will discover that they are not just obnoxious regulations but rather good habits, ones that will become automatic and will ensure you day-to-day fun with safety.

# 8

# BASIC TRAINING ON THE FLAT: UNMOUNTED

DURING HIS PERIOD OF ELEMENTARY EDUCATION every pony must be taught many things that most riders, used to finished mounts, tend to take for granted. If your pony is "made" or "finished," a knowledge of how a pony should be educated will help you maintain his level of schooling—or raise it. If he is green and "unmade," such knowledge as this book gives will enable you to train him.

Basic training on the flat consists of unmounted or on-the-ground work and mounted or in-the-saddle work.

Unmounted, the pony must be taught to wear a halter, to stand, to move over, to walk on and trot on a lead rope, to back, to be tied, to lunge, and to load willingly.

At a midway stage preparatory to mounted work, he must be taught to accept the bit in his mouth and to accept the saddle and you, the rider, on his back.

Then comes basic mounted training at the various gaits: walk, trot, and canter.

The rein-back and the half-turn on the forehand are also included in basic training.

Many people underestimate the importance of the early lessons on the ground. In my view, they are vital: as important as any that follow mounted. For one thing, they instill in your pony a fundamental respect for, trust in, and receptivity towards you, his trainer, and the person who is going to ride him. Personally, I'd rather start with a pony that has been properly schooled in hand and is an ignoramus mounted than with a pony that is good under saddle

but deficient in the basic "civilities" of routine handling. That is part of the fun of working with a young as well as a green pony: you can shape the armature before you even begin to apply the clay. You have a better chance of training your pony to your own standards. You may make mistakes, but they are your own, not just fresh clay over somebody else's hardened clay on a well-hidden armature. Most mistakes can be avoided if you look and think and talk things over—and read!—ahead.

Most phases of this basic work on the flat follow one after the other in an orderly way; many of them dovetail and ramify. Some aspects of training, "surprise-proofing" for example (see Chapter 10), begin when your pony arrives, whether wet and innocent at birth or full-size and already "schooled," and never stop. Don't forget that even if you have chosen your pony because he has already certain accomplishments and you needn't begin at scratch every encounter you have with him is nonetheless going to be a schooling session. You either teach him something new or reinforce what he has already learned or undo his previous training—for better or worse.

The earlier in the pony's life his basic on-the-ground training begins—from birth week on—the better for you and for him. Schooling problems increase in direct ratio to the increase in the pony's size and degree of greenness. The fourteen-hand four-hundred-pound three-year-old that has never been tied poses a different, far tougher problem than the thirty-inch fifty-pound foal—or the forty-six-inch eighty-pound weanling.

If your pony, full-grown or otherwise, is to have basic training, you must teach him three things simultaneously. Just as the novice driver must learn to start, steer, and stop the first time he is at the wheel of a moving car, so your pony must at the start and in combination learn the following:

• He must learn that "Ho" means to stop—to stop and stand still. You wouldn't head down a steep hill on skis without knowing at least a snowplow stop; you wouldn't take off in a motor boat without knowing how to cut the engine. Don't teach your pony to walk on until you and your youngsters can stop him.

• He must learn to "Move over." His response to this command (voice and touch) at a standstill will simplify his obedience when you want him to move on at a walk or a trot.

• He must learn to "Walk on" and to "Trot" on command—on voice command in-hand now in unmounted work, on voice and leg command later in mounted work.

Even if the pony you have acquired knows these three R's already, a quick refresher course will establish you "boss" once and for all, fix you in his one-track mind as the one he must respect and obey.

Start this lesson with a hungry pony; you'll see why later.

The first step is to gain your pony's confidence so that he will come up to you whether in stall or pasture and willingly let you put on his halter. Remember, never chase your pony. Teach him to come to you—the last few steps in the paddock, head to you in the stall. Take advantage of his inquisitive nature, as suggested in "Basic Safety Rules." Pony Pals at High Hickory do this by pausing when they open a stall door and saying "Come, Pony." A carrot regularly at first, then occasionally, rewards obedience until a pat and "Good pony!" are enough.

A pony can be "whip broken" always to face you when you enter his stall, but this method is neither necessary nor desirable for a child working with a pony. In whip breaking, one touches a whip to the pony's rump whenever he turns his rear. I feel that patience and carrot-kindness achieve the same result less harshly and as quickly. (The only time I would sanction applying a whip to a pony's rear would be as a once-and-for-all cure of a people-kicker. A wisely selected, properly handled,

sufficiently exercised pony will not kick people. If your pony has this vice, it must be corrected; but the correction should not be left to a youngster.) The pony should respect but not dread a whip: the child should use one as a visual, not an applied, aid in lunging. Fear is no adequate substitute for trust and confidence.

## HALTERING

Start the first lesson by putting your pony's halter on him in his stall. If you are awkward about haltering (or bridling) do not practice on your green pony. Gain experience on some steady patient "oldie"; and don't be embarrassed about asking to be taught. Many good riders just never have the opportunity to learn handling and stable management. This is what we suggest to the Pony Pals:

Pick the halter up by the noseband. Slip this over your left wrist with the head strap undone and to your right and with the buckle on the near side of the halter cheekstrap to your left. Put your left hand on your pony's nose, and with your right hand reach under his neck and grab the head strap. With your right hand gently raise the head strap until the nose band is in place over his nose. Now move your left hand up to the buckle and hold the halter in place by that. Carefully bring the head strap behind your pony's ears so that you can grab its end and slip it through the buckle. (Do not flip or bang the strap against his ears, which are sensitive, or you may make him "head shy.") Adjust the head strap so that the noseband fits below the cheek bones but above the sensitive nose cartilage. You should be able to insert a finger or two (but no more) under the noseband and to insert at least your clenched fist under the jaw strap in the throat latch area.

If you are lucky enough to have had your pony from foalhood on, he is used to being handled and haltered by the time he is ready for his basic training. (See Chapter 14, "Raising a Foal.") If not, when you groom your pony spend some time gently rubbing his head and gently tugging his ears. This will help in haltering and later when you come to bridling.

## "Ho!"

Control over a pony in a halter only is very limited unless he obeys voice commands; and obedience to voice command depends on his associating cause with effect. You want him to work out this formula:

"Ho! + pressure on my nose from that halter = pain."

and then this one:

"Obedience (stopping or standing still) = pain stops."

Your pony should learn to obey voice command once and for all by one sharp first impression rather than by a weak impression that permits him to get away with disobeying. Once a pony discovers that he can bolt, not even a powerful, experienced professional can control him on lead rope and halter alone. The pony who succeeds in dragging a young handler or breaking away has in his mind the chain of association: "Command = no pain; no pain = do what I please."

A disobedient pony is often a loose pony, and a loose pony can be a danger to himself, to other animals, to property, and to people. Remember that whenever he is out of his stall or his paddock you are responsible for your pony, and saying "I can't hold him," "I can't control him," does not lessen your liability. This is another illustration of the importance of pitting your brains against his brawn, of *never* letting him discover his own strength; and it emphasizes how many pony problems can be avoided or simplified or solved by proper handling early enough.

If obedience is not taught effectively, you may be in for endless trouble and frustration.

Realizing now the paramount importance of this first lesson, be prepared—unless your pony has already learned it as a foal by imitating his well-schooled dam—to make it a sharp lesson: probably the sharpest lesson, and the only intentionally severe one, in your pony's entire education. You can administer it right in the stall or paddock. If your pony does not know the command "Walk on" you can teach "Ho" while he is at a standstill.

Instead of the usual lead rope, for these first few lessons use a lead shank (rope or leather) with about twelve inches of chain on the snap end. Put the chain through the near side ring of the halter, pull it over the pony's nose, and snap it to the off side ring. Now any pull on the shank will be on the chain directly over his sensitive nose, and will be felt.

Let your pony move on either of his own accord or on your command and then say "HO!" Say it loudly and firmly and at the same time give one quick light jerk downwards on the lead shank.

Your pony will stop. He will undoubtedly sit back a bit on his haunches and jerk his head up . . . but he will Ho! Praise him immediately; pat him, give him a carrot, make a big fuss over him—all the while standing still yourself, as Ho! means not only *stop* but *stay stopped.*

Repeat this, using the lead chain more gently or more severely as needed. Once or twice with the chain over his nose should be enough. Now you should be able to get obedience without the chain over his nose and with the snap fastened to the usual center under-ring.

If at any time in the future your pony gets rambunctious or if you're in a situation where you fear he may be unruly, put the chain over his nose as a safety precaution. The mere weight of your hand holding the lead rope puts pressure on the chain, so never abuse him by using this method harshly or unnecessarily.

### "MOVE OVER!"

Now that your pony knows that "Ho" means stop, teach him to "Move over." There will be many times when you will want a loose pony to obey this command on voice alone: when you're working around him in a box stall, when you want to squeeze in beside him from the rear in a narrow area such as a straight stall in a barn or a trailer, when he's cross-tied on the barn floor, when you're grooming, lots of times!

A combination of voice command and hand pressure teaches your pony to move over and, since this initiates a response later to be required in mounted schooling—movement of his body away from pressure against his side—it serves a double purpose. For this reason you will apply pressure with your hand now where you will later apply it with your legs, just behind the girth area.

Before you ask your pony to move his hindquarters away from you as you hold him on the lead rope, consider a few things. The movement you want him to make can be compared to what happens to a ruler if you hold one end in your left hand and push the other away from you with your right. Or it is like the drawing compass used in school: your pony's front

122

feet are the metal point stuck in one spot, his hind feet are the pencil that moves in an arc. If a grown-up is explaining this to small children a rough sketch scratched in the dirt may clarify ahead of time what the lesson is supposed to accomplish.

Stop your pony facing a fence or wall so that he has room to move away from you in any direction except forward. See that he is standing relaxed and square before you ask him to "Move over." He must move his hind feet to obey, and he cannot if he's braced back on them or is gawkily standing on three legs, resting one hind.

You are not going to frighten your pony into moving away, so do not suddenly jab him and do not use a sharp object like a stick. As in all schooling except the initial "Ho," start out gently and increase in severity only if you have to.

Now, lead rope in your left hand, order "Move over!" as you repeatedly press your right hand against his side just beyond the girth area.

Be pleased with any movement away from your hand as you give the order. Praise the pony, then ask for another few steps (from the other side, if he has swung clear round). Don't be concerned if he moves more than his hindquarters. (This is an introduction to the half-turn on the forehand, but our concern now is not to get him to pivot on his forehand but to move his hindquarters away even if he moves his front feet as well.)

Repeat the exercise from the opposite side. Be generous with your praise and let your pony relax. He now knows "Ho" and "Move over" and in this same brief lesson is ready to learn to "Walk on."

a race for the last musical chair; you will very likely see that the handler is looking back at his pony. Probably both he and the pony have their feet braced and are leaning against opposite ends of the lead rope in the direction each wishes to go. When you have to walk or trot your pony in hand in the show ring, keep this in mind.

The pony will walk on willingly if, initially at least, you take advantage of a few other tricks: "Lead" him where he wants to go. If he's in his stall, lead him out. If he's in pasture, lead him in—to water or to feed. (Now you see why it helps to start this first lesson with a hungry pony rather than one who has just eaten a full dinner.) If you lead your pony this way a few times with the voice command "Walk on" you will avoid any battles. He will associate "Walk on" with reward (feed, freedom, etc.); by the time you have to lead him some place where he may not want to go, he will be conditioned to obeying.

He should now be eager to move on. Give him the command "Walk on" and start walking on yourself—out of the stall, into the barn, around the paddock. If he is reluctant to move, have someone shake some feed in a pail at a slight distance ahead of him to coax him forward as you repeat "Walk on." Praise him, let him have a mouthful of feed, then make him stand on "Ho" while your assistant moves farther away with the feed. Again ask "Walk on," and again let his reward be feed. Now have your assistant go out of sight, and then order "Walk on."

Don't look at your pony, and don't pull. Should he balk, ease up on the lead rope. Repeat "Walk on"

## "WALK ON!"

While your pony is relaxing for a moment, think of what your eventual goal is in asking him to "Walk on." Although you seldom see an example set, the proper way to lead a pony in hand is to walk at his side with his near shoulder beside your right shoulder—not with your shoulder at his head or with you at one end of the lead rope out as far as it will go and your pony at the other. You want a brisk lively walk, so don't dillydally; you are not Epaminondas dragging butter home on a string!

Your pony will walk on more willingly if you allow a little slack and do not look back at him as you lead. Notice next time a pony refuses to lead out of the line-up in a model class or after a speedy dismount in

**Robin practices "Walk on" as she leads her new—and very green—birthday pony out from pasture after school.**

and turn sharply to your left, pulling his head around; bring your left hand in a quick slap against his side with the words "Move over." This will force him to move to keep his balance, so you must be quick to say again, "Walk on," praise even a few steps, and *go on with him.* Keep repeating "Walk on," go with him—even if it's not where you intended to go! After one or two tries like this, he'll associate "Walk on" with moving on—in a straight line—and will walk on where you want him to.

There are of course other ways of getting a green pony to "Walk on." You can put a long rope in a noose around his rump with its length running on through the halter so that the pony's resistance to your pull on the rope results in tightening of the noose and pressure around his hindquarters. You can carry a schooling or lunging whip in your left hand and use it behind you on your pony's side as you lead. An assistant can threaten with a whip or even apply it from behind. Two assistants can follow with a lunge line or rope stretched between them, or even a board, to discourage balking. They can even push from the rear! In each method, voice command should come only from the person at the pony's head, and force should come from the rear. However, over the years our simple pacific method has worked with ponies and children of all ages and sizes.

Suppose, however, that instead of balking your pony tries to pull on past you. Tell him sharply to "Ho." If he hasn't really learned that vital "Ho" lesson (you do not now have the chain over his nose), pull down and to your left with the lead rope in your left hand and at the same time swing your body against him. Simultaneously yank with your right hand under the halter so that your right elbow jabs into the crook of his neck. Grab his nose so that your thumb and fingers dig into the soft parts on either side of the bone and squeeze. Sound complicated? You'll find you can do it in one quick movement. When you do get him to "Ho" by dragging back against him and half cutting off his breathing, put the chain over his nose and repeat the first step of the lesson. Repeat it severely so that he really learns what "Ho" means.

This cycle—"Ho", "Move over", and "Walk on" —has constituted one schooling lesson. In beginning work on the flat it may be all the schooling your pony gets. Perhaps at first you will teach these commands in one fifteen-minute period devoted to just that; later, you can repeat the periods several times

a day, but interspersed with feeding, grooming, and shifting to pasture. Gradually they become not schooling sessions as such but a part of routine handling, before and after you begin more complicated training like lunging, driving, or mounted work.

## "BACK!"

As soon as your pony becomes familiar with "Ho," "Walk on," and "Move over," which takes only a few days in most cases, teach him to back up. His knowing this command will come in useful when you handle him in the barn or paddock, when you open a gate or door towards you, when you teach him to drive, when you trailer him, and when you school him in the saddle.

Since you are going to be working with your pony in hand and in a halter rather than a bridle, your standard of backing will not be so strict as in later schooling when, mounted, you ask a proper rein-back. At present all you want is for your pony to move back willingly a few steps on a comparatively straight line. But you want him firmly to associate the voice command "Back!" with a rearward movement so as to simplify your more advanced, exacting schooling later.

To make your task easier, pick a corner of the paddock or ring where your pony cannot go forward or sideways but will have room to back. Walk him along the fence to the rail corner, ask him to "Ho," and then—before he stands so long that he is anchored to the ground—ask him to "Back!" Put your left hand on his nose and, as you pull down and back with the lead rope in your right, press down and back with repeated gestures with your left. Stay facing forward, but lean and step backwards yourself. If need be you can put your body weight into your signals. The Pony Pals have found here, as in leading, that on foot this method is more effective than to face a pony and tap his chest or forelegs with a switch. He will soon back without your hand on his nose, on just a slight tug on the lead rope.

Be patient. Remember that your green pony must have time to sort out his feet for this rather unnatural step. (A free pony almost never backs.) You don't want to set him back on his hind quarters: his body weight must be evenly distributed if he is to move his hind legs in proper sequence rather than drag his hind feet backwards.

When he backs even a few steps, praise him. Say

"Walk on," and move forward to a halt. Right from this start, get into the habit of ending your backing not with a halt but with a few steps forward and then a halt, so that he will learn to halt squarely.

For the time being, you will not make more stringent demands so far as backing is concerned. Your pony has already learned enough to help you in many operations. You will now be able to back him into place for the cross ties on the barn floor, back him out of a trailer, or back him into the shafts of a pony cart, on command.

## "TROT!"

Once the pony obeys the basic commands "Ho," "Move over," "Walk on," and "Back," you can introduce him to the wider world around him. You can now begin to surprise-proof him on foot. (See Chapter 10.) The possibilities are limited only by your own free time and powers of endurance.

A nonriding youngster or a rider who is not competent to school a green pony in the saddle can derive a lot of pleasure and feel a sense of achievement from doing such schooling in hand. If you have access to larger fenced-in fields than your pony's paddock or pasture, a timid child can develop a sense of security by working within such bounds. Quiet surroundings and a minimum of distraction help at times, but you can't school a pony in a vacuum: and to develop capability around ponies youngsters must be shown how to cope with certain crises that may arise. For instance, what if a pony gets loose? What is a child to do? It is a good idea to learn how to cope with this situation under conditions that are not potentially disastrous as they would be at a crowded horse show, on a neighbor's lawn, or on a road with heavy traffic. With the pony's basic on-the-ground training well in hand, you can begin to broaden his exposure—and yours.

Now is a good time to begin trotting in hand. Obedience to the command "Trot" in close contact with you on the lead rope is good preparation for work at a distance on the lunge line.

To teach your pony to trot in hand, take advantage of his feeling peppy some day when he's been asked to "Walk on." If you sense that he would like to move on a bit faster, slack off a little on the lead rope and, without looking back at him, go into a jog yourself. As you do so, say "Trot!" If you have done much work with your pony in hand, he is by now accus-

Surprise-proofing and unmounted schooling go together. Galaxy (note yearling-length tail) looks on calmly despite the racket and movement of bulldozer and dump trucks during tennis court construction. Already she is used to being led on either side.

Green Tuffy gets a lesson in "ponying" in preparation for mounted lead-line work. Should rider drop his lead rope, Tuffy would still be under control. Later Eric ponied Tuffy alongside Peggy at a walk and a trot.

tomed to keeping beside you, stopping and starting when you do (even without voice command), and hurrying or slowing his walk as you vary yours. Now he will hurry to keep up with you—at a trot.

After a few strides at the trot say "Walk" and slow down yourself with a slight backwards pull on the lead rope. In all transitions, give your pony time—and space—to "shift gear" from one gait to another. Do not make him change from a trot to a standstill at this stage.

If he starts to play around at his faster gait, settle him down with a soothing, drawled "Walk". If he's really peppy or naughty, bring him down with a "Ho!" and a more forceful jerk on the lead rope. ("Ho" should by now be firmly equated with instant obedience.)

While your pony's walk may be about the same speed as yours, you may find that even his ordinary trot is much faster than your jog. Extend yourself a bit rather than hold him back. While he is trotting repeat the command "Trot trot" sharply and frequently in rhythm with his step. Praise him heartily so that he understands that clearly this is what you want him to do when you order him to trot. His breaking into a trot on voice command will make things simpler when you teach him to lunge or to be "ponied" or led by a rider on another mount.

## TYING

You see them at any horse show, in any stables, in any television Western: horses tied up to a fence rail or a hitching post. There they stand, docile, the rope hanging slack, waiting patiently for their riders to emerge; maybe even dozing. Such a sight is so commonplace that nonrider and horseman alike we take for granted the animal's compliant acceptance of this cobweb captivity. But if you once see a "problem tier" you will never again be so blasé about a pony's submission to so weak a control.

After all, being tied up goes against the pony's most natural instinct—to be free! His inborn reaction to any fearful situation, any menace to his freedom, is flight, rearing, or kicking. Tied up, he suddenly finds that he cannot move at his own will, cannot back or run off. Even if he has accepted some human being as his master, that master is not necessarily nearby at the other end of the tie rope. Even for the wee foal properly trained in babyhood, being tied for the first time may be a traumatic experience.

A properly trained, people-trusting foal should be tied for the first time under careful supervision, with the security of his dam near by, or a familiar Pony Pal to reassure him. If he has already learned "Ho" as he

**This wee foal accepts being tied up and groomed near her dam. Robin's gentle touch on Galaxy's chest steadies her while motherly Star looks on.**

runs free but copies his dam, he will relax even more quickly. We will easily establish his initial and lifelong acceptance of this "unbreakable" restraint.

And unbreakable it must be. A strong tie rope with a heavy-duty snap, a sturdy halter, and a firm post or tie ring are vital. Once again, the cause-and-effect association is critical. For the pony who fights against being tied up and succeeds in breaking loose—whether because of a broken rope, a broken halter, or a broken fence rail—will fight and break loose over and over again.

When we speak of a pony that fights against being tied up, we do not mean a pony that is wild or unbroken, or that the pony resists as you lead him to a tie ring or struggles as you tie the knot. The fight doesn't begin then. Only when the knot is tied and the pony moves, maybe only a step or two, and feels the unyielding halter around the back of his head, only when he comes up against the fact that he is tied, does the fight begin.

A well-trained pony may under some odd circumstance pull back and break a halter or rope; but that is a far cry from the to-the-death contortions of a confirmed halter-breaker. The problem pony feels fear and panic. He bursts into unreasoning struggle against the tie rope and against the pressure of the halter on his poll. The more he pulls, the greater the restriction and pain—and the more frantically he pulls. He may rear and twist, may get a foreleg over the rope, may sit down or fall over backwards. You have to see such frenzy to believe it possible in a tame animal—and you can think yourself fortunate if something (your rope or halter) breaks before a neck or leg does.

As often as not, once free, once no longer tied up, this problem pony just stands shaking or walks off a few feet and starts grazing. He willingly lets himself be picked up. His desperate fight against being tied up has nothing or little to do with any desire to gallop off or with distrust of his handler or fear of his surroundings. He may be amenable in all areas except this single one.

At a large stable, such a problem pony might be merely one out of hundreds bought and resold over a period of months, to be "killed or cured" or passed on "as is" to an unsuspecting buyer. The professional expects a few exceptionally bad animals—and hopes for a few exceptionally good ones—to balance his average. But you can't figure that way. For you, the pony is not "expendable." Not only can you not so easily recoup any financial loss, but if you do decide

to sell it may take months, and meanwhile routine expenses will continue. Your pony funds, your facilities, and your time may be involved, preventing your getting a replacement. Your emotions (after all, you wanted *this* pony) may be involved even longer.

**The inconvenience of a pony that won't tie: A tailgate lunch is more enjoyable if you don't have to hang onto your pony.**

It is not impossible to live with a pony that won't tie. The Monks put up with this failing for years in Dingbat, an otherwise top 4-H project. But they could never escape certain inconveniences. Dingbat could never be tied on a trail ride or cookout; he couldn't be tied to be groomed, or to be left in the trailer between classes at horse shows. The Monks's barn was papered with notes to the blacksmith and veterinarian and pony-sitter warning that Dingbat, the chestnut with the blaze and patched halter, must never be tied. When Dingbat was "sadly outgrown," the family found it difficult to locate a buyer who was equally willing to put up with this fault.

So if you find that you face this problem, the best thing is to solve it—for your convenience, safety, and future pleasure.

With a new pony, the first thing is to recognize that there may be this problem. As I said earlier, most of us assume that a pony ties. Don't! If you neglected to check out this point in your search, don't neglect it now that you have your pony at home. If he accepts being tied up, it is because some early handler has done what is recommended here in "Raising a Foal" and has saved you a lot of work. If he gives even an inkling that he will be a problem, there are several things that you can do:

Avoid tying your newcomer until you have time to give him a real, once-for-all-time lesson. Meanwhile, when you groom him have someone hold the lead rope (or hold it yourself: a long one will permit you to reach even his hind feet). Don't be discouraged. Everything you do to develop his trust and confidence will help, but it will be a slow continuing process.

The first time you tie him up, take certain precautions. Choose an enclosed area—outside rather than in a stall with low overhead or on the slippery barn floor. If your pony does panic you don't want him skidding on artificial footing or whamming into the sharp corner of the tractor scoop, but neither do you want him galloping off cross-country if he breaks free.

Have a strong tie rope, a sturdy halter, an unbreakable hitching post. (For this trial it is possible to substitute a piece of string for the lead rope so that if anything breaks it is the string. The disadvantage of this device is that the pony may associate breaking the string with success as much as breaking something sturdier, a cause-and-effect association we do not want.)

For this first trial the tie rope I prefer is a neck rope. Twice as long as an ordinary lead rope, this has a regular snap at one end. A metal cylinder about an inch long with a threaded collar holds a screw eye large enough for the snap to hook into. With the screw eye loosened, the cylinder can be slid up or down on the rope and fixed into place by tightening the screw through it. You put the snap end around the pony's neck at the poll and adjust the size of the loop or noose thus made by fixing the cylinder in place at that point. You then run the long end of the rope through the halter ring beneath the pony's jaw.

Both the noose end of the neck rope and the halter should be covered with sheepskin (or a fleecy tubular girth protector) to prevent your pony's neck from being rubbed. Each time you use the neck rope you must check that the cylinder is securely tightened in place so the noose cannot slip and choke him. A wildly struggling pony can break even this rope (especially if the screw is always threaded into and weakens the rope at the same spot), but it is an additional safety measure often used in tying and trailering. In this initial test the fact that the neck rope first takes the strain may prevent a halter's being broken.

With either device, be prepared for trouble. Be

Tying a pony with a halter hitch soon becomes automatic. Star stands quietly by one of numerous trees at High Hickory that have tie rings at pony height.

prepared to untie the pony immediately at any sign that he has not learned to be tied. If you can delay this test until you have taught him in hand what "Ho" means it will help, but time may not permit.

Now tie up your pony as you ordinarily would with a halter hitch or safety release. Keep the knot loose with the end of the rope free of the loop so that you can undo the knot quickly if need be. (Have a knife handy in case the knot jams.) Stay close by, ready to act promptly but calmly if your pony pulls.

If he stands quietly, test him: cautiously see if he is bothered by your waving your arm around him, by someone's pushing a wheelbarrow behind him. Move a few yards away from him and take off your jacket. If he does pull back, don't rush to his head. Get behind him with a reassuring "Ho." The crux is not whether he pulls back but what his reaction is when he can pull back no farther.

You can quickly tell whether, even if not surprise-proofed and therefore a little spooky, he accepts the limit of the rope and settles down or whether he is going to fight the limit and panic increasingly.

Let's hope that all you experience is anti-climax. But if coming up against the limit makes him pull more, don't wait. Free him before he breaks loose. Undo the knot and give him slack even if you have to cut the rope. It is better for him to associate freedom with your being at his head than with his besting the rope.

If your pony really blows up, there may be little you can do except keep out of the way of flailing hooves and thrashing body. If he reaches this explosive point it will not be safe for you to attempt to release the rope.

The best means of quickly curing this problem is to tie the pony in such a way that his pulling creates pressure not on his poll but around his body. A rope of soft strong cotton twenty or twenty-five feet long is best; the more common manila can be used but is more abrasive. A piece of tubular sheepskin or fleece (such as two girth protectors joined together) should be slipped over one end. Put this end around your pony's middle just at the withers and tie it under his girth area with a bowline. (A nonslip knot is essential!) Run the remaining length of rope between his forelegs and through the center ring of the halter. Allow about three feet (depending on the size of the pony) and tie the end securely around your hitching (or snubbing) post at ground level. Now when your pony pulls—and he will; if he doesn't, you make him—he will cause the rope to tighten about his body. He will soon learn that he creates the pressure himself: that when he pulls he feels discomfort but that when he stops and stands he feels none.

With the tie low down on your hitching post, the only pressure on the halter comes from underneath and on his nose, where a normal pull on the lead rope in hand would be. This keeps the pony's head in a more natural position and makes it hard for him to rear.

Another version of this method calls for tying the rope high above the pony's head; another, tying it to the tail rather than around the body. Solutions like whacking a pony from behind if he pulls back merely substitute one fear for another and make the problem a double one.

Most of the time when you are controlling your pony you are there close to him. You have him in hand; you are on his back with saddle and bridle; you are lunging him. He should still be under control when tied up, but in his one-track mind it may be remote control as far as you are concerned. At first (as when teaching a puppy a prolonged "stay") you must be present all of the time, giving the pony the opportunity to fight being tied but reassuring him when he struggles and praising him when he stops struggling. Gradually you can increase your distance and prolong your absence, but as with all training and care you are responsible. Do not tie your pony, or leave him tied, in such a manner that he can hurt himself.

With any pony problem, if the quick cure is a rough one avoid it if you possibly can. For most problems in schooling a large yearling or full-grown pony, the best long-range solution is to go back to the very beginning, to the basic steps for training—those for work with a young foal and those for work in hand. Analyze the problem, and remember that for permanent success any "cure" must be followed up by kindness, firmness, patience—by frequent, repeated, consistent brief sessions which gradually make your pony trustful and obedient to your voice commands. With slow careful training, along with "just plain growing up," most problems vanish; and both you and the pony should enjoy the training process.

## LUNGING

One of the most useful things you can teach your pony unmounted on the flat is to lunge.

Lunging permits controlled exercise of any pony even by a small rider or a nonrider. It permits schooling of an immature or an injured pony not up to weight on his back. It permits schooling of a green pony by a mounted rider or schooling of a green rider on a finished pony. It permits schooling or riding in a very restricted area (crowded show grounds) or a very open area (an unfenced field) where it would be unwise not to have this degree of control. Its importance as a means of working down a pony has been emphasized in "Basic Safety Rules."

To put it simply, in lunging your pony moves around you in a circle on a long line. You stay in the center and he moves on the perimeter at a walk or a trot (later, in advanced lessons, at a canter). You control him by giving voice commands and by making signals with a long-lashed lunging whip.

Again, you can compare your pony to the pencil of a drawing compass and yourself to the metal point.

**Lunging here is practiced not as schooling for a green pony but as a safety precaution—a release valve for bucks and high spirits before her little rider mounts.**

**The handler holds the lunge line coils in one hand, the whip in the other. Whichever way the pony circles, the whip signals from the direction of the hindquarters.**

The lunge line you hold in one hand and the lunging whip you hold in the other make a moving sector, with your pony on the arc. Or think of a piece of pie: your two arms make the wedge, with the pony the broad edge of piecrust. As he moves on the edge of the circle you keep the wedge the same size by keeping your arms a constant distance apart and by pivoting on the center spot.

Properly done, lunging is one of the finer equestrian skills and a joy to watch. As in all perfectly executed movements forward (except the "shoulder in") the pony's body from nose to tail follows the line of direction, a continuous curve, and his hind feet track his front. (He "tracks up.") His carriage of head and neck is free and easy, his body balanced and relaxed, his step springy and light, hocks moving well under him, and the cadence is even and rhythmical. Transitions from halt to walk to trot and reverse are smooth. The pony moves quietly away from his trainer out to the circumference of the circle at the start and he stays there when stopped unless commanded to come in.

Though you can move the whip and send subtle signals through the line, in lunging more than in any other schooling you control your pony primarily by your voice. Here, especially, pitting strength against strength would be futile. At this distance—you are many feet from your pony—you might indeed find yourself the loser!

LUNGING EQUIPMENT AND TACKING UP

Lunging equipment, like the rest of your equipment, can be very complicated or very simple. You need three basic items: a cavesson or halter of some sort; a long piece of line of some sort; a long whip of some sort. Elaborate lunging cavessons, lunging surcingles, cruppers, side reins, elegant beautifully balanced whips and a conventional lunge line—all (if you can find them in pony size) are "proper" (and expensive), but not necessary.

A lunging cavesson resembles a bridle rather than a halter in cut, with browband and cheekstraps and one or two throat latches—but it has no bit. A center strap may run from the noseband to the crownpiece. The most distinctive part is the noseband or cavesson itself: this is thick and stiff, usually in rigid curved sections. Softened with chamois-covered padding on the inside, the outside noseband has heavy metal plates with swivel rings or Dees at the center and sides. The plated under-section buckles on two sides and should be carefully adjusted for size and unbuckled when the cavesson is being put on or taken off. The throat latches should be adjusted to prevent the cheekstraps from hitting either eye during lunging. Because of the combination of metal plates, padding, and rings, the cavesson is a heavy piece of equipment, and you will want to avoid bangs and bumps either to yourself or to your pony while tacking up.

But if you decide not to invest in "regulation"

**Sturdy construction of a lunging cavesson shows here: center strap, double throat latch, metal plates covering the padded nose band. Cavesson is worn over a snaffle bridle, its reins secured around the pony's neck.**

equipment, it's good to know that you can use your everyday halter.

As for the regulation lunge line and the regulation lunging whip—with children, it is actually preferable to use a plain twenty-foot or thirty-foot dog-lead of webbed cotton (as strong as regulation line and more comfortable to the hand) and a bamboo pole or an inexpensive driving whip, either of which is lighter to handle than the regulation item and quite long enough for work with a pony.

When your pony is started under tack, you can lunge him in saddle and bridle. You will want your reins secured in short fashion through the throat latch or to his mane; unless you are trying to accustom him to flapping leathers, you will want the stirrups run up short and secured. When lunging with a bridle, do not fasten your lunge line directly

to the bit on the side that will be on the inner part of the circle. You can run the line through the inner snaffle ring on under your pony's jaw and fasten to the far or outside ring; you can run the line through the inner ring and on through the outer and bring it back to fasten on the inside ring; or, you can run the line through the inner ring all the way up one cheek around his poll, down the other cheek, and fasten it to the outside ring. Each arrangement prevents your simply pulling the bit through his mouth, and each requires your undoing and changing the lunge line each time you reverse direction on the circle. I prefer the second method.

The formal lunging cavesson can be worn "bare" or over a bridle with a schooling bit or an ordinary snaffle. Adjust the throat and jaw straps carefully so that the cheekstraps do not pull into your pony's eyes (especially the outside eye) as you lunge him. Buckle the noseband well above his nostrils. If the cavesson is worn over a bridle, its cheekstraps, noseband, throat latch go under the corresponding parts of the bridle.

In the method most commonly seen the lunge line is attached to the top center cavesson ring—or, if the pony lugs to the outside, to the side rings on the metal noseband. I prefer to fasten the lunge line under the noseband as one does with a halter. Since there is no ring there, you must have a lunge line that ends in a swivel with a leather strap and buckle end. By securing your line here you eliminate some of the pressure on your pony's sensitive nose, pressure which might for one thing make him want to lug off the circle. You are not going to be controlling him by force on the lunge line any more than in most of his other schooling; and the pony harrassed by constant, even if unintended, pain on his nose will not be in a cheerful or relaxed—and receptive—mood.

As you will have gathered, if you are going to fasten your lunge line under the pony's nose—and if your training plan has no place for side reins, draw reins, dummy jockeys, and so on—lunging in just an ordinary halter is not such a handicap.

If your emphasis in lunging is on exercising your pony from motives of safety, certainly use your regular halter. With smaller ponies and smaller children I have always done so. Where the main object in having a pony is to let children do things themselves, the simpler and shorter the preparation the better. High standards of pony management must be maintained, true, but a child should not spend more time cleaning stalls and tack or preparing his pony for schooling or riding than he does in fun—whether that fun be work on the ground or work in the saddle.

In keeping with this stress on simplicity, while we now use a cavesson on larger ponies and put boots and "bells" on, we still work the small ones "bare." Even if you can find small-pony-size brushing boots, galloping boots, and rubber bell boots to protect coronet and fetlock from over reach (ideally you should have two sets of each in order to have a clean dry set each day), you may not have time to put them on and take them off and keep them cleaned and oiled. Those extra fifteen minutes are better allotted elsewhere—

Instead of using boots you can protect the pony's legs with bandages. While more time-consuming, the process of bandaging is good practice towards what you will have to do for trailering or veterinary work or stable wear to prevent stocking up.

Bandages are applied in a special way for exercise. Whereas bandaging for travel or stable wear protects as much of the leg as possible from knee or hock to coronet, exercise bandaging begins below the knee and stops above the fetlock so as not to interfere with the action of the joints. Bandaging may protect your pony's legs from a bang from his own hoof or from a stone tossed up as he works. But the more the trainer is doing alone the more important it is to keep things simple. Know the maximum and the minimum means of attaining your goals, and find your road somewhere in between.

### LUNGING PROCEDURE

If you have never lunged a pony, let alone trained a green pony to lunge, here's a trick the Pony Pals use at the novice stage.

One youngster is the pony on the snap end of the lunge line, another is the trainer with the remainder of the line coiled in one hand and the lunging whip in his other. A third child can be included as the assistant who initially leads the green pony on the circle in either direction. Since you not only have to teach and control an "ignorant" pony but also have to manipulate a long whip, an equally long lash, and an even longer lunge line, a little practice with a cooperative two-legged beast will help. It will give all concerned an idea of the difficulties you can encounter with a real pony that won't "wait a minute" while you straighten things out.

Such rehearsal will give you a chance to learn how

"Want me to come in and show you?" Schoolmaster Tuffy stands patiently as Kate shifts lunge line and whip to opposite hands.

to feed out part of your long line with one hand while you move the pony away from you and use your whip properly with the other. You start out as if the lunge line were simply a very long lead rope, its extra length carefully coiled in your left hand. In that same hand you also hold the handle of the long lunge whip and the tip of its long lash. (By now your real pony is surprise-proofed so that he is not disturbed by the movement of the whip alongside his body as you walk to the lunging spot.) You "Walk on" and "Ho" slightly off center in the lunging circle.

It is at this point—in the course of transferring your whip to your right hand, paying out the lunge line without dropping or tangling the coil, and starting your pony walking quietly out and away from you on to the circle—that problems often occur. Your two-legged pony won't be bothered by your awkwardness. (With small children and small ponies, the problem of coping with a lot of surplus lunge line can be avoided by using the shorter web dog leash.)

Now, whether you are practicing with a stand-in or working in earnest with a real pony, this is the procedure:

Hold your pony only by the lunge line in your left hand. Step back a few steps off the center with your left arm extended. Say "Walk on," and raise the whip quietly at a right angle behind your pony's rear. Since you do not give with the lunge line he has no place to walk on but in a small circle around you. Gradually pay out the line as you back away to the center point, thus enlarging the circle as he walks around.

If you have an assistant, you may stop in the very center of the circle while this assistant, his hands on the outside cheek strap, leads the pony to the circumference as you pay out sufficient line. *All* commands must come only from you, the handler, in the center. We like the assistant to walk on the outside of the circle, on the far side of the pony from the person with the whip. In this way, it is very easy once the pony is moving satisfactorily on the circle for the assistant to walk off on a tangent from the lunging area. If he is walking on the inside between the pony and the trainer he must duck the rotating lunge line as he moves to the center or move off the circle behind the pony.

Walk your pony once or twice around the circle, urging "Walk on, Walk on." Then ask him to "Ho." You want him to stand on the circle and not head in towards you. If in earlier lessons you have effectively taught him that "Ho" means stand still, he will stay there.

Ask him to "Walk on" again, and praise his obedience. As he moves, you pivot on the heel that is towards him and under the hand in which you hold the lunge line.

We are going to want to lunge the pony both clockwise and counter-clockwise. Most of us find it easier to do one than the other. (For right-handed people it is easier to manipulate the lunge line with the left and the whip with the right hand.) Therefore it is a good idea to get some practice in the direction we find less comfortable before there is a real pony on the other end of the lunge line.

In correct, traditional lunging the handler stands in one precise spot, moving only to pivot. (He's the fixed point of that pie-shaped wedge.) You don't have to be quite so fussy. If walking in a smaller concentric circle helps you to keep your pony moving on his big outer circle, go ahead and walk. What you want to avoid is tension on the lunge line, either from you or from the pony. Ideally, with your pony circling you want a very slight catenary through the line from his head to your hand. Watch out in case his coming in or circling irregularly lets the slackening line droop down so that he or you might step on it. Be prepared to move back a few steps and slightly towards his rear and coil up any slack if need be.

At no time do you want to feel as if you're a swivel with your pony whirling around the outside like a bolo. Take steps to lessen the likelihood of your pony's getting going and trying to head off the circle:

**Resistance shows in head and neck carriage and outward jut of pony's jaw. Later, pony's body will curve along the circle, hind feet "track up," and lunge line have a slight catenary from nose to trainer's hand.**

First, before your lunging session let him gallop around and act up while free in his paddock. Later, lunging can be used to give him this release; now, when lunging is the lesson, he should get this necessary release while free.

Second, lunge within an enclosure. Even confining your lunging circle on three sides, for instance using the end and two sides of a ring or field, will make it easier to keep your pony in bounds. With a paddock just the right size or a specially made circle of snow-fencing the problem may never arise. An open field should have some visual limits: you can indicate corners or entire sides with saw horses and planks, oil drums and boards, or jump wings.

When the pony is lunging, try to prevent his lugging off the circle by setting up slight vibrations on the lunge line. If you are prompt to praise him when he does what you want, he will be more likely to realize what is expected of him in what must otherwise seem a pretty senseless maneuver.

What if the pony comes in off the circle? You must be quick—quick to realize that he is about to come in, quick to recognize the inward turn of his head and shoulder, quick to move your whip at eye level towards his nose. Usually a green pony remains on the circle while moving and comes in only when you have made him "Ho" and then remove your attention from him because you're busy straightening out the lunge line or something of that sort. The way to eliminate this problem is to emphasize in hand that "Ho" means stand still—and to become more adept with line and whip yourself.

I have occasionally heard of a pony's charging in at his handler. If yours should do this, use your whip *as a whip*. Check your equipment to see that it is not causing pressure or pain. Then back track and do some more basic schooling in hand with voice commands. Give the pony more free exercise before his schooling on the lunge. Be sure that the charging in, lugging off the circle, balking, or rearing is not simply your adolescent saying, in the only pony way possible, that he's had all he can take, physically or emotionally.

Problems of this sort diminish with progress in overall schooling. Keep your sessions brief. Recognize every concession or accomplishment, reward it with voice praise, and exploit it by ending the lesson on a good note. (Often the secret of success is knowing when to quit.) Your pony will be aware of your pleasure; and when you have him in hand to walk back to the barn, pat him enthusiastically and give him a concrete token of your appreciation in the shape of a carrot.

Try to lunge him always in one certain area separate from the paddock or pasture where he plays. Establish a firm routine, if your own schedule permits, and your pony will come to recognize a working session. Some breeder friends of ours have a Welsh pony stallion that is in great demand both as a stud and as a saddle pony for a small adult. They believe one reason for his outstanding twofold success is that they follow two markedly different routines in his training. For breeding work, distinctive stallion tack is put on in one section of their elaborate barn. For pleasure riding, they use a distinctly different bridle and saddle and do grooming, saddling, and so on in another section. This is yet another example of how association with certain sights, sounds, actions evokes certain responses from the pony. Your pony has learned, early, to come *towards* you when you hold out your hand. Now, if you set up a lunging routine with repetition and consistency he will soon learn to move *away* from you when you begin work on the lunging circle.

It is important when lunging, as it will be when you start mounted schooling, not to work your pony on too small a circle. The radius of the circle should be from ten to fifteen feet depending on the pony's size. Circling repeatedly puts unequal stress on his inner and outer legs with much strain on his hocks and pasterns. The deeper the footing and the smaller the circle the greater the inequality and the strain—and here again, if moving your central pivot point means your pony is circling on better footing, move while you lunge him. Try also to divide your lunging session so that frequent changes of direction total up to a balance of work on both hands.

You can change direction in any of several ways. In the early stages when you have stopped your pony on the circle you can walk out to him, picking up the slack of the lunge line in coils as you approach. Once at his head, you have him make the half-turn on the forehand that you taught him with "Move over" in his stall. While he stands on the circle—facing now in the opposite direction—you move back to the center paying out your lunge line as you go. Later you can stop your pony on the circle, call him towards you on "Come here," and stop him with "Ho" after a few steps towards you. While he stands facing you, shift lunge line and whip to opposite hands. Then step off the center to your whip side, raise the whip behind and towards your pony's rump, and command "Walk on." Once he has walked across the center and is curving towards the circle in the new direction, you return to the center point and lunge as before. Or, of course, you can call your pony all the way in to the center, have him stop close by you while you change line and whip, and start him out on the circle as you did at the beginning of the session. You may find that your pony, like some of ours, will add a new word "Reverse" to his vocabulary if you use it regularly when changing hand.

GAITS ON THE LUNGE

Now that you have your pony lunging—working at a walk or a trot on the circle—what, other than exercise, are you looking for?

The most difficult gait for him to do properly on the lunge is the walk. He should not sloth along (any more than in hand or under saddle) but should move energetically and smoothly with impulsion generated by his hind feet reaching well forward under him. He should move quietly into the trot without any shifting of his head and move rhythmically, again with his hocks well under him as he strides. His hindquarters should not swing stiffly out or in off the circle.

Perhaps you can't judge some of the finer points; but you can tell if he's going smoothly, alertly, and with a certain *joie de vivre*.

Perhaps while you're still working on the walk and

**In not-yet-completed arena, footing is too deep and too soft; Lutine Bell goes into a "protective canter" to maintain her balance.**

the trot some of this *joie de vivre* will spill over into a canter. Don't snag him down. For a stride or so say "Canter can-ter" so that he associates this voice command with what he's doing—this new gait. Then quietly say "Trot trot." Chances are he will settle down; he may only have gone into a canter to catch his balance. You can slightly vibrate the lunge line so that he feels the vibration on his nose, but do not try to yank him down to a slower gait. Such brutality may do damage to his neck and spinal column; moreover it may also be ineffectual, in which case you will merely have created a situation where your pony is suddenly disobeying you and you can do nothing about it.

Give him time to obey. Remember, he has to shift legs from one gear to another. I always think of the moment when a diver takes the board to perform a complicated dive. He has to prepare some mechanism of mind and body to trigger the complex maneuvers he must click through in the air. Something like this must go through your pony's relay system before he can transpose obedience to command into action.

Remember: when problems or "failures" do occur, you never have to "save face" with your pony. You may have to go back a step or two on your schooling ladder to reestablish yourself as boss, but you must do this without resentment or grudge. If your pony makes you mad, just don't stay mad!

Much of your work on the lunge line will be done at the trot, with frequent reverses to develop diagonals equally and with frequent periods at the walk to keep the pony cool and relaxed. Sweating on the neck and shoulders or between the buttocks is often a symptom of distress rather than the result of warm weather and work. The Pony Pals chant:

> School, school,
> Avoid a duel.
> Don't be a foo-ool,
> Don't lose his cool.

Jump-rope sing-song, but sage advice.

At this stage, cantering on the lunge line is mainly accidental—that is, you let your pony do it if he wants, to get excess action out of his system. When you are ready actually to school at the canter, you can continue to take advantage of his having learned the voice command "Canter," as described above. Even if initially he has gone into the gait of his own accord, let him keep at it for increasingly long periods before you say "Trot." Soon you will be able to put him into the canter on command.

At either stage it is important that your pony go into the canter *from* the trot, not *through* the trot. He should not, because you have forced him (by waving your whip, for instance), fall into a canter to save himself. Do not make him go faster and faster at a trot until the only way he can keep on his feet is to sprawl into a canter—counter canter, disunited, or correct.

To put your pony into a canter when *you* want him to canter (and at this stage it will still be from a trot), you must realize that while you may think of correct leads in terms of the leading foreleg your pony actually starts his canter with the opposite hind leg.

The canter is a musical gait; you can hear the three beats and feel the pulsing rhythm. It can be considered a lateral/diagonal gait, lateral since two opposite legs work independently on each side preceding and following the diagonal work of the other pair. On the left lead, the sequence is: off hind, off fore and near hind together, and near fore. On the right lead, it is near hind, near fore and off hind together, and off fore.

In each combination of three beats, the last leg to strike or reach forward is the one we speak of as the "leading leg." To a spectator, this leading leg is clear as it moves well in advance of the diagonally working opposite foreleg. Many people use this one part of the canter to determine which lead a pony is on. Some never go beyond this point in observing or figuring (or, if in the saddle, feeling) how all the legs work in a canter. It is for this reason that many riders do not realize how the pony starts his canter—with the opposite hind leg.

(Beginning Pony Pals sometimes ask the difference between a canter and a gallop. The gallop may be called an extended canter, extended so that the diagonal legs have a separate footfall and make it a four-beat gait. The feet hit the ground thus: near hind, off hind, near fore, off fore. In both the canter and the gallop there is a moment of suspension after the last beat when all legs are briefly airborne. Then the hind leg that initiates the whole sequence hits the ground well under the pony and propels him forward again.)

To put your pony on the correct inside lead, therefore, you must signal him at the moment when the outside hind leg is coming under him as part of his diagonal at the trot.

Long before you start asking for the canter, watch his footwork at a trot. See if you can analyze the gait and catch the count for the outside hind/inside fore diagonal. (Children whose time in the saddle is limited to lessons can learn a lot from just looking!)

When you are ready to ask for the canter, at this moment in his movement give a light flick of the lunge line and of your lunging whip (still keeping your wedge-shape angle) and say "Canter." It is particularly important that your pony's head and body be curving on the curve of the circle at this moment, just as a runner moving to the left looks towards his left shoulder.

Sometimes a pony will favor one lead and resist going into a canter on the other. By reversing direction you will put him more readily into a canter on the favored lead. Once he canters and is praised for "obeying," he is more likely to comprehend and cooperate on the other lead—and, later, to canter on command from a walk.

Now that your pony is walking, trotting, and cantering on the lunge you have a means of regulating the amount of exercise he receives. You can now follow a daily routine that will develop his muscular coordination and strength along with his obedience and receptivity to training. As with all other pony work, feeding, grooming, free play, lunging, and surprise-proofing go hand in hand. Each is but part of the whole, and each part contributes to and affects the others. Your pony will soon be ready for basic training on the flat under saddle.

(Loading, which is also part of training on the flat, is discussed in Chapter 16, "Fun beyond Your Own Backyard.")

## TACKING UP

By this time you are eager to *ride* your pony. Your work on the lunge line has prepared him for mounted work—all that remains is to tack him up and ride!

If your pony has already been backed and ridden under tack, he will be used to being saddled and bridled. If not, or if he has any unpleasant habits when being tacked up, you will want to start from scratch. Ponies that have not been properly prepared for tacking up may puff or blow, may even bite back or cowkick when girthed. Some raise their heads high in evasion, try to move away from their handler, or refuse to open their mouths for the bit when bridled. Since we want a pony to stand quietly when saddled and to lower his head and take the bit willingly when bridled, we are particularly careful how we first introduce our young ponies to tack. As in all work we "take time."

At this point, a saddle and bridle may still be unfamiliar objects to your young pony, strange shapes to be suspicious of even close by on a fence rail or on your arm, let alone on his own body. Take time to let him investigate the sound and scent and feel of bridle and saddle before you put them on him. He must accept these foreign objects as objects before he accepts them as his tack, and he must accept them as tack on his body before you give him the added novelty of a rider on his back and the problem of balancing a strange weight as well as coordinating his own still awkward limbs.

If you've been working with your pony for some time, all your grooming and handling and deliberate lolling over him and playing around him will have made him pretty indifferent to almost anything you do. Nevertheless, and especially if you are uncertain whether he has ever been tacked up before, start with these basic steps:

### BRIDLING FIRST

Your pony is accustomed to wearing a halter and to having his ears gently pulled and scratched. He will not mind having his ears briefly flattened back when the crownpiece of the bridle is slipped back over them, but while he is wearing his halter take time to open his mouth once in a while and put your hand in behind his front teeth and in front of the back teeth on the bars (See "Your Pony and His

Health," Chapter 6). This will help when you come to slip the bit in.

Long before any formal bridling, a pony that has grown up with children may have been "ridden" bareback with lead rope-reins attached to a halter. Little Tuffy was ridden thus as a three-year-old by four-year-old Robin; a year later they got their first bridle with bit the day before their first horse show. Top Rail Stardust proved another story. Attempts to ride her as a three-year-old in halter only meant that this 12.2 pony went where she willed. Such limited control was not enough for her. She took eight-year-old Robin crashing through head-high brush and bramble. Yet two years later, after schooling only by Robin along the lines described in this book, this same pony took second place in a large bareback "command class" in which figure eight's at a canter with change of leads, stops on command, counter canters, jumps over a saw horse, and other challenges were all done in halter only with a single lead rope kept on one side of the pony's neck. Your pony may be one that can be ridden in halter only, or with a bit attached makeshift fashion to his halter; but eventually you will need a proper snaffle bridle with a snaffle bit, as explained in Chapter 4.

Ideally the first bit your pony feels in his mouth will be a schooling bit, with one or two joints plus small dangles to stimulate saliva and encourage his mouthing it. We have found that a thick but light jointed snaffle secured to the side rings of the halter with string works equally well for the initial introduction.

When you first bit your pony, have him in his stall with his halter on. A child assistant can hold him on a lead rope, or you can handle him alone. Tie the right ring of the bit to the off side of his halter, rub a little molasses or honey on the mouthpiece, and, as you open his mouth, slip it in gently. Then tie the left ring on the near side of the halter. Be very careful not to bump his mouth or teeth with the metal or you may create a problem pony who is justifiably reluctant to be bridled.

When you remove the bit, now or later when it's part of your bridle, be equally careful. Nothing is more brutal than to drop or yank a bit from a pony's mouth in unbridling, but an astonishing number of "horsemen" are guilty of this brutality out of sheer thoughtlessness. Your young pony may playfully hang on to the bit with his teeth as you slide it down and out. Don't force: let him grip it for a minute or two, then praise him when he releases it.

Any child or short adult appreciates a pony that holds his head low for bridling. You can encourage your pony to do this by giving him a piece of carrot held very low—right in your hand along with the bit, even—just before bridling, and after. Teach him to expect gentle handling and a knee-level tidbit, and you will develop a pony that bridles willingly, and with his head where you can reach it.

Leave the schooling bit in your pony's mouth only briefly the first few times. Let him mouth it for five or six minutes while you watch. He'll probably toss his head and worry it with his tongue. He may be too surprised or annoyed to eat, but more likely he will soon accept a handful of grain. (If you let him eat hay, it may clog or ball up until he learns to manipulate the strange object in his mouth.) Either way, he'll soon ignore the bit.

While a jointed metal bit which encourages salivation (and thus a soft mouth) is preferable for this initial bitting, a soft rubber snaffle is more desirable once you start riding. You may find such a bit with a straight bar, or jointed; but it should be of the soft flexible rubber not the hard vulcanite type. A straight bit eliminates the wishbone effect a jointed one may have on palate and bars. Rings come in many styles; we prefer an egg butt or Dee snaffle, but a full-cheek may prevent the bit from pulling out on either side while your pony is being schooled on indirect or open rein.

Whatever the style, the bit must fit your pony's mouth properly and be neither too wide nor too narrow.

Once your pony is used to the bit in his mouth, you can put on bit and bridle together. Bridle as you do any schooled horse (remember, you should practice this elsewhere ahead of time so as to spare your "baby" any fumbling on your part), but do so with the cavesson or noseband unbuckled and with the cheek straps adjusted approximately ahead of time. This will lessen the amount of fussing around the pony's head the first time he's bridled. Once on the cheek straps must be adjusted more accurately so that the bit causes a slight wrinkle of the corners of the lips. The cavesson should rest just below his cheek bone and buckle with space for a finger to be inserted. The throat latch should be fastened with enough slack for your hand to be inserted on edge—and not so tightly as to be uncomfortable for the pony when his chin is close to his chest.

In these early stages do not lead your pony in the conventional way by the reins under his jaw or over his head. His bars are exceedingly tender (he may even be teething), so you want the only pressure on the bit to come through the reins from the rider on his back. This point should be stressed with children, who may tend to correct instinctively by a yank on the reins as they would with a lead rope. It is better to put the bridle on over the halter and attach a lead rope or lunge line than to lead by the reins. If you must hold or lead your pony in bridle only, do so by the cheek straps.

### SADDLING NEXT

The standard scene of a pony being saddled for the first time takes place in a dusty corral. *The captured pony stands tense. From his high-held head to his close-clamped tail everything in his rigid body screams fear and resistance. One leathery cowboy tightens the twitch cutting into the pony's nose. He reaches to adjust the red neckerchief blindfolding the pony's eyes—and barely ducks a wildly striking forefoot. His tanned partner swings the heavy saddle over the fear-humped back and clomps it into place. Swiftly he reaches under the sweat-soaked belly and grabs the cinch from the other side. The pony cowkicks, his raking hoof catching the hairy wrist. Both men curse. A jerk, and the cinch is tight. The first cowboy swings aboard. His partner yanks the blindfold off and jumps clear.*

*The pony explodes. He dives and twists and rears. Both cowboys yell. Still the pony bucks and arches. The rider fans his hat and rakes his spurs. The pony stumbles. He staggers and gives in. His head sags. Sweat weeps from his flanks as he stands subdued. The cowboy dismounts. One more pony has been broken to saddle.*

Even today such scenes actually occur. In some parts of our country "horsemen" still *break* ponies to saddle. Even where the violent act no longer exists, the terminology—"breaking a horse"—still does. But breaking implies a crushing of spirit as well as of will, and genuine horse-lovers avoid the phrase even as they even more consciously avoid the act. Schooling, training, teaching, working—"breaking" your pony to saddle should be just one more eased-into stage in the peaceful progress of your pony's education.

Preparation for saddling goes along with all the routine things that you have been doing since you got your pony—handling, grooming, blanketing,

haltering, surprise-proofing, bitting. Perhaps your trusting pony lets you go right up to him while he's lying down in pasture or lets you sit astride his back when he's lying down. Perhaps you ride him bareback.

If your pony has not been handled in this way, or backed, take time to prepare him for something—the saddle—and someone—you—on his back. Put pressure all over his topside and girth area as you groom. Put an arm across his withers and lean on him. Do this from both sides, of course. There is no reason for a green pony to expect to be saddled or mounted from one side any more than from another except as your habits condition him. Put both arms over him and hang your weight on them. Spring up and lie over him on your stomach with your feet dangling for a second or two.

Habituate your pony to a person's being above him. Lead him by a rock or fence with people on it. Get him to stand parallel to a step or mounting block while you climb up on it. (Use your half-turn on the forehand with "Move over" to put him into position.) Try grooming him while standing on a box so that you are higher than he is.

Spread your rub rag out over his saddle area and flap and drape it conspicuously around both sides. Exaggerate this with a saddle pad or empty grain bag.

If you blanket your pony, he is accustomed to the encirclement of the surcingles on his sheet. Tighten the front one for a few minutes every so often. It will help even more if he's used to the complete belt of a cooler surcingle or body roller.

**A happy owner shows her pony their brand-new saddle. Used to being dressed up for make-believe and to being ridden bareback, Tuffy was from the first utterly indifferent to a saddle on her back.**

As I've suggested earlier, let him see his saddle before you're ready to put it on his back. Let him get used to its sound and smell on your arm or on a rack. Exaggerate the noise as you pull down a stirrup iron and slap the leather against the skirt under his very nose. Later this won't bother him when it happens on his back behind him. Let him nose a saddle on another pony's back. If as a foal he was used to seeing his dam under saddle, he's probably sniffed one already. (The Pony Pals firmly believe that one schooled pony tells a green one not to be alarmed, when such nosing takes place. Perhaps some sort of reassurance does come across telepathically, from another pony's acceptance of or indifference to what the green pony must regard as an outlandish object on his back.)

After this preliminary work, before we really saddle up a green pony for the first time, we put the saddle only—without girth or stirrups—on his back several times. Do this with your pony in his familiar stall. Have him on a halter and lead rope with a friend at his head to steady him. Do not have his bridle on. Any corrective restraint should be with voice and lead rope, but don't hold him tightly. Let your pony face a corner or his manger. If you're relaxed, he will be too.

Don't try to sneak the saddle on to his back. Let him see it and sniff it; raise it up and down a few times where he can see it. Then raise it carefully and put it gently on his back. Use your familiar commands—"Ho," "Easy boy," "Good boy." Hold the cantle and pommel so that you can keep the saddle in place if he shifts position. You do not want it to slide or fall off and frighten him. If he turns back to nose it, let him.

When you remove the saddle, lift it up and off. Praise him again. Let him sniff it while you perhaps flap the skirts a bit. Praise him. Repeat the whole procedure. After a few experiences like this he will be familiar with the feel and weight of the saddle on his body before you do anything about girthing up.

With this careful approach, your pony's not likely to act up when you saddle him completely. But, as always, take precautions:

Exercise him first. As with anything new, saddling for the first few times should be done after he's let off steam on the lunge line or in his paddock, not when he has been pent up and is raring to go.

Again have him in his stall with your helper at his head. Plan to put the girth on separately at this stage

so you won't risk whacking him as you lift the saddle into place. Buckle the girth on your side and pass it close to his elbows to your assistant's outstretched hand on the other. Or, if you must work alone, go around to pick it up yourself. Now tighten the girth slowly, a hole at a time, until your pony feels a gentle pressure in a circle around him of saddle and girth.

You do not want to tighten the girth fully at this stage. Therefore, since a loosely girthed saddle that slips is a hazard, keep a hand on the saddle so it can't twist under his belly if he shifts or jumps. Praise your pony and pat him. If he is indifferent—maybe even eating hay—move him around a bit, but don't let the saddle scrape the wall lest it startle him.

If your pony seems nervous, stop and reassure him. When you undo the girth, ease it free so it does not whack his legs as you let it go under him. Undo the girth on the other side. (Later, when you remove the saddle with girth attached, be sure the girth does not drag and whack his back or sides.) Lift the saddle off and again let him sniff it if he wishes. Above all, reward him with voice and a carrot tidbit.

You will soon—the second time, the fourth, depending on your pony—be able to tighten the girth to a normal degree. You want always to be able to slip your flat hand between pony and girth, to feel a little "give." Youngsters who so often have to be reminded "Check your girth" may be so concerned with the danger (saddle slipping) of a too-loose girth that they do not realize the hazards (billet popping, stitches breaking) of a too-tight one on an active pony. An inexpensive mohair girth has more give than a leather one, while a combination leather-and-elastic stretch girth offers more flexibility. (As Pony Pal Sandy once said, "After wearing stretch jeans I'll never go back to regular denim. I bet Cricket feels the same way about girths.")

Now, with your saddle securely girthed, you can lead your pony around in the outside world. Be careful to allow for the skirts as well as for his sides when going through doors and gates. From this point on, slap the saddle seat now and then and generally "make noises" from the saddle area. If your pony is relaxed, trot with him in hand.

The next step is to tack up your pony with stirrup irons on. At a standstill, accustom him to the slap of irons being pulled down; he's heard this before, but now it's behind him on his own body. Walk him so he feels the leathers and irons dangling and banging as he moves on the lead rope. Jog him with the irons swinging. Steady him with voice praise and fuss over him when you put him up.

Lunge your pony now with his saddle on. The first few times, lunge him properly with the irons run up and secured. Then, at a walk and later at a slow trot, lunge him a few times with the irons dangling. This is improper, but there might be a time when your pony would be moving with irons loose, and you may as well expose him to such agitation against his sides while you can see his reaction and calm him if necessary. (It's also good preparation for legs moving against him when you ride.)

Do this as a separate schooling session for four or five days until your pony is utterly indifferent to having the saddle on his back at any gait. When he has reached that stage, he is ready to ride!

# 9

# BASIC TRAINING ON THE FLAT: MOUNTED

## BACKING

NOW AT LAST YOU ARE READY TO MOUNT YOUR pony! All the patient ground work you've been doing leads up to this exciting moment when you "back" or mount him for the very first time. Backing is a major step in schooling, the initial one in mounted work on the flat.

Backing a green pony for the first time may be done in one of two ways: The rider may be lifted into the saddle with a leg-up from an assistant, or he may mount conventionally under his own steam. In either case, preliminary surprise-proofing to accustom the pony to your suddenly being first higher than he is and then actually on his back pays off here. Whichever method you decide on, plan ahead.

Where small children and green ponies are concerned, we feel one can't be too cautious at this point. We don't want a rider to get hurt, nor do we want a pony to learn at this crucial moment that he can "dump" a rider.

Though so far it's always proved unnecessary, we insist on at least one and preferably two assistants at this point. This is a good time to include a nonriding parent or older child. (So often the mother is the only horse lover. This was true in Pony Pal Lootie MacFarnold's family, but Lootie often quotes her father's response to an appeal for help on B-day: "It sure is nice," he said, "to be asked to do something with that hay-burner besides pay the feed bill!")

Even with older riders who are doing most of the schooling of their ponies on their own, it is best to

In-foal Stardust is backed for the very first time. Dave helps eight-year-old Robin in this important step.

have a friend on hand when backing for the first time.

### LEG-UP PROCEDURE

This is the procedure followed if you have a leg-up:

Back your pony, this first unpredictable time, in a small enclosure like a field or paddock. (Never, of course, in a stall or low-roofed building.)

When Star accepts her rider at a standstill, she is led forward a few steps and patted reassuringly.

A youngster backing a green pony for the first time is relaxed herself when she knows her pony obeys "Ho." Ability to do a "safety dismount" helps, too—although after 39 inch Tuffy, 12.2 Star seems "pretty high off the ground."

Careful preparation made this pony indifferent to Robin's sliding around on her the very first time mounted. Star's attention is focused hopefully on Dave's pocketful of carrots.

Have your pony on a lead rope, bridled over his halter, and saddled. He has of course been regularly exercised all week and today he was well lunged before being saddled.

You are the rider. Have your helpers quite clear as to what their duties will be.

Assistant Number One will hold the pony by the lead rope. He will stand by the pony's head on the off side, stroking his nose but ready to apply pressure over the nostrils if necessary. Once you are mounted, his job will be to hold the pony quiet, to lead him on "Walk on" or stop him on "Ho"—all on *your* voice commands.

Your pony must learn, of course, to stand without being held while you mount. It's most annoying to have a pony move about while a person is trying to mount or to start off before the rider is set and signals him to do so. Chances are that your pony is so used to standing still when the person working him in hand says "Ho" and stops that he will stand now while he's mounted for the first time. If he doesn't, correction of this fault will come at a later date. First things first, and right now getting on your pony is the point at issue.

Assistant Number Two will give you a leg-up on your count of "One, two, three." His only concern is to give the leg-up strongly and smoothly so you clear your pony's back and ease into the saddle. (Again, practice on a steady old pony beforehand if you aren't adept at this sort of gymnastics.) Once you're in the saddle Assistant Number Two will step back. He can stay on the near side by your leg to act as a "pickup man" rodeo style if your pony should really act up.

You, the rider, will pick up the reins loosely in your left hand. You also grab either a fistful of mane or the pommel along with them; and, with your right hand, the cantle. You stand in close with your left leg

**142**

bent back up and kept that way for your helper to hold as he gives you a leg-up. Your sole concern is to spring up on "Three," to swing your right leg clear of your pony's rump, and to land lightly in the saddle without a thump and without banging your legs against his sides. Keep your left arm stiff and support your weight on it as you move your right hand forward and swing your right leg over the pony's rump, and ease into place.

You are mounting on the near side now, simply because this is probably the side on which *you* are most adept. In future schooling you will deliberately mount from the "wrong" or off side also.

All voice commands to your pony during this backing session should come only from you the rider. With a reassuring "Ho, boy" or "Ho, girl" to your pony, you count "One, two, three" to your leg-up man; he heaves—and you are on your pony's back.

**Robin dismounts from the off side rather than end up between the two ponies. Unless ambidextrous, the rider is likely to find working from the "wrong" side more awkward than his pony does!**

CONVENTIONAL MOUNTING PROCEDURE

This procedure is only slightly different. Assistant Number One stands on the near side, holding the pony by the lead rope and nose (or by the cheekstraps and nose if no halter is used). Assistant Number Two waits on the off side, gripping the off stirrup, ready to put weight on it to keep the saddle from slipping as you mount. He will stay on the off side to act as pickup man and will walk along by your right knee.

You will pick up the reins, grab the mane or pommel and the cantle, and mount as you ordinarily would. Be careful not to dig your toe into your pony or you may mount high into the sky! not on to his back. You may choose to put your left foot in the stirrup once or twice, then put it in and spring up on it once or twice without swinging your right leg over the pony's rump, to test his reactions. With either method, be certain to land lightly in the saddle and not tighten your legs suddenly against his side. Again, voice commands come only from you, the rider.

### IN THE SADDLE

At last you're in the saddle! This is a thrilling moment, and tenseness begets tenseness. You may find yourself saying "Easy, boy!" to calm yourself as much as your pony. While both reins are still in your left hand, reach forward and pat or stroke his neck with your right. (Children may need to be reminded not to let their heels go back into the pony's sides.)

Let's hope that at this moment your pony will just stand still and accept the new weight on his back. If so, pat and praise him; but keep leg pressure off his sides. If he does not stand still, don't be too demanding. Let him move on a bit and have your assistants move with him. Try to keep your legs a little more forward than usual. At this stage keep your feet out of the stirrups.

A quick dismount is preferable, on this occasion, to letting any problems such as bucking or kicking back develop. If your pony really acts up, you have not spent enough time in preparation. Dismount and do more work on the unmounted steps described earlier. So, hop off. Calm your pony. You can then try mounting again and sitting in the saddle a bit longer. You can say "No," or "Behave yourself"—words he knows from general handling—but if he still refuses to accept you calmly, don't scold him or lose your temper. He's just not ready for mounted work yet. To have backed

**143**

him even to this extent is progress; and by dismounting and doing more ground work you may prevent him from learning to buck you off.

At this crucial stage, the emphasis is on not letting the pony discover his own potential. What he doesn't know—that he could dump you!—can't hurt you. Do everything to keep him from having the perfectly normal reaction of bucking you off when he finds that you have suddenly landed on his back.

Nearly always, with a properly prepared pony, brief pressure on the pony's nose from Assistant Number One and your vocal reassurance are enough to counter this instinctive objection, and the strongest reaction you may feel when you're first in the saddle will be a hump in his back—a hump of uncertainty.

Your assistant may have to raise the pony's head with the hand holding the lead rope under his jaw. Lifting the head thus forces the pony's weight back on his hind quarters and makes it impossible for him to buck. Should he attempt to crowhop or rear, your assistant should quickly move him forward—and in a circle. All this time your voice should be calm and reassuring, but loud enough for your pony to hear at a time when he's concentrating, not on your voice, but on that strange hulk—you!—on his back. (The Pony Pals, noisy as they may normally be, often have to be reminded to "speak up" their first time in the saddle.)

Here as with all schooling it's important that the first session be a pleasant one—for the pony. Should he "misbehave," he's not being "bad": just normal. You should not punish; you should correct—and at this point correction can only consist of reassurance and familiar commands like "Ho" or "No" or "Behave." If you make him associate this stage of his training with pain and punishment you will foil your own ends. If you have been following the guidelines in this book, at this stage you will have earned your pony's trust and obedience and will find yourself sitting in the saddle on a green pony who is merely standing there waiting for you to tell him what next.

What next is for you to pick up your reins loose and long, one in each hand but with no pressure, and to say "Walk on," with no leg aid or pressure. As you give this command, the assistant walks on, and the pony with him. "Ho" and "Walk on" and "Ho" again are carried out repeatedly in this same manner, with your pony doing things he is used to doing in hand, but making the mental transition to the commands' coming from the rider on his back.

Your young pony has now to make a major adjustment. He must contrive not only to balance his own body at different gaits but to balance it with a top-heavy, live, shifting weight on his back. He may wobble and stagger under you as he walks—he may cross his forelegs and zigzag and seem unable to walk a straight line. He may carry his head unusually low or unusually high. As he regains his balance and poise these faults will right themselves.

Don't ask too much of him in these first mounted sessions. Keep them brief. As brief as five or ten minutes. It may hardly seem worth tacking up—but remember that at this stage with a green pony tacking up itself is still part of the training.

Mounting and dismounting, letting your legs rest normally against your pony's sides, letting him feel the movement of the bit in his mouth when you pick up your reins, tightening the girth from the saddle, adjusting your stirrup leathers while mounted—all can be part of his early lessons in backing. As the pony gets used to your weight and movements on his back and your legs against his sides, as his back and leg muscles strengthen under you, you can increase the time spent mounted. And of course two half-hour sessions a day are better than one overly long one. A green pony is frequently a young pony; and in any case he must not be overworked physically, mentally, or emotionally.

## WALKING

Now your pony has accepted you on his back. You are ready to start *riding* him! For added control, you may once again take advantage of the familiar and do this initial riding on the lunge line. Your decision whether to do this or to go directly to riding free—or to do a combination of both—may depend in part on your facilities. If you have nothing but huge open fields, work on the lunge line will give additional control and security for even the best rider at the beginning walk and trot. It has the disadvantage of keeping your pony working on a circle.

We've had no problem in going directly to free work even the first or second time mounted. However, your pony should work in some sort of enclosure, if possible one with at least visual limits such as trees at the edge of a field, or shrubs at the border of a yard. At High Hickory a pony trotting towards the puppy pen in the play yard "sees" something that will make him think "stop" before

For the first time Stardust and Robin work free under saddle. Both reveal tension and uncertainty. (Needless to say, adult supervision is right there!)

Six weeks later—what a difference in confidence and balance on the part of both pony and rider.

**Less than sixteen months later, ridden only by Robin, Stardust and her nine-year-old owner won their first pony hunter championship.**

the child rider asks him to. The ponies know well that the stretch from the puppy pen leads out the gate and on down the path into the woods, left to the meadow or right to the turnaround: the twelve-foot metal gate across this stretch can be closed and makes them *think* "stop," as well as providing a physical barrier. Even a track worn in the grass may provide a pony with a visual limit. But it is better to set up corners or side rails by resting bars on barrels or boards on pails; the psychological effect is as often as not beneficial to the rider as well. Because such devices limit areas where ponies can move on without stopping, the ponies expect to be told to

walk or to stop. By the time they are ridden where they can trot on endlessly—even around and around a ring—they are used to obeying their small riders and never get out of hand.

Wherever you ride, whether free or on the lunge line, the same principles apply. Right from the start work should be on a light almost loose rein with the rider's hands slightly farther apart than when riding a finished pony. Use an "open" rein so that the direction (or pressure) is towards your hip rather than towards your belt buckle. When you use one rein, give a little with the opposite rein.

Your green pony will be very much on his

forehand. He may travel with his head low. Do not attempt to raise it by pulling up or lifting with the reins. Your goal is a free, rhythmical walk with a low reaching-forward head carriage. As his condition as an athlete improves, he will bring his hocks in under him. He will come off his forehand and his head carriage will improve—but this will result from and must originate in impulsion from his rear end.

Possibly your pony will carry his head too high, becoming ewe-necked and concave-backed. Again, do not try to correct this forcibly. Forget about martingales and other such tie-down devices. Frequently this faulty head carriage is caused by nervous tension and immature development or weak muscles. (Not, we trust, by having had his mouth abused.) Again, this will usually disappear as your pony's coordination and muscular development improve and as you work with your hands and legs to encourage flexion and impulsion.

The only part of a martingale I like to use is the neck strap. Taken up by forefingers alone along with the reins, its tautness or slackness gives a clear indication of whether the rider's hands are steady at the trot. It can also be grabbed in case of trouble. Usually riders are told "Don't hang on" or "Let go of the mane." At High Hickory, a pony's mouth comes first, and a Pony Pal is often advised to try to keep his knuckles on his pony's neck or to pick up some mane or the neck strap.

Try to have very sensitive hands, to give "commands" by squeezing rather than pulling the reins. (Ça va sans dire! an experienced horseman will say; but youngsters have to be reminded.) Be quick to give when your pony gives. If he tosses his head, do not pull or jerk; rather, fix your hands; your pony soon learns that he is only fighting himself and that you give when he does. Remember that at a walk a pony uses his head and neck—just as you use your arms—to balance himself. You must "follow his mouth" if he is to move freely and evenly.

Your pony already associates moving with hand pressure behind his girth area and moves forward in hand and on the lunge on "Walk on." Under saddle, he will rapidly associate pressure from both legs given with voice commands to go forward and will soon walk on and later trot on willingly.

Start off with the least possible leg pressure. A light touch first, a firmer one if needed—always keeping in mind your long-range objective of a pony who will respond to signals imperceptible to an onlooker.

Let your pony know ahead of time that you are going to ask something of him. For instance, when you mount now do not let him move off until you are ready and ask him to. Take time to fix reins and stirrups and sit for a minute at a standstill. Then give the familiar command "Walk on" a fraction of a second before you give a preparatory indication with your hands—a slight squeeze on the reins to move the bit in his mouth and alert him that an order is coming. Almost simultaneously you will squeeze with your legs and give with your hands so that he can walk on as you ask it aloud again. Gradually you will eliminate the first and then the second voice command—and your pony will walk on conventional aids. Praise him with a "Good pony," not with a pat: you want the bit and the reins steady.

## HALT

The uneducated rider mistakenly thinks that to stop or halt you "pull on the reins." Rather, you should "fix" your hands and let your pony come up to them.

To ask your pony to stop, again give him warning with a set of signals fractions of seconds apart. Say "Ho." Close your hands on the reins and fix them (instead of following his mouth as his head and neck move in a balancing swing). Straighten your back, raise your chest, and sit into your saddle. Maintain your leg pressure close against his sides to bring him up against the bit, and he will stop as you say "Ho" again. His reward is your easing of your hand and leg; but do not let go of the reins or lean forward to pat him. Praise him with your voice only and maintain your halt.

If he has halted squarely, with all four legs evenly under you, let him stand for a minute (increase the length of pause each time) and then ask him to walk on (by reversing your aids: easing of the hands and pressure with the legs only enough to make him move forward).

Remember that in these early transitions from walk to halt, from halt to walk, soon from walk to trot, and so on, your pony may need a bit of time to "sort out his legs." His not obeying instantly is often not disobedience but rather his not being in the right physical posture to obey.

If you're an experienced rider you will know where each of your pony's legs is at each beat of the walk or trot. A child rider may not know that the walk is a four beat, but even beginners, informed that a trot is a diagonal gait in two-time, are aware of the strong beat as they count "Up, down, up, down" as they learn to post. Youngster and pony alike will benefit if the rider listens for the footfall of each gait as well as feels each step, and tries to figure out which foot is under, forward, or back. The only way to make what the Pony Pals call a "Thelwell halt"—true and square with "a leg at each corner"—is to know where those legs are. The time necessarily devoted to walking your green pony now can contribute to improve the rider as well as the pony.

You can work on halts in both directions, near a fence and away from it, until your pony comes to a halt from a walk and stands without moving until you ask him to move on. In early training your voice commands help; as he progresses you will omit them.

When your pony comes smoothly to a halt, you can begin work at the trot and, with the same aids, work on decreasing speed or on bringing him from a trot to a walk. In his early schooling do not bring him from a trot to a halt, but bring him down through a walk.

**Galaxy "rubbernecks" at a standstill. A pony can just as easily walk or trot on with his head turned away from the direction of movement.**

## CIRCLES

Once your pony is moving more steadily and responsively under you on the undemanding "straight" track of your ring or the edge of your field, you can begin to work him on large circles. ("Large" is of course relative under saddle as it was in lunging.)

A young rider may mistakenly think that turns and circles are made by the reins only and not understand the proper use of leg aids. Think of it this way: The early use of open reins is similar to use of the handlebars of a bike. When one hand comes back the other moves forward. The handlebars can turn completely at a standstill, spinning the front wheel fully, but the rest of the bike need not move. In like manner a pony's head can be turned, rubbernecking back, with rein alone, without his body's moving. The rider who has had his foot sniffed by a pony nosing back to the stirrup has first-hand knowledge of how flexible a pony's neck can be. You may have seen a true rubberneck forging stubbornly ahead with his nose yanked back to his shoulder while his rider vainly tries to turn him in another direction;

you may or may not have noticed that the rider's legs were jammed forward rather than applied correctly to demand a turn from the hindquarters.

It is because leg aids are so important in turning that you avoid making small circles or sharp turns till your pony learns what leg aids mean as he goes straight ahead. Since he has already learned to move over from hand pressure behind his girth area on either side, you can take advantage of his conditioned response as you apply leg aids to circle and turn.

Remember that a pony's body should always follow the line of direction: straight on a straight line, curved to the right on a circle to the right, curved to the left on a circle to the left—with his hind feet tracking his front. On a circle you should just see the inside eye as his forehand curves "ahead" of you. Slight pressure with an open inside rein will make this possible.[1] (Later you will maintain pressure on the outside rein as well; but for now, give a little.)

Just as on the lunge line, you want his hindquarters curved behind, not shifting in a straight line off the circle. To achieve this bend you will apply pressure with your inside leg against the girth and

1. (Remember that while *near* is always your pony's left and *off* his right, *inside* and *outside* depend on which way you're moving. *Inside* applies to the side towards the center of a circle or ring; *outside*, to the side away from the center or towards the fence if you have one. *Inside* and *outside*, therefore, change with every change of hand or direction.)

pressure with your outside leg behind it. This "wrapping your pony around your inside leg" keeps his hind feet tracking in the steps of his forefeet, and combined with proper rein maintains a body-long curve. Otherwise your pony could crook his head and neck but move around the circle with his body stiff as a board angling outward on a wider circumference. Many riders are not sensitive enough to feel this curve on a large circle; it is apparent to them only when they execute a small one. To the observer on the ground it is more obvious, for he can follow behind to see where the hind feet step. (The Pony Pals like to check their hoof prints when first riding on a rain-swept stretch of driveway or ring.)

You are beginning to use your legs more as you ride, and your pony may misunderstand them. If at any stage during work at the walk he breaks into a trot through loss of balance or excitement, don't overcorrect him. A calm voice command to walk and your seat still in the saddle—sit heavy, don't post—will probably be enough to settle him back down to a walk. Be sure you have not used too strong legs against his side. You want to keep them light so that his sides will not be deadened but continue to be sensitive.

If you have taken the edge off your pony by lunging him before mounted schooling, such an increase in speed or a change in gait is usually a self-saving error, not deliberate naughtiness or a desire to "take off." However, now as through all his past and future training, frequent halts and transitions to slower gaits will promote obedience and prevent him from thinking that, once started, he can just move on continuously at whatever speed and whenever he wants.

Your pony should still be working in a place that is at least "visually enclosed." Wherever you school, vary your routine. Don't always start or stop in the same place. If you always trot in one direction your pony will come to expect this and will trot before he is asked. He may also anticipate walking as he approaches certain visual limits; so that sometimes you should ask him to trot on. Clearly at times you take advantage of his anticipation; at other times you counteract it, depending on which course works to your benefit.

**Makeshift fencing temporarily indicates the boundaries of a ring and provides visual limits for both pony and rider.**

A reminder for young riders: In these early stages you must, as always, be careful about riding close to trees or fence posts or any obstacle you will have to circle or avoid. You cannot signal a green pony at the last moment and expect instant accurate obedience. Even a green pony will never bump himself—but even a wise old pony will not allow an extra inch or so for your knee—or for your head. With a green pony especially you must think ahead, must give him time—and room—to carry out your command. While a highly schooled horse could come from a trot to a walk precisely at point E in the dressage arena (see sketch), your green pony might take from halfway after K to halfway before H. He may be very willing, but simply not have the coordination or experience required for performing with finesse at this stage.

If keeping to work at a walk for some half-dozen sessions seems dull, bear in mind that throughout his entire career your pony's walk is going to be a most important gait. "Never underestimate the power of a walk!"—the Pony Pals parody. You want a walk that is free-striding, powerful from the hindquarters, rhythmical and smooth, not poky or slow. Such a walk can be developed during explora-tory excursions beyond your schooling area to keep your pony (and you) eager and fresh-minded. Older riders will appreciate that even top event horses and endurance horses work only at a walk for weeks at a time to "leg up" during early conditioning.

If you have an understanding riding companion, there's no limit to where you can take your pony now—up hill and down hill, over any sort of terrain. Of course you will have to avoid noncooperative riders like the plague. Don't expect your green pony to walk if your companions are the sort that ride along with you at a walk for a while and then go galloping off.

Like skiing and swimming, riding is a sport where some sort of buddy system should be practiced; and schooling is one phase of riding which should *never* be carried out alone. With a tiny child and a wee pony the "riding companion" may be a parent on foot. Adults or older riders on horse-gaited mounts may not want to be slowed down by a child on a middle-sized pony, and it's often unfair, if not unwise, to ask them to take the responsibility. The older child or small adult schooling a large pony is more likely to find others doing the same thing, so the problem of "responsibility" does not come up.

At High Hickory we're fortunate in having several paths with stonewall or post-and-rail limits where a small rider can "go out alone" and still be within sight and sound at a stage in schooling for a pony and riding for a child when it would not otherwise be safe to do so. But supervision, whether immediate or remote, means just that: Some responsible person must check, look, and listen regularly to see just what the youngster schooling alone is doing.

## THE HALF-TURN ON THE FOREHAND

The half-turn on the forehand, like the rein back, is done only from the halt.

"I just pretend Tuffy's Daddy's ship tied up by the bow and my leg's a tugboat pushing her stern over," Robin said years ago. I have used the comparison in teaching older children how to do a half-turn on the forehand. In this movement your pony moves his hindquarters in a 180-degree turn while pivoting on his forehand. He has been to some extent prepared for this by your using your hand against his side when you ask him to "Move over" in his stall or on the cross ties. Now, mounted, you want him to do it more precisely.

It is a movement done from a standstill. You, the rider, have to do several things at once: you have to prevent forward or backward movement, you have to create movement to one side only and with the hindquarters only, and you have to turn the pony's head ever so slightly in the direction in which he will eventually face. It will be easier if you work alongside a fence.

Halt your pony with your left side parallel to the fence, but about a pony-length from it: you don't want him to bump his nose as he pivots. You want him barely to move his front feet, pivoting on the right fore, and to move his rear by stepping with his left hind crossing in front of the right hind. After his half-turn on the forehand he will be facing in the opposite direction—his right side will be parallel to the fence. To accomplish this:

With both hands, prevent his moving forward while with a little more pressure of the left hand you bring his head slightly towards the fence. With your right leg close to the girth, apply enough pressure to prevent his stepping backwards. With your left leg, apply pressure behind the girth to move his hindquarters to the right, away from the fence.

**Practicing a half-turn on the forehand: purpose, to bring rider and pony parallel to sawhorse blocking a driveway.**

**Star, well surprise-proofed, calmly lets her rider pick up and move the sawhorse some distance.**

**Half-turns on the forehand come in handy when you want to open a gate easily without dismounting, as Eric does here.**

**Unless pony is parallel to the gate, the latch is a long awkward reach for a rider.**

At this stage in a green pony's training, the half-turn on the forehand is obvious in its exaggerated "cause and effect," "ask and receive." You ask, and your pony steps; you ask, and he moves. With an unschooled pony the most important thing for success is for you to ask—and *wait*. When you ask with your leg you must give your pony time to lift his left hind leg, to cross it forward and under him in front of his other hind leg, to put the weight on it, and then to shift his opposite hind leg.

He will be using muscles in his haunches and loins that he hasn't used before, and he will be moving in a sideways manner that is not "natural" to him. He must have time to assimilate your command and transfer it to his body. If you give him time, he will do so once he comprehends. But if you repeat your leg signal before he has had a chance to obey you he will move either backwards or forwards in confusion. Signal, wait, signal, wait will eventually become signal, step, signal, step, and your pony will have made a smooth, steady half-turn on the forehand. Once you have completed this movement, praise your pony and ask him to walk on in the new direction. Stop, and repeat the process in reverse. After a pause on completion, always end by walking on.

## THE REIN-BACK

The more common term for a rein-back is "backing up." The common picture is one of a rider sawing and yanking on the reins and the pony stiffening body and outstretched jaw in bewildered resistance—if he finally goes backwards, he moves with spraddled hind legs, his rump swinging from side to side.

This is a far cry from a correct rein-back. The importance of a relaxed jaw and low head carriage in backing is one reason why we don't teach it too early. However, you should now teach him to back a few steps without resistance, if not yet to back fluidly at dressage standard, for his safety and yours may at some time depend on his backing willingly and straight.

Teaching the rein-back is another time when your schooling is simplified by working in a corner of your ring (or at least beside a building) with fencing directly in front of as well as alongside your pony to provide a psychological directional signal. It is also one of the few times when we would use a crop. Most of all, it is another time when your pony's intelligent trust enters in: you are asking, not forcing, him to back.

If you are schooling your pony alone, work on foot first. Stand facing the same way as your pony. Hold the reins under his jaw with your right hand as if you were leading him. Maintain constant light pressure on them. But at no time, now or ever in a rein-back, do you pull. If you have already taught your pony to back on voice command, he will do so on "Back." If not, now with your other hand or with the crop tap his chest in light staccato fashion and say "Back!" (One school of thought advocates tapping the

forelegs, but that can sting and be painful to the pony.)

Just as you will with your hands and legs when you are in the saddle, you are asking your pony to move but not letting him move forward. Since your hand does not yield (and the fence and wall are there to enforce it) the only way he can move is backwards.

Be satisfied with any movement backwards. Praise him and ask him to "Ho." Immediately walk on. (Always end a rein-back with a few steps forward.)

Teaching the rein-back may be easier if you realize that your pony moves his legs in diagonal combinations. "You mean, when he backs up, he walks backwards at a trot?" a Pony Pal puzzled aloud; then added: "It does sound like two beats, not four, if you listen."

Achieving a rein-back is also easier if you do it from only the briefest of halts at first. After a long standstill your pony is "set"—feet rooted to the ground!—and must be warned that "something is coming." If you are ever asked to back for a judge after a long line up in the show ring, remember to "wake your pony up" by subtly moving the bit in his mouth to prepare him for your command. Note too that to move his legs correctly in alternate pairs your pony must be balanced so as to step back with one hind as he steps back with the diagonally opposite foreleg. (Actually, the hind moves a split second earlier.)

If you have an assistant, you can do the rein-back mounted, your helper close by to tap your pony's chest if asked.

With reins adjusted so there is gentle tension, close your hands. (Do not pull!) Sit deep into your saddle, straighten your back, and apply equal pressure with both legs against the pony's sides. Say "Back!"

By now, of course, your pony associates your leg aids with moving forward. But in this lesson, with any movement forward he comes up against your hands. When this happens in the halt, you cease the leg pressure. Now you continue it. Your pony may sidle or shift his rump sideways—or he may step backwards. If he backs, praise him, and reward him by ceasing.

If he does not move backwards, continue asking from the saddle while your helper now gives two or three light taps. Your pony will move. Don't be concerned about sideways motion. Once he gets the idea that going backwards is what's expected you can straighten him out, as long as you are initially satisfied with only a step or two in the right—backwards—direction. Now halt him and walk on. After a few strides forward, halt and ask for a rein-back again.

In future lessons you can correct movement to one side by stronger application of your leg, slightly farther back, just as you can direct him to either side if you want him to back other than in a straight line.

Should your pony thrust his jaw out or raise or twist his head, forget about backing for the present. Your insistence might lead to his balking or jibing or even half-rearing and wheeling. Recognize these first signs of confusion or uncertainty—they are unlikely to be signs of stubbornness, but that may develop if you don't know when to stop. For the time being, create a situation where you can praise him: ask him to go forward (he understands that) and end your schooling on a good note.

Of course, you can teach a pony to back on a loose rein (or a lead rope) by using your crop severely on his forelegs. Ponies "taught" in this way practically run backwards on a loose rein—but they would still resist if *asked* properly to back. If your pony resists when you give him his first formal lesson, spend some more time on the walk and the halt; then when he understands your aids better, has a better foundation, return to work on the rein-back.

## MOUNTED WORK AT THE TROT

Since your pony is already fit from daily work on the lunge line, he will soon toughen up under a rider, but keep this additional burden in mind during the first few mounted sessions. Then, depending on your progress at a walk, you can go on to work at a trot.

Your green pony may seem to have better balance right from the start of work at the trot than he did at a walk, partly because of your mounted schooling at the walk, partly because at the trot he always has a diagonal pair of legs under him for support. Unless he misbehaves and you want the additional control of weight in the saddle by sitting to the trot, it's easier on him if you post.

Of course you will change diagonals with regularity. Even if your pony seems distinctly rougher at one diagonal than another, do not favor the smoother one or you will further develop the difference. Youngsters may think of diagonals as reserved for horse shows, something to be marked on a judge's score card, not for ordinary riding: but horsemen conscientiously alternate whenever they post. In ring work you can post to the outside diagonal, but which you use does not matter so long as you are consistent. It helps if you pick up the desired diagonal at a trot before you start to post. You will also find when circling that your inside leg moves less against the saddle if you're on the correct diagonal.

Initially at the trot you will still want your pony's neck low and his head reaching forward. As he moves, he will carry them slightly higher than at a walk, and steadier. Because of this, your hands will be steady, with no slack in the reins. Contact and collection will come later.

Put your pony into a trot from a walk, not from a halt. As you walk, let him know you are going to ask something of him by a slight shortening of the reins. This will move the bit in his mouth and prevent sloppy reins at the higher head carriage of the trot. Now your hands give slightly as you apply increased pressure behind the girth with both legs and simultaneously give the familiar voice command Trot! Sit into your saddle for a minute; then, as the pony strikes off into a trot, pick up your diagonal and post on.

Should your pony become excited by this faster pace and by your movement on his back, reassure him with your voice. Ease him back into a walk by fixing your hands, keeping your legs steady against his sides, and sitting back deep into the saddle as you say "Walk!" Let him have a little extra rein, and walk on. If you do not feel secure about giving him extra rein, you can give him the same feeling he would have with extra rein if you ride with the reins still short but your hands farther forward than usual.

Throughout this schooling be lavish with voice praise. Keep pats and carrots for breaks in the schooling session, as you don't want to let go of the reins and upset the pony's balance while you are working. Follow the same program you did at a walk: trotting on straight stretches, walking on curves, lots of transitions from trot to walk to halt, and the reverse. Go to large circles at the trot (half the paddock space), to the diagonals of the ring at a trot, to the length of the center line at a trot—turning left one time and right another. Always give your pony time to obey your commands and, remember, avoid doing anything so routinely that the pony anticipates it—or gets bored. Continue to vary ring work (whether your "ring" is a dressage arena, a paddock, or a field) with work in the open, in company. Nothing will dull or sour a pony, green or finished, more than sheer routine without a change of scenery.

Throughout his schooling, one reward that your pony will truly appreciate will be the walk on a free rein which, while not allowing him to drag along like a dullard, gives him the full use of his head and neck. If you do not yet feel secure riding almost on the buckle, you can still give him this amount of freedom by bridging one rein so that you can shorten up quickly if need be.

Of course from his point of view the best reward is probably the end of the lesson, when he is untacked, cleaned, and turned loose. In fact many ponies are so eager for this reward that they try to head back to the barn or leave the schooling area whenever they're near the gate. As a trick to avoid this annoyance, the Pony Pals tack up but do not mount in the paddock. They lead their ponies to the riding area and mount there. When they are finished they halt facing away from the exit, dismount, run up stirrups, loosen girths, and then lead their ponies back to the barn. They also make a point of riding past the barn without stopping during a lesson. We also try not to ride a pony just before feeding, when his mind is especially likely to be on food, and we avoid making those gourmet sounds of graining that set up Mess Call whinnies among the resting ponies that might tempt a working pony to misbehave. By such machinations, you can keep your ponies from being either barn- or herd-bound. They would be impossible of course in a highly organized, tightly scheduled stable: one advantage of having a pony in your own back yard is flexibility.

At High Hickory, when a green pony is ready to be ridden "outside," off our hill and possibly in strange company, we provide one or two emergency brakes.

Even the most experienced rider needs more than a snaffle on an unmade pony in case the unexpected makes his mount take off. With a large pony we may put a second snaffle rein through a running martingale and attach it to the bit rings below the regular rein. This second or emergency rein may be carried like a curb rein, slightly looser than the snaffle in use, or it may be knotted and lie free on the pony's neck ready to grab if needed. In either case the martingale is thus brought into play only if needed. (An interesting commentary on this

**Still without a bridle, but with an "emergency brake" attached to the halter, pony and rider prepare to ride outside the playyard. Border Collies, waiting patiently with Pony Pal Susie, provide surprise-proofing against dogs encountered cross-country.**

device is that we once tried it on a teething pony whose bars were so sensitive that she could not stand the additional weight on her gums. She tossed her head and fussed until what had seemed to us an insignificant increase in weight was removed.)

The other device is more economical and more convenient in that it fits a pony of any size, even the tiniest. It consists of an ordinary dog choke chain, a small piece of string, and a rein-long piece of clothesline. We tie the center of the chain to the center of the bridle noseband, slip the ends under the cheek straps, and fasten the clothesline to the large end rings now under the pony's chin. This is similar in action to a chain lead shank over your pony's nose for work in hand, and is not to be used lightly. The dog chain has the advantage over a running martingale in that it does not play on the bars of your pony's young mouth. Again, the line may be held along with your snaffle rein as a curb rein would be or it may be short enough to lie, knotted or unknotted, on the pony's neck ready to be pulled on if necessary.

In our sixteen years of schooling ponies at High Hickory I can't recall either of these emergency brakes ever being put to use: perhaps because of the very fact that they were available. (They made for conditions in which they weren't needed; knowledge that "help" was there made for a relaxed rider and therefore a relaxed pony.) But just as you wisely go to a stronger bit when you hunt even the mildest pony for the first time, so you wisely go prepared with an unmade pony. The best emergency device, however, is thorough schooling and "surprise-proofing"—which is what this book is all about.

By now your pony is "legged up" and "backed up" to his rider's weight and is fit for longer periods of mounted schooling. As always, his feed should be proportioned to the amount of work he is doing, with allowance for feed for growth as well as for energy. (See Chapter 5.) You should find that the more you work your pony the more fit he becomes. Since it thus becomes almost impossible to "work a pony down," the need continues to take the edge off him before mounted work. Whereas previously you have used lunging as a means of schooling in itself, you now use it mainly as a safety device; it's a way for the pony to let off steam. If you "lunge" him free in his paddock, you must draw a clear line between chasing him around (possibly, heaven forbid, by throwing something at him) and making him move free on voice and whip command. You must not ruin a trusting pony that comes willingly when called by deliberately using threats to achieve this action.

The pony that has been thus active does not need quite the warming-up period at a walk when first mounted that the pony just out of a stall does. You may go more directly to work at a trot, thus eliminating the freshness some ponies show at the start of a training session. Try to keep it a slow trot by slowing your posting. If the pony remains over-eager, small frequent circles will help settle him down. Such circles, turns, and changes of direction require him to pay attention to you and to his own balance, so he's less likely to "build up steam" than if he were moving on one long stretch. If your pony is one that is excited by trotting, settle him with work at a walk: and always intersperse trotting with walking and halts.

Gradually you will spend more and more of your schooling session at the trot, and you will no longer use such an open rein. You will begin to ask your pony to take a feel on the bit. Instead of letting all his motion or power "run out at the front" as it seems to in the early stages when he moves with a low, stretched neck, you now continue to ask for it from his rear (with your legs and seat), but hold it in at the front (with your hands). The young pony that seemed (and was) overloaded on his forehand will begin to have better head and neck carriage as he corrects his weight distribution from the rear.

If he carries his head too high, it may be that he has stiffened his jaw. Little squeezes of your hands on the reins will help him relax but you must be quick to respond to his dropping his nose and flexing at the poll. (Pony Pals get the idea of how to squeeze by practicing on old tennis balls.) In the opposite vein, your pony may start hanging on the bit instead of carrying it lightly in his mouth. You will need to keep your hands very light but steady, a little high; but do not try to pull his head up. Use *your* legs and seat more strongly to make him use *his* legs more strongly—and farther in under him.

Do not spend any session merely nagging away on points of refinement, however. If you are a serious older rider, you may work with more finesse and patience and have only your pony's reaction to consider. If you're helping a younger rider, you have his retention span of interest in such fine points as flexion and contact to consider as well as the pony.

While this elementary work on the flat is progressing, other important aspects of your pony's education are being undertaken as well. (See Chapter 10 on Surprise-Proofing again.) Thus many of the problems often associated with schooling a green pony are avoided or solved.

Remember that some of these problems—shying, bucking, balking, or rearing—may be caused not by meanness or freshness or fear. They may be caused by your making too great demands. Remember that sweating is often a sign of stress. Nervous sweating may mean that a pony is being pushed beyond his powers of endurance. Where some ponies try to speak up by acting up, other ponies never openly rebel, but their bodies reveal their inner tensions. Just as you strive to bring a pony in cool after any ride, so you want to *keep* your pony cool *during* a workout. Learn to distinguish between his being hot from judicious exercise and the day's temperature and his being "in a lather" from nervous and mental if not physical fatigue. As with a child who's big for his age, you must remember that a green pony—however big or well-developed—is still an adolescent.

## MOUNTED WORK AT THE CANTER

Long before you even have a pony, galloping cross-country is a thrill you dream of, or perhaps your dreams are of peaceful hacks along a stream or slow canters through daisied fields. Riding in the open—off the limits of the lunge line, beyond the confines of paddock or ring—is a goal you work towards from the time you first start mounted schooling.

When to start riding in the open? That depends as much on your riding setup as on your particular pony's temperament and progress. At High Hickory we've always started green ponies in the open right from the start, but three factors help determine this: (1) Unusually, in our immediate neighborhood open riding is *safe*. (2) We buy a pony, not to train quickly and resell, but for one particular child; and since we want the pony to "last" we do not rush his education but think in terms of four years, eight years—not four months, eight months. (3) There's a supervising adult with interest, experience, time, and energy to devote to pony activities.

If in your neighborhood the only safe riding territory is a field or ring, then that is where you should ride until your pony is well schooled. If you have riding country within safe access of the barn, you can ride in the open as soon as you feel secure at a walk or trot. At a walk or trot—because that is all you will do in the open at this early stage. However, you can ride endlessly, anywhere, if you keep at a walk.

To say "Keep at a walk" is simple; but with a green pony it is good sense, not cowardice, to worry about his taking off and even running away; and of course ponies never run away with a rider at a walk or a trot. They run away at an extended canter or gallop. Therefore, even though a pony is not ready for sustained schooling at a canter and though he wears one of the "emergency brakes" suggested above, both he and his rider together should be given some brief experience at the canter, early on. There will be certain psychological advantages. Beginning riders consider learning to canter a high point in education, and beginning trainers may regard mounted schooling at the canter in the same light. A brief pretaste of the canter under controlled conditions will serve to reassure novice riders and novice trainers alike. For it helps to know that a canter is no cause for excitement or speeding or trouble and that if you train your pony properly he will obey at this gait as at any other.

Before you request it of him, your pony may break into a canter spontaneously during your mounted work at a walk or a trot. He may do it merely to

regain balance lost because of poor footing or because of his rider's shifting. Don't make an issue of this. Allow him enough strides to shift back into a trot. If he continues to canter, do not pull him down with the reins but rather fix your hands, keep your weight in the saddle with your shoulders back, and repeat "Trot!" in your usual tone of voice. If necessary you can slightly close his leading shoulder with a light squeeze on that particular rein. Be quick to post on as he resumes his trot. You do not want to fuss over his unauthorized canter but neither do you want to stop his work forward or pull him down to a walk.

Overreaction to mistakes or misbehavior of this sort calls attention to a casual act which was not intended to be naughty, and your displeasure may set up a defiant attitude in the pony. You must be tolerant about occasional deviations. But you have to learn to detect the difference between what the Pony Pals call "Testing. One, two,—" on the part of a pony and a good-natured skip for joy. The former needs an unemotional "No, no" so it doesn't develop into an equine nosethumbing; the latter, if simply ignored, is something from which any vivacious four-legged youngster will himself settle down— and you do want a pony that has some spirit! A relaxed attitude on your part will keep your pony from associating the canter with defiance in his one-track mind, and when you are ready to school him at the canter he will be as nonchalant about it as he is about walking or trotting.

## A PREVIEW OF CANTERING

Now, for the first time, you are going to tell your pony to canter. From your lunging and riding you know about leads and the importance of being on the correct one when cantering. And of course you must know the aids to obtaining these leads before you can school a green pony to canter. The schooling session that is also a riding lesson for a green child who has not learned to ride on a schooled mount can be total confusion for a green pony.

You may choose to canter your pony, this first time, in the ring on a circle—the conventional place for a lesson. But you need not. You may equally well choose a quiet path in the woods. Personally, I prefer such a path—a long gentle uphill stretch. Free ponies tend to canter rather than trot uphill, and learning to canter there seems a more natural and relaxed experience than a lesson in the ring.

If there are visual limits ahead to help you bring

the pony down to a walk easily after a short distance, so much the better. Don't choose a path that opens up into a wide, gallop-inviting field. At High Hickory we use a favorite T path. How many times I've waited at the junction, on foot when a small child is schooling a tiny pony, mounted when another is schooling a larger pony. Along with the seeming dead end of the path, I myself form another "visual bound." My familiar voice can reinforce the rider's commands. If need be, I can move forward to block the path (though I have never yet had to do so).

At last, you are going to tell your pony to canter. He already obeys the voice command on the lunge. Two things—that conditioned response and his natural preference for cantering rather than trotting uphill—work in your favor now as you order your first "Canter!"

Since you are going to put him into a canter on the straight, not a curve or circle, it does not matter which lead you go on. Nevertheless, you still have to ask for either a right or a left, so from the beginning use the aids which you will employ when a specific lead is required. Here again it does not matter which aids are used: lateral (left hand, left leg) or diagonal (left hand, right leg).

To say it does not matter is not to evade the issue. For decades authorities have argued as to which method is better—to start a green horse with one and switch to the other, or to start with one and stick with it. Really, consistency is what matters. (After all, if you are consistent about it you can condition your pony to canter every time you pull his ear or tap his shoulder!)

For this first canter under saddle, you'll want your pony eager—not over fresh and full of bucks, but not tired from a long mounted workout. Plan this new step for the middle of your schooling session.

Walk out towards your chosen hilly path and some distance ahead pick a point of departure. Plan your course. (Plan to ask the pony to canter at such and such a white birch, for instance, and to bring him down to a trot again by the time you reach that fallen pine.) Do not expect to have the canter depart from a walk as you will in later schooling. At this time, be prepared to get it from a sitting trot.

As you walk on, pick up your reins in the familiar "something is coming" warning to your pony. Up till this moment, this preliminary form of collecting your pony at a walk has been followed by your signal to trot. Now, as you push forward into a sitting trot, it will be followed almost immediately by your canter signal. Whether you use aids diagonally or laterally, the important thing for your pony's understanding is that you now use one hand and one leg more strongly, not with equal emphasis as in your trot signal. As you apply these aids, you give your voice command "Canter!"—and let your pony move on.

He may quite likely continue forward at a trot. Do not bring him down to a walk (as you will in more advanced lessons), but do not post. Posting would indicate that you meant him to trot. Instead, keep sitting and repeat your canter aids as he moves on. If he now canters, praise him and encourage him to continue, repeating the command he obeys on the lunge line. He may canter faster than desired, but follow his mouth and do not try to check him. After ten or twelve strides more stop using your canter aids and give your voice command "Trot." Sit deep, upper body back, and repeat "Trot" until he changes back.

If you sit quietly as your pony canters so that you don't excite him with banging legs and bouncing body, he will willingly come back to the trot. Should he seem to take hold or pull and refuse to return to the trot without fuss, you have the visual limits of the end of your path and/or your assistant waiting ahead. You have also the effective voice command "Ho!" which you (and your assistant) can use sharply indeed. But remember: "Ho" is an emergency device. Don't misuse it. Do not say "Ho" unless you want and are going to insist on a full halt. If you want a walk or a trot, say "Walk" or "Trot." "Ho" does not mean slow down. It means "Ho: Stop, and stay stopped"—and must never be used to mean anything else. As a last resort, you have another emergency brake, the device we suggested your green pony wear in the open. But it's most unlikely that it will be needed.

Remember, the pony will need time and room to come down from his canter to a trot. Give him time. Trot on smartly a few steps. Then ask him to walk. "Good Pony!"

Now walk back, in a roundabout way if possible, to the start of your slope, and canter again. If your pony went into a canter the first time, use the same aids you did then, requesting the same lead. If you now succeed again, it may be that this is your pony's favored lead—and/or that you applied the aids when his hind leg was in the right position for him to strike off on that particular lead. A third time, ask for the opposite lead.

If your pony did not canter the first time and does not go into a canter the second time on the same aids, go quietly back to your starting point and try this time with the aids for the opposite lead. He may favor and go into that lead more readily.

Just as the pony may favor one lead and be stiff on the other, so may you, as far as giving the aids goes—influenced perhaps by your right- or left-handedness. This inequality, along with checking on diagonals at the trot, is something to guard against in working in the open. Later, you will work equally on both leads; if anything more on the one your pony favors less. For the present accept the one he prefers and use the aids you give most readily. What you want just now is a few short canters so that you can bring him back to a walk.

If you have difficulties in putting your green pony into a canter, they may be those you would have with a well-schooled pony. Perhaps you gave a clear canter signal, but did not release the pony with your hands so that he could move forward in response. Perhaps you gave up just when he was finally about to go into a canter, and therefore jerked on the reins so that he certainly did not go into it. (Be a little more patient. If necessary steady your hands with the neck strap or a bit of mane, as jabbing his mouth will truly confuse and discourage him.) Perhaps you did not ask for a canter on your chosen lead when the opposite hind leg was under you and did not apply your leg behind the girth strongly enough. A review of what to watch for when asking your pony to canter on the lunge will clarify the timing of aids with footwork for which you must strive.

Just as on the lunge, although you go into your canter from a trot you do not want it achieved by forcing your pony so fast through the trot that he falls into a canter from loss of balance. If he gets upset or excited, stop trying to make him canter. Walk. You can try again another day. Make it clear that the walk is the gait you now want, and praise him. Walk home. End your ride on a good note.

If he has cantered for you, do the same thing!

Your purpose in this preview has not been to teach the pony to canter. It has been to teach him to come back from a canter and to be reassured, yourself, that he will do so.

If your pony is still not ready in regular schooling sessions for anything but work at a walk or a trot, you will continue at those gaits only. It may be some weeks or months before you school at the canter. But thanks to this preview of cantering, whenever you extend your horizons by rides in the open where you intend to keep at a walk, you can do so confident that an occasional break into a canter is no cause for alarm.

## REGULAR SCHOOLING AT THE CANTER

What if your pony is ready, in terms of physical maturity and preliminary training, for serious work at the canter? You can now work on this gait as you have on walking and trotting, with emphasis on your pony's going when and where and for as long as you ask and not otherwise. School as you did on trotting so that he does not think that, once under way, he just keeps on going; so that he is alert and aware of the possibility that you may at any moment ask him to come back to a trot or a walk.

If you do not have a ring and are doing all your schooling in the open, you must constantly school so that the canter does not become synonymous with excitement or speed. You must make certain now that the pony remains calm and does not anticipate a canter, by never cantering the same stretch repeatedly or in the same manner. If schooling regularly on your special path, never canter from beginning to end. One day walk half way, then canter; the next day canter half way, then walk; another day, walk part way, canter, trot, or walk the rest of the way. You are still not concerned about eliminating the intervening trot before or after the canter. What you are striving for is a pony that goes into the canter—and out of it—as relaxed and willingly as a walk or a trot.

What if you have no path or safe schooling area in the open, and for that or for some other reason prefer to school your pony to the canter in your ring or paddock? Again, you have choices: briefly to introduce the canter with emphasis on coming back to a trot and walk; or to school routinely either with a "free" rider and pony or with rider and pony on the lunge line.

If your green pony is small like our thirty-nine inch Tuffy or eleven hand Galaxy, with a correspondingly little and very young rider, you will almost certainly choose to do mounted ringwork for the canter (as earlier for the walk and trot) with your pair on the lunge line. Although the pony will be bridled under his lunging gear, the rider should steady his hands with neck strap or mane, keeping only the lightest pressure on the outside rein. No matter how good the rider may be the lunge line should be fastened to the cavesson or halter, not to the bit. (You know ways of fastening the line to the bit, but this is not a time to use them.)

For the first few times cantering on the lunge, your rider should be strictly a passenger. He must sit passively while you, the handler in the center, put the pony into a canter. Simultaneously you both should give the voice command "Canter!" (This carries over into later sessions when, still on the lunge, the rider uses both voice and conventional aids.)

After a few "passenger" sessions, the child can become a rider and coincide his use of leg and hand aids to start and stop cantering with your commands. Eventually, still on the lunge line, he only will give all commands. Although from the center you could keep the pony going indefinitely at a center, from now on it is the rider who must get the results. Your main role is to supervise and to provide the additional control and safety of the lunge line.

Emphasis is on the pony's cantering calmly and *coming back* to a trot and a walk. Thanks to unmounted schooling on the lunge, he goes readily into the correct leads. As in all cause/effect situations, his quick association of the familiar correct lead with the new signal his rider gives from the saddle works to your advantage in mounted work when off the lunge.

Since a small pony's strides are short even at the canter, you can enable your little rider to canter on a large circle by following around on an inner circle as you lunge. (See the section on lunging in the preceding chapter.) You can follow this lunge line technique of schooling the pony-under-rider with any size pony, of course. We have found it a safe, successful way to start regardless of the rider's size or age. After several sessions on the lunge, when control and confidence are established, rider and pony work free in the traditional manner.

What if, skipping the step above, you are going directly to free mounted schooling at the canter in a ring or paddock? The advantages of your pony's cantering on voice command on the correct lead on the lunging circle still carry over. If you wish you can do limited introductory work for safety's sake in preparation for walks in the open; or with a pony ready in terms of age, physical development, and basic preparation you can do free mounted work on this gait regularly.

Certain locations in your ring are strategic spots at which to put your pony into a canter easily on the desired lead. Instinctively he canters on the inside lead on a curve—inside foreleg leading so that the outer leg will not cross in front of it and trip him. If you are moving on a circle, theoretically any point is equally useful—but if you are making your circle at the end of your ring, three sides of your fence make certain spots visually more helpful: i.e., any point at which you are moving into an enclosed curve, or when you are circling into the end of your ring, not out of it.

Marking your enclosure, be it field, paddock, ring, or arena, with the internationally accepted dressage letters will give you a frame of reference understood and used by most horsemen. More important, the letters will be routinely useful in schooling and right now will serve to pinpoint these favorable locations for an easy canter depart.

The Pony Pals have used various makeshift portable markers. They have painted the letters on red pails and plastic cider jugs. They have propped lettered boards against rocks, trees, or sticks driven into the ground. They have ridden to a generous neighbor's grassy ring with a knapsack full of corrugated-cardboard squares painted and punched with loops of string to hang over fence posts and remove at the end of the session. You could use pieces of white rag or people's jackets—anything to stand out as you ride around. The standard (and apparently illogical) location of these unalphabetically placed letters and future references will be plainer if you "let your fingers do the walking" on the explanatory diagram.

These spots are best when you are putting your pony on to the correct lead: on to a right lead, H and F when tracking to the right; on to a left lead, M and K when tracking to the left. If you go diagonally from F to H, you can put your pony on to the right lead at H; diagonally from M to K, on to the left lead at K. If you go diagonally from H to F, you can put your pony on to the right lead at F; diagonally from K to M, on to the left lead at M. In nonalphabetical terms, you can put your pony on to the correct lead in the direction you are about to circle or turn towards, at the point where you start your turn or curve.

Now at last you are in the saddle, your pony relaxed and responsive under you at the middle of your daily schooling session. You are ready to ask a first canter on command of him.

```
                          C


          H-                                        -M




          E-                    X                   -B




          K-                                        -F


                          A
```

Moving down the long side of your ring tracking to the left, you will want a canter on the left lead. You decide in advance to request your canter at M. Pick up your trot on the opposite side and as you come out of the curve at F go into a sitting trot. At B, ask more strongly with your legs and seat than you give with your hands, and just as you enter the curve at M give your pony your canter signal and simultaneously your voice command Canter! Give with your hands and move with him as he strikes off into a canter. Praise him and repeat "Canter, good boy, Canter."

If he goes into the wrong lead (was the proper hind leg under him as you applied your aids?) or canters disunited (were you forcing and letting him move on so fast that he just sprawled into a canter?) bring him quietly back to a trot. Let him know that "trot" is what you now want, and praise him for obeying.

Now try for a canter again. Trot on to F, and between B and M prepare and ask for your canter. Remember that, as with most aids, you do not apply them in one, two, three order but almost simultaneously.

Again, when the pony canters praise him. If he is on the correct lead, continue cantering on a large circle (about half the width of the arena). You must be sensitive enough to feel whether or not he is going to break back into a trot—and, equally important, whether or not your urging him on with canter aids and voice command is going to *keep* him cantering. At this beginning stage it is more expedient to *tell* him to trot rather than vainly attempt to continue his canter. For these first few times you may be satisfied with even a few strides of the canter, but never with letting him trot if you are telling him to canter. Just as you are concerned with his coming quietly down to a trot from a canter, so you are concerned with his going into a canter more than with his maintaining it. The maintaining it will come.

While working on a circle makes it easier to put the pony into a canter and keep him at a canter on the correct lead, the circle should be as large as possible. The smaller the circle in proportion to his size, the greater is the strain on your pony—even more now that he is cantering with weight on his back than when he was lunging unmounted—and the more difficult it is for him to move on the curve with his entire body curving in proper alignment.

In future sessions, vary cantering on the full circle with cantering the curve at the end of your ring and continuing down the straight to the beginning of the next curve.

Here come back to a trot, posting around this curve and down the stretch out of it. Part way down the straight, go into a sitting trot and at the beginning of the curve go into a canter. At the end of the curve this time come back to a sitting trot and then walk around the ring. Change direction, and after a rewarding period of relaxation on a loose rein work on a canter on the opposite lead.

Later in your schooling program you can move on a rough figure eight, working at a trot on the diagonals of the ring and asking for a canter as you go into the curve at each end. (At a later stage yet—much later—you will round off this rough figure eight so that it consists of two contiguous circles at the meeting of which you will come to a half-halt and make your change of leads.)

Now, as you ask your green pony to come back to the trot, use a softly resisting hand, one that no longer follows but is still. Just as no turn is made by hands alone, neither is any transition to a slower gait: you must also convey to your pony through your back (raise your chest), your seat (your weight in the saddle and your shoulders back!) and your legs (closed lightly against his sides) the fact that you want him to stop cantering.

Since you are keeping the actual amount of cantering down, break up your training periods with review of work already mastered: stopping on "Ho"; standing at a square halt; not moving on when being mounted or dismounted; walking, turning, and trotting on nicely in hand. Learning new material is very demanding on a young pony; he may find a brief spell of cantering coupled with work at the sitting trot (more tiring than a posting trot) as exhausting now as a much longer period will be later on. By way of reward he will be gratified, more than by a pat, by a loose rein and the opportunity to stretch and relax his neck.

Let your pony know that you are pleased with small successes. As he learns to go smoothly into a canter and out of it when, where, and as you ask, his understanding of what you want will grow. So also will his ability to maintain the canter on either lead as long as you demand. For him to maintain a relaxed rhythmical gait without hanging on the bit, it is important that you follow his mouth with light hands. If you do not feel at ease working on a long rein, you can use a shorter one but make the necessary adjustment by keeping your hands low and forward, quick to give when the pony flexes and relaxes his jaw.

Should your pony show a tendency to rush at the canter, you can slow him down by working on successive circles along your ring. To make a circle at each letter, while not requiring a change of lead as would work on a serpentine or figure eight, demands his full attention and will take his mind off simply going full speed ahead.

Since the canter has a three-beat footfall, you do not want to hear or feel a fourth. Correct such a fault by obtaining more impulsion (asking for more with your seat and legs but not "letting it run out the front end" with your hands) or by bringing the pony back to the trot and starting over again.

As your pony's understanding of your hand and leg aids increases at the canter and slower gaits, your use of all voice commands in mounted work should decrease. Eventually they will be eliminated entirely. Your aids will become more and more subtle and imperceptible to the onlooker; your transitions will become smoother, with no upward movement of the pony's head.

When you come down from a canter to a trot, keep your pony moving forward strongly. Don't let him change from a canter to a sloppy trot that fizzles out into a poky walk. Make a smooth transition into a good steady trot and only after moving on make a smooth transition to a good brisk walk. A young rider may have to be reminded of this frequently.

Young riders (and old ones, too), at the canter particularly, sometimes tell their ponies one thing with their hands and another with their legs. In reaction the pony with sensitive sides may take off with too much speed and seem hard to stop or control. The pony with a sensitive mouth may stop, lug on the bit, or start throwing his head up, and seem hard to make go. Occasionally a small pony is so sweet-natured that rather than act up in confused resentment against the conflicting commands of rough hands and banging legs he develops a protective insensitivity and merely plods along. In the case of the "cute baby pony" bought to "grow up with" a child, this is fortunate for the safety of a novice rider, if hard on the poor pony. But if the child is able to improve in skill in such an unlikely situation, frustration lies in store, for the pony will be indifferent when in time he feels a more properly applied leg or hand aid. The child then resorts to a crop or to deliberate kicking, and another undesirable situation results.

A young rider needs regular instruction on another, schooled mount, especially if his own pony is green, just as a top horseman seeks out coaching in a situation where he can concentrate on how he is doing, not on what he is asking his mount to do. However expert parental supervision may be, a young rider—and therefore his pony—will benefit from periodic instruction under an impartial, disinterested outsider.

Brief schooling sessions keep both children and ponies eager and hard working. Slumping and yawning are a sign of overtaxation in the child, as are dragging hind quarters, scuffing hooves, and a concave back in the pony. Such a collapse during transitions or after a canter calls for a change of activity or scenery so that neither rider nor pony will go sour.

To maintain steadiness in your pony and self-confidence in his rider, work at the canter should be interspersed casually with work at the trot. With larger ponies and bigger children it's easy to forget that schooling still involves green ponies and children. The supervising adult must realize that while an older child may be sophisticated enough to hide trepidation, trepidation may exist. It has helped more than one rider (young and old) to learn, often with some disbelief, that famous professionals often feel similar "butterflies in their stomach" when working a green horse and are not ashamed to admit it.

We must never overface either a young pony or a young rider. If your child feels insecure schooling at a canter, let him school longer at a walk and a trot. The pony too will benefit, since a tense rider cannot develop a relaxed mount. As confidence at one pace grows so will readiness for progress at another. If a child (or pony-riding adult) feels tense and fearful and shows it by impatience or anger or bullying his pony, he may not be ready for the work he is trying to do.

A nonriding parent whose riding child is being supervised by someone else should be aware that if his child shows irritation or displays of temper directed at pony, family, or inanimate objects it may be because he is afraid. Riding parents with aspirations for their child's prowess and vicarious pleasure in it may have to make a special effort to be receptive and open about such a possibility and to realize that even an apparently communicative child may not admit to fear if questioned directly—especially if he feels that his parents and siblings will look down on him if they know.

Sometimes of course fits of irritation and temper are a by-product of a completely unrelated problem involving school, friends, family. Vented on the pony, they require solution elsewhere. So long as that problem remains to torment the child, his relations with his pony should be ones of love and fun—only. He should not be involved in the more demanding, mature relation of schooling. For his own well-being and self-respect as well as for the pony's sake, he should not be allowed to take his frustrations out on the pony.

This perhaps sounds moralizing and irrelevant to schooling ponies. But over years of work with many youngsters and many ponies I have found that it is impossible to separate consideration of the youngster as a rider from consideration of the youngster as a child, in his working with ponies.

Such problems as parents must watch for in children, older riders have to watch for in themselves. It's understandable to be out of sorts because of a low physics grade in college, an unjustified reprimand from the boss, or an argument with an in-law. But at such moments it may be better to forego schooling and just go out through the woods for a long quiet walk or a nice easy canter on your pony.

# 10

# "SURPRISE-PROOFING" YOUR PONY

ONE OF THE MOST IMPORTANT QUALITIES IN A child's pony is acceptance of the unexpected. At High Hickory we spend a lot of time familiarizing our ponies with as many strange sights, sounds, and experiences as possible to make them "surprise-proof."

Much of this proofing is done from the ground, thus providing a fine opportunity for the nonriding sibling or parent to share in the fun. Some of it, like lunging, ties in with age-old training methods. Some of it is necessitated by the increasing mechanical or motorized hazards that a rider faces today.

Most likely to accept the unexpected is the pony with the edge taken off him before the child gets on his back. A brief lunging without a rider gives him a chance to get any "kinks" out of his system. Do not be concerned if your pony acts up—bucks, kicks up his heels, canters at first instead of trotting—while you are lunging him. This is the time for him to do it. With ponies that are free to romp in pasture, you may have none of this play on the lunge line. At High Hickory we seldom do, but we stick to the routine lunging nevertheless and have found, with a green pony particularly, that the mounted schooling session that follows goes more smoothly for both pony and young rider.

When lunging, stress stopping on command as much as moving on command. The pony that knows what "Ho" on the lead rope or lunge line means easily transfers obedience to the mounted aids (leg, hand). Often the voice command can be an added safety device for the child. This emphasis comes into use in all our "safety" training.

Your pony's willingness to stop on voice command will also come in handy if you drive or jump him. One way to avoid a pony's rushing a series or round of jumps is to pull him up frequently after only one or two jumps in a schooling session. In this way he learns that a series of jumps does not automatically mean *Go*, but rather *Go if asked*, and *Stop if asked*. The result is a smoothly paced round when several jumps are to be taken, and a quiet willing jump if only one is required.

Continue this stress on stopping on command when riding cross-country. Although certain trails may be especially delightful for lengthy trots or long canters, make it a point to interrupt such stretches with frequent stops and changes of gaits. A Pony Pal may go off during a lesson with directions such as "Walk to Picnic Pine. Canter halfway along that path. Stop. Canter to the Ski Gate. Walk to the stone wall. Stop. Then trot to the turn-around." The ponies learn that they may be asked to Ho at any point. Thus a pony is less liable to associate any one area with a fast speed, and less liable to develop an automatic reaction which could result in taking off or running away.

Although responding well to voice in all other situations, Top Rail Stardust was unwilling to stand still after being mounted. To correct this eagerness to move forward before being told, Robin, with a Pony Pal holding Star, would mount, repeating "Ho," and then quickly reach forward to give her a carrot. As there was an increasing delay in giving the reward there was less need for the pony to be held. Wise Welsh Star soon associated a tidbit with her rider's settling into the saddle and would stand patiently till, stirrups and reins adjusted, Robin signaled her to move on.

This voice command plays a vital role in some of the more "violent" surprise-proofing; but you must always introduce your pony considerately to a new situation—don't plunge him into it. As in all schooling, work slowly; reward often. (At High Hickory we're great believers in carrot handouts.) It's much easier to go up your training ladder a rung at a time than to have to go back because you tried to skip. For instance, don't start out to whip-proof your pony by suddenly and violently cracking the lunge whip under his nose: you may terrify him for good. After days of the schooling described below, he should no longer mind such a sudden motion—but it will be because he has learned to accept it and because, even when it is unexpected, he will associate it with reward not punishment. But first you must teach him.

It is invaluable for a pony not to be afraid of moving sticks or fluttering objects (such as horse show programs held by spectators at the rail). We work on this during lunging. Hold your pony short on the lunge line or lead rope and let him see and smell the whip. Accustom him to its moving slowly about his head—where he can see it. Reward with voice, pats, and tidbits. Depending on your indi-

vidual pony, perhaps all you will achieve the first day is his sniffing it instead of flinching back. Don't go too fast. Gradually (how to define gradually? not only slowly within a given period, but slowly in terms of the number of periods—days, weeks, months—depending on you and your pony)—gradually move the whip over greater areas of his head and body. Gradually wave it more and more wildly over and around him. Always reward his calm acceptance. At all costs avoid striking him accidentally.

At High Hickory we never use a whip for punishment, so our ponies have no conventional association of them with pain.

Besides sticks (crops, canes, umbrellas, fishing rods, and rakes), flapping objects are among the unexpected your pony should learn to accept. Following the same procedure as you did with the lunging whip, introduce him to such things-in-motion as blankets, saddle pads, plastic sheeting, clothes on the line, jackets being taken off by a child on foot or on horseback, being tossed up or down by the rider to a person on foot or vice versa, and being reached for and lifted from a fence. At High Hickory one jump has a large flag mounted by it; the bright stripes may hang limp or may suddenly flare out as a pony goes over the bars. On a path, a pony may encounter colored crepe paper, streamers, or rattl-

**Stardust stands calmly on a slack line while the whip is waved around and touched all over her body.**

165

**High Hickory is a windy hilltop where ponies would have a good excuse for shying or spooking. Eric introduces Stardust to black plastic sheeting preparatory to surprise-proofing.**

**The sheeting is flapped deliberately (and blown by the wind) in front of and behind Stardust and against her body.**

Stardust stands quietly (note slack lead rope) with the plastic draped over her. The sheeting still rustles and crackles in the wind as well as with the pony's movements.

A flapping flag that may billow in her very face is ignored by Stardust as she willingly takes a jump without wings.

Brightly colored pennants draped from tree branches flutter in the wind as Lutine Bell approaches and is allowed to stop and sniff.

Lute then walks quietly under on a loose rein. Thereafter the pony goes under, back and forth, without any hesitation.

Have a child move the handlebars, ring the bell, or rattle the carrier. If your pony needs it, pat and calm him. Have the bike rider move off—and go on from this quiet start to scrunching stops. See if a baseball bat or butterfly net in the bike rider's hand bothers your pony. Is the pony as calm about bike activity under the saddle, at a walk, trot, or canter, as he is on the lead rope?

Uncertain footing, mud, marshy grass, a white line on the highway you have to cross, hardtop itself, an exposed culvert, a wooden bridge, water—all are things many ponies object to. Welcome, indeed create, the opportunity to face your pony with any of these while you have the time and properly controlled circumstances to cope with them patiently. In introducing the pony to walking over tricky footing, realize that he may suddenly jump rather than walk through. When leading over a stone wall or a brook, be certain to be to one side of your pony and not in front of him. Hold your lead rope or reins in a single coil in your left hand and your right about six inches from the halter, or your reins pulled long over the pony's head, in the same two-handed manner. If it is necessary to give him extra slack, you can let go with your right hand and still have control. Don't hold your pony by the halter or bridle: if he suddenly lunges forward you may be jerked off your feet and forced to let go. Often, too, your pony must have slack merely to keep his balance.

ing foil plates dangling from a tree on an easily broken string, the string itself being safely above the level of the rider's head. A pony learns to walk, trot, or canter under or through these bright flapping things, steadily—to go where asked, when asked, as asked, no matter what. If your pony is hesitant, lead him through the first few times. And don't forget the reassuring reward.

Accustoming your pony to bicycle activity is wise, and another way to include the whole family in pony activities. Introduce your pony to the bike. (A typical amused response to this advice is: "How do you do, Bike?" "How do you do, Star?") Let him look, sniff, and finally nose the stationary object.

Followed by "wish I had a pony" pals, Pied Piper Stardust goes over a wooden bridge. Hoof beats sounded so hollowly that one child said she expected Billy Goat Gruff to pop up.

Water is no problem to this pair. Although this pond is belly-deep with steep sides, Lutine goes willingly in and through without hesitation or change of stride.

For many ponies a ditch, brook, or even a puddle is cause for shying or refusal. Agile Lutine takes a trappy runoff in stride, going along willingly on a loose rein.

As Tuffy investigates the sheep's water tub, Robin, lead rope coiled in her left hand, slacks off with her right.

Occasionally a pony needs to learn that the children-on-foot he accepts so happily are the same youngsters suddenly four feet higher on a fence rail. Pony Pals jumping up and down, waving their arms for balance on our long "bouncing board," are soon ignored by a pony trotting past. Familiarity with the noise and scurry of someone hitting on the tennis backboard soon breeds indifference.

Ponies are alert and notice changes in their daily surroundings: that huge pile of gravel dumped by the paddock gate while they were in the far field; the tent just set up in the play-yard; the lawn chair dragged out to the lunging circle. The coon cat that goes out daily with the Border Collies to bring in the ponies and sheep is a cat-of-a-different-color when she tightropes across the top bar as a pony is being ridden into a jump. Full-grown Border Collies milling around are one thing, but even brood-mare Star with foal at side looks askance at those strange tiny things called new puppies.

**Surprise-proofing includes such taken-for-granted things as a hand on the rump or a whack on the neck during moments of pony-play. Here Robin clowns on Tuffy.**

**Stardust sniffs an early lamb. Ponies often find alarming the sight, sound, or smell of other animals, but our ponies are well surprise-proofed by chickens, ducks, and cats as well as dogs and sheep.**

Of course, when we praise the desirability of a pony that accepts the unfamiliar, we do not mean that we want a dull, unobservant animal. The alert,

noticing pony needs a rider who "stays awake"—but such a pony is a safer one for a child because he can be schooled not to be frightened by what he observes. The lethargic, dull pony that "never pays any attention to anything" may actually be a risk. If such a pony ever meets a situation that does scare him, he will not have learned to respond to—and obey—his rider under frightening circumstances.

Many hazards are noisy ones: power saws, tractors, car horns. We go out of our way to bring the ponies near, in hand or under saddle, when farm machinery is in use. The sound of a hay-baler in the field below has us hurrying down the hill to expose a pony to this "danger." Sometimes the peaceful isolation of High Hickory seems a handicap in schooling. (We used to joke about installing loudspeakers and piping the recorded blare of a crowd to the pony paddocks; now we are working on a tape recording which will enable us to do just that.)

As these surprise-proofing ideas show, your

**Lutine, exposed to bulldozers, chain saws, power tools, and tractors, finds nothing to fear in this piece of heavy equipment.**

pony's developing this most desirable trait—acceptance of the unexpected—depends mainly on two things: exposing the pony to as many strange sights and sounds as possible, and developing in him the idea that when the unexpected happens he turns to his rider for assurance and command. (Remember that all training takes advantage of your pony's one-track mind.)

Naturally, there's always the possibility of the pony's being startled by something to which you have been unable to expose him. However, if your emphasis has been on obedience under stress, his reaction will be less extreme than it might otherwise have been.

Top Rail Stardust's reaction to the sudden flushing of three pheasants one after another under her very nose illustrates what I mean. When the first bird whirred noisily up from deep grass Star shied—and stopped. Each time a bird drummed into flight, Star half-jumped sideways—and stopped. A less trusting, less "What do I do now, Ma?" pony would undoubtedly have bolted under such rapid, repeated alarms. Star responded to the child on her back, although she had only been under saddle some dozen times.

# 11
# TRAINING YOUR PONY TO JUMP

THROUGHOUT THE SCHOOLING IDEAS SUGGESTED in this book, emphasis is on the *willing* pony. Perhaps in no area of riding is willingness so important as in jumping. Nothing is more unpleasant to ride (or watch) than a reluctant jumper, a pony whose very approach to the jump is sullen or over-anxious, whose attitude is refuse-or-shy-if-I-can or bolt-and-bounce-before-I-get-whacked. Nothing is more satisfying to ride (or watch) than the pony whose approach is calm and relaxed, confident and certain, responsive and reliable, the pony whose steady eagerness shows his willingness to jump what he's asked, where he's asked, when he's asked, and how he's asked.

From the parental standpoint as well as the horseman's, such willingness in a child's pony is a great safety factor. Willingness to jump eliminates many of the hazards inherent in jumping and, along with athletic development and experience on the part of both rider and pony, puts jumping in its proper perspective as just one phase of the overall picture of riding, not an area of special danger. Certainly there are added challenges, and risks increase under certain conditions and sought-out situations, but just as every person should learn at least rudimentary "survival" swimming and just as every rider should be able to negotiate an occasional low jump, so every pony should be schooled to jump at least minor obstacles. For the sake of all concerned, whatever the extent of jumping, we want a willing pony.

How can we achieve this goal? By laying the basic foundation in unmounted schooling, then building slowly and patiently on this foundation in mounted work. Much of the groundwork can be done by a child or adult who is not an experienced rider, but for mounted schooling, in this above all areas, the combination of green pony/green rider is to be avoided.

No pony will be (or long remain) a willing jumper if every jump means a thump on the back or a jab in the mouth from an insecure rider. The green pony has to learn to approach his jump correctly, to take off and balance himself over the jump, to land and move on smoothly—and then to do all this with the added complication of a rider on his back. If the rider cannot control his own balance and weight, and cannot adjust instantly to the irregularities and inconsistencies of a green pony, he cannot be anything but a hindrance to the pony he is supposed to be schooling. (And remember, every time you are on your pony you are schooling him, intentionally or not, by commission or omission.) Even the experienced rider must not only not make mistakes himself but be quick to allow for any mistakes on the part of the pupil/pony under him.

This chapter, then, on schooling your pony to jump is not a riding lesson on jumping. Anyone doing the mounted schooling of a green pony over jumps should not only be experienced over fences but should have some knowledge of what schooling a green pony entails—in time, patience, mental and emotional stability as well as physical ability. He should be not only proficient as a horseman but mature as a person, able to differentiate between correction and punishment, to realize for example that refusals are often instinctive self-preservation on the part of the pony and not deliberate disobedience. He must be able to admit "This is my fault," and not automatically blame the pony; to ask "Why?" He must be mature enough to say "I have time"—in terms of weeks, months, years. He must be able to recognize day-to-day progress, to develop a pony seemingly imperceptibly on a long-range plan and not be impatient for instant success. He must be considerate enough to school according to the physical, mental, and emotional ability of the green pony.

Here is where the schooling of the small pony should be strictly supervised. With ponies up to the weight of adult riders, schooling is simplified, but with the smaller breeds mounted schooling must often be done by children of the size who will eventually enjoy the finished pony. Unfortunately, most youngsters are not mature enough to school. Least fit of all, perhaps, are "child prodigies" in riding, for the very aggressiveness, daring-do, and athletic ability that make them good little riders may make them impatient, overeager, and intolerant of green pony mistakes. Schooling by youngsters should be under adult supervision, as it takes only one snatch or jerk by a (however understandably!) frustrated child to ruin a potentially good pony. Schooling sessions over the jumps, as on the flat, should be kept brief and—by hook or by crook—should end on a good note for both child and pony.

As stressed before, crops and spurs should not be necessary aids on a child's pony. Certainly in developing the willing jumper they are not necessary aids. In reschooling the problem jumper, by going back to scratch and following the ideas below, you should do away with the need for them. (Of course reschooling an unwilling jumper in many instances takes longer than training the unspoiled green pony.)

Before you consider schooling your pony to jump, stand back and take a look at the total picture.

Is he fit to jump? Here is where your veterinary routine, your blacksmith program, your basic stable management, all play a part. Negelect in any of these areas may cause troubles: lack of fitness, or general exhaustion; sore legs, bad feet, outright lameness; girth, back, or mouth sores from poorly fitted, patchy tack or overbitting. Such discomfort will prevent any pony from being willing.

It may be alarming to see a child on a "hot" pony, one whose "hotness" is caused by overfeeding of non-pony diet and lack of exercise. It is also upsetting to see the all-too-numerous ponies who are easily controlled by youngsters not because of proper schooling or riding but because the ponies themselves are weak from malnutrition, if not on the verge of starvation. Half the grouchy "sluggish" ponies some owners complain about would be improved by decent, sufficient feeding. An undernourished pony can hardly be a happy willing one. To do well in any work your pony must, of course, be physically fit, well conditioned, and on a diet adjusted to allow for growth as well as for activity asked of him.

## UNMOUNTED SCHOOLING

The willing pony over jumps is the pony to whom jumping is all in a day's work (or play), not a once-in-a-blue-moon ordeal.

Here is where unmounted schooling plays a helpful role in training the green pony to jump while fitting in easily and economically to a backyard situation. With jumping as with all phases of schooling, you can invest in devices and equipment and expensive layouts. The pony owner with a small paddock and a converted garage for a stable may long for a jumping chute and an outside hunt course. But a single jump—two standards and bar—costs fifty dollars and up, so most people will feel that do-it-yourself is called for here. Costly paraphernalia are not necessary. The pony you work over a fallen log or a discarded hot-water boiler or a pile of tires salvaged from the dump may turn out to be the better jumper for the very variety of obstacles which ingenuity and make-do produce for his training.

When can unmounted schooling over jumps begin for the green pony? Almost from foal-hood on—not seriously, of course, until at least three years, and even then lightly as young legs and baby bone are not up to work. But the foal running free with his dam will leap fallen trees and natural obstacles quite casually and may well be led over a bar or two on the ground from the beginning of his early lessons on the lead-rope.

Use of voice commands as an aid has been emphasized in earlier chapters. Teach your pony even now the voice command for jumping to be used later on—"Hup!" or "Over!", for instance. Voice command will of course be replaced by other aids in mounted schooling, but on occasion will still be used by the rider (or his assistant on foot).

The aids to jumping are, for us, voice, hands, legs,

body weight and balance. Aids, in a different sense, are the example given by a schooled pony leading over the jump ahead of a green one; the choice of direction (your pony will perhaps jump more willingly headed for home, for instance, or coming in for feed on a lead rope); and rewards (of praise, carrots, pats, cessation of demand). In jumping, undesirable aids include not only crop and spurs but whips, wings, and threats from an assistant on foot. Do not let anyone "help" you by waving his arms or a whip behind your pony as he goes into a jump. Do not try to funnel your pony over a jump with wings.

Your pony's first introduction to jumping, whether unmounted or under saddle, should be to a solid bar on the ground. (The bar on the ground is obviously a jump in its simplest form and is commonly used in schooling in a series or *cavalletti*.) Place a solid bar on the ground across a path or wide gateway that your pony goes through frequently, either loose or on a lead rope. He will think nothing of going over this and will soon step over it nonchalantly if it is raised a few inches or even a foot. When you are leading your pony over the bar pay no attention to it; walk on as usual. But as you approach it give your voice command: "Hup!" If he wants to sniff it, let him; do not attempt to yank him over. Use your voice command "Walk on," and he will soon ignore the bar and take it in stride. Lead over it at both a walk and a trot.

Never place a bar in a gateway so narrow that a pony's jumping it would injure him or risk his coming over on top of and not beside the person leading him. Have your lead rope long enough for the pony to move his head freely if he jumps rather than steps over the bar.

Some ponies truly love to jump, jumping playfully when loose, so that a fallen tree or a few bars left set up about the pasture provide a source of play. Other ponies that turn out to be great jumpers under saddle struggle over a low bar in a gateway as if they weren't used to having four legs. Neither behavior is indicative of how the pony will jump for a rider. However, the more your pony learns to handle himself and balance himself free over jumps the more skillful he will be under saddle.

If you are willing to walk, you can introduce your young pony to a great variety of jumps on the lead line. Go devious routes to take him to pasture so as to have him go over a few obstacles en route. At High Hickory an energetic youngster will run alongside by side with the pony and pop over a low picket fence or a row of red pails with him. I detour sedately, only the pony taking the jump. Here as in all future schooling the height of the jump is important only in a negative way: Keep it low.

Keep it low! School your pony to go willingly over a variety of jumps from a variety of footing—uphill, downhill, sand, mud, water. Praise and reward him. Make jumping pleasant, and he will soon take anything willingly on voice command. (This comes in useful in trail riding and in the show ring when you must dismount to lead your pony over an obstacle.) When your pony jumps such a variety willingly on a lead rope, he will not be likely to cut out or refuse similar jumps under saddle. If he learns that "Hup" means to jump, he will obey the voice command just as he does "Trot" or "Canter" or "Halt" on the lunge line.

When your pony is working nicely on the flat on the lunge line, you can put a long bar across the curve of his circle. Start with it on the ground and lunge him over it at a walk and a trot. He will become so accustomed to it that he will continue to circle over it unconcernedly as you gradually raise it to the point where he must jump rather than take it in his stride. You can use your voice command "Hup" just before he goes over the jump. The end of the jump towards the inside of the lunging circle must of course rest on a support low enough not to catch or entangle your lunge line.

Right from the start, use solid substantial jumps in schooling. Even your basic bar on the ground should be heavy enough not to roll or shift should the pony hit it with his foot. Heavy poles (both natural and brightly painted), railway ties, sections of telephone poles, make fine ground jumps if you can leave them permanently in place. (If you have to move your jumps, lighter weight must be a consideration.) Your pony will pay more attention, correct his own carelessness, and learn better judgement if he bangs a foreleg or kicks a hind foot against a heavy bar that does not give way.

## MOUNTED SCHOOLING

Even before mounted schooling over jumps with the additional weight of a rider is begun, you must be careful not to overdo. The younger the green pony the more important it is not to do too much. Two or three jumps once or twice a day are plenty at this stage.

In later training the rule "Don't overschool" is no less important. Regular schooling is needed, but practice might be every other day with "The higher, the fewer; the odder, the better" as your slogan: drains, fallen trees, ditches, stone walls, small brooks or man-made water jumps, posts-and-rails, low chicken coops, lobster-crates, small oil drums, a bar with a row of pumpkins under it, and stacks of car tires with a wooden bar or "rider" on top. These can range eventually from one foot to two feet six inches depending on your pony's height, for the first year or two. Thereafter a good ratio of height of jump to size of pony is to start with a three-foot jump and take off one inch for every inch the pony is below 14.2 hands.

Except in later work when you use several low jumps set at one or two stride intervals to teach your pony to adjust his stride without changing pace, jumps are best set up individually, not in a series. In early work when you end your mounted schooling over cavalletti (spaced three to five feet apart depending on size of pony) with a low jump at the end, be sure that the higher obstacle is placed at least nine feet after the last ground bar to allow for a stride before take-off.

The use of such cavalletti with a higher obstacle can provide excellent mounted training in a limited space. Obviously, to jump well and safely your pony must look at the jump, and the "little horses" supply an excellent means of getting him to look down and judge his stride and take-off. Vary the one obstacle as much as possible and change its position at the ends of the cavalletti so your pony can take it from both directions.

When to start mounted schooling over jumps? Clearly, any schooling over jumps of a young pony will require not only physical maturity but his having developed good balance under saddle, obedience, and an even pace in flat work. Beginning schooling over fences with a rider can go hand in hand with this elementary work on the flat if you observe the restrictions suggested here.

**Olympic and World Champion Bruce Davidson instructs over cavalletti at a clinic sponsored by the Ponkapoag Pony Club. Lutine's tail action is like that of world-famous Nautilus.**

175

Lutine Bell's first experience over "proper" jumps was in a show ring. Concern for a green pony's mouth shows in the rider's hands.

In the very beginning stages of mounted schooling, it is better to work on a slightly loose rein throughout than to throw away contact suddenly and disturb your pony's balance. It is also better to grab the mane or a neck strap worn for just such a contingency than to grab the mouth via the reins in case of misjudgment—either yours or the pony's.

Although your hands must be quiet and gentle and although you must not interfere with your pony over a jump, you cannot be hesitant or undecided as you approach. You will communicate this uncertainty to your pony. He is then liable to stop or to jump incorrectly. The old saying "Throw your heart over the fence and your horse will follow" has bearing here, too. In these early stages, with a calm confident pony, you should not head into a jump unless you intend to take it. Later, or to reschool a pony who tends to rush his jumps, you may work on

circling over and over past the obstacle until the final calming circle places him in position to take the jump on command. Later, too, you may bring your pony up to a jump, halt him in front of it, back, and then go over it. However, even if you approach a jump at a walk slow down in the last few yards so that your pony knows in advance that he is going to be asked to stop, not expected to jump. Until he is better schooled it is as well for him not to have any uncertainty about whether or not he is going to be asked to jump if he is headed for an obstacle. (If he is going calmly and quietly, he will pull up if needed as willingly as he will jump—and if you are working on this halting concurrently on the flat.)

Wings, as I have mentioned, are to be avoided in setting up jumps. If you have a ring, you can put jumps along one side of it, but with careful schooling right from the first bar on the ground, even this

**A carefully schooled pony jumps even a single oil drum. Ridden only by Robin, Stardust not only was always in the ribbons but never once refused—truly a willing jumper.**

one-sided "boxing-in" is not necessary. With proper progression in training, room to run out on either side or both sides of an open jump does not prove a temptation.

Running out or refusals are a sure sign that you are pushing the pace. Never "overface" your pony: never ask him to jump something more difficult than he is ready for in terms of physical, mental, and emotional readiness. If he starts refusing, you should go immediately back to smaller fences—not only for future training, but for the particular fence at the moment of refusal. Better to drop your two-foot fence and have your pony go over it willingly at one foot than to "win" a battle over the two-foot that sets the pony back.

Avoid arguments. Remember that refusals or running out are often common sense on the pony's part, stemming from self-preservation, not deliberate disobedience. Such a situation calls for correction, not punishment. Sometimes the correction will be asking your pony to take the same jump with a proper approach; other times it may be asking him to take the same jump lowered. Just remember, you don't have to "save face" with your pony! Strive always to end your schooling sessions with a good note.

At this early stage, even if you let your green pony determine his own take-off point, you should coincide your own command—voice and/or legs—with his action. He will thus learn to associate taking off *with* your command and eventually will take off *on*

your command (even if it should not be a take-off of his own choosing).

It is easy to understand why you should not interfere with your pony over the jump, but many riders fail to realize the effect of interfering with him in the approach to the jump. By interfering I mean frantic kicking, jabbing with spurs, whacking with a crop on the last few strides. Such "aids" distract the pony just when you most want him concentrating on the jump. They are certainly not conducive to making jumping a pleasurable experience. With schooled animals as well as green, the pony that is batted and egged on by crop and spurs often comes into the jump completely unbalanced. You want your pony to jump because you signal him, not because you painfully force him.

A young pony is a curious creature, so introduce yours to new obstacles before asking him to jump them. Lead him or walk him around them letting him sniff and nose them with outstretched neck. Soon he will take the strangest contraption for granted and jump it willingly without such preliminaries. This sort of surprise-proofing in the early stages pays off, just as does surprise-proofing on the flat. The more your pony is exposed to and can investigate and accept as an everyday commonplace, the better. For instance, once in a while, leave an old mattress in the pony paddock, or the carton the television set came in, or the old white washing machine the junk man is going to haul away.

Familiarity with unexpected objects that may be incorporated into challenging jumps will result in a relaxed pony—and therefore in a more willing

**Letting a pony look things over gives the rider a chance to check footing.**

**177**

**This jump provides two challenges: Up and on to a bank—or**

**Off and down in a slight drop. A green pony can be brought in at a trot from either direction.**

jumper. Tenseness and shying (and refusals) are closely related and are often based on lack of confidence. Your schooling must develop confidence in your pony—confidence in his rider, and confidence in himself.

Do not be impatient to jump high. "How high can he jump?" puts the questioner instantly into a certain category—not a top-ranking one—in a true horseman's opinion. What is important is *how* the pony is jumping, not how high. You want to be working for variety and width, not height.

At this point, a youngster must make a decision. Either you are going to indulge in certain fun, larking about on ponyback with your friends and riding carelessly, or you're going to forego all that,

set a long-range goal, and work towards it steadily. As with any goal, what you don't do may prove as important as what you do do. (For the boy or girl with only a green pony to ride this may prove a very difficult choice; lucky the child who also has a finished pony available to provide the safety valve of fun and relaxation after a schooling session.)

If you decide to work towards a long-range goal, "just one more" must be out of the question. "Proving" what your pony can do must be, also. While other pony owners are cavorting around on the trails, taking the outside course over and over, and entering every class in the show, you may have to be an onlooker or a stay-at-home. If you do ride in company you must choose your companions (equine and human) carefully: they must set good examples to your pony-in-training.

Just as you should not be in a hurry to jump great heights, so you should not be in a hurry to jump your green pony from a canter. Most of your schooling should be done from a trot. If your pony wants to slip into a canter before and after the jump, try not to let him. If on the flat you are developing a good stride with thrust and impulsion from hindquarters well under your pony, he should be able to take the jumps asked of him at this stage from a trot. From a trot he can best judge his take-off and best balance himself, and keeping him at this pace will avoid anticipation and rushing. Just as in your early work over the cavalletti you strive for evenness of gait with no change of pace or stride, so you want the pony to come into any jump in the same steady manner. The calmness of his gait on the approach to an obstacle will reveal a lot about his temperament and the success of your schooling. Also, it can be a real advantage to have a pony who can jump a good spread from a trot.

Introduce your pony to as many spread jumps as possible. Instead of raising your cavalletti, for instance, put two side by side like parallel poles. Build your stone wall low and wide, rather than high (do have a telephone pole "rider" on it). Do the same with your ditch or water jump.

A good program might go from work over a heavy pole (about four inches high) to railroad ties (about eight inches) for several weeks or months to jumps increased by a few inches at a time to about eighteen inches for another period of months. (Even for a 14.2 h. pony, two feet should be tops for the first year of mounted schooling over jumps.) Progress to two feet and then begin to broaden your jumps. You

Jumps such as this, on the beautiful course at Last Laugh, provide variety and spread with or without height.

A few standards and bars, comparatively light-weight and portable, can provide a variety of jumps.

Springy turf offers ideal footing. Space for galloping on before and after a jump tests a pony's responsiveness when asked to pull up in approach or on landing.

can do this to existing jumps by placing both a take-off and a landing bar in front of and after the obstacle. By placing these from one to three feet away you can increase the difficulty of the jump and teach your pony to spread himself over the jump. He must be able eventually to do this in the unexpected situations of the hunt field, the challenges of cross-country eventing, and the contrived trickiness of the show ring.

A take-off bar is helpful in establishing a ground line for your pony with certain types of jumps (e.g. a single pole as opposed to a chicken coop, which sets its own ground line.) It is much better for him to take off a little too far away than to come in too close to the jump and have to "take off on his forehand." Where the rider does not regulate the pony's length of stride and speed, such a bar helps him to make the necessary adjustments himself for proper take-off. Of all phases of jumping—approach, take-off, suspension, landing—it is the take-off that matters most. With proper take-off—from the rear end with hind legs engaged under him—your pony can if necessary make corrective movements during suspension for safe landing (to allow for unexpected width or for tricky footing on the far side not visible before take-off, for example).

If you are mathematically inclined, a certain scale for placement of the ground line or take-off bar can be worked out. One and one-half the height of the jump is generally measured—four to four and a half feet in front of a three-foot jump, for example.

Regardless of how you create height and width in your jumps, the more patient you are about increasing them the less likely you will be to have to go back. If your pony gets excited at the prospect of a jump or if he has to be forced over, you are probably pushing him too fast. Any step upwards should seem all part of the day's riding, not a special "promotion." Just as you make a special effort to prevent boredom by the variety and placement of your jumps, so you must resist the temptation to "skip a grade" or ask too much of your green pony too soon. Think in

**Solidity of this permanent obstacle contrasts dramatically with moveable ring jumps.**

**Lutine Bell shows that a pony can handle solid, horse-size obstacles with aplomb—when she is no longer green.**

terms of his lifetime of usefulness, not in terms of this year or next.

The "don't's" in teaching your pony to jump can't be emphasized too much. Let's review them:

Don't overschool or overface. Don't try to advance too quickly. Don't punish a green pony: correct him. (Never "correct" him with your reins by yanking the bit and jabbing his mouth.) Don't blame the pony for the rider's faults: loss of balance or mistimed aids, whether leg or hand, that put a pony off stride and cause a faulty jump or a self-protective runout or refusal. Don't underestimate how much a pony, especially a green one, is influenced by your movements on his back. Don't

be left behind—better to be a little advanced than to risk a pound on the back or a jab in the mouth.

Don't school if you are in a bad mood—admit it and quit for the day. Be tolerant. Your pony's mistakes are just that most of the time, not naughtiness. Training is teaching, not punishing. If your pony knew so much that he never made mistakes there'd be no need to school him.

Keep an overall perspective: Compare your pony's accomplishments of today with what he could do two months ago, not yesterday. (Like the successful dieter, don't weigh yourself every day!) Apply standards for a green pony, not a finished pony, when you evaluate his work.

Enjoy your schooling sessions for themselves, not just for what you hope the final results will be. If you don't enjoy the problems and challenges of schooling, don't try to work with a green pony either over jumps or on the flat. Let someone else do the training, and you stick to finished animals. . . . Just realize that a "good" pony represents years of work on some horseman's part, and should command a good price.

Supplement your training sessions with "homework." (In this case it's the teacher, not the pupil, that has to do it.) Read books: Fillis, Seunig, D'Orgeix, Wright—(See the Reading List at the end of the book). If you can't pick the brains of a professional horseman whose horses you admire, at least ask him to suggest authors whose writings he considers still valid today. Look at photographs and pictures. Investigate movies produced by organizations like the American Horse Show Association or the United States Pony Club or by breed associations like the Welsh Pony Society of America. Go to horse shows and cross-country events and watch ponies in action over jumps. Analyze approach, take-off, "bascule," landing. Talk training with other pony owners. Know your goal.

What do you want to *avoid?* A pony who props or bucks over his jumps, who rushes with his head in the air, whose every bunched muscle screams overexcitement, who comes into his jump too fast and overcollected, who won't pull up between jumps or afterwards, who shies out or refuses. . . .

What do you *want?* A pony clever, handy, agile, obedient, who will jump freely with proper use of head, neck, and body, who will jump powerfully and smoothly with the least effort necessary to clear any obstacle, who will continue on quietly or come to a halt instantly; a pony who will jump anywhere, any

First time off a drop bank for a four-year-old pony (and for her rider). Confidence works two ways: yours in your pony, and your pony's in you.

After jumping, both wonder "Was it really that much of a drop?" Stone revetment can be taken as a bank as well as a drop jump.

time, anything you ask him to jump—willingly.

As you school your pony towards this goal, you will get a perhaps unexpected bonus from the time, effort, and imagination you put into making your pony a better athlete. For as he improves in physical condition and in gymnastic ability over jumps and on the flat he will improve in beauty. Granted, his conformation will not change, except for such faults as were caused by underdeveloped muscles and awkward movements. But just as the person who moves with *joie de vivre* and exudes good health looks more beautiful than the person who slouches and is listless, so your fit, willing pony will seem more beautiful. The benefits will mushroom: The pony who is in top shape and up to what you ask of him will perform more willingly and you will have a better ride. Jumping your pony will not be an occasion for grim determination or butterflies in the stomach but, for both you and your pony, just one more source of day-to-day fun with safety, and maybe a little bit of glory, too. . . .

# 12

# TEACHING YOUR PONY TO DRIVE

THE PONY THAT "RIDES AND DRIVES" HAS AN added selling point if you must eventually part with him, but, more important, he can provide additional pleasure during riding years and long after he is outgrown under saddle.

Driving makes possible not only work with a two- or four-wheeled cart but sleighing and ski-joring. Besides participation in pet pony in harness or fine harness or roadster classes, it opens up such specialized activities as pony racing or chariot driving. It makes it possible for the pony owner to include nonriding friends in horse shows. It opens up a new range of ideas to creative youngsters who enjoy costume classes: with a pony that drives you

"I feel like a Laplander driving a reindeer!" Pony Pals exclaim, sleighing with Tuffy. Brakeman keeps the sled from running up on Tuffy's heels at a stop.

can enter as Santa with his reindeer and sleigh, a settler with his covered wagon, a Roman with his chariot, a Swan Boat and operator, or Cinderella and her pumpkin coach. It makes possible participation in affairs such as spring and fall carriage drives or sleigh rallies sponsored by various pony organizations. Driving provides an opportunity to include the whole family in backyard fun. Boys who may not care much about equitation enjoy roadster events at shows and pony racing at tracks (but may have to share the reins with father). One grown-up pony owner I know regularly enjoys an evening drive after his day at work.

If you're a do-it-yourself pony owner, your driving pony can earn his keep around the barn by hauling bags of grain, bales of hay, bags of shavings, and loads of manure. More than one back yard pony has willingly pulled a small garden or snow plow, hauled rocks for stone walls or logs for the fireplace, and is as appreciated for that as for the ribbon won for "pet pony in harness."

Driving also makes possible another form of exercising a pony for the small rider. Instead of lunging your pony before he is ridden, or when the rider is away or not free to ride, drive him instead. Here nonriding youngsters or adults can help out.

Driving is also just plain fun—so much so that it may be the choice for the day's activities just as often as hacking cross-country. Small friends or casual visitors who for various reasons cannot be allowed to ride can share a pony cart drive. Swim suits and picnic lunches, a halter and lead rope, are easily

Nonriding youngsters from The Learning Center for Deaf Children wait while Tuffy is hitched up. Hundreds of boys and girls have had fun with the pony cart.

More cart than pony, but with typical Shetland strength Tuffy easily pulls this work wagon with its ball-bearing wheels.

stowed aboard a cart, even books or a sketch pad and paints if a long outing is planned.

Suggestions for teaching your pony to drive given here are "backyard techniques." They incorporate some traditional professional ideas but assume that you will be working with the most limited equipment. You do not even need to own a driving harness or a pony cart when you start preliminary training. I'm speaking here more as a mother whose youngster has taught three ponies to drive just for day-to-day fun than as a professional with a fine harness show pony in mind. However, let me stress one point here:

Just as you or your child must learn to ride fairly well before schooling a green pony under saddle and must jump competently before schooling a green pony over fences, so you must know how to drive before training a green pony to drive. Even a child can teach a pony to drive—but such work should be done under knowledgeable supervision.

Before you start to train your pony, if you do not drive you might get a friend with a trained pony to let you follow our procedure. Using Tuffy or Galaxy, who already drive, a Pony Pal who has never driven a cart learns first to drive on foot—the pony alone without the added complications of a cart. Later, with an experienced driver beside him, the green child learns to drive pony and cart—learns to allow for the width of the wheels, the length of shafts and cart, the rigidity of the same in turning. He learns to drive by and around obstacles before taking the reins alone. Driving is neither difficult nor complicated, but a few sessions of this sort avoid even initial problems.

There are three periods in your pony's life when you can start teaching him to drive: (1) As a youngster before any mounted schooling begins. This is often recommended, as a late yearling or two-year-old can drive before he can carry weight, and many horsemen believe this develops a good mouth. (2) Concurrently with the training on the flat that your mature pony is beginning under saddle. (3) With an older pony of any age whose mounted schooling has long been considered complete.

We followed the first approach with Galaxy, the second with Tuffy, and the third with Top Rail Stardust. Choice was determined more by time and equipment available and by what was being done with other ponies at the same time than by any firm belief in the superiority of one approach over another. The one thing I am firmly convinced of where driving is concerned is that *all* your handling of the pony from the moment you get him, whether foal or aged veteran, helps prepare your pony. Galaxy went through long months of careful groundwork, was hitched up and drove like an old hand the very first time. Top Rail Stardust, never given any specifically driving groundwork, was hitched up on the spur of the moment and also drove off as calmly as if she'd always been in the shafts—credit due to the daily training and surprise-proofing she'd always had.

Whichever your approach to teaching your pony to drive, the first time you hitch pony to cart there must be no mistake—for the pony that has a terrifying experience between the shafts or bolts with the cart will never forget it, and may be ruined for good. No matter how steady and reliable a pony seems, one should be prepared for possible trouble. With proper overall training it is less likely to occur.

Ideally, training of your pony to drive begins with his basic work on the lead rope and on the lunge line. Here the value of voice commands—which are used in driving—stands out. "Ho," "Walk on," "Back,"

"Trot"—these are all orders you can teach any age pony to obey in hand.

Again, surprise-proofing is invaluable. The pony used to cars, bikes, motorcycles while on the lead rope or under saddle is not going to be spooked by traffic—and a pony and cart on the road are part of traffic, subject to the same rules of the road as cars. The pony accustomed to a branch being dragged along side, behind, or against him by a rider or a person on foot, the pony used to a buggy whip being flicked all over his body and snapped around him, is not going to be bothered by traces or shafts against his side. One reason why Stardust went so calmly when first hitched up was that she was thoroughly accustomed to being ridden beside, behind, and in front of the pony cart with Tuffy pulling it.

One stage of training your pony to drive will be to lead him while someone else pulls the pony cart rickshaw-style alongside, behind, and in front. For the show ring, you may want your cart well-oiled and squeakless, but for this preliminary stage the noisier the better. You may even want to tie on a few sleighbells or tin cans! This stage is also an ideal time to seek out rough noisy going underfoot—crushed stone on a driveway, mud puddles, grass, hardtop, a wooden bridge—a familiar cart going over different surfaces sounds different. If you don't have your pony cart yet, this can be accomplished with such makeshift "rickshaws" as wheelbarrows, tricycles, lawnmowers, the traditional little red wagon—anything that can be pulled along on wheels near your pony. Leaving the pony cart out where your loose pony can investigate it and step in and out of and over the shafts is another way of accustoming him to the contraption. As always, when you introduce anything new and frightening, sight or sound (think from the pony's point of view, not yours!) do it gradually—and be by the pony's head to reassure him.

After such surprise-proofing and work on the lead rope and lunge line, you can proceed to driving on foot. Some horsemen go from lunging to work on the circle with long reins; I don't recommend this, particularly with young ponies. With a child doing the schooling, it is simpler (and more satisfactory) to go directly to driving from behind the pony. I believe in working in very close to the pony's rump—no need to work at a long distance behind as some handlers suggest for fear of kicking. By this time your pony is thoroughly used to being worked around, used to his tail being firmly tugged, to your

**Galaxy is held by Robin while Eric drives Tuffy. Although the rope is slack, Galaxy looks leery about this new procedure.**

**Eric drives the tractor behind, beside, and ahead of Galaxy—just as an uncooperative motorist may overtake, pass, and pull in ahead. Only a pony well surprise-proofed against traffic should be driven on the road.**

**Encouraged by voice and untroubled by the familiar noises of the pony cart, Galaxy moves on unhesitatingly.**

**Even on a turn, Galaxy travels beside the pony cart—no pulling back or reluctant dragging.**

leaning on his rump, to a grain bag or blanket being slid off his rear, to the lunge line coming in contact with any part of his body or legs. He knows the reassuring sound of your voice and responds to "Good pony," "Easy, boy," or other soothing phrases, and respects your firm "No!" or "Behave!"

When your pony has reached this point—after days, weeks, months, depending on you and your pony—he's ready to drive on foot.

Equipment? With Tuffy, it was at first an ordinary halter with a lunge line attached to make long reins (lines, as they are more properly called in driving). These went through a loop high on each side of a homemade canvas girth (actually a piece of lunge line just tied in place each time) so as to keep the long lines from sagging between her head and her rump. You could saddle your pony, run up the stirrups on the leathers, and put your lines through the irons. If your pony is not responsive to a halter only, and has been bitted, you can long rein him with his riding bridle, substituting long lines for reins.

Galaxy started out from the very beginning with "proper" harness, a set belonging to thirty-nine inch Tuffy that had to be let out as growing Welsh filly outstripped the mature Shetland. A bridle with blinders, a harness girth with togels and lugs to run leather lines through were used at the start. Later, adding breastplate and britching, Robin drove her in full regalia, still on foot.

As you'll have deduced from the above, it is not

necessary to drive your pony with blinders (except as necessary to meet class requirements in a show). Some ponies drive better without them; with a surprise-proofed pony they certainly are not needed. If you and your pony drive around the countryside for the fun of it, it may increase his enjoyment to go in an open bridle; this obviously affects how he moves on, so you in turn benefit. If you do use blinders, be sure they fit so that they do not rub the pony's eyes or face.

As with any new schooling, do not ask too much of your pony the first time you ground-drive him. Be satisfied if he just walks on a straight line for a few yards, stops on voice command, and walks on. See

Gal moves lightly and completely at ease during an early driving lesson. Like many ponies, she enjoys this work.

A pony must not move when driver or passengers get in or out of the cart. Galaxy stands quietly on slack lines as Debby and Robin get out.

that he stands until told to walk on. The first few times it may help to have someone at your pony's head with a lead rope fastened to the halter (worn under the driving bridle), but all verbal commands should come only from the driver at the pony's rear. If you are working alone your pony may be briefly puzzled at orders from the rear. Your hand against his rump along with voice command is better than slapping the reins. Just as in mounted work at High Hickory we never use crop or spurs, so in driving we never use the buggy whip. Strictly speaking, a long driving whip should be carried in hand or in cart whip socket whenever you drive, but consider it an emergency device. If you carry it in ground-driving, use it as a visual aid only.

Increase what you ask of your pony at each session, beginning with a brief review, asking

something new before he tires, and ending on a note of accomplishment. From driving in the straight, you can go to large and small circles, to figure eight's, to driving around obstacles such as trees or barrels or cars. You can go up hill and down, as far from home as your own energies permit. "Drive" your pony along the road to accustom him to passing and on-coming traffic. Just remember you are no longer a pedestrian (although you may feel very much one before your jaunt is over) and keep to the right. Occasionally drive your pony with longer lines in preparation for the distance away you will be in the pony cart.

You'll be fortunate if you have other pony drivers

Pony cart traffic in a show ring may startle a novice. Galaxy, with Robin's familiar voice reassuring her from behind, soon settled down in her first class in harness.

187

nearby so that you can work your pony, still on foot, in company with ponies driven to cart. Later, too, when you are driving hitched up, you will find it helpful to your pony's schooling to seek others out. Galaxy's first time driving in company was in a show ring with fifteen other rigs—each man out for himself, of course: a bit of a challenge for a youngster that had pulled a cart only three times previously. Total schooling had had its effect and Galaxy settled down to perform nicely. (Of course this time she did not place.) Stardust's first time in company was easier, at a well-attended carriage drive which more closely approximated her brief experience in the shafts.

# 13
# MAGIC MOMENT: BIRTH OF A FOAL

RAISING A FOAL IS A RARE AND DELIGHTFUL EXPER-ence. Many a top-ranking horseman has never known this pleasure, for schooling and training green horses and ponies can be a thing quite apart from breeding and raising; the most experienced rider may never have handled anything younger than a three-year-old up to weight in the saddle. But all horsemen, young or old, dream of bringing their own stock along from birth, and every horse-crazy youngster longs to raise a foal of his own.

Raising a foal is enjoyable even if you get the foal "ready made." We were amazingly fortunate in that we actually saw our foal—Stardust's—born.

Through all the months of waiting and wondering—was Top Rail Stardust in foal or wasn't she?—I don't think I ever thought we would actually witness the birth.

I thought that, if there was going to be a foal, it would greet me some morning at Stardust's side, *un fait accompli:* like my ewe Mascara and her twin lambs, or, nightmare of nightmares, I imagined some disastrous birth like my Floss's lambing. And into what station wagon could we ever haul Star to drive her off to rescue if no vet could come?

Bookworm Robin, just eight and full of tales in which twin foals cost the life of the dam, repeatedly asked if her pony was likely to have twins. After the foal was born, the first thing she asked was, Would there be another?—not wanting it, fearing it.

But—from one day to the next we found ourselves with a healthy frisky foal that galloped in tiny strides around its grazing mother—and all of us saw it born!

No warning. None of the straining or biting at her flanks or restless pacing you expect. Just Star and little Thelwell Tuffy side by side under the pine in the meadow by the outer field, with a gray drizzle sifting wetly down, when I went to get them. I put Tuffy into her stall, and as I shut the door Star went into her box and lay down. Oh *no!*

"Out of there, girl," I told her. There was a clean foaling stall ready in another shed. Would she make it?

Star got up and came out. She walked back and forth a few times—a white balloon under her tail now—and then she lay down by Tuffy's door.

The foal was coming! Its forelegs in the balloon, clearly—but the head? Then that came, and half the foal was out.

I was taking no chances. Gently I freed the tiny nostrils of the wet membrane and stepped back.

Robin was jittery with excitement, crooning reassuringly to her beloved Star. Eric, yellow-slickered, was frantically trying to get one of three cameras to take pictures in the rain—frustration.

Star was so good. Her labor seemed not too difficult. (I am glad, when I think of Floss.) Part of the time she had her head up and looked around towards her flank or tail as if in wonder, and she seemed glad we were there. Trusting pony. We patted her and stroked her neck.

A final surge, and the foal was completely out, its lower half encased in membrane. Dark and wet in the dusky drizzle, it struggled more to get to its forelegs than to free its hindquarters.

Suddenly Star sagged utterly, her neck stretched and flattened out, her eye rolled back. For one awful

**Was she or wasn't she? As spring wore on, it was increasingly obvious that Top Rail Stardust was in foal!**

moment I feared she was dead. She was limp. That powerful gray parcel of energy was limp. I put my hand on her neck and spoke her name. She lifted her head—those liquid dark eyes!—and I stepped back with Robin and Eric. There Star lay with her neck arched, looking back, the foal by her hindquarters, a picture I'll never forget.

There was none of the immediate care (licking, biting of the navel cord, etc.) that there is when a Border Collie has pups; but soon both ponies were on their feet, Star nuzzling and the foal—a filly or a colt?—wobbling about almost blindly, and the rain drizzling down.

Since even the calmest, kindest mares can become fierce and nasty with motherhood, I was very leery of stepping in now. But we had to get that wee pony foal under shelter. How would Star react to our interfering?

Shortly, we had no choice but to do *something*. The foal persisted in heading in the one direction in which it could get into trouble, into and under a big coil of wire that was leaning against the back side of the sheep shed. If it got under that, or tangled in it—its little hoofs were only about the size of a 35mm. roll of film. If Star went into the narrow space after it, she'd get frantic and we'd have a frightened rump to contend with in the wet dark.

Eric ran for a lead rope. I took Star and had Robin get the foal. Tiny and fragile though it was, it was strong and heavy. Robin hugged it about the middle, half-lifting, hauling it along. By Star's special foaling stall, I had her let it go.

Star, as I see now, looking back, was still an uncertain enough mother, and uncommonly enough attached to Robin, not to be so fiercely protective as she might have been a few hours later. We did get

**190**

pony dam and foal into the prepared shed, where Star now gave calm attention to a good feed and drink while the foal made reassuringly loud slurps as it nursed like an old-timer.

"Put iodine on the navel." It sounds so simple in the books. The books don't mention what the foal—let alone the mother—is doing while you apply that stinging stuff. Of course, my iodine spilled completely.

Neighbors, responding immediately to a "happy emergency" call, arrived with excited whispers and the iodine and a bag of carrots for the mother. We all muddied our way back down to the barn by flashlight, and I allowed one brief peek. Imagine. I'd have been thrilled just to see an hour-and-a-half-old foal, let alone own one. And we had seen ours born! What is more, it happened to have happened on Mother's Day.

After everyone left, I put the iodine on. I decided it was safest to do it alone, counting on Star's knowing me. Without too much trouble I was able to struggle the foal back to pour on the iodine in the dim light. From the way it wiggled about when I let go, I must have covered the right territory.

Now I knew for sure it was a girl—a filly foal. A little bay, brown to bloodred, with a fringe of black mane that looked as if someone had just undone braids. A little broom tail of black with white at the dock, constantly flipping. One white hind pastern (left) and one ring of white around the left front coronet. And a big pear-shaped star on a dish-faced head—miniature Arabian indeed, this tiny Welsh pony.

Suddenly, as I knelt in the fragrant warmth of hay and horse, the shine of my flashlight on the water bucket became the glint of show ring lights on a

**Stardust and her wee filly a few days after foaling. The foal's bright bay and splashy star contrast with the gray of her dam. In maturity Galaxy too is a gray.**

silver trophy, the drumming rain on the roof the patter of applause. Blue, red, yellow rosettes blurred brightly in the cobwebby shadows beyond the rose gray mare and her tiny foal. Names of ancient Welsh ancestry whispered with the rustle of straw underfoot: Dinarth Henol, Coed Coch Glyndwr, Tan-Y-Bwlch Prancio, Prydydd, Lowri, Revel, Madog, Pioden—

For one dreaming flash all the magic of the age-old Welsh breed brightened our rough stall. Then Top Rail Stardust touched her future champion with a gentle nicker, and I got to my feet.

Outside, the rain fell soft and gentle. A special word to Tuffy, and a last peek at Stardust and foal, and then to bed. Our little world at High Hickory was the richer because we had witnessed the miracle of birth.

**191**

# 14

# RAISING A FOAL

A FOAL CAN COME INTO YOUR LIFE IN VARIOUS ways. (1) You may decide to breed a beloved mare of good health and bloodlines, carefully arranging stud service with your own or someone else's stallion. (2) You may want a certain pony—Connemara, Welsh, New Forest, or other registered breed or crossbred—and find that, foal at side, she is available only in a "package deal." (3) You may buy a mare that has already been bred and will foal sometime after you become her owner. (4) Rather than a young or aged pony, you may want a foal and conduct your search for the ideal pony (see Chapter 2) with only this particular age group in mind, investigating foals at the dam's side or in the next· weanling stage when (and only when) they may be separated from their mothers.

If you buy a pony mare with foal at side, find out whether the mare has been "bred back." Don't be surprised if the pony still nursing that bouncing youngster is already in foal again. Economics call for a brood mare to produce each year; to accomplish this, a mare is bred back during her first heat a week after foaling. (During the last few weeks of gestation, she may be sent to the stud farm to foal, so as to be where the stallion is available.)When we bought tiny Tuffy, she had an even tinier foal at side, but she had not been bred back.

If you are starting to raise ponies on a planned breeding program, buying a bred-back mare with foal at side results in a three-in-one-start. However, you may not want yet another foal the coming spring; so check. If you buy a mare with foal at side

and are prepared to keep it, consider weaning and raising problems. Remember, disposing satisfactorily of a foal or yearling later may be difficult if you have bought one simply to get its dam. If you want a foal as such, buying one "ready made" with or without its dam or as a weanling is obviously less of a gamble than buying an in-foal mare or breeding your own. Buying young stock is always a gamble, though. Judging this age group is a skill acquired only through experience of young animals, and a horseman's ability to judge a mature pony does not necessarily qualify him to judge a foal or yearling. Here, particularly, buying from a respected breeder with an established reputation to uphold protects you.

Like children, ponies as foals, weanlings, and yearlings go through various stages of cuteness and gawkiness. Just as it's hard to be certain that the pretty roly-poly toddler will develop into a well-built adult, so it is hard to see beyond the heart-warming charm of a foal and predict the desired conformation of maturity. Again as with the children, many animals that mature into satisfactory-looking "adults" pass through discouragingly awkward, homely stages. Let an experienced pony breeder help you evaluate the potential.

If you breed your own mare to a stallion whose parents and whose offspring, perhaps, you have seen, the element of gamble remains. You breed for certain desirable traits of both sire and dam that you can see in these mature ponies—size, color, head, disposition, jumping ability—but you still have to sit back and wait, praying for, at the least, a healthy normal foal.

You can also acquire a foal as we did: because you want a certain pony. We bought Top Rail Stardust *in spite of* her being in foal. A common arrangement in such a case is for the return of the foal to the breeder at six months, or for the payment by the dam's purchaser of an additional sum (usually the equivalent of the stud fee or more). Agree in advance as to who is to pay for veterinary care, extra feed, and transportation; at the end of six months, you will have made a small investment of money and a much larger one of your time. The biggest investment you make will be one of affection for the foal; so be warned.

We certainly had no intention whatever of keeping Top Rail Stardust's foal. High Hickory is geared to raising Border Collies and a few sheep, not ponies. One eight-year-old girl did not need three ponies; we would have Star, and we'd never part with outgrown Tuffy; a third—unrideable for at least several years—would be ridiculous—

However, we wanted Stardust, and the arrangement mentioned above—paying an additional sum or returning the foal at six months—would provide Eric and Robin with what might be a once-in-a-lifetime chance to enjoy a foal, with no worry about how to dispose of it once it was weaned. (Top Rail Stardust, a Coed Coch Glyndwr/Madog mare, had been linebred to Coed Coch Prydydd, and the foal would be a peculiarly desirable fourth generation which the breeding farm wanted back as part of their permanent herd.)

Parting with the foal would of course be hard, but, we reasoned, with Stardust and Tuffy as consolation we would surely survive the wrench. We ought to have known better!

Don't (I therefore suggest) buy a mare with an unborn foal on this either-or basis. If you know you can't keep the foal, fine; you can build up resistance to make parting possible. But if it's "maybe," you may do what we did—spend six months churning over whether or not to keep a foal that we loved more and more each day.

If your foal is "in dam," alert your vet as to the possibility of your needing him on the predicted foaling date. You may not need him. I wish you the easy "magic moment of birth" we shared with Stardust on Mother's Day. Welsh ponies, like most native breeds, do foal easily; pasture foaling in warm spring weather is the most natural, convenient of "arrangements," far safer than an inadequate, none-too-clean stall: the mare must have room to move around. Nevertheless, years of aiding in lambings, Border Collie whelpings, and other animal births have shown me that complications are always possible. If you have taken on the responsibility of breeding an animal, you must follow through on the attendant responsibilities of gestation and birth.

Concern for your foal should begin before the service of your pony mare by the stallion of your choice; it should carry through the prenatal year as well as from birth on. Riding of the in-foal mare will be somewhat restricted. All vets emphasize "no jumping"; but regular exercise is good. You will want to watch gates and doors to avoid bumping, and other ponies to avoid kicking.

Immediately after the birth, attended or not, your vet will give shots to both dam and foal. Possibly he will give the newborn an enema; early bowel movement is vital and, as with your grown ponies, an indication of state of health. For instance, scouring or diarrhea in the foal may occur at about a week, when the mare comes into season. Washing the foal's bottom will make him more comfortable. Should this scouring continue for more than a few times, or commence at any other time, you should consult your veterinarian right away.

You will want to limit visitors for the first week or so, as with any new baby. The most easy-going pony may change personality even with her beloved owner or stablemates. She may be fiercely protective, sometimes only at first, sometimes for weeks, maybe always with strangers. Proceed with care until you see how she feels.

Stardust, who calmly let us handle her foal right from birth on, went into a frenzy the morning after foaling when Tuffy, till then her buddy, somehow got into the paddock and looked in the window of Stardust's stall. Star circled, half-reared, stomped, bit—all at her foal, rather than at Tuffy—and our veterinarian (who had come to give the routine shots) said that in such circumstances mares sometimes kill their own foals. Fortunately his prediction of continued trouble did not materialize. In the greater freedom of the paddocks Star relaxedly let the foal and Tuffy make friends through the fence. Sooner than expected (and by their own doing) they were sharing a field, and from then on it was more usual to see the foal grazing beside Tuffy than beside her dam. Yeld mares like Tuffy, who have had foals but are now open (not in foal) and without a foal at side, sometimes jealously cause trouble, after foaling; before foaling, one is often warned against running an in-foal mare with a gelding.

Aside from a few routine precautions, you will find that your foal is a pretty rugged little animal! Tiny Galaxy raced and cavorted, skittering through woods and underbrush, not only leaping stone walls but scrambling along them. Foals are like children: it's amazing the bumps and bruises they survive. Inevitably they'll cut a nose on a wire opening no grown pony ever thought of poking through, or they'll rub shoulders raw trying to barge through a post-and-rail fence to get to their dam, though the gate is wide open just five feet farther along.

Remind your children that if a silly frantic foal gets into trouble it is quicker and easier to lead the mare to the foal than the other way around. Once calmed by the presence of his dam or a person he trusts, he can usually extricate himself. In many ways success in training a foal depends on the transferral of the foal's trust and affection from his dam to you and his other handlers.

## TRAINING YOUR FOAL

The demands your pony makes on you as a foal are less than at any other time. Until weaning, the dam supplies the most nourishing food—her milk—and shares her hay and grain ration (be sure to give them a feed tub big enough for two heads), and teaches her child where the best grazing and water are. If there are other ponies or such hazards as stray dogs she will protect him, or teach him to be unconcerned about what he may initially regard as a menace, a chipmunk for instance. The foal will spend his days eating, playing, and sleeping.

Don't be alarmed if you see him flat out. Those little sides *are* going in and out, and at your voice he'll lift his head. He's not dead, just dead tired—but in an instant, he's up and off in wild antics, sniffing at a dragonfly, snorting at a rock, exploding in a buck, galloping like a miniature stallion to skid to a stop under his mother's neck.

Perhaps the most important part of your pony's education comes during these early months. You want to encourage his confidence, his inquisitiveness, his trust, his obedience. The sooner you start handling him, the better. Galaxy was, as I have said, handled from within minutes of birth—perforce—

picked up and carried, a tiny leggy armful, by an eight-year-old child while I led calm, trusting Star.

From then on, whenever the foal was concentrating on nursing and we fussed over Star, we would gently stroke the foal. Galaxy got used to being touched before she was truly aware of it. Soon the gentle pat on the back became a stroke, and the stroke on the back extended down the legs and under the belly. While still tiny enough to be less powerful than the people around her, Galaxy was held gently but firmly—and never had occasion to learn that she could be boss.

In fact, Galaxy spent the first two weeks of her life being picked up and carried a few feet, over and over again. Millwood Hunt invited pony and dam to be a "star attraction" at the annual show. This seemed a wonderful chance to boost ponies in general and the Welsh in particular and to make a contribution to the show: it would help with publicity. (New England newspapers actually gave two-column headlines to the promised appearance on both sports and society pages: this tickled all concerned.) But what if we had trouble getting her to the event?

Daily, like the muscle-building boy with the growing calf, we picked Galaxy up. On the morning of the show, with Stardust and Tuffy in the rented-for-the-occasion two-horse trailer, we picked her up and popped her through the escape hatch into the open storage space in front of the stall partition, under the nose of her dam.

The show committee had put up snow fencing at Raceland, and within this enclosure, at one of New England's most beautiful shows, Top Rail Stardust

**Visitors like Leslie prepared pony mare and foal for hundreds of spectators two weeks later when they were star attractions at a show.**

and High Hickory Galaxy made their debut. The interest and delight of spectators and competitors alike was most rewarding. Children and adults submitted suggestions for a name. (Galaxy was just "the Foal" then and remained just that for months.) Everyone wanted to take pictures and "just touch." It was amazing, particularly in that horsey milieu, how many people—children and grown-ups, horsemen and nonriders—had "never seen anything so tiny" as our little Welsh foal.

Regardless of how you get your foal, once you have him handle him as much as possible. The more people, not only you and your family but friends and visitors too, that handle him, the better—under supervision, of course. A foal used only to small children and women may react to a six-foot man as if this were a member of a different species. Remind visitors that even the best-natured foal is a baby, with the unpredictable responses of a baby. An inquisitive nuzzling can become a nip; good spirits may manifest themselves in a playful kick—considerably more painful that that of a human baby. Also, just like a bitch with puppies, the family-loving dam may be suspicious of and hostile towards outsiders.

In the early months, your foal will spend most of his day in complete freedom. Most breeding schedules are worked out so that foaling takes place in early spring, in order that foals can be outside in fresh air, warm sunshine, and green grass. These are the days to have fun with your foal—just watching!—and to make friends.

Try with your foal the procedure we use with our Border Collie puppies: Make a point of calling your youngster, catching him, fussing over him, and *letting him go*—at a time when you do not need to catch him for any purpose (such as tying him up or shutting him in a stall). The pony (or puppy, or child) who thinks being told to come means only loss of freedom is not going to be eager to obey. The foal who learns that the approaching child means something nice—a friendly word, a carrot, a scratch behind the ears or along the neck, and then release to go back to grazing—will come up equally willingly when the child has a halter or bridle in hand and work is in sight.

Add some sort of call to your pony vocabulary. The Pony Pals always carol: "Come, Pony-ony-onies!" (I've heard funnier calls, from yodeling to whistling and hand clappings) when they go out to hay, grain, or bring the ponies in. This call promises something good, and even tiny Galaxy responded to it from early foal-hood, cantering in from the fields with her older companions. Such a call may save you both time and steps when your ponies are out of sight but not out of hearing.

Your use of the pony dam will be less restricted after foaling than it was during late gestation, although you may have to stick closer to home because of the foal. You will want to bring the dam back into riding condition gradually, and feed to compensate for her nursing as well as for her working, of course. Some of the best riding fun Robin ever had with Top Rail Stardust came right after Galaxy's birth. Within a few days, and with the veterinarian's okay, Star was ridden quietly with the wee foal scampering alongside, all around High Hickory. Later, while Robin rode Star I'd hike along with Tuffy on a lead rope and Galaxy free. (We were lucky in having miles of paths which we could use without meeting another person or having to cross a road; otherwise it would not have been safe to have a loose foal galloping along.) Perhaps this exercise served as a substitute for the strenuous play some foals get running in a herd, and helped make Galaxy the well-developed filly she became. As for Star, with the addition of motherly whinnies of reassurance and pauses for nursing, her schooling went on as with any "single" pony.

It was a delightful sight to see a Pony Pal on Tuffy, Robin on Star, with Galaxy prancing about them, a lively shadow. If Star went over a low jump the foal would soar after (the Welsh ability to "jump like a deer" shows up early).

If you have other ponies, however, problems of jealousy may arise.

As mentioned above, Tuffy's intrusion the morning after Stardust foaled drove Stardust into a frenzy that took the form of attacking the foal. This problem, by great good luck, sorted itself out. But there might have been another kind of crisis. Often a yeld mare like Tuffy will be possessively troublesome. While the dam can protect her baby against other mares (and be downright unkind towards another mare's foal), trouble is best avoided. Fortunately, again, Tuffy was disposed to be friendly towards the newcomer, while Galaxy on her side was, within a few days, more often grazing next to Tuffy than near her indifferent mother. Possibly she thought thirty-nine-inch Tuffy was another foal.

Require obedience of your foal right from the start. While he is tiny enough to hold in your arms

**With the veterinarian's approval, Robin resumed schooling, with the wee foal scampering alongside Star.**

**The pause that refreshes: the foal interrupts Robin's ride to nurse her dam.**

196

**Tiny halter is worn only under supervision, lest the foal catch a leg in it.**

and is still weaker than you, teach him that you are master and that "Ho" means to stand quietly.

Get a halter on him early. It may be hard to find one small enough, but putting a halter on a tiny foal that someone can hold is easier than struggling later with a strong six-months-old. Never leave a halter on an unsupervised foal. Check the size of the halter frequently; you'll be surprised at how fast the foal grows. Make sure the noseband fits, with no loops that a little foreleg can get caught in while the foal is grazing, or a hindleg while he is going through one of the enchanting contortions he goes through to scratch behind an ear.

Since leaving a halter on is so dangerous, it's helpful to be able to come up to your loose pony foal to put the halter on in the field. Children may find it easier for one child to slip a lead rope over his neck while another one puts the halter on, until the foal is completely relaxed about the headstrap's going back of his ears. Gentle rubbing and handling of the ears and all parts of the head makes haltering and bridling easier.

Since a foal should not be permanently separated from its dam before about six months of age, we'll assume her presence at any schooling session. If your pony foal comes to you as a weanling, we'll hope someone else has already followed such procedures as these. However, they can be applied to a colt or filly of any age.

Make any pony routine a training session—but only if you are not in a rush. Don't tackle anything new, or any training, unless you have time to spare, if need be, to follow through should a problem arise.

From the very outset, voice commands obeyed by your pony dam on a lead rope are copied—and learned—by your loose foal. Before she herself was put on a lead rope, Galaxy already knew "Ho," "Walk on," and "Come" from imitating Stardust. Instead of walking your pony straight out to pasture or from one field to another, make the normally uninterrupted walk a practice for "Walk on" and "Ho." Lead twenty feet, then stop, then walk on.

Certainly your foal will run free to where you take his dam. Take advantage of that fact when you first put him on a lead rope. Avoid any arguments: "Lead" him where he himself wants to go—up to his mother's side; but add a little tug on the rope to your voice command "Walk on." From day to day you can increase the separation between foal and dam, still following but in an increasingly distant or roundabout manner. Make the foal stand for a longer pause while his dam moves away, until he is told to walk on after her. Make him stand while she is led out of sight around the barn corner; then walk on to reunite them. Gradually he will accept his dam's lengthier and lengthier disappearances.

Avoid any tugs-of-war with your foal. Permanent injury can be done to a little neck or back. A frantic foal may rear and fall. If you haven't a pony dam or an outgrown pony like Tuffy to act as a steadying aid, always have someone at hand to help you. Even nonriders in your family will enjoy sharing in this early groundwork. A little pressure on the foal's rear, an arm around a little rump, or someone with an encouraging voice merely walking behind can help the person leading. (Professional trainers sometimes use various rope loops to accomplish this phase of work, but such devices are better avoided by the novice and are unnecessary with the patient, firm but loving approach of the "this pony is mine" handler with a long-range plan for his pony's development.) If the foal pulls back, head high, neck rigid, forefeet ready to come up off the ground, don't pull. Ease up: let the foal settle down, soothe his tenseness, and start again.

Don't try to lead him any great distance the first time. Be content with a few steps forward. As in all your schooling, reward any cooperation with praise—a pat, a word, a carrot tidbit. Take advantage of the pony's intelligence and of his unspoiled disposition. You'll find that a foal has certain puppy-

**197**

Our Welsh foal at three months is as big as our
Shetland at seven years. Later, when full-grown,
Gal measured a little under her 12.2 dam.

Green Star's mind is more on her foal than on
Robin's work in hand.

**Soon Star relaxes and leads on nicely, foal prancing behind.**

like qualities that make training a delight.

While your foal is tiny, teach him what "No" means. Any tendency to nip should be immediately discouraged. This would be the only case in which I'd condone a child's hitting a pony—and then the correction should be instantaneous, a light, brisk tap on the muzzle.

Some people believe that carrot- or sugar-feeding makes ponies into nippers. Our ponies have been rewarded with carrots for years without taking to nipping. We may need to discourage sniffing of carrot-filled pockets with a "No," but apparently the rewards are commonplace enough so that no bad habits develop.

The playful wheeling and kicking out some foals indulge in when being "picked up" in pasture can be avoided if you always stop just before you reach your foal. As with your grown ponies, let him come the last step or two to you. Never chase him if he moves away. Rather, pretend to walk away yourself, or sit in the grass and pretend to ignore him. Ponies, young and old, are friendly and curious; if you go up slowly, with frequent stops, and hold out your hand, your foal will make his approach. With a tiny foal, it

often helps to stoop down or kneel so that you are closer to his level. When children go to fetch him, stress that their movements should be slow and gentle.

Because of the deep friendship that developed between Galaxy and Tuffy, we did not have the

**Ponies are affectionate. Galaxy lavished love on Tuffy, whose company she preferred to her dam's, but here she noses Star.**

problem of an upset foal or an unhappy mother when Star was ridden far off alone before weaning. If you don't have the rare good fortune to have a baby-sitter like Tuffy, a frantic youngster trying to get to its mother by any means may prevent the mare's being ridden except with the foal along, which may limit your riding to the paddock or home pasture.

Fencing and stalls that are adequate for mature ponies are often not sufficient or safe for an upset foal. Foals may climb, barge into, go through, jump out of, get entangled in, any fence or any stall door or partition not specifically designed to resist such assaults. Proper facilities must be a consideration when you decide whether or not to have a "backyard foal."

Certainly at High Hickory we are not really geared for proper weaning. There is not the complete separation (out of sight, out of sound) there ought ideally to be. Where we have post-and-rail fence, it is lined with stock fencing because of our sheep—perfect wire traps for scrambling foal legs. Neither three-foot fences nor stone walls were a deterrent to an unwilling weanling dead set on getting to her mother and nurse.

A few horsemen suggest gradual weaning: most recommend complete and permanent separation at about six months. The Arabs, according to one authority, believe that a healthy lactation period should equal the duration of pregnancy. (Few horsemen let a foal nurse that long: either the mare has been bred back, or she needs to maintain her freedom and condition for work.) Despite our efforts, little Welsh Galaxy was obviously a proponent of the Arabian theory.

If we had had a colt rather than a filly foal, weaning might have been simpler. Colts tend to "horse around," climb up on their dams, and pester them. Before long the mares will bite them, kick out, drive their male offspring away in no uncertain terms. Sweet Star is so good natured that even though she would squeal with pain when toothy Galaxy nursed, she would never, alas, be "mean enough."

At long last, after applying alum with vasoline and then vicks vaporub, by seeing that Galaxy stayed with Tuffy fields apart from Star, by preventing her ever being near her mother when she was hungry or thirsty, we finally triumphantly completed the weaning process—at about twelve months.

When children are doing the schooling of a foal, the cautions stressed in previous chapters hold good. Play and work should be under the supervi-

sion, not necessarily of a horseman, but of a mature person. A youngster's mistakes are often those of overambition, impatience, lack of judgement—even if the youngster has had considerable pony experience he is nonetheless not an adult. One moment's explosion into crossness because of frustration, temper, exhaustion can undo the patient labor of a month and also create new problems. A child needs to be reminded of this—before the explosion can take place.

A child may be so keenly aware of the final goal he is aiming at that he can't appreciate the slow steps forward that are actually being made. Progress may be so imperceptible from yesterday to today that the child may have to be reminded of the progress made from two weeks ago to today.

Keep a notebook, and take pictures, so that there can be an objective record of progress.

Like the pony he is schooling, the child may need praise for the slightest accomplishment. A child who has ridden only schooled ponies or schooled one pony satisfactorily may have forgotten—interestingly enough—how slow the stages of schooling were, and thus he may apply standards of "perfection" wildly beyond the reach of his pony. Neither youngster—the child or the foal—should be allowed to school when tired or hungry or in a bad mood.

**Now too large to run free with ridden ponies, Galaxy is taken in hand on surprise-proofing expeditions. On this one she was led over a pile of soft, shifting sand.**

200

Right from the start, take advantage of every opportunity to train and surprise-proof your foal. Our blacksmith was cooperative: even when trimming was not needed, he would pick up Galaxy's feet and let her investigate his equipment. When bulldozers, dump trucks, and tennis-court-rollers clanged and roared around High Hickory, we led Galaxy up close to watch. Whenever we had the trailer (we were then renting one) we fed her a snack or a meal inside.

At horse shows, Robin showed the foal in "in hand" classes, to give both herself (she was eight) and the wee Welsh experience of the bustle and commotion of exhibiting. At home, when a child was driving the pony cart someone would lead Galaxy alongside; later, a passenger would hold the lead rope and let Galaxy jog along behind.

Sometimes the surprise-proofing merged with make-believe. Pony Pals dressed Galaxy up as a patient with leg bandages—as a knight's charger with trailing finery—as an old witch with a paper-bag hat. Nothing phased her. (We have one picture of Robin reading to Gal, the foal half asleep, "tucked in" with a grainbag, her head in Robin's lap.)

From the start we encouraged lolling and leaning on the foal so as to put weight briefly on her back, and reaching over and across her body, with the result that when Galaxy was older it was not a shock

**Napping Galaxy is too drowsy to respond to curious Mirk. Minutes later she fell asleep with her head in Robin's lap.**

to have Robin astride for a few seconds at a standstill. Remember that all your early handling of your foal is aimed at the pony's calm acceptance of the rider on his back when he is older.

Your foal will not be ready for lunging, bitting, ground-driving, or other more serious schooling for some time. Meanwhile, continue your daily handling, feed well and often, and look forward to the challenge of more advanced work. Have fun with your foal!

# 15

# FUN ON A PONY

GAMES AND EXERCISES ON YOUR PONY CAN PROvide fun all year long. When icy footing or deep snow limits the amount of active riding, many of the following exercises can be carried on in a sheltered paddock or inside the barn—even in a large roomy stall. (At High Hickory, because our pony barn is low roofed, we have a strict rule of "No one on a pony's back inside a stall.") If, like one of our neighbors, you have a stable with a tremendous main floor, you can even play indoors those games on ponyback that are done at a walk.

These exercises not only develop dexterity, strength, and balance in children but accustom their ponies to all sorts of motions on the part of their riders. Before you start the exercises, make certain that the pony is surprise-proof. Be sure he is used to waving objects, to pressure on his rump. Reach behind you as you sit in your saddle and put your hand all over him—*firmly*. Often a pony will fidget at a light, uncertain touch; a firm hand tickles less.

Note that in many cases these exercises are done by the mounted child *only* with someone at the pony's head. Since there are usually "extra" youngsters around any pony, these games are doubly good in that they can include nonriders as well as several youngsters sharing a pony. In many exercises a nonrider helps by holding the pony while the mounted child goes through the stunts with his reins dropped on the pony's neck.

Note, too, that in every case at the start of an exercise the rider takes his feet *out* of the stirrups *before* he does anything else. Thus if he accidentally kicks his pony he still has his reins for control. If he

loses his balance he can safely slide to the ground. He *drops* his reins *last* and picks them up *first*. In each exercise, whether at progressive steps throughout with a green pony or at the end with a schooled pony, the rider finishes by patting his pony, picking up and adjusting his reins, and then, without looking and merely by turning his toes up and in, rather than by raising his legs, puts his feet back in the stirrups. (Some of the exercises can be done bareback, some really require a saddle.)

Fun on ponyback of course includes such groundcovering games as Rescue the Maiden, Tag, Cowboys and Indians, and Treasure Hunts. The fun described is of a much more stationary sort. Directions are given as they would be by the Pony Pal assistant or "instructor."

### NUMBER 1

*Exercises without reins*

For the beginning rider (first time on a pony, even), a most elementary exercise is to sit or ride at a walk *without reins*. Youngsters (and adults) often consider the reins a device to keep them on their ponies. A little time spent at a standstill, then at a walk, later at a trot and a canter, without reins improves balance, hands, seat, and confidence. So, with a Pony Pal at your pony's head (not necessarily holding him), drop your stirrups. Drop your reins evenly on your pony's withers. Put your hands on your head. Put your hands on your shoulders. Clap your hands over your head. Behind your back, etc., etc. With several youngsters riding in a group this can be a lively "Simon Says" game. Done at a trot or a canter it can be challenging to older, better riders.

*Dismount at a Walk*

This is a safety exercise, done first at a walk, eventually at a trot, even at a canter. At a walk, take both feet out of the stirrups. Reins in your left hand. Both hands on your pony's withers. Supporting your weight on your arms, swing your right leg straight over your pony's rump and, saying Ho!, slide to your feet, facing the way he is moving. (If you are following the training suggestions already given in this book, your pony learns to come to a standstill as you dismount when he is moving—a great safety factor.) Then immediately move on at a walk or jog. (In games such as Musical Chairs or similar gymkhana events, winning may depend on having a pony that will lead on rapidly after a dismount.) Stop, and mount.

**Exercise No. 2. Safety Dismount (at all gaits)**

**With an assistant close by to reinforce "Ho" if necessary, Pony Pal Karen swings off Galaxy in a safety dismount.**

*Lying Down Backwards*

Having made certain that your pony is surprise-proof and doesn't mind pressure on his rump, have a Pony Pal hold your pony *under* his muzzle—ready to raise the pony's head if he should move forward or shift his hindquarters. (A timid child will soon do this exercise with confidence in the instructor and the pony, even first time up, but may need the assurance of another Pony Pal's hand on his knee and shoulder. Stress should be put on the rider's keeping his lower legs in place so that his abdominal and thigh muscles do the work.) Now, feet out of stirrups. You can hold the reins by the very end or, better, drop them evenly on the pony's neck. Hands on your knees. Keeping legs in place, lie back until your head is on your pony's rump. Just pretend you're lying on a bed! Relax. Count to ten, or look for bluejays, or recite "Ride a Cock Horse" . . . anything to encourage limpness. Now sit up. *Don't* let your legs swing forward as you do so, or your hands jerk the reins and your pony's mouth. Pick up and adjust your reins. Feet back in the stirrups.

**Exercise Number 3. "Lying Down Backwards"**

**Robin on Star, Susie assisting.
(Border Collies: Airlie and Guess)**

203

*Toe Touching*

This may be done without reins and stirrups or without stirrups with the reins in one hand. Keep your legs in place, in either case. Reins in your left hand, raise your right hand up over your head and then reach over and down to touch your left toe. Change rein hands. Raise your left hand high, reach over and down to touch your right toe. Don't let the opposite foot slide back as you reach for your toes. Keep both heels down. Get your seat out of the saddle, rather than moving your foot forward, in order to touch your boot.

Again, with better riders, this can be done at a trot, then at a canter, and the toe-touching time can be prolonged. Another version is to have the rider reach out and around his body with his inside arm to touch the letters on the fence rail as he goes round a ring. (Letters can be utilized for many games and exercises—figure eight's, circles, serpentines, relay races, and drills of all sorts.)

Toe-touching develops one-handed control, with the body bending forward and down and twisting from the waist, and is a good prelude to games like Toss the Ring in the Basket and Flag Snatching.

**Exercise Number 4. "Toe Touching"**

**Robin and Janie, the Pony Pals;**

**Star and Tuffy, the ponies.**

*Heels over Head*

Feet out of stirrups. Drop your reins. Put your hands behind you on your cantle, thumbs turned *outwards* away from your body, so that you can support yourself when you lean back. Swing your legs up and together over your pony's neck until you click your heels together. Lower them and pat your pony.

The secret of this (and the next exercise) is to keep your legs *straight* and to *swing* them up. If you bend your knees as you raise your legs you'll kick your pony. Lean back slightly on your arms and think about raising your feet, not your knees.

If you find your legs unexpectedly heavy, or if your pony raises his head as you swing them up, start by raising your legs only to the point where you feel the strain or where your pony begins to be upset; then lower them and praise your pony. You will find that he soon accepts your strange antics. Of course the Pony Pal holding your pony must allow (and encourage) him to keep his head and neck normally low.

**Exercise Number 5. "Heels over Head"**

**Robin up, Janie assisting at Star's head.**

*Cut-Under.*

This exercise is more difficult because it requires strength from the rider's arms as well as coordination. Here the secret is to keep your arms stiff and your weight above the saddle (and slightly to the off side) throughout. (With the emphasis on physical fitness and the practice of push-ups and pull-ups in schools today, youngsters may not find the cut-under so tricky as adults may. Some of our keener Pony Pals do push-ups, pull-ups, deep knee bends,

**205**

and straight-knee toe touching in their bedrooms at home just to improve their riding.)

To begin the cut-under, drop your stirrups and your reins. Put your right hand on your cantle, and keep it there. Put your left hand on your left knee and *keep it there*. Swing your right leg over the pony's neck. You now slightly resemble a side-saddle rider. Put your left hand *over* your right knee and on the pommel. Supporting yourself on stiff arms, turn over on your stomach. With one motion, and the greater part of your weight on your left arm,

shift your right hand to the pommel *as* you swing your right leg over your pony's rump. You are now back in the saddle. This last part is somewhat similar to mounting, and if you support your weight on stiff arms you will land in the saddle without thumping your pony's back.

Neatly done, this is an impressive trick, one that gives children lots of merriment and lots of challenge and that puts most of them on equal footing regardless of riding ability.

## Exercise Number 6. "Cut-Under"

**Robin up, Janie at Star's head.**

Exercise Number 7. "Kick-Back"

Robin on Star, with Janie.

NUMBER 7

*Kickback*

Less complicated, but also requiring some strength and coordination is the kickback. Drop your stirrups and your reins. With your thumbs pointing forward and outwards, grip your saddle skirts or knee rolls close to the pommel with your hands; if your thumbs are out, your upper arms and elbows will be close to your upper body as you lean forward. Supporting yourself on your elbows, in one motion swing your upper body forward and swing your straight legs backward and up over your pony's rump. In order to kick your feet together in the air in this kickback, your entire body will be clear of the saddle, and you will be briefly supporting your whole self on your arms. Again, come back gently into your saddle to avoid bumping your pony.

The kickback, like the cut-under, is usually better done when done with a certain amount of speed; you swing your lower body and legs back and up, rather than lift them.

As the photographs show, a pony with a good disposition and tractability makes fun on a pony possible even with some strange acrobatics. Observe the basic cautions emphasized here, and note that there is always a Pony Pal "assisting." Such playing on horseback is one more illustration of how ideal a pony is for a family.

# 16

# FUN BEYOND YOUR OWN BACKYARD

BESIDES THE DAY-TO-DAY "BACKYARD" FUN THAT you have with your pony, there are many kinds of activities that you can participate in away from home. Gymkhanas and horse shows come instantly to mind, as do hunting, trail riding, clinics, rallies, trials of all sorts, and—most challenging and exciting of all—eventing. Some information about horse shows, gymkhanas, and eventing is given later in this chapter.

Many youngsters belong to such organizations as the United States Pony Club or the Horse Project of the 4-H Club. Many are junior members of such general groups as their state Council of Horsemen or, say, the Green Mountain Horse Association, or of breed organizations such as the New England Welsh Pony Club. These groups sponsor activities geared specifically to the interests and ability of the young rider. Most carry on with indoor meetings and educational programs during months of limited riding. Treasure hunts, picnics, overnights, breakfast-, lunch-, or supper-rides, and workshops often spice their programs, providing a youngster with a pony a chance for fun with his peers beyond his own doorstep.

Beside one-day affairs, there are many which cover several days away from home and involve overnight stabling. Many commercial riding centers and stables offer courses of varying lengths for the rider with his own mount, as do many private camps emphasizing or specializing in riding. (Of course some of these establishments provide mounts, but others expect and allowance is often made for the youngster who brings his own pony to a session.)

The young rider may participate in special divisions in endurance or competitive rides, ranging from short-mileage to two-day affairs to long-distance treks of a week or more, with overnight stops at the same base or at different stops along the route. Well-known among such exciting events, and specifically tailored to the young horseman, are the U.S. Pony Club regional rallies and resident clinics and the 4-H Horse Camps.

While your own backyard may be near enough to some activities scheduled away from home for you to hack (or ride) over—for a swim in a neighbor's pond, for instance—participation in most such events is possible only if you truck or trailer your pony some distance. In the early days of pony ownership you may find it more practical to rent a trailer or pay someone else for vanning. However, while a child may fervently declare that he'll "never ask for another thing" if only he gets a pony of his own, "a trailer of my own" soon heads the Christmas list; and the piggy bank into which allowances, newspaper-route money, or baby-sitting and berry-picking profits clank bears a new sticker conspicuously lettered "Pony Trailer." Some advice on choosing a trailer is given in Chapter 17.

Whether hacking over or trailering makes entry in these outside events possible, happiness and success in the venture depend largely on the same ingredients: You and your pony must be in the necessary physical condition to participate and at the proper level of schooling for both rider and mount. You must have certain necessary equipment in good condition. If you are vanning, your pony

**Pony too young or too green over fences to hunt?
Robin and Lute, relegated to the sidelines, look on
as Old Northbridge hunts Millwood.**

**Bruce Davidson, top international horseman,
talks to absorbed riders at a Ponkapoag Pony Club
clinic. Our participant described this pose as
"croaching," a good portmanteau word for
crouching and coaching.**

Robin and Star, still going strong after a cross-country outing, come uphill and through a gap in a stone wall, with the rider out of the saddle to spare her pony's back.

Water-rat Lutine enjoys swimming as much as her rider. Back home after a triple success at the University of Massachusetts Horse Trials and Dressage Show on two days of record-breaking heat, Robin and Lute cool off.

**When other footing is still too icy, a muddy turnaround provides a place for work to keep a pony in condition.**

must load and unload easily so that you can transport him to the site.

Much of the advance work in readying for any of these events is the same regardless of whether you and the pony will be away for a day or for a week. While in many cases a youngster will be accompanied by a parent or some other grown-up, often he and his pony will be on their own. Robin's and Stardust's week at a 4-H Horse Camp one summer provided just such an independent excursion into the wider world of horses. Southern New England Horse Camp in Worcester County, Massachusetts, with fifty boys and girls age ten and eleven, each with his own pony or horse that had been his 4-H project for the past year or longer, proved an ideal adventure for a child away from home on her own with a pony for the first time.

For these young horsemen, camp was limited to a week's stay. Workshops on English and Western riding, jumping and hunt seat equitation, fitting and showing, schooling and retraining, trail and obstacle riding crammed each day. Youngsters of course did their own grooming and stable work. Since riding with other pony riders in the same age bracket is special fun and since having your beloved pony along the first time away from home is like having your "security blanket" or favorite teddy bear, what better introduction to the away-from-home extended activities could a ten-year-old have: The weather cooperated, the beds were comfortable, the food was good, the counselors great, and in the little horse show that climaxed the week Top Rail Stardust lived up to her past performances by taking a blue in

each class in which she was ridden. From the start there was happy talk about "next year."

Preparation for an adventure like this—for you and your pony—should begin well in advance. Just as your pony should not stand idle during the school week and then be ridden hard and long over the weekend, so should he not be expected to participate in a full strenuous schedule for days in a row without preliminary conditioning. If he is going to do well on even a fifteen- or twenty-five-mile trail ride, if he is going to carry you through a two-hour workship in the morning and a three-hour workshop in the afternoon daily for a week, you must start weeks ahead to toughen him up.

At the same time that you are getting your pony muscled up by trying gradually to approximate the type and amount of exercise your special adventure will demand of him, you will be getting yourself into good condition, too. No 4-H Horse Camper had trouble sleeping at night, but even the child who "rides all day"—in playful off-and-on rides—will find four to six solid hours in the saddle amazingly strenuous and likely more than he is accustomed to. So, without making it an alarming routine, and without eliminating the fun, some schedule of regular exercise should be worked out well in advance of the actual event and adhered to faithfully. It is better to work your pony regularly and steadily half an hour every day than not at all for five days and several hours on the sixth.

Along with this conditioning should go the opportunity for the young rider to become as independent and as self-sufficient as possible in the total responsibility for his pony. While youngsters with ponies should always be under adult supervision, supervision of a duo ready for activities beyond their own backyard should be as slight and as unobtrusive as possible. Stable chores should be competently done voluntarily, rather than of necessity, at a parent's instigating "Time to water." Performance of chores could be checked off on a chart rather than by "Did you hay?"

Some provision must be made for the possibility that things may go wrong away from home—a pony go off his feed, reins get broken—the sort of thing that wouldn't unduly concern a child in his own surroundings but could away from home. He should be aware that he may have to adjust feed proportions, should know to whom to turn for advice, and should feel assured that he should never hesitate to ask for advice and help.

It may be wise to recommend tact and diplomacy to the young rider who is used to one teacher at home, when he goes for the first time to a camp or clinic. Make it clear that for every instructor there's a different way of teaching, and that while away he should follow the advice of the new instructor, whose tutelage he has asked for by the very fact of coming. Later, if he so wishes, he can compare and evaluate, and choose either to follow the new methods or return to his old. An outspoken child may need to be warned not to pipe up: "But that's not how Mrs. Sugdenson said to shorten my reins" or "That's not how I was taught." (At High Hickory we always use the "safety dismount"—both feet out of both stirrups before any other step. 4-H Camp taught the more formal way of dropping only the off stirrup, swinging the leg over and keeping the body weight on stiff arms and only then dropping the near stirrup and sliding to the ground. One little camper is convinced that dismounting as her 4-H instructor taught helped her win a blue ribbon, though she decided to return to her old safety dismount for everyday riding.) Foresight on such small matters as this one of open-mindedness will help make any away-from-home pony experience a happier one, for it will lessen the trepidation that inevitably tinges the most eager anticipation for a first-time participant.

### LOADING

You and your pony may be in ideal condition for your special event, but that will avail you nothing if you can't get him to leave home! A pony's reluctance or outright refusal to load can spoil any trip—at the last moment. Practice loading ahead of time. Having your own trailer simplifies this: if you don't own one, you will find it's worth the additional expense to get the one you're renting for a day or two extra, beyond what you need for actual trucking. Make a point of feeding the pony in the stationary trailer right in your driveway occasionally; then unload him without driving at all. Thus his associations with being loaded will be pleasant ones exclusively. (The way to a man's heart may or may not be through his stomach: certainly the way to many horse events via trailer is through a pony's!)

If loading is new to you and/or your pony, several bits of advice may help:

Your pony may go more willingly into the trailer if a stablemate is already aboard. (But if another pony

**Lutine, neck rope in place, looks on as trailer tailgate is lowered.**

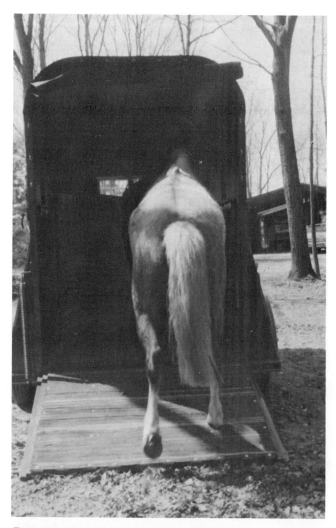

**Despite the dark interior, Lutine walks willingly aboard. Rainflap has been rolled up overhead, center partition swung to one side.**

**"Good girl, Lute!" Voice praise and a handful of grain reward Lutine for loading willingly.**

School only when you can, if need be, devote an hour to it.

School your pony to load when he is hungry. You may coax him aboard step by step the first few times with handfuls of grain—always repeating the command "Walk on" or "Come up." Eventually he will walk on or come up on command whether or not you have a container of grain to entice him. Grain and carrots failed to coax one pony we worked with, but we found that a bucket of water when he was very thirsty was an excellent lure until he got over his initial fear.

Don't be impatient. The pony may be almost aboard and then back off—He may have three feet on, the fourth about to step up—and a sudden motion on your part will back him out in a hurry. Have a lead rope long enough to give him slack without fighting him, let him calm down, and start over.

The firmer and more level the loading ramp and the steadier, the more willing your pony will be to embark. He will be quite right in mistrusting wobbly or ramshackle footing or in hesitating to load when he can't see the interior of the stall for contrast with sunlight outside or light blinding him from the front windows of the trailer.

In practice sessions, praise any slight progress he makes, even if he has only timidly put two feet in the stall and stopped there: do not try to force him beyond that point in this lesson.

Occasionally someone will give a loose pony complete freedom of a trailer, allowing him to go in and out on his own to eat. This does teach the pony to feel at home, but does not teach him to load when led and on command; it may even develop bad habits of backing out before the handler wishes. Do not permit your pony to start backing (or, worse, to try to turn to get out) before he is told.

Except for the rare case, if you have been schooling your pony according to the ideas in this book your pony will follow you aboard even a strange trailer calmly and confidently.

Of course there are problem loaders, and of course there are many ways of forcing a pony aboard a trailer, most of them guaranteed to make the animal unwilling ever to load nicely. At any show grounds you will see "rare cases" being loaded by a crowd, never by just one handler (whereas our goal is one pony/one child). Someone at the pony's head pulls while two helpers use a pole or lunge line to pen him from behind. Or, when he balks part way

is known to be a bad loader, don't let your green pony watch him fuss.) Your pony may load more willingly if, instead of going into his stall ahead of him, you lead him into it by walking into the adjoining stall yourself. Some ponies dislike being cramped or dislike crowding; so shift the lead rope around the center post and reach across to tie him up. Always use your halter hitch or quick-release knot. Once the pony is well aboard, have someone shut the trailer door or raise the tail gate promptly but quietly behind him. Do not let spectators or "assistants" stand in the pony's line of vision, as their movements may frighten him: have them stand well behind his rear.

Teach your pony to load only when you have time to spare. Never load for the first time, or with a problem pony, if you have only five or ten minutes.

in, someone whacks him with a broom from the rear so that he plunges into the trailer. Or you will see a neck rope being used like a winch: when the pony is part way in the rope is tied to an inside stanchion at the shortest possible length; when finally to relieve the pressure on his neck the pony moves forward a step or two, the slack is quickly taken up; this process is repeated till he all the way in and the tail gate up. Most such "cures" have to be used over and over, every time you load.

Should your new pony turn out to be a rare case, a problem loader, how can you cure him once and for all, or with perhaps an occasional booster shot?

First try to analyze why he is a problem. Is he green and untaught? Is he full-grown and mistaught? Willful and cagey, has he learned that he can get away with not loading by exerting his sheer physical strength against you? Has he had a bad experience traveling in a rickety trailer or noisy van with a driver who took corners too fast and slammed on the brakes? It can be an eye-opener to follow in a car behind a horse-trailer. I have seen ponies constantly shifting and trembling because of noise or wind or lack of space: even seen them so thrown off balance that they ended up sitting on their rears with one foreleg or both in the manger or over the center partition. All too often the driver—indifferent or unimaginative—has been unaware of any unusual commotion behind him.

Often problems in loading are related to problems in tying. I have seen one pony plunge and rear in a moving trailer basically because she was a problem tyer. And the means of solution to the two problems are related: gradual development of confidence through familiarity in the area of fear—and Xenophon's age-old advice.

That solution of course takes weeks, even months. Meanwhile, there may be times when you have to load your unready pony; and this is the method we have found more successful:

Have the trailer ready in a familiar paddock or enclosed field, with the ramp down as firm and level as possible and the center partition swung to one side and secured so as to allow as much stall space and as wide an entry as possible.

Take time to protect your pony's legs and head with proper travel gear—leg bandages, bumper cap, sheepskin-wrapped halter. You will also want your lead shank with the chain on one end and your schooling whip or switch.

This session, like all other schooling sessions, is intended to convince your pony that it's pleasanter for him to do what you want him to than not. It is going to be one of the rare times when you use your whip not as a visual aid as in lunging but on your pony, as punishment. Because of the very rarity of this method, it will be effective without being harshly applied.

The chain of the lead shank may be used either over the pony's nose, as in your initial teaching of "Ho," or, as a more drastic resort, fastened in the same way but under his upper lip and around the gum. In the latter method it is trickier to keep the chain in place, as it slips the moment you give any slack, but you must remember that the slightest pressure on the lead shank is pressure on the chain on an acutely sensitive part.

All commands and controls should come only from the handler; and this is one time when the handler should not be a small child. It is a problem pony situation and should be dealt with by a mature person. (If you're seriously studying this book, you probably "qualify.")

Now with your pony in one hand and your whip in the other walk towards the trailer as if you expected no resistance. The instant you feel any resistance apply the whip behind you sharply, at the same time saying "Walk on." If the pony walks on, fine; go right into the trailer with him.

If he doesn't, use your lead shank to keep him from backing. Realize that he will swing his rump away—possibly his feet off the ramp. This is one reason why you took the trouble to bandage him. He may try to pull back or plunge or rear. If he's too far out of position to go into the trailer, circle around and start over. This time say "Walk on" and apply the whip immediately. Try to walk on into the trailer and be sure to praise and fuss over any concession your pony makes.

If he does load, he may instantly try to back out, so be prepared to say "Ho!" But this is a lesson in loading, so don't get into a second fight over his staying. Jump the gun the first few times by ordering him to back out if he shows signs of doing so. You can then load him again and make him stay inside a little longer. The main thing is to get him aboard and be able to praise him for obedience in that regard.

Some difficult ponies acquiesce after one or two light switchings. With the rare real problem, be prepared to do battle if necessary! One of the best ponies we've ever had in every other respect, but one with the worst "emotional" problems, put up a full hour's resistance; but she now practically trots aboard.

Every pony, like every person, is different. If you get yours full-grown, you will reveal yourself as a person as well as a horseman according to your ability to differentiate between the timid pony who is willing but fearful and the cagey pony who is just pitting his one-track mind and superior strength against you. Sensitive handling does not mean babying, nor does it rule out drastic methods when they prove truly necessary.

### TRAVEL BANDAGING

During travel your pony's legs and tail should be protected by bandages. (Knee caps, hock boots, and poll pads or head bumpers are other protective devices: sheets or blankets are sometimes worn during travel time also.) When learning to load his pony, a youngster can learn to bandage, but a grown-up should check the final work, as too-tight or too-loose bandages can cause trouble.

Youngsters usually enjoy bandaging. Besides protecting, bandages neatly applied lend a dressy look to your traveling pony. (Our bandages were gleaned from several sets of red, white, and blue, so Stardust went off to 4-H Camp looking like the Fourth of July.)

Bandages, usually made of wool or cotton and similar to an ace bandage, may be put on over a roll of cotton batton or may be put on the bare leg. They

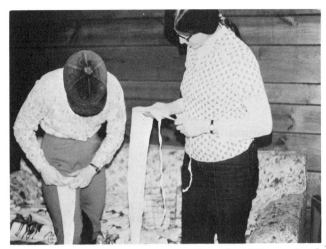

**Tapes are straightened out before freshly washed bandages are rolled and used or put away.**

**Bandaging takes practice; here, just for practice, it is done without the usual cottons underneath.**

**Home after an outing, two partners show Grandma one result of their day's activity. Lutine was as carefully bandaged for the return trip as she was for predawn departure to the three-phase rally.**

should be neatly rolled up, with the tapes and sewn part inside at the center or beginning of the roll.

Commence bandaging just below the knee or hock, with a short flap left exposed, wrapping the bandage downwards around the leg to the coronet, unrolling a little at a time. At the coronet or fetlock joint the bandage will naturally turn upwards. Continue unrolling, working upwards, till you reach the knee again. Before making your final turn, fold the exposed flap down and cover with the upcoming bandage. The tapes will now be in your hand and can be tied in a surgeon's bow on the side of the pony's leg and then tucked in. We finish off with a strip of masking tape over the ties. Tying off on the front or back of the leg may cause painful pressure on the tendons, so avoid this.

Never sit or kneel to do legs, even those of the best-natured pony. Squat or crouch.

When removing bandages, untie and unwind loosely without attempting to rewind. Just pass the bandage from hand to hand close to your pony's leg in loose coils. Once they are off, give your pony's legs a brisk rub with your hands to restore circulation.

Tail bandages should be used to avoid rubs and should be removed immediately on unloading. You may want to wet your pony's tail to make the hairs lie flat, but never wet the bandage itself, as shrinkage could well injure the tail and would at the least spoil its appearance. Start at the root of the tail (near the body) by putting your hand under the tail with a length of bandage in it. Hold on to this length until you make one complete turn and secure it. Keep your first two turns high on the root of the tail, then work evenly downwards. Just above the end of the tail bone, tie the tapes neatly but just tight enough to hold the bandage in place.

Removing the tail bandage is a quick easy operation: put both hands around the bandage close to the root and slip it off with a firm downward pull.

GETTING READY TO GO AWAY

The pony kept out on grass or used to free choice as to stabling may find it hard to be confined to a stall at a camp or clinic. At 4-H Camp when Stardust found herself in a slat stall surrounded by four other strange ponies with still others across the aisle in the Pole Barn, she showed her uncertainty by at first refusing to eat or even drink. Some ponies used to lingering over their food in solitude may start

**Mastering bandaging is serious business for a child who wants to be self-sufficient before she and her pony go off to camp on their own.**

bolting their grain; others may chew wood, or pace. Others equally used to roughing it in the open may decide this is the life and be spoiled forever!

Youngsters love to have their ponies make friends with other ponies in new situations, but they should be warned that sniffing and nose-touching may end up in sudden (surprisingly startling!) squeals and attempts to bite or kick, whether the ponies being introduced are under saddle or on a lead. Children riding side by side should be warned not to turn their ponies' heads away, for this instinctive "correction" of a pony that puts its ears back merely swings the more dangerous rear end closer and may precipitate kicking. Better for each rider to keep his pony straight, pushed up to the bit, and to rebuke the mood so fortunately indicated by those talkative ears with a firm "Behave yourself!" and continued watchfulness. Even a pony that has seemed indifferent to other horses in the show ring may reveal uncertainty, irritation, or downright dislike of the situation (as much as of another pony) when asked to ride side by side in pairs or by threes, to travel at a walk or trot counter to other moving ponies in the ring work, or to have ponies passing close in front or behind in crossing figure eight's and other exercises. Sometimes all the ears-back pony needs is the familiar voice soothing him and reassuring him with an "Easy, Boy," or "Trot on." One of our goals is a happy pony with a happy rider, and those weather-vane ears are a good indicator of success or failure.

Before any extended absence from home with your pony, one-time dates on your calendar should include veterinarian, blacksmith, and saddlemaker. See that routine health care is up to date—negative Coggins, shots for tetanus, shipping fever, encephalitus, etc., just as you are better for having your tetanus booster, and polio immunization. Schedule your blacksmith's visit to ensure good feet for your stay. (The group sponsoring your special event usually provides a source of emergency care.)

Tack should be in tip-top condition, not only well-cleaned, but with all stitching and leather strong and flexible.

Oil the safety clasps through which your stirrup leathers run and keep them open. (Never ride with them closed. If you ride correctly you will not lose a stirrup, and better the leather should come off than risk failure of a safety clasp to open in an emergency. Such failure might result in dragging.)

If your saddle does not have D's (metal fittings shaped like the letter D), your saddlemaker or repair man can put some on your saddle—in several locations so that you can carry a raincoat or sleeping bag behind your cantle, in front of your pommel, or to either side of your seat behind your saddle skirts. Most hunting saddles have such D's so that hound couplings, wire cutters, a flask or sandwich case may be attached.

If you plan to carry supplies on your away-from-home, experiment ahead for your comfort and your pony's. I well remember one childhood overnight on which several ambitious young riders carried all cooking, eating, grooming, and sleeping gear in grain bags slung in front on each side of our legs. My bags contained the knives and forks, among other noisy sharp utensils, and both my mount and I were well pricked before our enforcedly slow ride came to a weary end. Most of the fun of an overnight is in the actual riding, so it is better for supplies to be trucked to the campsite and have as little equipment as possible carried by the riders (even leading a separate pack horse is not much of an improvement). Then the riders can "move on" at a trot or a canter or take an occasional fence comfortably.

For short trips, a knapsack on your back or over your shoulders may not be too awkward, and some of its edible contents can be replaced with treasures—wild flowers, special stones, interesting cones or feathers—found on the trip. Less cumbersome is a small insulated picnic bag such as the ones Pony Pals use. They carry nearly frozen cans of drink and a chemical "cold" can in one, sandwiches and bathing suits (nylon tank suits take no space, dry almost instantly) in others tied to the D's with ordinary shoelaces. These bags are soft and compact and can be squashed close to the seat so they do not bump and bother the ponies or riders. Midday as well as overnight stops can be arranged at a friend's: this gives children a chance to extend their riding territory on their own and parents a chance for a discreet safety check.

For such trips, a halter can be worn under the bridle with lead rope attached and ending in a loop around the pony's neck. Of course a lead rope can be coiled and attached to a D, worn as a belt or shoulder sash, carried in a knapsack. But your pony's wearing his halter is more convenient than your carrying it to put on over a bridle or having to remove your bridle for brief stops. Having a halter and lead rope so convenient eliminates the risk of a youngster's tying up a pony by the reins and chancing broken tack.

Fortunately, little special equipment is needed for such special activities beyond your own backyard. Usually all you have to do is put some mark of identification on items you already own. You can splurge on brass identification plates for saddle and halter, or you can mark the underside of the leather with magic marker or pyrography needle. Letter wooden handles in the same way; use bits of colored ribbon or string on lead ropes, conventional name tapes on jackets and hunt caps, decal or stencilled initials on water buckets, grain barrels, and tack chest.

It is mostly a matter of replenishing normal supplies, at your tack shop: but normal supplies are numerous—and bulky—enough. Packing Robin and Top Rail Stardust off to camp for one week was as complicated as packing two children off for two months. Besides providing for possible extremes of weather and temperature, besides bedding and towels, work, play and show clothes, reading, writing, and swimming material for the rider, the pony had to take along everything but her stable. Tack, of course, and its cleaning kit (saddle soap, sponges, bit polish, etc.), grooming kit (curries, brushes, hoof pick, etc.), broom, manure fork, rake, wheelbarrow, water bucket, feed bucket, lead rope and cross ties, feed measures, first aid kit—and, of course, the inevitable supply of carrots.

If you and your pony are going to travel to any extent, a tack chest will prove very handy, particularly one designed to hold a saddle as well as

Tack chest with saddle rack, bridle hook, and removeable tray keeps equipment organized at a ten-day Pony Club clinic in Vermont. Chest has castors for easy moving. Web guard across stall doorway is a handy travel accessory.

grooming supplies easily accessible. At Horse Camp, riders' trunks were placed by their beds in the dormitory and tack chests were placed by the stalls in the barn aisles (although saddles and bridles were generally kept in special sheds).

Just as inanimate equipment must be properly cared for, stored away, or returned to its place for continued daily use after any special event, so your pony must be properly cared for on return home after a period of intense activity. Rider and pony may both welcome a day of rest on their first day back home, but on the following days exercise should be gradually tapered downwards, not suddenly cut down drastically or eliminated. Continued intensive riding like that of the camp, clinic, horse trials, or endurance ride may not be possible or desirable, but your pony must be conditioned away from the peak ("let down") just as he was brought up to that level.

In this way you and your pony will be easily and happily ready even on short notice for your next adventure away from home.

## HORSE SHOWS

*"Contestant Number Fifty-four. Mr. Rupert Jones on Bully for You. In a four-way tie for first place."*

*The announcer's voice crackles over the loudspeaker. A ripple of applause. The spectators inch to the edges of their seats in the bleachers. Below them the ring is a mass of color: red geraniums, evergreens, white standards, green-and-white striped poles, startling against the tan-bark. Resplendent in red, the top-hatted ringmaster raises his long horn and brassy notes rise to the rafters. A gleaming chestnut prances through the in-gate, his black-coated rider hat in hand. A salute to the judges—and, accelerating, horse and rider circle. Silence throbs as they fly the first jump.*

The show ring is also called the show arena, with all the arena's associations of gladiatorial combat. No one ever enters a class at a horse show, even the tiniest rider, even if he tells himself it's farfetched or premature, without some hope of coming out with a ribbon. (Blue for first, red for second, yellow, white, pink, green—on down; there can be ten.) "Just for fun" is more fun if you place.

Throughout the country, shows if "recognized" are run under and if "unrecognized" modeled after the rules of the American Horse Shows Association.

The A.H.S.A. rates various divisions: for example, a show may be entirely an A show or be A in one division or B in another. The annual A.H.S.A. Rule Book runs to over three hundred pages; if you're interested in showing you should become a member and know the rules, for shows "go by the book." The Association governs conduct of shows, duties and qualifications of judges, stewards, and other officials, class definitions, tack and apparel of competitors, and so forth.

For pony riders, there are the A.H.S.A. Hackney and Harness Pony Division, the Hunter and Jumper Pony Division, and three divisions for Shetland, Welsh, and Pony of the Americas respectively. You and your pony can compete in lead line, in model, halter or in-hand, on the flat, either hunter or jumper over fences, equitation, equitation over fences, breed classes, and driving or in-harness. (In equitation classes your horsemanship is judged, not your pony.) Championships are offered in pony divisions, as well as ribbons and trophies in each class.

If you have never seen a show, attend several as a spectator before entering one. Read the prize list for scheduled shows to know what classes count towards championship and reserve and what the class restrictions are. Riders may be restricted by age or by experience as determined by ribbons previously won (maiden, novice, limit). Ponies may be restricted by sex (stallions barred, mares in foal only, etc.), by age (yearlings only, etc.), by size (under 11.2, over 12.2 but under 14.2, etc.), by breed (Welsh, Connemara, etc.), or by type (pleasure, hunter, pet, model, etc.). There are open classes with no restrictions, too. (In any under-saddle class suitability is considered in judging; in any children's class, the smaller the pony the greater the emphasis that should be placed on suitability and temperament.)

You may send in advance entries, filling out a

**Number tied around her waist, a four-year-old and her suitable little Shetland get their first show experience in a lead line class at Raceland.**

blank with information about your pony and yourself, to be signed by your parent (unless you qualify for one of the all-too-few "adult to ride" pony classes); you will also send a check for your entrance fee (stabling if overnight) and drug test fee, as well as a photocopy of your negative Coggins test if required. If post entries are allowed you may wait to enter at a slightly higher fee on the day of the show.

On arrival, in either case, you will pick up at the entry desk a number for all your pony's classes and one for all your equitation classes. Cardboard or cloth, these numbers tie around your waist or arm or clip on the back of your jacket collar. Be sure to wear yours so the judge can see it, and know it in case you're "called."

Thousands of shows—indoor and outdoor—are held annually, and in recent years there has been a formidable increase in the size of classes, particularly in the number of junior and amateur/owner entries. Classes with over fifty entries must be divided; and so very high are the numbers that the A.H.S.A. makes provision for redivision of either split if that still has fifty. Today it is very hard to find such a thing as a small show.

In fact, the very popularity of showing has led to a situation which is making showing unpopular with many horsemen and causing concern among exhibitors and officials.

Lutine takes an artificial log in her first indoor show. Even if not claustrophobic, your pony may need to become accustomed to a covered arena.

Classes, not riders, are scheduled. They may start late and run over the estimated time, delaying all that follow. An exhibitor may after much pre-dawn effort arrive well on time to be ready (tacked and warmed up) for the first—eight A.M.—class, only to wait forty-five minutes for it to commence. A last class, scheduled for four o'clock, may begin at six; do young riders forfeit their entry money and their high hopes to get home when planned, or risk their family's ire and late late barn chores? Even the best-organized show may drag on long after dark; the A.H.S.A. has found it necessary to rule that "No class shall be started after midnight."

Classes on the flat are so mobbed (forty-eight or forty-nine; you wish there'd been fifty!) that a rider may not even be observed by the judge. Overworked judges lament that they cannot make helpful comments—how can they give careful heed to one pony or one rider out of hundreds? Their score cards are hardly ever posted and when they are may need translation. Risk of injury to rider and pony increases when rings are so crowded that "Keep to the rail" and "Do not cut corners" are rules impossible to respect (and even "Don't run over the judge" may be difficult). In classes over fences competitors ride individually, but large entries throng the in-gate.

Not only is showing itself less and less a civilized, personalized affair: the show grounds are more hectic. More vans, more trailers, more trucks, more exhibitors' cars, more spectators' cars, more grooms and helpers, more litter—more people. Practice areas (for warming up before classes) may be unfenced and unsupervised, with riders as well as spectators seemingly oblivious of the vulnerability of people on foot among ridden horses and ponies.

Horse shows are not merely highly competitive: in many ways they are now big business. Aside from the frankly commercial element (concessions, tack and trailer sales, paid ring crews, coaches, trainers, announcers, and so on), in many classes cash premiums totalling thousands of dollars are offered along with ribbons and trophies. You meet entrants, products of our affluent society, who are there not just to win a ribbon but to "make expenses," to "be in the money." Even children today in some classes judge achievement by money earned—four-figure yearly totals. You meet entrants who consider that if you don't win, what you do is go buy a better mount—not that you try harder! (Result: winning horses and ponies change hands for astronomical sums.)

220

Perhaps this is part of the current commercialization of all sports and our lack of clear-cut amateur/professional standards, scrupulously observed. At any rate, for people who want to enter "traditional" shows, it's hard to find one that is low keyed.

As a novice rider or a junior rider with a green pony, you ought to be able to show in a relatively relaxed manner. But it may be hard to find a show where you are not badly outclassed. Since in A.H.S.A. ones ponies may show green one year only, experienced riders try to give potentially top mounts experience at unrecognized shows, greatly stiffening and increasing the competition for the novice rider on a backyard pony. (Besides cash stakes, many riders aim for annual high-point awards and horse-of-the-year awards. Competitors may travel constantly "on the circuit" from one show to another, cramming in as many as possible to pick up the necessary points. Such "pot hunters" and "point chasers" are even found in lead line and short stirrup divisions!) If you do decide to show, do so at a show suitable to your ability and your pony's ability—and looks. It must be realized that there is a tremendous gap, as far as top-level showing is concerned, between a show pony and even the best of backyard "just for fun" ponies.

The Pony Pals know a show pony: Amelia's Licorice Lad. He came with all sorts of championships from another part of the country, four thousand dollars worth. Boarded at a big stable, he is given mounted schooling daily by adult professionals. Amelia shows him weekends. She is never allowed to ride him in the open, and one after another the Pony Pals have stopped asking her on pony picnics and trail rides. "Daddy says he's too valuable and Mummy thinks he'd get a blemish," Amelia says cheerfully to her peers; but to me she once said wistfully: "I've never ridden outside the ring. I think I'd be afraid on Licorice." Amelia is a pretty little rider; but so long as she is confined to the hothouse experience of showing she will never become the versatile horsemen that many youngsters with "just ponies" are.

Smaller shows (unrecognized or schooling ones) include open 4-H or Pony Club shows (some limited to members only, still have hundreds of entries) or Hunt Club or neighborhood riding club shows.

If you can find one of these, it will give you a chance to take your pony over strange fences in different surroundings and gain group experience in flat classes. Expenses like entrance fees are lower

**A local show gives a green pony experience over fences in an outdoor ring.**

(there won't be any stake classes or prize money) and your riding outfit, while it must be appropriate, may be less elegant than for a top recognized show. At such smaller meetings you'll enjoy the camaraderie of competing with others who share your love of ponies.

## GYMKHANAS

Rollicking fun on horseback—with the very name intriguing. Gymkhanas have the festivity of party games, the exuberance of children at recess. The audience is noisier, lustily cheering contestants on:

> "Ride, Roger! Ride faster, get in there!"
> "Come on Jenny! There, there!"
> "Hilda, you dope, that way—Head for the chair!"
> The rooting section jumps up and down by the white-railed ring. As the blare of music abruptly stops, their yells sound over the general hubbub. The three finalists in Musical Chairs hear nothing. Arms flapping. legs flailing, they drive their ponies in to the center, intent on being first to reach the two remaining chairs.
> A roar of cheers goes up, muffling groans. The ski-jacketed judge removes one chair and centers the other.
> Roger hugs his pony and leaves the dusty ring. Music again drowns out the shouts. Jenny and Hilda take the rail, cantering their ponies collectedly, eyes on the one remaining chair, ready to turn and race in, each ready to win with her pony!

The gymkhana (pronounced jimKAHna) developed from the rough and ready games of tribal horsemen—Tartars, Khirgiz, Cossacks. (Every country where riding is taken for granted has a playful version of its serious business of war, hunting, cattle raising, bronco busting—our rodeos are a case in point.) The wildness has tamed down, but the challenge and fun and often the element of speed remain.

Gymkhanas may be held under A.H.S.A. rules; these are organized with much advance planning and work and are highly competitive. The Association offers an annual Horse of the Year award in the Gymkhana Division. A prize list offering classes to count towards this might include Keyhole, Figure Eight Stake, Cloverleaf, Quadrangle Stake, and Pole-bending competitions or Scurry, Figure Eight Relay Rescue and Speed Barrel competitions, as well as a Gymkhana Riding competition.

But gymkhanas can be very informal—more romping and games than a straight horse show; this kind can be simply and quickly put on. Since the results of many games are objective, highly qualified judges are not required. Gymkhana games included under "Miscellaneous" on 4-H Show prize lists are often the most exciting part of the show for competitors and spectators alike. Since there is no widespread advance advertising promotion, entries come from a much more limited area than at horse shows, and there is a "neighborhood" feeling of familiarity and friendship which is not developed even by seeing the same competitors over and over on a show circuit.

In gymkhanas ponies and horses compete in the same class. You will usually be at an advantage on your well-trained pony. Quick turns (on a dime, not a quarter), obedient halts, willing work in hand (if you have to run on foot leading your pony by the reins), surprise-proofing (balloons bursting won't spook your pony), closeness to the ground (for quick dismounting and remounting) may determine success.

So will some skills that are not equestrian—skills like being able to untie and lace up two shoes quickly, in the Sneaker Race. This means that the ribbons are spread around a bit farther, but the ability to keep calm, think quickly, and work efficiently is part of successful competition at any level.

If you and your pony enter a gymkhana for the first time, avoid mass games like Balloon Bursting in which all riders mill around trying to pop everyone else's balloons while protecting their own, or the Unsaddling Race in which, once bareback, competitors race to the opposite end of the ring. Try a few of the more orderly games first: Egg in a Spoon, Command class, or Sit-a-Buck, where riders stay to the rail. Then if your pony is going quietly you can enter scurry games like Musical Chairs and the Costume Race.

For most gymkhanas you enter your pony when you arrive, for all classes at once or one at a time. The elimination of advance entries simplifies the putting on of a show, even if it adds to the bustle on the day of the show.

Put on your own gymkhana some time. You can include all your friends, since most of the games can be played at all gaits. Musical Chairs can be open to beginners at a trot as well as to advanced riders at a canter. One of Tuffy's first blue ribbons from a 4-H gymkhana was won at a walk! Gymkhana games are adaptations for ponyback of ones all children play on foot. If you need inspiration, see the Reading List at the end of this book, or any book on games. Of course rules must be spelled out ahead of time and the "judge's ruling" be accepted as final. The Pony Pals have found putting on an impromptu gymkhana an enjoyable way of earning money to contribute to some worthy cause on a small scale, modest entry fees going to the U.S.E.T. (United States Equestrian Team) or the S.P.C.A. (Society for the Prevention of Cruelty to Animals), for example.

Two Welsh ponies—raised at the same farm, together again only by chance—pair off successfully in a gymkhana class. (Alice on Crownridge Blue Chip, Robin in hunt cap on Top Rail Stardust.)

## EVENTING

*Hooves drum under you. The gleaming bay body*

**Jumping out of dark woods into a sunny field, Robin and Lute aim for the best landing and the most direct approach to the next obstacle.**

*drives forward, the black mane ripples under your hands, as you canter on. Wind stings your face as you push into a gallop. Sunlight glints across the wooded trail ahead. Birches and pines flash by. Sweat—your's or the pony's?—whitens the reins as you shorten up a bit and increase speed. Suddenly the woods open out, the wide field glistens green and gold before you—and you break out of the darkness of the woods. There, beyond the spectators crowding the course markers on the hill, the final flags flap red and white against the sky.*

*"Come on, boy!" Your pony senses your urgency. He lengthens his stride. Hoof beats, heart beats mingle. One last surge. You burst across the finish line—you and your pony!*

Throughout this book the stress has been on learning to do a variety of things. We want both the rider and the mount to be versatile. For both, eventing is the test!

Eventing, Horse Trials, One-Day, Three-Day, Two-Phase, Three-Phase, Mini-Trials, C. T.—these are all names for an exciting sport, *Combined Training*, which combines the thrill of fox hunting with the challenge of horse showing. For a rapidly increasing number of riders like our Pony Pals at High Hickory for whom crowded show rings have lost their charm and for whom opportunities to hunt dwindle with the encroachment of urban sprawl, eventing is a joy.

Combined training is considered the complete test of horse and rider. (If you're training your pony yourself, it is a way of evaluating what you've accomplished and what you can do.) Originating in the military in the days when cavalry was vital and an officer's charger had to be obedient, bold, and fit, C. T. today is a mushrooming sport which civilians have taken over officially under the jurisdiction of the United States Combined Training Association and similar bodies throughout the world and unofficially by riding organizations everywhere. The best known example of a sanctioned event of the highest standard is, of course, the Equestrian Three-Day Event at the Olympic Games. At the opposite pole, the most *un*known and informal are the mini-events the Pony Pals put on the last day of Pony Camp at High Hickory.

At whatever level, combined training events consist of three separate tests: a dressage ride or test, an endurance test, and a jumping test. Divisions for sanctioned combined training events include training, preliminary, intermediate, and advanced; while nonsanctioned ones may have novice or pretraining divisions, which, like training, may be broken down into Junior and Senior by age of rider. (As with any riding, to know the rules and support the activities, join the official organization—especially since many nonsanctioned C.T. affairs are "not yet sanctioned" ones that follow the official rules of the U.S.C.T.A.)

Entries close well in advance of the date of an event and are limited in number of competitors. You compete individually in each phase. Riding order is precisely scheduled. You will know days in advance that you ride your dressage test promptly at 8:35 A.M. and your cross-country at 10:47 A.M. Order for stadium jumping depends on your standing after these two. Dressage tests are available in advance (from the event sponsors, from the A.H.S.A., or from your U.S.C.T.A. Omnibook listing all events for the year), while your score sheet with the judge's comments may be picked up at the close of the event. For both cross-country and stadium jumping, "walking the course" is important preparation for deciding just how you will tackle each jump as well as the overall ride. Part of the challenge of eventing is seeing how you and your pony can handle at speed a cross-country course you have "cased" on foot. The cross-country is usually open the day before, so if you're fortunate you can walk it then as well as on the day itself. Stadium courses may not be walked until permission is given during the event.

Hunting attire is usually worn for the dressage and stadium jumping, but a sweater or jersey is often substituted for a jacket and a colorful silk cover worn over a hard hat during the cross-country.

In dressage, your pony wears a number on his bridle. In the other two phases, *you* wear a pinny with the same number. (These you pick up when you check in on arrival, along with an envelope of other pertinent information.)

Dressage is most simply defined as schooling or training but with emphasis on the finer points of a horse's education. Experts break this training down into the most basic Débourrage, the wider range of Dressage, and the higher and more limited achievement of Grand Prix or top-level dressage. Whereas "equitation" applies to the rider, "dressage" applies to the horse, and in dressage rides, while obviously how you ride affects how your pony goes, it is the horse not the rider that is being tested.

Dressage has been compared to ballet. In eventing then the program you ride is choreography planned to test your horse's athletic ability and schooling in performing designated movements on the flat and the impression he gives of being in obedient but willing harmony with his rider. In tests of varying degrees of difficulty (or training level) you and your pony earn numerical scores for transitions, for impulsion, for halts, for "tracking up" on the straight and on circles—for how well he executes all the things you've been working on at home! (The pony you've surprise-proofed won't lose points for shying at the white line laid out in chalk in the grassy arena, or jump out of the arena over the low boundary fence, or shy at a wall mirror if the test is indoors.)

Tests include work at the walk, trot, and canter; changes on the diagonal and circles; and, at higher levels, shoulders in, etc. Though the horse and not the rider is being judged, space on the judge's score sheet includes room for remarks that may apply to

Wooden "flag" and number indicate direction and order as Lutine Bell takes the star jump during the cross-country phase of a Novice Horse Trials at Trailmare Farm in Hopkinton.

the rider; and notes on "position and seat of rider" or "correct use of aids" contribute to or deduct from points given under "general impressions." During dressage, as always, you and your pony must ride as partners.

The cross-country phase tests speed, boldness, and jumping ability at a distance of specified length (about a mile in novice divisions) at a specified speed (reasonable and with much leeway in novice) over some twelve or fifteen natural obstacles (under three feet in height and spread in novice). The cross-country (or X C) is also called the "test in the open" and clearly is the one phase of the three that cannot be held indoors. The obstacles, even if man-made, are those that a cavalry officer might have to take if he were carrying an urgent message as the crow flies—stone walls, banks, slides, drops, water, tree trunks, gates: solid permanent obstacles that would prove no obstacle to the ideal charger. Not all are found at novice level.

The stadium jumping tests the horse over colorful artificial jumps requiring precise athletic response. At casual glance, the jumps and the course may resemble show-ring competition, but the resemblance is superficial. The test is not of style but of the horse's ability to complete the course after what he has gone through in the fast strenuous cross-country phase. Stadium requires fast obedient agility over a tight challenging course, all the more demanding after the bold forward flight required in the open. The stadium jumping is a test to see whether, unlike the horses who Carried the Good News from Ghent to Aix, your horse—or pony—is fit to carry on after the rigors of the cross-country.

Only a fit mount and a fit rider can pass the "complete test" of combined training—and a true part of eventing is the preparation that goes into it.

Conditioning is a continuing process that must commence months before your first scheduled trials. It must be carried out regardless of weather according to a well-thought-out plan so that your pony reaches his peak of fitness at the right date—and so that he is let down properly and gradually afterwards. To compete in one-day events, your pony will not follow the same regime as would a horse entering top-level three-day affairs. But like competitive endurance rides such trials are something he must be worked up to systematically. And if your yourself are to be in shape, you'll need the conditioning working with your pony will give. As with all your pony activities, eventing will affect your feed schedule: your pony will need to be taken off grass and/or his hay must be cut back and his concentrates increased as you demand more of him.

For any one aspect of combined training, one could write a book! I can only hope that the little that is said about it here will make you want to know more, and that most of all you and your pony will give eventing a try.

The thrusting power of a pony's hindquarters shows as Lute is about to take the second element of step jumps on a cross-country course at Stonehenge Farm in Dover.

For a novice, jumps downward may be more alarming than ones uphill, but: "Throw your heart over, and your pony will follow."

# 17
# CHOOSING A TRAILER

ALMOST INVARIABLY, FULFILLMENT OF THE WISH for a pony of one's own is followed by the wish for a trailer of one's own.

Of course a trailer is something of secondary importance. If there must be a choice, it is far better to put your money into a good pony and good tack and proper feed: and to all the little pony owners who complain to their mother and father: "Why can't I have a trailer?" it might be pointed out that there are many thousands of horsemen three or four times their age who have never had and who never will have trailers of their own.

Nevertheless the convenience and emancipation that come from having one's own trailer, as opposed to the uncertainty and questionable availability of hiring someone else's trailer or of having one's ponies "vanned" —and fitting into someone else's schedule—are certainly great. Suddenly you are mobile, free to go to show or a clinic or a friend's on the spur of the moment, free to load when you are ready and free to go home when you want. Anyone who has waited impatiently to load at dawn or has hung about wearily after his part of a show is over for another van-sharer knows what a relief this is. New responsibility is yours with ownership, however—if a parent, you will find that your role as groom will now expand to parent-groom-chauffeur-of-horse-trailer.

For years I longed for a trailer of my own. Then the time came to buy one. For months I looked at trailers, under trailers, into trailers. The more I talked with trailer owners and dealers the more I realized how little potential owners, myself in-

The Pony Pals always pack reading material— homework or The Lord of the Rings—as well as a picnic lunch. Alicia, Robin, and Lutine Bell relax between classes.

226

**Pinny on, Robin waits on the step of our new trailer(!) until time to saddle her New Forest/ Thoroughbred pony for a hunter pace event.**

cluded, knew about the subject. This chapter embodies some of the facts culled from talking with hundreds of fellow-horsemen and dozens of trailer dealers. These facts helped me as I was finally—"o frabjous day!"—in position to have a brand-new trailer of my own. Since according to several dealers women outnumber men in buying and hauling horse trailers, my point of view will perhaps be helpful.

The decision to buy a trailer made, you then have to decide whether to buy a new one or a used one. This decision may be easy: it may be arbitrarily determined by the amount of money you have or are willing to spend. New trailers seem to start at well over one thousand dollars and go on up; used trailers seem to start at two hundred dollars and go on up. Sometimes what may strike you as an extravagance in spending a little more initially will pay off in the long run in return on your investment if you decide to sell, in ease of operation and comfort while you own the trailer, and in peace of mind and assurance of safety not only for your ponies and horses in the trailer, your children and other passengers in the towing vehicle, but for everyone else on the road.

What do we look for in buying a trailer? Where do we look? And when do we buy most satisfactorily?

Trailers come in various sizes and in various "horses"—one, two, three, or four, for instance. Since the more common variety (recommended even for the one-horse owner) is the two-horse trailer, the information to follow will deal with that. Trailer heights start generally at six feet, increasing in six inch multiples. Trailer length follows in proportion, with short bodies or stalls in the lower versions. (A low price may indicate a short-bodied,

low-roofed trailer with narrow stalls—a point to keep in mind.)

So, if you have one pony, do you buy a one-pony trailer? Almost unanimously the answer is No. No seems equally unanimous when you ask about buying a two-pony trailer. For one thing there is the matter of resale value (here you haven't even bought a trailer and we're talking about selling it!). Your children may give up riding after the pony stage, or may move on up into horses. In either case the small pony trailer will have been outgrown and you will face a smaller, more limited resale market. On the other hand if you give up horses, a horse-trailer's value is automatically there even three or four years later. If you raise ponies or know that you will never truck anything bigger than a twelve-hand pony, there's something very nice about a small trailer behind: but the problems of loading, handling a loaded animal, and so on are lessened with a horse-size trailer. Good horse-size trailers haul with equal ease.

Even if you have ponies, the seven foot is the size most usually recommended. Don't take offense, as I was told some customers do, if your trailer salesman asks what sort of horse you have. Thoroughbred or Registered Welsh or part Quarter Horse or just plain plug—the question isn't asked out of snobbery. The salesman can advise you better as to size and style if he knows whether you are planning to truck a seventeen-hand horse weighing close to a ton or a midget breed weighing two hundred pounds only.

horse, where your riding interests lie, and why you want a trailer, they can better meet your needs— needs you may not really know yourself, if it's your first—with some version of the two basic trailer styles.

These two basic styles are the so-called Thoroughbred or Hunter type and the so-called Western or Quarter Horse type. Put most simply, the first style is boxier, its top squarer, at the towing end, while the second style is more rounded or egg-domed there. Interior differences will be described below, but perhaps it should be pointed out here that when a "Thoroughbred interior" with a "Quarter Horse exterior" is created on a Quarter Horse undercarriage, an undesirable toe-tripping difference in floor level between stalls and front space is often produced.

How do you go about buying a trailer, new or

used? By reading the advertisements in horse newspapers and magazines, your telephone classified pages, your city newspapers, your stable, grain, and tack store bulletin boards, signs on trailers at horse shows, your 4-H and Pony Club newsletters, and by word of mouth. Breeders and stables often sell trailers as a side line, as do some car or truck dealers. The most satisfactory source, probably, is the representative of an established manufacturer, a representative who has had experience himself in trucking horses so that he looks at the trailer from a horseman's point of view. Trailer dealers who handle horses themselves are usually aware of the safety features so vital to safe and happy trailering. And they are interested in repeat sales.

Since any of the features to be discussed would apply to used as well as to new trailers, I'll not make a distinction here.

Look at as many trailers as possible. There are dozens of makes, most with half a dozen models or more to choose from. If possible, talk not only with dealers but with owners using the various styles you see: find out what they like and dislike about their model, and then decide which will be best for you and your pony. But remember, as my trailerman says: "'Best' is a nebulous word."

When is the best time to buy a trailer? Obviously, so that it will be there when you actually need it. If you want a new trailer for spring, order before March. Once good weather rolls in, so do orders for trailers too, apparently, and unless you're taking one off the line at a lot you may have to wait till May for your special order to be filled. In the fall, students going back to school, families giving up showing, dealers with end-of-the-year sales of outgoing models may be good sources. If you must have any of the many individual features that are available (color, trim, attachments, etc.), allow four to eight weeks for delivery. If you're not too fussy, you can look at a trailer, go through the necessary formalities, hitch up, and drive off.

What is the most important requirement in a trailer? *Safety features:* (1) for the ponies inside; (2) for you and your passengers in the towing vehicle; (3) for all other drivers on the roads you will be hauling over.

Safety features for your pony include proper head height, proper stall width, sturdy chest bars (preferably made of metal, not wood which might splinter if the pony crashed against it); no exposed wiring for him to chew; no inside handles, hooks, or projec-

tions for his halter to catch on (with resultant panic and injury to him, not to speak of the most minor damage likely: a broken halter).

Safety features for the trailer tow vehicle include a heavy duty hitch, often a ball type that matches the trailer's in size. The hitch, best welded on, should be up to hauling the total tonnage and tongue weight of a loaded trailer. (Many lightweight hitches, merely bolted or clamped to a car, are designed only for such lightweight tows as a sunfish or snowmobile.) The trailer itself should have emergency brakes operated from the driver's seat or activated by a breakaway release on the hitch. Heavy safety chains secured with safety hooks provide additional security.

Load levelers, equalizer bars, sway bars, or similar hauling devices should be considered in terms of your own towing vehicle and trailer combination. Spare tires should be carried for both trailer and car as they usually are not interchangeable; a scissor jack rather than a bumper jack is required. A rearview mirror designed for towing can be permanently or temporarily attached to your car's righthand side for safety in passing and pulling back in as well as in backing. All equipment—trailer, towing vehicle, and connecting parts—must be checked regularly.

Safety features for the trailer include the basic box: a properly balanced, all-steel construction; a sturdy undercarriage; a strong axle with springs to absorb shocks, and wheels with tires that are at least four- or six-ply, wall included, inflated to thirty pounds. Welded and gussetted construction, rather than pop rivets, and box tubing are desirable. (Fiberglass roofing is available in some makes of trailers, and claims are that it is stronger than steel, cooler in summer and warmer in winter. Condensation may be a problem.) The roof should be one piece or the seams so welded as to be waterproof. (One new trailer I looked at was leaking like a sieve.)

The floor should be of boards spaced slightly apart. Although you see "tongue and groove" advertised as a selling point, I consider this highly undesirable and even dangerous. The slight gaps that one sees between floor boards are meant to be there, to allow for drainage and to prevent the floor boards from rotting out. Interestingly, oak, so good for house flooring, should be avoided for trailer flooring: it becomes more slippery when wet and dries out less well than, for instance, fir or hemlock, or soft woods. Having used a rented trailer with a steel floor, I would never buy one—or even use one again.

Various mats are available to go over the floor boards. Some are spongy and light and easy to remove for cleaning underneath, and soft under a sore horse. One generally rated high is the tire-tread mat, three-quarters inch to one inch thick, of wired-together strips. The matting is stiff and awkward to handle for cleaning but it allows for drainage of urine and does not become slippery underfoot as might the solid rubber sheets. Such standards also apply for matting needed for tailgate ramps not equipped with cleats to provide surer footing for horses, especially in backing out.

Two partners I talked with who handle standardbreds "housebreak" their horses so that they stale before loading, not in the trailer. Many horses hold back during a long trip; geldings and stallions particularly must have sufficient length of stall. (Whether you succeed in housebreaking your pony or not, always try to give him time to relieve himself before loading after a show, a hard ride, or a hunt.) Another dealer/breeder uses no floor mats—"A shoe can get caught in them"—but just scatters sand directly on the boards. Some people use mats only, others use bedding of straw and/or shavings over mats. I heard amazement expressed at how careless many owners are both about mucking out trailer stalls after use, and about occasionally removing matting and hosing out with the trailer slightly tipped up on its front jack wheel.

Chest bars are used on the Thoroughbred or Hunter models rather than the solid partition front with manger seen in the Western or Quarter Horse models. Chest bars are placed for the average-size horse—fifteen hands—and adjustments (involving permanent welding of supports) may need to be made if you trailer such extremes as a tiny Shetland and a huge Thoroughbred. (We have special brackets for the adjustable bar to be put into when we truck thirty-nine-inch Tuffy.) Some chest bars swing, some drop to one side (usually on the center partition), others swing and/or lift out completely; I prefer the last. Steel bars are, I think, best protected by padding. Planks are used, the wood covered by padding or, with one owner, by a length of inner-tube; but in case of trouble some makes could splinter or break. (But in case of trouble, argue proponents of planks, how do you cut or remove steel bars?)

Here perhaps it is time to consider the "in case of trouble," for this merits concern.

As a blacksmith who trailers a lot and has gone through many models said to me, "I'm glad to have you pass on my bad experiences, and not to have anyone learn the hard way as I did." Among his experiences was that of having a horse go through rotten floor boards on the return trip from a horse show; others will be mentioned later.

"In case of trouble" . . . because in choosing a trailer we can't always assume an ideal pony as loader or passenger. Something may go wrong to change your perfect pony in a flash, or your next pony may not be so perfect. You can love a pony or a horse to doomsday, but he may have some quirk that requires mobility of thought where the safety factor is concerned.

Most people would drive trailers differently and take corners more carefully if they had ever ridden in back with their animals. Open side vents cause rumbles in going under overpasses or by trailer trucks, and a trailer with a straight axle or Dead X passes every bump on to the pony.

In the Thoroughbred, the front of the trailer or the space beyond the chest bars is open so that the handler can open the bars, go through, close the bars, tie up his horse, and walk out a full-size side door. In the Western type, the stalls end not with a chest bar and a "room" beyond but with a solid partition which provides in its upper half a manger and in its underpart, accessible from outside only, a tack storage compartment. In the latter type a handler must either let his horse go in alone and go around to tie him up or must tie up in close quarters with his horse and then step up and stoop out of a small escape door. At a recent demonstration of loading at a local clinic, the horse was loaded alone, but before the handler went around to tie him up, from the front, he had half turned around and got stuck. If there is only one such escape door, the handler must always squeeze out past his horse when using the other side. This can be dangerous. It also means that the handler cannot reach or work around his horse from the front or head but must always approach him through a small window, through the escape door, or through the rear loading door.

With the open space (perhaps twice the size of a telephone booth) in the front of a Thoroughbred, with the chest bars as "stopping" point, there could be the possibility of a horse's going on beyond the bars, but it is possible to leave the bar in place and duck under if you are loading a green horse.

In the Western, it seems common to have a grate or spaced-grill partition dividing the manager and the forward part of the center portion from wither height to top of trailer. Most horsemen seem to feel, though, that if the horses are tied properly there is no need for such head and shoulder dividers. (In one new demonstrator model, spacing is such that a horse could get its head through—and caught!)

What is "properly tied"? In any trailer, this means with a little slack. In a Western, usually directly over the manager to a ring on the far side of the manger top. In a Thoroughbred, cross-tied to rings on the side of the center partition and on the outer wall. Thus secured, passenger ponies can eat from the manger or from a hay bag slung high in the center front space.

All types of two-horse trailers have a center partition dividing the interior into two stalls. Like the stall sides, this may be of plywood or planking (most rarely, metal), and, again like the sides, it may be lined with metal "kick plates." Like six inches or so of the stall side, the partition may be topped with padding covered with colored leatherette or plastic. The partition may be swung to one side at the loading end or may be completely removed. (Horse trailers double for all sorts of work!)

With a difficult horse, loading may be easier with the additional stall-width swinging the partition aside gives. (Here a tailgate loading-ramp trailer has an advantage over one with dutch doors; the latter has a permanent center post from floor to roof for securing the rear doors and even with the partition swung aside or removed this post divides the trailer, cannot be moved, and limits the width through which the pony can be led.) In a drop-tailgate trailer, the opening is the full width and height of the trailer itself, with no obstruction when the partition is removed. Some people like a half-partition, believing it gives an animal more room to straddle or spread his legs. However, unless a half-partition is needed for a specific reason (such as allowing a foal to nurse its dam while traveling), a full partition is safer. You can of course truck a single pony or horse with the partition removed, making the trailer one big stall.

Perhaps no one aspect of a trailer gives so much choice —or caused me so much pause—as the rear or loading end. Two basic styles exist: the drop-down bottom-hinged tailgate and the regular swing-open, side-hinged doors. Both basics are available in different varieties and in combinations.

Dutch doors (as tail doors are usually called) come in full length, in partition height, in midsection height in combination with a partial or mickey-mouse tailgate, and even in removable styles to use over regular tail gates. The dutch door-partial ramp combination makes it possible to close a horse in while the small ramp remains down. However, assuming that the only reason for having such a midsection door shut would be to keep a horse inside, the same purpose can be accomplished by hooking tail chains across. (Better trailers provide covered tail chains with two sets of hooks in two locations at the stall ends for adjustment to the size of horse or pony.)

Unless used in combination with this small ramp below them, dutch doors mean a "step up" trailer. This is popular in the Western models—Western horses apparently think little of hopping up even on to a pickup truck, to say nothing of hopping up less than a foot into a horse trailer. But one point was stressed by most other horsemen I have talked with—professionals who handle many mounts, not just one or two personal mounts: a horse is much more likely to walk on into a trailer when he has already walked part way up a gradual incline (the tailgate ramp) than when he has to make an initial step up to go in.

I have seen what can happen when there is a step or drop from the rear floor of the trailer to the ground. A green horse panicking backwards, still tied by a neck rope, got its hind feet out and under the trailer—and was trapped, getting badly cut up on its hind legs before it could be cut free. I have also seen a pony load for the first time up a very steep ramp far more willingly than any pony in my experience has ever gone up into a step-up trailer for the first time. For one thing, a firm ramp presents consistent footing, regardless of mud or dirt beneath it.

Ultimately, of course, loading into a trailer boils down to schooling: so welcome the chance to load your pony into trailers of all sorts.

Some people consider dutch doors a help in "funneling" a difficult loader aboard. But more often they seem to be something that may swing into the way, or something that a troublesome horse can get behind and become caught on. (I have always been partial to dutch doors for the privacy they afford for changes in a costume class! But now, with some extra rings welded in place, I plan to rig a curtain in the space ahead of the stalls for such occasions. Dressing room trailers are available; their extra length is more than I care to haul.) Partial dutch doors, and top dutch doors of metal (rather than canvas rain curtains) strike me as a genuine hazard both to horses and to people—something to bump a head or shoulders or withers against. Granted that a certain amount of common sense and attentiveness should be expected, one should still try to eliminate potential sources of injury. For instance, it is all very well to say that an escape door on the front side of the trailer should always be opened before you walk around to load a horse from the rear: a child may forget, load the pony, and then be stuck in the stall, unable to squeeze back out past a fractious beast, and unable to escape because there is no inside handle. And it's not only youngsters who forget.

Just as I feel strongly that there should be an inside handle on every door, so others take the opposite line with equal fervor, arguing that (as mentioned earlier) a halter might get caught on a handle and the horse be injured in his struggle to free himself. But properly recessed handles could both prevent that from happening and provide the necessary safety for the handler.

But to return to rear ends. The other basic style, the drop-down tailgate, also has its varieties. It comes with straight sides or wing sides. It comes mickey-mouse size, as mentioned, or full size. When it comes "just plain ramp tailgate," you unscrew or unbolt the two securing latches ("dogs") at the outside top corners of what is roughly a four foot by five foot by three inch combination of thick wood and metal, grab the top edge (about head level if you're five six), and back off as you lower it to the ground. One dealer, a Greenbay Packer in size and physique, yelled to another rugged male for help so he wouldn't "bust his back" when he was showing me a trailer in this cumbersome style. Clearly such a tailgate, awkward and impossibly heavy, is a two-MAN job, not a parent-and-child operation.

Easy-loading springs make the magic difference. Such springs attach to the sides of the trailer and to the top corners of the ramp tail gate. With this "spring assist," raising and lowering a necessarily heavy, rugged, well-constructed tailgate is an easy job even for a youngster. If, like me, you decide on the full tailgate for ramp loading, along with nonslip matting on sturdy well-secured cleats, put this "spring assist" on your *must* list.

Adequate lighting is important as a loading aid and an indirect safety factor. Whether you have one inside light or more, be sure to have your dome light as far forward in the trailer as possible, to lessen the effect of outside floodlights and headlights, and enable your pony to see what he's walking into after dark. A dome light in a more central overhead position casts shadow as soon as his head has passed under it and is therefore less desirable just in terms of him. In a Thoroughbred or Hunter type of trailer, where you can stand and work in the space in front of your pony, a high dome well forward will give light for your operations. (Many people fasten a tack chest to the floor in this area.) Such lights work when parking lights are on or when the towing vehicle is moving.

Clearance, stop, and tail lights, along with directional signals and reflectors on the tailgate, are legal requirements.

Of course there are many other features to think over in choosing a particular make or model beyond these first basic safety factors affecting your pony. I shall mention a few, most of them optional equipment or "extras."

A rain curtain for the top opening of the rear end is desirable if you trailer a lot regardless of weather. Usually rolled close to the top of the roof and secured by straps (or stored in the car trunk), this curtain lowered and snapped into place will keep rain from being sucked through the rear opening into the interior (and on to your pony's rump) while you are driving. You may want it dropped in cold weather with a tired pony blanketed inside: in summer, it may stay up.

Just as you want to adjust louvers (side vents and front windows) so that no wind blows directly on your pony, so you want circulation of fresh air at all times. This is essential. Some trailers have a one-piece front window that opens like a door; others have a fixed window (usually of shatter-proof plexiglass) in the front with small side windows that open; yet others have a large louvered window screened inside—in the best models, carefully placed so there is no danger of draft on the pony's chest. Side vents and windows operate, preferably, from outside, to avoid accidental opening or closing by and injury to the equine occupant. The trend seems to be towards big, almost "picture"-type windows, because, for one thing, "some horses and ponies like windows," while for those that don't, that are bothered by things "rushing past," the owner can easily block the window or cover it temporarily while under way. Certainly generous windowing makes for better-lit interiors—and hence more willing loading.

Such items as a saddle rack, pull-out or stationary, in the storage compartment of a Western model; a spare tire in the compartment or mounted, perhaps with a tack chest, over the right-hand (off-traffic side) fender; a brush tray on the door; trailer gravel guards; blanket racks; chrome trim—any or all may be important to your way of pony-ing. You can, for a price, obtain extra height, extra length, extra-stall-width, a lock on your hitch, a light in and a lock on the tack compartment, two-tone or tri-tone paint jobs.

Besides the walk-through model with the chest bars, there are also walk-throughs with swing-away manger door units. In some models, parts of the mangers fold and lift or push aside in the middle for narrow passage through a single center door providing exit over the trailer hitch itself (and therefore, in my view, inconvenient). A manger per se has certain advantages; but no make that I have seen provides for easy cleaning. Those in use have usually been edged with stale feed. The storage space underneath them that seems such an inducement is lost when the door connected to the manger pushes back; a saddle or broom stored beneath blocks operation or gets shoved around; hay drops into this storage space below. Some people like fixed mangers and the solid partition below them; other people have had experience with young stock getting their feet into the manger and not being able to get them out.

Some trailers have exterior tie rings, but—with all deference to Western riding habits—most of the horsemen and trailer dealers I have talked with strongly advise against tying a horse to them—or to any part part of your trailer or car (door handles, for example). If your trailer has exterior tie rings, use them for hanging a hay net, or a duffle bag for discarded vests and gloves and raincoats, or your class numbers, or even a bunch of daisies. Best put your horse up in your trailer.

So, having weighed the pro's and con's of these various features of safety, convenience, and appearance, the next thing is to find the one trailer make and model that combines the most of them at a price you can afford. Economy, Standard, Special, Custom, Deluxe, Super Deluxe—whatever name the model bears there are certain basic specifications and certain optionals or extras. Compare the items listed and the costs carefully. Having decided that the basic strip model with a few vital safety "extras" is all you can afford, you may find that these necessary extra features bring the price up into the next trailer bracket, without a proportionate increase in style and resale value.

# 18

# PONY BREEDS

"NATIVE" PONIES ARE PONIES INDIGENOUS TO A certain region or country, able to fend for themselves in their natural habitat. Perhaps robust is the best term for such hardy breeds which, without help from man in providing food and water, shelter and care, have survived and developed down the ages. More such breeds are found in Great Britain than in any other part of the world; they are the breeds we know best in North America, and traditionally if illogically we refer to them as "native."

## PONIES FROM THE BRITISH ISLES

### SHETLANDS

Merrylegs, the "little fat gray pony" in *Black Beauty*, "cheerful, plucky, and good-tempered," must have won many friends for Shetlands. This diminutive creature's shaggy mane and forelock, his combination of toylike charm, useful strength, and affectionate nature endear him to children and adults alike.

The Shetland ("Sheltie" or "Equus microscopus" or "mighty atom") is so small that he is often measured in inches rather than the traditional hands. He can be as tiny as twenty-four inches without deformity or loss of conformation (such as is seen in the miniature Falabella).

His is not only the smallest but one of the oldest breeds. For centuries this pony ran on his native Isles north of Scotland looking like a midget draft horse and laboring like a full-size one—in pits, or carrying peat and seaweed—and sharing roof and affection with the family dog on the island crofts.

Over the years the breed was "improved" in several ways. First the harshness of nature on the Shetland Isles, where constant sea winds and boisterous storms dwarfed vegetation and ponies both, winnowed out the weak so that only the fittest survived. Then in the sixteenth century, legend has it, Arab studs swam ashore from the shipwrecked Spanish Armada and mated with local mares. And much more recently in the late 1940s, outside blood was deliberately brought in by the Shetland Pony Stud Book Society (one of the oldest, founded in 1891).

Today, both here and in Great Britain, there are really two types of Shetland, the "Island" and the "American." The latter, with a top size limit of forty-six inches, has a finer neck, a higher head, and slimmer more delicate limbs, and is in general a much more "artifical" pony. The Island type has retained the original Shetland's deep girth, short strong back, and short legs with good knees, hocks, and feet. Both reveal Arab descent in their pretty heads with large bright eyes, small ears, and generous nostrils and their profuse manes and tails.

The Shetland has a heavy winter coat which makes him resemble a Teddy bear but sheds out to a fine satiny coat in summer. Typical also are his piebald and skewbald colors—which are "allowed" only in this one pony breed. (These parti-colors, considered to be indicative of his prehistoric origin, are more usual in the United States, where paints, pintos, Appaloosas, and other spotted horses are

**Like Merrylegs, Robin's tiny Tuffy has won many friends for Shetlands and has given her owner "day-to-day fun with safety and a little bit of glory, too."**

popular, than in Great Britain, where solid colors like bay, brown, and the rarer gray are preferred in Shetlands and the purebred Shetland has black as a foundation color.)

To some extent the very things that helped the Shetland endure over the ages—his minimal demands for food and space, his rugged strength, his charm—have worked against him. Imported into the United States in the last century, he was the victim of a brief "pony boom" some years ago, when every Shetland owner seems to have bred indiscriminately and prolificly; a pony which is mainly suitable in size to toddlers only was overproduced and sold to uniformed parents. As a result the Shetland gained an undeserved reputation for bad temper and "hotness."

The Shetland is very versatile: as a lead line or short stirrup pony, as a pet pony in harness, or as a work pony on a small scale. Popular in the show ring in pleasure driving and roadster classes, he is also a favorite in pony racing, sleigh rallies, and pulling contests. He lives to a ripe old age (forty is not uncommon), and what with his good feet and strong legs it's usually a useful old age.

WELSH

Of all the breeds now found in Great Britain and North America, the Welsh pony has the most ancient pedigree. Two thousand years ago Roman invaders found this pony already living in the mountains and valleys of Cambria—Wales. There were even recognized studs.

In order to survive, Welsh ponies had to overcome rough, trappy terrain, a harsh climate, and sparse grazing. Against odds, they flourished, developing sure-footed fleetness, imperviousness to cold and wet, and overall stamina. By the time Henry VIII ordered that all horses under fifteen hands be destroyed, natural enemies had already weeded out all but the hardiest of stock. The royal edict drove ponies off common grazing all over the British Isles. With the tremendous power of endurance and keen intelligence they had already developed, the Welsh survived both this wholesale official massacre and the more random attacks of shepherds and sheepdogs who zealously guarded their limited grazing. Driven off, forced to hide in the most desolate regions, the Welsh not only survived but managed to continue reproducing as a distinct breed.

Like most ponies, the Welsh has played many parts in the course of history: from the exciting one of chariot-racing in crowded arenas to the humdrum one of pulling ploughs on isolated farms to the tragic one of pit work in the eternal darkness of the coal mine. He has been the pampered plaything of royalty and the casually cared-for playmate of ordinary boys and girls.

The Welsh pony is generally conceded to be the prettiest pony in the world. Spirited but not mean, intelligent but not "smart," rugged but not coarse, while he is unmistakably a pony with a pony's charm, he often strikes one as a "miniature Arab." In fact the Romans brought Arabian stallions to Britain with them, and these strains show up in the Welsh pony's high tail carriage, beautiful way of moving, and elegant head. The head, with large liquid eyes, is slightly dished, tapering from a broad forehead to the muzzle—never a Roman nose! The tail, mane, and forelock, not so fluffy as a Shetland's, are generous and long, giving when windblown a certain wild quality to even the gentlest of pets. A good neck, a shapely body—muscular with good withers, a perfect sloping "riding" shoulder, a short well-coupled back, and strong hindquarters—are typical. These points of conformation, along with strong well-proportioned legs of good bone—"model hocks and limbs"—with neat dense hooves, contribute to the Welsh's appearance as well as to his exceptional jumping ability.

The Welsh Pony may be any color: black, bay, or chestnut, roan, cream, dun, or palomino (never piebald or skewbald). Grays predominate (tracing back to those long-ago Roman Arabian studs), and many a Welsh that is bay or black when foaled turns roan or gray, and some turn "white" with age.

With both the Royal Welsh Pony and Cob Society and the Welsh Pony Society of America ponies are registered either in Section A (ponies up to 12.2 hands) or Section B (over 12.2 but not more than 14). First imported here in the 1880s, Welsh ponies are unquestionably the most popular and up-and-coming and one of the most numerous of all breeds registered in the United States.

Aristocrat among ponies, the Welsh is peerless for beauty, temperament, athletic ability, and sheer versatility. He is *"le seigneur des poneys"* in the eyes of French horsemen, too. The breed excels in many fields: in the show ring in model, in-hand, and breeding classes, in harness of all sorts, in Western, English, saddle seat or hunt seat, pleasure or trail, on the flat or over fences, you name it!—pony-clubbing, 4-H-ing, eventing, hunting, backyard funning, name it again! The Welsh is a consistent winner at all levels, and nearly all the top professionals in the horse world regard him as the most desirable child's pony.

He also offers a unique advantage to a family who want to share a pony among different-sized children, or parents and children. For, while so suitable to a small child, he has enough substance to carry an adult for schooling purposes, as well as the strong but comfortable action at a trot to keep up with a horse, and zest in harness for driving fun. Because he can hold his own in the stiffest of competition from other breeds, adults can show him with pride. The same pony is often exhibited by parents in certain classes and by their children in certain others. Action and speed make the Welsh excel in pony racing and sleigh rallies, two of the rare equine areas in which men and boys outnumber women and girls.

### NEW FOREST

Wild "horses" living in the great forest that once covered much of southern England were mentioned in the days of King Canute (1016) and recorded in Domesday Book (1085). Today the very old "New" Forest consists of sixty thousand acres of crown land, and fifteen thousand ponies still live there. Although they roam wild, they belong to various "commoners," renters of land with common rights dating back to Norman times. They are rounded up at autumn "pony drifts" supervised by "Vederers." About five hundred are sold each year, mostly for children's riding ponies, some for export. (Lutine Bell's sire,

**235**

Solent Harbour Master, was one such export.)

Originally the New Forest pony was a crossbreed of uncertain lineage with Arab, Highlands, Fells, Welsh, and other blood. But, as an official of the New Forest Pony Breeding and Cattle Society puts it, "owing to the mysterious power of nature to grind down and assimilate all these types to the one most suited to the land, New Forest ponies are still fairly of one type and they are rapidly becoming more so. For the last twenty-five or thirty years no outcrosses have taken place." The Society, though the breed is so ancient, only opened its stud book in 1959.

What are the New Forest characteristics? Hardy and sound, these ponies have a good forehand with well sloping shoulders, good legs, and good bone. They tend to have a large head, but, as with many top jumping ponies and horses, this is not necessarily detrimental. At one time the New Forest averaged 13 hands, but, like other breeds that go oversize when fed young on good grazing, many are now up to 14 hands.

Temperamentally New Forests show a steadiness of disposition and an intelligent, fearless curiosity.

Because of the varied terrain of their native habitat, they have always been used to all sorts of footing—fields, bogs, streams, high heather, rabbit warrens, and woodlands proper; perhaps this is one reason why they are so resourceful and reliable cross-county.

Bays and browns predominate. Our Lutine Bell, whom the Pony Pals describe as a "pine-needle roan" with chestnut dapples, is often miscalled a gray: she has the yellowy white mane and tail often seen on such New Forests.

A note on shows in the New Forest itself: There are classes for Forest-fed or non-hand-fed mares that remain out or "run" on the Forest year round rather than wintering on a farm or being stabled as riding ponies. There is also a unique "Veterans" class: first place once went to a pony of twenty-two years. The youngest in the class of sixteen was twenty, the oldest thirty-two, and all were still in use. Several were broodmares and "schoolmasters," but two were hunting, one for his seventeenth season and the other, at twenty-three, still serving as whip and taking any fence. Another twenty-year old worked on the annual cattle drifts and colt hunts (round-ups). All worked regularly in harness and under saddle on their owners' small holdings. Younger ponies take part in polo, racing, driving, gymkhanas, and jumping events as well as hunting—typical New Forest versatility.

## DARTMOOR

A breed of ponies native to Dartmoor, in southwest England, was first mentioned in the year 1012. Through the Middle Ages they worked carrying tin from mines in Cornwall. When the mines closed, the ponies that were not kept for farm use were left free to roam.

The Dartmoor is a pretty pony with a nice head that is rather short from eye to muzzle without much tapering of the nose. Erect "prick" ears are characteristically small and alert, and the eyes are quite large. Several features make the Dartmoor a comfortable riding pony: sloping shoulders, narrowness through the forehand, a neck that is strong yet neither thick nor heavy, and low free action. The Darmoor has ample bone and tough, well-shaped feet. Surefooted and a good jumper, he is now popular with children, but has long been used in harness and under saddle by farmers and shepherds, even though, with a 12.2 h. height limit, the pony may be "hard to see for the rider."

Bays, browns, and blacks are the usual colors, with a rarer chestnut or roan. No white is permitted except for a star or fleck on the forehead, according to the Dartmoor section of the National Pony Society (established in the United Kingdom in 1899).

At one time there were three distinct herds on the windswept moor (the moor in *Great Expectations*, *The Hound of the Baskervilles*, so many stories—). One was dark brown with a light mealy muzzle, another bay with a mealy nose, and the third all gray. The Leat, a 12.2 bay stallion sired by a 14.1 Arab (Dwarka) in 1918, exerted a tremendous influence on the breed and may be responsible for the resemblance many Dartmoors have to a miniature middleweight Thoroughbred hunter.

## EXMOOR

This pony from another great stretch of English moorland (the *Lorna Doone* country) is easily distinguishable by his mealy muzzle, wide-apart prominent "toad eyes," and pale underparts. It is claimed that the Exmoor coat is different in texture from that of other breeds, being harsh and springy in winter, with no bloom, but hard and "shiny as brass" in summer. No markings are permitted; brown, bay, and dun are *the* colors; some people even consider that any color other than brown is a blot on the Exmoor escutcheon.

Authorities consider the Exmoor the nearest direct descendant of the aboriginal British wild horse. Like the Norfolk Roadster, the Galloway, and other breeds that were widely sold for meat, it nearly became extinct. Certain primitive qualities are suggested today in the Exmoor's stocky build; although he usually has a nice head, sloping hindquarters often detract from his looks. Wide low withers, thick shoulders, and a strong neck make him unsuitable for tiny children, but since he goes up to 13.2 in size and is a good jumper he is popular as a second pony.

## HIGHLAND

The smallest pony breed, the Shetland, is well known to Americans. The largest, also Scottish, is very unfamiliar unless one happens to have seen it in paintings by Munnings or in photographs of "carting deer." This is the Highland or Garron pony. Besides his traditional use in carting deer or panniers of grouse, the strong and docile Highland hauls timber and sledges hay to snowbound sheep and cattle. He is often towed behind a small boat from one island to another; he penetrates where larger horses cannot in hilly country and does a horse's job. His steady temperament makes him reliable for such patient mundane labor—also for a pony-trekking mount to be used by tourists of dubious riding ability. Critics complain that the Highland is not fast or a good jumper; proponents claim that he is a good mover, a reliable sturdy hunter capable of carrying a sizeable adult but gentle enough to be ridden by a child.

The Highland has both cart-horse and Arab blood. Thickset, with short powerful limbs and a short back, he has velvety intelligent eyes in an attractive head, and even the mares have stallion-like crests. He may be black, brown, gray, with no white. Particularly pretty are the bright chestnuts with silvery manes and tails. Duns commonly have an eel stripe and even zebra markings on the legs, pointing to early Scandinavian as well as Celtic ancestry.

## FELLS AND DALES

Though the Fells and Dales of northern England are separated by the Pennine chain, these two breeds were originally one and were bred as pack ponies. In the eighteenth century they carried lead from mines to seaports, often transporting loads of two hundred and twenty-five pounds sixty miles a day, in droves of twenty ponies called "pack horse gangs." They are still used in mines and for sledging peat, carting wood, and other general light harness work. Like the Highland, they are popular for shepherding and deerstalking.

Because of the introduction of heavier blood, the Dales is larger, with abundant bone and rather straight shoulders that make him better for harness than saddle. His short neck and hairy heels give him a cart-horse look. Black and dark brown are common, with occasional grays and bays—never chestnuts; white appears only in a star or fetlock.

Unlike the Dales, who do not run on the moors, most Fells ponies (except in-foal mares) live out all year. They are gentle and kind. They stand thirteen to fourteen hands, have good necks and better riding shoulders than the Dales, and are popular for trekking and long-distance rides. Manes and tails are usually wavy, and in winter the legs are feathered with silky hair. Black is the best color, with no white; while duns are very unusual, bays and grays are sometimes found. A light color around the eyes and a mealy nose suggest a relationship to the Exmoor, though the Fells is a darker pony. Hooves are hard with a characteristic blue horn.

There are not many Fells or Dales today; they are numbered in the low hundreds, with only a few registered stallions. Efforts are being made to save the breeds, each of which has its own society.

## CONNEMARAS

The Irish Connemara pony, introduced to the United States only twenty-five years ago, ranks third in current registration, second only to the Welsh Pony and the P.O.A.

The Connemara has been described as a coarse miniature Thoroughbred because of his compact deep body, his good frame and abundance of bone, and his intelligent head. Add to these points of conformation surefootedness and great jumping dexterity, add ability to survive on minimum forage, add docility and affectionate good nature that make him easy to train, add finally a size (13 to 14.2 and frequently over) that makes him an ideal "general" family pony useful for hunting, pulling, and driving, and you have the explanation of his popularity.

The Connemara was not always thus. We can see his ancestors on sculptured stones of the fifth century—short legged, looking small in proportion to their riders. There were many trials and tribulations before the breed was "standardized." One theory is that as with other breeds of the British Isles Arabian stallions from the Spanish Armada contributed their genes, but a more likely one is that these stallions entered Ireland through early trade with Arabia and Morocco via Spain. In any case, the early ponies were rough specimens, despite their merits. In the nineteenth century, government schemes for improvement of horse breeding introduced other stock in such a hodgepodge way that the Connemara breed was in danger of disappearing, but it was rescued and preserved by the creation in 1923 of the Connemara Breeders Society in Ireland. While other outcrosses failed, upgrading with Welsh blood worked. Today England and the United States have their Connemara Societies, and outcrossing is no longer permitted.

Colors seen are black, bay, brown. Roans and chestnuts and yellow duns with black points are said to show the influence of Norwegian or Western Islands ponies. Grays, however, predominate. Like P.O.A.'s, Connemaras are checked for height by their breed society as they mature to see that they do not go "beyond size."

## BREEDS FROM OUTSIDE THE BRITISH ISLES

Ponies from countries other than Great Britain and Ireland are mostly not represented outside their own land. However, we do have in the United States a few examples of the next two breeds listed:

The Hafflinger is a pony from the Austrian Tyrol, reared in the same central stud as the famous Lippizan Horses. His recorded history goes back to 1811 only. He is heavy in build, large-headed and rather long-bodied, and stands from 12.3 to 14 hands. Coats are always chestnut with thick manes and tails a striking flaxen contrast; there may be white in a star or blaze. The placid Hafflingers—sure of foot and tough like most mountain ponies— usually work as pack or all-round draft ponies, but are capable of jumping under saddle.

The Norwegian pony, a miniature draft horse, has not changed much since the days when the Vikings bred his forebears. Dun with a black dorsal or eel stripe and zebra markings on his legs, he is compact, stands 13 to 14 hands, and is sturdy enough to plough and pull on a farm in his native mountains.

There are other breeds that are less well known (even in the British Isles: for instance the ponies of Lundy and of the Quantock Hills), with no society to protect and promote them, no studbook record of their breeding.

In the ninth century Norse settlers introduced to Iceland a pony now known as the Icelandic Pony. Like the Norwegian Loften pony, now extinct, it has had infusions of Scottish blood; it looks and moves much like a primitive Shetland. Icelandic ponies stand between 12 and 13 hands, are always gray or dun, and have a ground-covering ambling trot that makes them good for riding. Not surprisingly, they are rugged and hardy.

Another tough weight-carrying pony, always gray, comes from the Camargue, a region on the Mediterranean coast of France which is empty and desolate even in our day. About 14 hands, the Camarguais has a large head, large bones, large feet, rather straight shoulders, a short neck, a thick mane and tail. He is used for herding bulls by "cowboys" of Southern France, and for trekking. Like the Camarguais horse, bred and trained for Provencal bullfights, this pony is of ancient lineage. The breed is known to American youngsters through the film *Crin Blanc* (*White Mane*), in which an affectionate Camarguais pony swims to death with his young master.

Not as well known to Americans is the French pony Français de Selle. Like the United States, France has long imported ponies from the British Isles. Indeed, raising of imported Connemaras, New Forests, Dartmoors, and Welsh has been so successful that French stock is exported to the British Isles. Recently France became the only country in Europe to have a reciprocal agreement with Britain, Ireland, and Iceland: a pony registered in the French stud book of its breed can also be registered in the like stud book in those countries. Now French breeders have developed their own riding pony, Le Poney Français de Selle.

Using stallions of pure Connemara, New Forest, Welsh, and Arab blood on small domestic mares they have (like the P.O.A. breeders in this country) succeeded in creating a new breed. At present the stud book is still open but young stock, checked at two years, is constantly improving and becoming fixed, so a closed book is foreseeable.

As in many areas (among them equine activities) the Government gives French pony breeders strong support by supplying financial incentives and by supervising breeding standards. The French National Stud makes available top stallions, contributes towards breed competitions, and even partially subsidizes the schooling of green ponies.

Perhaps most important to the successful development of the Poney Français de Selle and to the well-being of all pony breeds in France (Merens, Hafflingers, Islandais, Norvegien, Highlands, Landais, and Pottoks as well as those previously named) is the existence of a national organization of pony breeders: La Fédération Française des Éleveurs de Poneys. The F.F.E.P., with Ministry of Agriculture backing, comprises eleven breed associations. It has its own headquarters (in Paris), its own logo and publications, and an active program of breeding, schooling, maintaining and issuing a stud book (Le Livre Généalogique Français des Races de Poneys). Under its logo, the Fédération publishes and provides information on "les poneys en France."

The United States has nothing comparable. In Paris at Fédération headquarters, for instance, its Président (talking with me and the Président of Le Poney Club de France) was able to give an impartial picture of the overall pony situation in France. In the U.S., there is no one organization, let alone one person, who could do this officially. We have no national all-breed pony organization; what few regional associations exist are in no way similar.

Like the French Fédération of Pony Breeders, Le Poney Club of France is unique. Unlike The Pony Club here or in the U.K., Poney Club means pony. The French avoid mixing ponies and horses in clubs as well as in shows. More and more of their Sociétés Hippiques have affiliated pony clubs. French government influence in things equestrian shows in the Poney Club as instructors must have a diplôme d'équitation d'état. There are, as here, non-governmental tests for riders (given by the French Fédération des Sports Equestres) but to teach one must pass certain government examinations.

Besides the exchange of information about the breeding and utilization of ponies in France and America—and the good will mutual interests can generate—this meeting of three "pony people" in Paris may have an exciting off-shoot: an exchange of young pony riders on an informal basis. As a start, Robin has been invited "to go stag hunting" in France and a French youngster will be our guest at High Hickory. Such international visits—similar in some respects to the team ones done on a larger scale by Pony Clubs of several countries, but by individual arrangement—has long been a dream of

mine. Fun beyond your own backyard, indeed! Perhaps through such exchanges, the new French riding pony, Le Français de Selle, will become a well-known pony breed in America.

Unlikely to become well-known here are the following breeds:

The *Viatka* is a Russian pony: strong, hardy, swift, about 13 or 14 hands, with good looks and conformation. Estonian *Obvinka* and *Kazanka* ponies are both of Oriental and Finnish blood. Poland has several breeds called Konik or Heecul (little horse); the *Konik*, with great endurance and power for its size (11 to 14 hands) is said to be a direct descendant of the wild horse. Iran has its Caspian pony, Sumatra its *Batak* or *Deli* as well as a stouter *Gayol*, and Australia its *Timor*. There are *Mongolian* and *Yarkandi* ponies, *Criolo*, *Bhutia*, and *Griffin* ponies; there are *Kathiawari* ponies in India and *Pegu* ponies in China.

Many of these are tough utilitarian little ponies tracing back to the pony of the steppes, the Przevalski or Mongolian—hardy, serviceable, versatile animals, but lacking the refinement and charm of our more familiar breeds. They mostly have the characteristics of the "Northern type" of pony, with prehistoric upright short manes, short thick necks, low-set tails, big out-of-proportion heads with unpretty Roman noses. (In the British Isles this Northern or "cold" blood shows up in heavy horse breeds but is rarer among ponies; some Exmoors and Shetlands have it.)

## PONY BREEDS IN THE UNITED STATES

### ISLAND PONIES

While we have no native breeds of great ancestry, we do have some wild (or semi-wild; more correctly feral) ponies on islands off the coasts of Virginia and North Carolina: Chincoteague, Assateague, Banker, Ocracoke, Cedar Island ponies. The Pony Pals like to picture the ancestors of these ponies swimming ashore from Spanish galleons wrecked off Cape Hatteras en route to the mines of Peru, rather than accept the more prosaic theory that they were imported by early settlers along with pigs and cattle.

Whatever their origin, the present-day Island ponies exhibit a great range of size and coloring. An abundance of piebalds and skewbalds among the various solid coats is ascribed to the introduction of Shetland blood in the 1900's. For the great part, the Island ponies are sturdy, athletic creatures whose occasional fine points indicate "good blood" somewhere in their past.

Most of them live wild year round, grazing on coastal marshes and dunes and even wading into the sea to reach inundated grass. Just as there are annual "pony drifts" in the New Forest, so there is an annual penning here, and some of the rounded-up ponies are sold to keep the herds from overpopulating the islands.

(Eleven-year-old Betsy Hilborn, a Pony Pal, went to see the wild ponies swim across the channel from Assateague Island to Chincoteague Island. It all began when she read Marguerite Henry's *Misty of Chincoteague*, she explained: "At first I thought the book wasn't true, but the characters in the book were so lifelike I began asking around. I found *Misty of Chincoteague* was part fact, part fiction." So she and her mother went to Virginia: "When we got to Chincoteague, the dock and shoreline were packed full of people. After a while I could see a herd of wild ponies on the opposite island, Assateague, about fifty or more ponies. Chincoteague ponies are about the size of a large Welsh pony. The Chincoteague Volunteer Fire Department, who are in charge, were driving them across the channel, which was about a half-mile swim. The ponies were driven on shore amid the spectators. Then they were driven through the streets to a big pen in the center of town. Later on the crowd was allowed to mingle with the ponies, taking their pictures and patting them—a dream come true.")

P.O.A.'S

During recent decades several attempts have been made to develop "new" pony breeds in the United States. Some results, such as the Americana, have been unsatisfactory; others have been successful—notably the Pony of the Americas with its carefully controlled stud book and active breed society.

Best known by his initials, the P.O.A. is a Western type both in breeding and in looks. He is the result of crossing Appaloosa horses with Shetland ponies and has been described as "looking like a Quarter Horse/Arab cross but exhibiting Appaloosa colors." As with the Appaloosa, the coat either of the rump area or of the entire body may have white on dark or dark on light in a spotty pattern described as "snowflake," "frost," "blanket," "leopard," and so on. Unique are the "varnish marks"—little areas of dark pigment around the nose, mouth, eyes, and jowls and under the tail. Markings, not always present in foals, may or may not appear with maturity, so a P.O.A. is checked when grown to see that he meets the society's standards for coloring and size. Minimum size is 11.2, maximum 13.2 hands, but within this narrow range the pony is remarkably sturdy and well-muscled.

One reason for the breed's popularity is the enterprising youth program of the Pony of the Americas Club. Another is the pony's versatility, his being up to weight for adults, and his success in all types of competition. Called "the using pony for youth," he is most frequently shown in stock seat and Western classes, but increasingly he appears in English classes too.

## HORSE PONIES

If a pony were to be defined merely as anything equine 14.2 hands and under, then there would be ponies among the horse breeds. Certain Thoroughbreds come within this limit, noteworthy examples being the stallion Chantain, so often used in cross-breeding, and Gay Presto, who was one of twins. Again, as Justin Morgan (the foundation sire of the Morgan breed) and his son Sherman were both about 14 hands, so today there are many pony-size Morgans. Moreover, most Arabs are 14.2 to 15.1, with many under 14 hands.

Nevertheless Arabs, Morgans, and Thoroughbreds, regardless of size, are classed as horses. Such "pony horses" may be shown either as ponies or as horses but may not be entered in both categories at the same show.

While there is no Arab Pony or Morgan Pony, there are an American Saddle Pony and a Hackney Pony—although really these too are simply smaller editions of two horse breeds. Their breed associations have no special pedigree or records for these ponies; they qualify simply if they do not mature beyond 14.2 hands. Like their larger versions, the American Saddle Pony is shown both three- and five-gaited under saddle and in harness and the Hackney Pony mainly in harness. Both, with their extravagant, artificial motion, are basically showring animals and the only pony characteristic they have is their size.

The Galiceño falls in a different category, officially. Though he has been pony size since Cortez introduced him into Mexico in the fifteenth century, and though he matures at only 12 to 13.2 hands, the Galiceño Horse Breeders Association, formed in 1959 to promote "the beautiful little horse with the proud history," claims that his "natural running gait sets him apart from the pony class."

Mounts used in playing polo are always referred to as "Polo Ponies," but polo ponies are a type, not a breed, and today they are usually horses. In the early nineteenth century ponies of 13 hands were used but eventually height restrictions were removed, and today they play to 16 hands and over. There have been attempts to standardize by breeding good pony mares to small Thoroughbred sires, thus aiming at agile animals with long flexible necks, powerful hindquarters with well-let-down hocks, and, most important, the courage needed for proper playing temperament. With the current burgeoning of interest in polo in this country, and the advantage of having mounts small enough to train and ride easily and maintain economically, we may see more polo ponies that are ponies.

## CROSSBREEDING

A crossbred pony is the result of a breeding between two ponies of different breeds (both purebreds, or a purebred and a mixed-bred) or between a pony and a horse. Goals in planned crossbreeding vary: to combine in the offspring the best points of each parent, to produce in the offspring a higher quality than is seen in one of the parents, to achieve a uniformity of type or a standardization of size, shape, and even color, or to increase or decrease the size of one or the other parent in the offspring.

In this country, although the Welsh pony is still used in upgrading, we seldom see crossing between pony breeds today. Rather crossing is between ponies and horses. Since we have no native breeds of ponies but many horses, it's easy to see why this is so. It's partly a matter of the ratio of horses to ponies and partly a matter of economics. In Great Britain, the more traditional cross has been that of a pony mare with a horse stallion. (As a result of five or six generations of pony crosses, a quality-type of riding pony has been developed there which can almost be regarded as a "breed.") For us, it has been more feasible to import one pony stallion, whose impact can be tremendous through twenty-five or more

breedings a year, than to import one or more pony mares, whose impact must be limited to one foal each a year. Of course in any country a herd of pony mares is cheaper to maintain than a herd of horse mares, but this advantage may be cancelled out if the market demand is for a large rather than a small crossbred.

Crossbreeding involves certain gambles, even more than pure breeding, since it may produce either a pony or a small horse. The cross of a small-breed pony with a small horse (with small-horse bloodlines) is likely to produce an offspring that will still be a pony at maturity. The cross of a large-breed pony with a small horse is less predictable: in this cross the same combination of sire and dam may produce a 12.2 pony one time and a 15.2 horse the next.

With those breeds (usually ones whose stud books have not been closed so long as the Welsh pony's) that tend to "go beyond size" on better feeding, the possibility that the crossbred may go beyond pony size at maturity increases. If you don't care, fine; this doesn't matter. But if you are striving for crossbred ponies, it does. (And if you are buying a green crossbred with plans to develop a mature pony, it does.) For example, the cross of a New Forest or Exmoor pony with a Thoroughbred results in a fine hunter type, but in such a crossbreeding your goal had better be an indifferent "either, or"; if you are breeding specifically for a pony you may just add to the statistics of thousands of failures. The foal may mature midway in size between sire and dam; on the other hand you may end up, not with the much-in-demand large "large pony" (14.2) but with the less-in-demand small "small horse" (14.3). In crossbreeding larger ponies the goal is generally a large junior horse (under 16 hands).

If you are crossbreeding a purebred and a grade or "breeding unknown," the gamble increases. In any breeding the foal's characteristics are determined equally by the stallion and the mare. (However, it is generally accepted that the dam affects the overall size of the foal—for instance, that a Thoroughbred stallion/Welsh pony mare breeding will produce a smaller cross than a Thoroughbred mare/Welsh pony stallion breeding.) Stallion and mare alike pass on an unseen inheritance going back many generations: therefore the better bred each is the more equally good and bad features will be blended in the foal. A "breeding unknown" individual may "look better than she breeds," for the likelihood of a throwback even to some primitive lack of conformation is greater than when the characteristics which we see and like in the individual are fixed and in the genes passed on in this side of the bloodline as well.

Fortunately for purposes of upgrading, if one parent is better bred than the other it is that parent's traits that will predominate. This is one reason why long-established breeds with centuries of recorded controlled breeding behind them—the Arab, the Welsh, the Thoroughbred—are so successfully used in crossbreeding.

Today as in the past these two horses, the Arab and the Thoroughbred, are the ones most commonly used in crossbreeding with ponies. Both in combination with the Welsh can be "hot" but outstanding crosses; both are said to "click" with the Connemara also.

At one period a cross of Hackney, Morgan, or Standardbred with a Welsh pony stallion was popular. Some fine crossbred ponies in this country are the result of a Hackney stallion/Welsh mare cross. We see less of these crosses on breeding farms today; rather there is growing use of the Thoroughbred-type Quarter Horse with his kindly disposition and good conformation.

So long as there were few ponies of any sort in the United States, the aim in crossbreeding was to provide more small mounts, more ponies. Now, with overall pony population and purebred pony registration both so much higher, the emphasis has shifted from quantity to quality and the aim is both to produce riding ponies of better quality and to produce good small horses with valuable pony traits.

One crossbreeding does not make a breed. Crossbreeding may develop a cross (like the P.O.A.), but five or six generations are required for sufficient standardization to begin to consider the results a breed—and many more before a stud book can be established and closed.

For many breeders, the first crossbred is the end of their breeding program, and they seldom keep their crossbred offspring for future breeding stock. Crossbred stallions, unless boasting an exceptional "extra" like palomino coloring, are (like most colts) usually gelded. The crossbred filly, on the other hand, is more likely to be used to produce a second cross, often on a private-owner basis, after she has had a chance to prove herself as a mature performer. For example, purebred Registered Welsh High Hickory Galaxy and her dam Top Rail Stardust were potential brood mare material right from birth,

**Multiple cross breeding unknown—A fine example of a "Just a Pony", Cecily's Jet who comes every summer to Pony Camp at High Hickory, ridden here by Shirley.**

simply on the basis of their remarkable bloodlines. Crossbred Lutine Bell was not automatically so. Now that she has proved herself outstanding in model, in equitation, over fences, in dressage, in hunting, in eventing, and as a member of the family! we're tempted to breed her to a carefully chosen Thoroughbred stallion, one with a good disposition, a handsome head, and an eventing background: our goal would be a second Lutine *in horse size* for an older Robin.

The initial crossbred may also be one of several other-breds. If both parents are of unknown breeding, it is simply a mixed-bred. If one parent only is purebred (or both purebred but of different breeds), the offspring is a half-bred: half-Connemara, half-Arab, etc. (Except for purposes of this chapter, the term half-bred used without special definition denotes half-Thoroughbred.) If one parent is a half-bred, the offspring could be a quarter-bred or part-bred. If one parent is a half-bred and the other similarly half-bred, the offspring would be half-bred. If a half-bred filly is mated to a stallion of that "half" breed, their offspring is three-quarter-bred.

Crossing repeatedly on this line will eventually produce an offspring so near to purebred again that much of the purpose and advantage of the earlier crossbreeding will be negated. (One field-hunter breeding program came close to this, as after four generations products of its original Thoroughbred/Clydesdale crossing approximated more and more closely to the Thoroughbred type itself.) When this happens, it is time to reevaluate the goal of the breeding program and either continue to refine or bring in a new infusion of the diluted blood of the original cross. (Thus a seven-eights Thoroughbred resulting from an original Thoroughbred/Connemara cross would be bred to a Connemara to strengthen such desired pony traits as ruggedness, bone, stamina, and evenness of disposition.)

In any program—even, or more especially, the one-mare backyard program—the crucial question is: What do we hope to get as a result? In crossbreeding ponies and horses, the question is: What does pony blood give that full-horse blood would not? Take our crossbred Lutine Bell again: Both pony sire and Thoroughbred dam contributed to her midway size and passed on good conformation. We credit her dam with her smoothness of gaits and the chestnut coloring she had as a foal. We credit her sire with her exceptional jumping ability, her boldness, her agility—and only native pony blood like a New Forest's could account for her love of cross-country (water, mud, any weather), her surefootedness in trappy territory, her awareness of hazards like woodchuck holes. Her sire it was who contributed soundness of hoof and bone and the general hardiness which enables her to live through New England winters with minimum care. The fact that she now looks like a dappled gray (a closer look reveals that she is a chestnut roan) with the yellowy white mane and tail characteristic of many New Forests we attribute to her sire; the faint star on her forehead, almost invisible now but obvious when she was a foal, comes from her dam. An interesting marking is lines on her legs which look almost like barbedwire scars. An old and respected horseman told us that these are "Tetrarch lines," evident in horses and ponies whose Thoroughbred blood traces back to The Tetrarch. We have since seen them in horses, usually Thoroughbreds and usually grays.

Since so many people with a passion for ponies outgrow them physically or succumb to "social" pressure to "move up to" a horse, it's good to know that many of the pony qualities they so like can be found in a crossbred horse. Even a small percentage—that dash!—of robust pony blood will contribute to a durable, pleasurable mount, calm, clever, sturdy, with good bone and conformation and a cheerful, affectionate disposition, tending to longevity despite a minimum of pampering. The purebred or crossbred pony owner who is tempted to breed might consider these points:

There is a demand for both first and second crosses. This effects the value of a crossbred, whether you are breeding to sell or to keep. As always, the demand is for a well-schooled animal ready to hunt or show. The price most people are willing to pay for a green three-year-old is seldom realistic; it is pointless to give a figure, since conditions vary so (location, year, etc.), but a rule of thumb seems to be that it is one-third to one-half of what it costs to raise the three-year-old!

Assuming that you already have the potential broodmare and the suitable stabling and acreage (fenced!) to raise a foal through its first three years, your expenses will start with your search for a suitable stallion. There immediately comes the cost of shipping to the stud farm, veterinary examination, insurance, and board for several weeks, quite apart from the stud fee (anywhere from one hundred dollars to five hundred dollars and up). Back home again, your in-foal mare will require increased feeding and supplements, particularly towards the end of the eleven months gestation. During this time your use of the mare will be curtailed if not eliminated. Foaling itself may require veterinary assistance; it will certainly require aftercare. Nursing mares need top nutrition, and even before weaning the foal has embarked on those years of his life when good food and plenty of it are of prime importance. (The best of care four years later cannot compensate for early deficiencies.). Veterinary care and at least minimum blacksmith attention are needed from the first year on. Since equipment for the mature brood mare may not do double duty for the growing child, you will need little things like foal-, weanling-, colt-size halters, etc. Raising a foal is more full of etc.'s even than keeping a pony or a horse. At the very least, quite apart from prenatal expenses, those first three years will cost you five hundred dollars; and of course this is assuming that you do mucking out, grooming, and training for nothing. Even if you added another fifteen hundred dollars to your selling price, that would hardly cover a groom and trainer working even one hour a day at below-minimum wages.

If you are crossbreeding to keep the foal, by the time it is a three-year-old you will—if all goes well—have a crossbred whose basic training has been handled the way you want it to be and whose future education will provide you with a mount as good as and perhaps better than—certainly bigger than—the pony dam you love so much.

Such crossbreeding (selling a foal annually, or an occasional yearling) might be a reason for and a means of keeping an outgrown pony "self-supporting" until a younger child or grandchild is ready for her. If "Must sell, owner going to college" means, not need for money towards tuition but reluctance to have a pony standing idle, how nice to solve that problem by having the pony produce while her rider is away from home! For many pony owners there is never an idle, or at least a quiet, year to devote to breeding. Crossbreeding to get a larger mount might ease the pangs of parting with an outgrown pony (do it at weaning time), or for a serious horseman, it might be the start of a long-range and more ambitious breeding program.

The goal in crossbreeding here could be to produce an Eventing crossbred—pony or horse—whose combination of qualities would contribute to success where a rugged cross-country phase demands bold-ness and stamina, where stadium jumping demands controlled agility, spring, and speed, and where dressage demands smoothness and beauty, with impulsion. Another goal could be a "fun" crossbred whose robust (that is, pony) traits would make him a pleasure for casual riding and easy keeping by a first-time, nonexpert backyard owner. Hail the Robust Crossbred!

## BREED SOCIETIES

By banding together, people interested in ponies have kept breeds pure and have saved breeds from extinction or extreme mongrelization; in rare instances, they have developed a new breed.

A breed organization (society, registry, association, club) may have many officers, a board of directors, a paid staff, and an enormous member-ship, or it may consist of two or three officers and the small nucleus of persons who started it and depend entirely on volunteer workers. Some societies have regular offices (for instance, the P.O.A. Club with its four hundred thousand dollar building). For others, headquarters may be a cardboard box on a kitchen counter. Some societies are nonprofit organizations; others certainly are not.

High on the list of duties of every breed society is maintenance of the stud book that it publishes annually (or less frequently, with the smaller groups). It draws up breed standards, determines requirements for registration, checks pedigrees, and ensures that only qualified ponies receive certificates.

A pony's certificate of registration (his "papers") is only as good as the particular ponies whose names appear on it. Unless a breed society achieves selectivity, registered "should-have-been-culled" mares can be bred to registered "should-have-been-gelded" stallions. Since most genetic defects are recessive, they cannot be seen even in good individuals; and if hidden faults are passed on by two poor individuals the recessive genes for the faults may pair off and the faults appear in the foal. The certificate can be more than just a piece of paper showing genealogy if the society keeps records of show or performance and sire and produce so that before breeding you can check what has been accomplished by ancestors and progeny as well as by the individual stallion and mare.

The longer a stud book has been "closed," the farther back all the ponies in a pony's pedigree have been registered. In an "open" book, criteria for registration vary (for example they might be size and color at maturity) and pedigrees may be pretty short.

With the exception of the "what?-bred" pony both of whose parents are of "breeding unknown," crossbred ponies may qualify for registration in one or more breed registries. (And if all you want is a "beautiful registration certificate" to hang in your stable, even the "what?-bred" can buy "an official registration" from a broad-minded all-breeds society that advertises that "any equine may be registered.")

A crossbred might be registered in a half-bred society such as the Half-Quarter Horse Registry or the Half-Welsh Registry of the Welsh Pony Society of America. In the Half-Quarter Horse Registry size would not be a consideration, but in the Half-Welsh the crossbred would not only have to satisfy blood requirements but also be pony-sized.

The same half-bred might qualify for both books and so be "double-registered." A crossbred with a minimum of twelve and a half per cent Arabian blood (or one out of eight great-grandparents Arabian) could be in the Arabian Part-Bred Registry. A Crossbred Registry offers listings to half-breds by a purebred stallion registered in the stud book for his breed, thus covering those whose breed societies do not have a partbred registry of any degree. Some crossbreds qualify not only for several breed registries but for "color" (such as palomino) or performance (trotting pony) registries as well.

Besides passing on applications for registration, the breed society files information as to a pony's sex, color, markings, breeder, owner, transfers of ownership, stallion service or mare breeding, foaling, gelding, and death. It may rule on names and changes of name and keep track of prefixes and suffixes, registering those that qualify as farm or stud names.

The societies concerned with the different breeds are responsible for seeing to it that their standards are upheld in breed classes in the show ring. Therefore they must educate and "recognize" breed judges, must insist that breed classes be under recognized judges, and must revoke recognition of judges who violate standards by placing ponies that are incorrectly or "artificially" shown.

As artificiality increases and strength, naturalness, and energy decrease, the numbers of a pony breed diminish. Just as working dogs are ruined when they are bred not for working ability but for looks and bench competition, so are ponies when they are bred not for use but for show-ring display. Therefore the societies must outlaw such show-ring falsities as excessively long hooves, heavily weighted shoes, and stretching. (In stretching a horse is trained to stand with his feet, not under him, but some distance back. There is only one time when a pony stands "stretched" naturally; and spectators at a Massachusetts show will never forget the day when one of our knowledgeable little Pony Pals was next to a pony that lined up and stretched, "parked," beside him in a Walk/Trot class. Loud and clear his voice rang out as he advised its rider: "Get off his back. He wants to stale.")

Show-ring success ought to equate with achievement of breed standards, not only in model and in-hand classes but in performance classes, for there is a close link between looks and ability. For modern riders, the emphasis is on *doing things* with one's mount—doing anything from tranquil hacking to tense endurance riding. The exaggeratedly artificial pony has only a limited appeal (witness the lack of popularity of the American Saddle Pony and the virtual demise of the Shetland when its artificiality increased). The lasting popularity of a breed depends on the development of good individual ponies and increase of their kind by judicious selective breeding; we don't want a "boom and bust" fiasco like that of the Shetlands.

A society should educate its members in the responsibility involved in breeding a pony. It should guide them in evaluating pedigrees, stress the need to geld all but the most exceptional colts and to resist breeding any but the finest of mares. It should encourage members to keep their breeding programs small enough so that they can sell selectively, and should provide them with "new owner literature" so that buyers can enjoy and take good care of their ponies, thus minimizing the danger of less selective resale. It should provide a realistic financial appraisal of what breeding entails so as to discourage members from engaging in it with the idea of great and immediate profit.

If you join the breed society for your pony, you will probably receive a magazine, an area club newsletter, and regional publications. While many breed magazines are of very restricted interest, others have such a wide appeal that they are handled by regular news-dealers and read by horsemen in general. Depending on the society's budget, there may also be film rentals, a field representative who works with 4-H and other youth groups, free literature for county agents, schools, libraries, and interested clubs or individuals.

Some societies in the United Kingdom run pony-management training courses and courses for training junior judges—a good idea! Here, the P.O.A. has a special endowment for scholarships.

Breed societies have an informational role. Nothing is more irritating, if you are keen on a certain breed, than to read inaccurate statements about *your* pony. (If anything said here about any breed displeases *afficionados*, it may be that the secretary of the relevant organization did not send requested information.)

You can obtain a list of breed associations, with their current addresses, from the American Horse Shows Association.

# 19
# PONY PROJECTS

YOUR PASSION FOR PONIES CAN BE CARRIED OVER into other creative activities. Here are some suggestions for "pony projects"—ideas for making things out of wood, paper, cloth, and other easily come-by materials.

Some of the projects are very practical. The equipment that every pony owner and horseman needs is, of course, available through supply houses or tack shops; but you can make some of it at home more economically and with the added fun of the making, the added pleasure there is in an "I made it myself" product. The creative process (banged thumbs, paint-spattered face, paper scraps, pasty clutter and all) as well as the finished product can be of value.

For the most part these pony projects require a minimum investment of money and material, though the sky's the limit if you wish. They are projects that can be worked on by a child alone or with friends, with adult help or without it. Some are strictly carpentry or strictly sewing or strictly pasting or painting; some a combination. Some are best made by the person who is going to use them; others make excellent gifts or saleable items for 4-H or Pony Club money-raising affairs.

Directions for one or two projects follow, but for others information is so readily available that the suggestions alone are enough. Patterns and diagrams can be made from paper or cloth (an old sheet or curtain for instance) before you cut directly into the material itself. Most catalogues from companies like Miller's, Kauffman's, or Beckwith's have illustrations on which patterns can be based.

**Pitch of roof shows these Sudbury 4-H'ers, painting their model barn a traditional red, are familiar with New England snow loads.**

Among the simplest, most familiar projects are:
• Bridle holders made from empty saddle soap or coffee cans, painted in any manner desired. Remove tops, nail through bottom on tack room wall at appropriate height, and replace top (or leave the can open to hold such small items as hoof pick or curb chain).
• Blanket or rug or girth holders made from a broom handle or thick dowel. Drill a hole at each end of the wooden bar, insert a chain or braided gimp, and hang on hooks. The bar may be sanded and stained, or painted in your stable colors.

Standards built indoors from scrap lumber during the winter by Pony Pals get a coat of white paint in the spring time. A freshly painted "picket fence" dries in the wagon.

• Save clean twine from hay bales and braid it by threes into lead ropes. Attach a snap hook at one end and back-splice or whip this part and the other end to prevent unraveling. (See any Scout or Navy or cordage company handbook on knots for directions.)

• When you've mastered braiding and back-splicing, make a set of rings from manila or hemp line (rope, to landlubbers). Paint an empty nail keg or pail for ring-toss games played on ponyback.

• Stuff old nylon stockings with rolled-up old magazines or rolled-up corrugated cardboard (tied securely first) to make trees or stuffers for your knee boots. Make a loop when you tie the stockings at the top so that you can hang them up when you are

A major pony project is building a real pony barn! An older Eric expands and maintains stalls and fencing put up as a ten-year-old.

wearing the boots. You can also make fancier stuffers of fabric cut in a tube; but nylons are quick, convenient, and slip smoothly inside your boots.

• Boot covers or boot carriers can be made of various fabrics, such as denim, duck, or Indian head.

• Save wooden boxes such as salt-bricks come in at your grain store. Sand and paint. Use them stacked up for storage shelves in your tack room, or nail them to the wall with a door or top attached by hinges made from an inner tube, or of leather.

• Or paste wallpaper inside a box, put a rug sample on the floor, make a stall in one corner, and give it to a Pony Pal for a horsey dollhouse-tackroom.

Pony Pals at High Hickory have enjoyed making, giving, and using several items that are variations on

Cut-away view of model barn built by Sudbury 4-H members shows a to-scale interior complete to clipboard on the tackroom wall.

one basic pattern: that of a book cover. Telephone books specifically for the numbers of Pony Pals, 4-H leaders, the vet, the blacksmith, etc.; scrapbooks for pictures and clippings relating to ponies; 4-H or Pony Club record books and portfolios—all can be made with soft covers to slip over existing books, or stiff covers can be made for loose-leaf pages.

These covers can be made of cloth (drapery departments are a good source of horsey designs) or of paper. Plain cloth or paper can be made vivid through various techniques, such as tie-dying, spatter-printing, and marbling. Directions appear in many "make-it" books or general craft handbooks. A youngster with a flair for drawing horses can work in water colors, acrylics, pastels, or felt-tips to

School daze are here again!

RAH    Aug. '73    NEH

**Pony projects can help towards pony extras— horse show entry fees, even a trip to the Olympic Equestrian Events. Sketches by Robin have appeared in Horse Play, The Chronicle of the Horse, and other magazines. "School Daze" was in a September Northeast Horseman.**

decorate both covers and end-papers.

Pony projects involving carpentry can of course be undertaken by girls as well as boys, but they provide a way of getting even the nonhorsey brother or father to share the fun of a pony in the family by lending a helping hand.

• Stall signs are easy to make and are a highly appreciated gift. Sand a 2 inch by 8 inch piece of soft pine. Drill a hole at each end for screws. Paint with white or basic stable color, preferably with outside paint. Letter the pony's name in a contrasting color. A quick solution to lettering problems for those who "can't draw a straight line" is to stick adhesive stencil letters in place, trace around them with pencil, remove the stencils, and paint in the letters.

This same short cut can be used for putting initials or names on metal or wooden objects. Monogramming can be a pony project in itself, whether of water pails, tack chests, feed tubs, or whatever.

One simple shape—that of a V-shaped trough or Λ-shaped roof—is used in several projects. Made of 8 inch by 5 foot planks nailed to two sturdy triangles

of pine (scrap wood in most cases), this shape forms a portable saddle rack. Supported by stools or tack chests at each end it can be used indoors or outdoors for holding or cleaning saddles. The same shape can be nailed between two trees for a permanent rack for summer. In a shorter length (to fit your saddle) it can be mounted with a diagonal support on your tack room wall.

Another easily made project is a wooden bootjack. Take a piece of wood about 10 inches long and about 5 inches wide; saw a V in one end big enough to take the heel of your boot. Attach a triangular wooden block about an inch high on the underside about half way so that the heel opening or V is an inch off the floor. Sand, stain, or paint, and keep near your outside doors. (One Pony Pal at High Hickory was so pleased by the ease with which such bootjacks removed not only riding boots but snowboots and rubbers that he made and presented an extra one to his grammar school homeroom.)

Handy bookshelves for a paperback horse library can be made from two horses' heads cut from plywood with a jigsaw for the ends. Connect with four dowels or two strips of wood to form the back and bottom. Sand, stain, or paint. Fill with your favorite books. (See Chapter 21.)

Other projects include making wooden squares about six inches square with a number or letter on each, to attach to your fence for dressage or games in the ring, and a wooden box with a hinged sloping top to hold notes, gloves, and a first-aid kit near your ring.

For youngsters interested in sewing—or with a mother or grandmother who sews—projects are many: saddle and bridle covers for both tack room and travel, cleaning aprons in bartender style with good-sized pockets; saddle blankets and even pads. Washable sturdy materials can be had in solid colors or designs, and both can have initials or borders appliquéd or embroidered on them. Saddle pads can be made of mattress quilting, and prove useful for purposes of economy or convenience when

Tuffy pulls a work wagon made into a covered Conestoga as a pony project by the young driver's brother.

Pony Pal Alicia strokes bold black letters on signs for the new dressage arena during Pony Camp at High Hickory.

sheepskin pads are wet or dirty or are being saved for a show. When fitted or contour sheets rip in the middle there is frequently enough good material at either end to provide two tack room saddle covers; the elasticized ends make the sheeting fit snugly over the cantle, and the dust cover can easily be laundered. Pony Pals go wild decorating such makeshift covers with magic markers, using horsey sketches and autographs à la plaster cast. Some riders have made saddle bags of canvas, leather, or vinyl.

For the youngster with a pony cart, a covered cushion and carriage robe may be a welcome gift. I confess that, while a robe may be *de rigueur* in driving classes in shows, the brightly piped red one that Grandma made is more often used for a picnic cloth on pony cart outings than in the show ring. However, that robe and the foam-rubber cushion covered in matching scarlet and gold—stable colors—are prize possessions . . . .

A project requiring only the most simple sewing is one of the most popular: sleeping-bag covers made from cotton with, on ours, lovely mares and foals hand silkscreened on it. These covers are similar to pillow cases and look like bolsters when in use. To make one, measure enough yardage to wrap around your rolled up sleeping bag with a slight overlap.

Fold in half lengthwise. Stitch (preferably by machine, but it can be done by hand) down the outside edges and across one end. Turn right side out and put on to your sleeping bag as you would put a case on a pillow. You can have a bedspread and curtains in a matching pattern.

Another project was suggested by my riders at a camp in Maine years ago. They indicated their ratings by the ties they wore—hand made in camp colors, with a boot, or crop, or hunt cap, or spur, as the case might be, embroidered on the tie-ends.

Craft-oriented projects are legion: illustrations for horse stories, modeling horses of clay or ponies of papier-mâché, doing wire sculpture in the shape of fighting stallions. Currently, six Pony Pals are working on a mosaic, in individual two-foot sections, which will eventually be mounted on the pony barn clerestory. Maybe it will never be finished; but the fun is in the doing. All such undertakings, instigated by a love of ponies, provide fun and comradeship. And instead of groans greeting rain or snow, it's more likely a discussion of what pony projects there'll be today. Have a good time with yours!

# 20

# A PLEA FOR THE WELL-ROUNDED RIDER

# (A Chapter Mainly for Parents)

I REMEMBER THAT IN THE DAYS WHEN I WAS teaching riding at a "snob" finishing school in the Massachusetts Berkshires a tweedy leather-skinned mother handed her twelve-year-old over to me with the exhortation: "I don't care what you stuff into her silly little head at this place as long as you don't ruin her seat."

That brand of fanaticism isn't very common. What is becoming common is the innocent parent who has never been in a saddle in his or her life and is suddenly faced with a child who lives, breathes, and sleeps horses.

In our affluent society sports are a major feature of life; and riding—riding and the cult of the horse—may well be on the way to preeminence among our sports. More people are riding than ever before; more stable their mounts in their own backyards. Horsemanship in all its aspects takes up a greater part of their daily lives. If youngsters were "crazy over ponies" in my youth, the craze is now becoming an epidemic. And more often than not the parent whose child has become an addict feels the bewilderment of a nice chickadee who finds that one of its eggs has hatched a bald-headed eagle.

All too often, I have seen a love of horses and riding intensify to the exclusion of all other interests. More than any other sport, riding gets an emotional hold on youngsters—especially on little girls—perhaps partly because it isn't just a sport but involves a close relationship with another living creature.

Some parents may breathe a sigh of relief that a preoccupation with riding is delaying a teenager's interest in the opposite sex. ("At least she isn't staying out late with a boy," one father commented as he helped unload a pony, saddle and other tack, blankets, picnic cooler, water pail, and hay net—all in the dark of a day that had started with the process in reverse long before the sun was up.) More often they are worried about such total involvement; and they are right. By the time a child gets over equine "funnel vision" it may be too late to develop the other interests and accomplishments that prove so important later in life.

One of the friends with whom I have discussed this problem over the years is the distinguished authority on child education, Dr. Fredelle Maynard, and her comment is this: "Though a child's real passion for ponies—or chess, or ballet—is a joy to parents and though it's tempting to encourage that single-minded passion even to the exclusion of all other interests, this is in the long run unfair to the child. He doesn't know what else the world holds. You do. And since there will be time enough later on for specialization, I think the parent's role is to direct a child's enthusiasm along many paths."

Some psychiatrists go so far as to say that the

person who is intensely concerned with athletic activity is more prone than others to middle-age neurosis and mental illness. I am not concerned with such an extreme. Certainly I do not advocate giving up riding. Never! I am not even thinking in terms of age—but of the person. I make my plea for the well-rounded rider.

There will always be hippomaniacs like the Dowager in Dylan Thomas's *Me and My Bike* ("Stir a hoof, Gregory, I'm waiting for me nosebag"). But I should like to see more youngsters who fall in love with riding realize that that *is* mania—and that to be a horseman you don't have to be like that, don't have to be "horsey." I should like to see their ardent pleasure in ponies and horses expand and enrich their lives, serve as a broadening of their horizons, not be a limiting microcosm.

Since a somersaulting horse caused me a back injury that changed my own career as horseman, I know all too well how vital it is to have other interests to fall back on.

To fall back on: not to take the place of—for they must be interests that tie in with the child's love of ponies (or for that matter of ballet or sailing or any other all-consuming passion). But these broader horizons, these peripheral awarenesses, must be developed *before* the need for them arises.

To accomplish this with your horse-crazy youngster, you need only take advantage of the intensity of that craze to spark other interests.

Take music, for instance. Your young rider may turn a deaf ear to Bach, but he'll listen at least once to the *Light Cavalry Overture*. If he already knows the opening bar "barroombarrumpparoomp-barump" of "The Storm" from watching the Lone Ranger, here's your chance to play the entire overture, and perhaps bring in the rest of *William Tell*—music, and story, and Swiss history. Music needn't be classical, of course. There's listening—and singing—fun to be had from "I've Got Spurs that Jingle Jangle Jingle," "Do Ye Ken John Peel?", "A-Hunting We Will Go," and dozens of cowboy ballads.

Any child would find the Cossacks fascinating as horsemen. Does yours know the Cossack hopak, or the Don Cossack Chorus? From the hopak to the prancing steps of the ballet *Rodeo*, a love of riding can lead to an interest in the dance, whether traditional or modern, whether as spectator appreciation or as active participation.

One delightful aspect of riding is the awareness of nature it develops—for the young rider off on his own with a knapsack on his back, picnic-full now, soon to be filled with "finds" from the woods or fields, or for the smaller child on a lead-line pony close to the forest floor (and with a mother glad to stop and rest!). The lady's slipper spotted, the rattlesnake plantain pointed out not only increase the joys of riding but can lead to a deeper interest in birds, beasts, and flowers. At High Hickory, a group of Pony Pals aged five up vie with one another each year to be first to spot "British soldiers" and "pixie cups" and mosses for their terrariums; each autumn they comb their riding territory for cones and pods to work into Christmas wreaths. A sixteen-year-old still adds to the pheasant, owl, and blue jay feather collection he began at lead-line age, and his science project for senior year is based on this and his subsequent study of ornithology.

And all this ties in with our new emphasis on protection of the environment. (As one seventh-grade Pony Pal phrased it in her research paper, "Horse manure is good for the ecology!")

Obviously, your efforts to make your child well-rounded will be influenced by your own areas of liking and knowledge. The uncle of one keen Pony Pal, Stephen, longed to interest him in philately, *his* hobby. Stephen, never out of his jodhpurs, couldn't have cared less about those old stamps—until his uncle had the idea of showing him some that pictured Lippizan stallions from Austria and harness racers from New Zealand. Now Stephen is collecting stamps himself—from Stubbs's *Mares and Foals* on a British stamp to Olympic riders on an Italian one (and he is learning a bit of geography along the line).

An interest in horses may make not only geography but foreign language come alive for children. In days past the grand tour was a usual part of a well-rounded person's education. Our twelve-year-old Pony Pal's trip to Europe for the 1972 Equestrian Events of the Munich Olympics included "more edifying" visits to museums and historical sites in France and Germany, and its influence is felt by all at High Hickory long afterwards. "*Dressur*: that's dressage, second day . . . That's Mark Phillips on Great Ovation coming in. The clock shows the exact second. *Richter*'s German for judge, and they posted each judge's score by his initial. They gave announcements in French, too," says Robin, going through her Munich photographs with the rest of us stay-at-homes, who had followed

252

A young collector of all things Lipizzan—stamps, statues, books, and paintings—is thrilled by the real thing: Robin, eleven, on the Lipizzan stallion Conversano-Almarina with Mlle Paster at Boston Garden.

During the 1972 Olympic Three-Day Robin photographed two competitors passing under the announcers' stand in the dressage arena in Riem (Germany). Horsemen or not, most Americans know Mark Phillips, shown here coming in on Great Ovation.

the Olympic Games on television. "Well, the word *dressage* itself is French," says Meg; "so many riding terms are, maybe I'd better keep on with it next year—."

Most Pony Pals seem to love to draw ponies (frequently in school when they should be doing other things). Encourage your young riders at home with sketch pad and pencil, canvas and acrylics, old brown wrapping paper and wax crayons or magic markers. When it's too wet or too hot or too icy to ride, suggest that they capture some aspect of riding fun in a craft medium—clay, papier-mâché, mosaics—as well as on paper.

The horse-centered child enjoys looking at pictures of horses; and this is a way of introducing him to the enjoyment of art. I don't just mean that you should put up reproductions of specifically "horse artists" like the masterly Stubbs, or Munnings, or Chao Meng-Fun ("the Munnings of the Yan

dynasty," who was an official at the court of Kubla Khan). Dürer, Daumier, El Greco, Velasquez all painted horses, too. You'll find polo games in Persian miniatures, war horses in the Bayeux Tapestry—two hundred of them in all sorts of situations, being transported by boat across the Channel, and taking part in the Battle of Hastings. Seurat's *Circus Horse*, Gauguin's drinking *Cheval Blanc*, Cracow's *Polish Lancers* all seize the horse in different roles and poses. Today's young Pony Club members could easily specialize in hunting scenes alone: Vernet's *Lion Hunt*, the elder Cranach's *Deer Hunt of Prince Frederick the Wise*, Uccello's *Hunt in the Forest*, Catlin's *Indians' Buffalo Hunt*—fox-hunting paintings and prints quite aside!

Perhaps your young pony-riders can see such works first hand. But if you take them to a museum, a word of advice: don't make their first visit an all-day affair. Pop in for a quick look at one or two

**Two Pony Pals in mufti spend a lazy summer afternoon sketching their favorite subject while Stardust and Galaxy mow the lawn.**

254

**Eric, written up in Seventeen and Yankee magazines at fourteen as an artist/athlete, combines his interest in ponies in both the enamels and the stories he has sold.**

specific "horse paintings," note some other (nonhorsey) works in passing, and then leave—go home for a gallop! Better for the Museum of Fine Arts in Boston to be remembered as the place where an Indian on his *horse* makes his "Appeal to the Great Spirit" than as a place of endless corridors. . . . .

But exposure to works of art doesn't necessarily mean a trip to a museum. Your own bookshelves or the public library probably include a wide variety of books with reproductions. ("I just leave my art books open on a table or counter," a Pony Pal mother told me, "though frankly the bathroom's the best place. When Elizabeth and Joyce have studied Rosa Bonheur's *Horse Fair* they'll flip through other pages of the book . . . even end up reading it.") The covers of your *Chronicle of the Horse* provide an opportunity to see and keep pictures of every period, many privately owned and otherwise unavailable to us. And then there is the daily mail—an unexpected source of art for the horseman. In the past month alone, from national weeklies, brochures about book-club offers, prepublication book announcements, and publishers' discount listings I have torn out a picture of a recently excavated Greek panel showing a Warrior on a Black Horse; full-color reproductions of Rembrandt's young horseman, studies of horses by Henry Moore and Leonardo, sketches of jockeys by Degas and Toulouse-Lautrec, and Franz Marc's expressionistic red and blue horses; and photographs of horse bits and

cheeks, horse brasses, whip handles in the form of prancing horses, and other pieces of unusual equipment. From the paleolithic cave paintings of Lascaux to horses by Chagall, Picasso, and Masson, these reproductions come unasked, part of a "sales pitch," valuable for their very expendability. They can be torn out, tacked up, pasted into a scrapbook, made into a collage, handled, passed on, discussed —and appreciated—for nothing. With young people, the lack of restrictions, the absence of "Don't touch," is of tremendous importance. Better the smudged reproduction, the battered book—and the well-rounded rider!

The same sources—museum, library, mail—that acquaint Pony Pals with paintings also provide examples of the horse in sculpture. Many children collect reproductions of photographs of statues— ranging from the T'ang Dynasty *Falconer on Horseback* to the frieze of the Parthenon to Mario Marini's *Horse and Rider*. They soon collect actual horse statuettes.

In sculpture and in painting, most children want their horses to be realistic. They will prefer Delacroix's *Horses Coming out of the Sea* to De Chirico's *Classical Horses*, which are also on the beach. It is the younger children—less inhibited in their own art work, and often more successful in capturing the movement of ponies—who can appreciate a less photographic treatment. For instance, an older Pony Pal will complain that the horse in Degas's

*Horse Clearing an Obstacle* doesn't have any ears or mane. A younger one will say: "It feels right."

And what about reading? There's such a wealth of material here that the whole next chapter is devoted to this subject. My point at the moment is that concentrated reading of horse books is likely to lead of itself to love of books in general: therefore don't worry if the child initially reads "only anything to do with horses." "If Hilda's not on a horse, she has her nose in a book about one," a mother told me. "But I don't complain. Her second-grade teacher thought she'd never learn to read. Then she discovered the C. W. Anderson books, then the Patsey Gray, then she got hold of *The Three Musketeers*—that starts off with a yellow horse, it seems. Now she's an omniverous reader. She's even doing book reports for the paper."

"*O what a day for riding, /For riding on a horse/ . . . . ./On a horse, of course!*" The eight-year-old chanting these lines from *Me and My Bike* as she trots off on her pony would pay little heed to *Under Milk Wood*. To her Dylan Thomas means several evenings happily and noisily spent tape-recording a family dramatization of the poet's hilarious and horsey play. When Robert Frost's poetry is read in school, the pony-rider who already knows "Whose foal is this" will tackle his other poems with more enjoyment and a sense of rapport. "The Centaur" may be the only May Swenson poem a young rider reads over and over just now:

My hair flopped to the side
like the mane of a horse in the wind.

My forelock swung in my eyes,
my neck arched and I snorted.
I shied and skittered and reared,

stopped and raised my knees,
pawed at the ground and quivered.
My teeth bared as we wheeled

and swished through the dust again.
I was the horse and the rider,
and the leather I slapped to his rump

spanked my own behind.

But the carry-over and exposure will be there; and future mature enjoyment of poetry and prose is more likely to enrich later years because of such happy, simple, horsey introduction.

Thus in art, music, reading—in history, too—in all possible directions use your child's monomania as a catalyst. Use his total involvement to generate new areas of excitement and discovery: new satisfactions, all extending from his passion for ponies.

**A passion for ponies? or for poetry? Either, neither, or both, you may recognize the feelings captured in this sketch, titled "Centaur" and done at age twelve by a well-rounded rider.**

# 21
# READING AND RIDING

Whether or not you have a pony of your own, you can make excursions into the world of horses and ponies through the pages of Books.

Of course some books subject-indexed under "horses" are merely stories that happen to have a "horsey" background. *Buckaroo, The Thirteenth Stone, The Intruder* are examples. So are a good many stories set in the past, for instance *Red Raskall.*

In some books of this class, especially ones with a "teenage romance," though the plot is laid against a backdrop of stables, the author could just as well have put the same people in the same situations, but dressed in tennis whites at the country club or on racing skiis at the halfway lodge. Reading *Crimson Ghost,* you suspect that Phyllis Whitney is a competent writer who simply thought that something to do with horses would provide timely material for a new book; it is a good mystery but doesn't carry conviction atmospherically. Even with some writers who concentrate on horses, you sense a foundation of book-reading rather than direct experience. "The scenes of Arabia in *The Black Stallion Returns* are like, well, like the result of the research we do for a school theme," a Pony Pal complained. "It's not like being really there in Australia in *Kilgour's Mare.*"

By contrast there are the really horsey books. In these the horse or pony is vital to the plot, not incidental, and the author doesn't have to go looking up technical information and local color. The world in which his characters move clearly exists outside the book; it is his world and he knows it by heart and firsthand. *Five Proud Riders, Fortune's Foal, Hobby*

*Horse Hill* are examples, as are Vian Smith's books: reading *Come Down the Mountain*, you can reach out and grab a handful of heather, or shiver in the predawn of a West Country morning climbing the hill to lead an old horse; in *The Lord Mayor's Show* you can rate the steeplechaser over a course. You know that Vian Smith has tossed hay, has rubbed down a sweaty back, has seen the Look of Eagles: his books make you smell the hay, wisp the flank, see the Look. With all such writers you "wish there was more."

## HOOVES ACROSS THE OCEAN

"Horsey" stories are set all over the world. *Bright Spurs* and *Outcast, Stallion of Hawaii* take place in Hawaii, as does *Pam's Paradise Ranch. High Hurdles* is set in Pennsylvania and New York, *Justin Morgan Had a Horse* in Vermont. *El Blanco* takes place in Mexico, *Gaudenzia, Pride of the Palio* in Italy, *Miss Pennyfeather and the Pooka* in Ireland, *Jumper* in Siberia. France, Canada, Arabia, India are not neglected. Most books, however, are set either in the American West (can one imagine a Western without a horse or a pony?) or in England, where children on ponies roam "the green hills and the heather where the tawny crested plover cries."

England is still the richest source of good books on riding and riders. This is partly because horses have continued to be a "way of life" there and partly because for those who seek this way England has long provided employment (girl grooms or "lads" long before such employment was "acceptable" in the United States) and training. (*The* place to go for a thorough foundation in all things equestrian has always been England, with its many centers offering courses leading to a B.H.S.I.—British Horse Society Instructor's—or A.I.—Assistant Instructor's—certificate. Only today are similar courses beginning to be offered at riding centers here. There is one American story about this kind of riding-center training, Don Stanford's *Horsemasters*, but it is still based on the British course and set in England.)

English children have long appreciated horses and been familiar with them. For them the horse is a horse, not a status symbol. Stories like *National Velvet*, *Moorland Mousie*, and *Five Proud Riders* illustrate this. The children put their mounts first. When Velvet enters the Pie in the Grand National it isn't for the prize or for her own glory. "It was the horse she was thinking of. Putting the horse in history, she called it." Velvet can "make a decision for her horse's good and throw away her own honours."

English stories take for granted a close knowledge of horses and stable management on the part of their readers. Jargon is seldom explained, yet does not cause confusion.

Today there are more and more knowledgeable American children who like this. They want stories to be solid and technically sound. There is a new enthusiasm for horsemanship—training, hunting, hacking, showing, jumping—as opposed to rough-riding and ranching. It is this trend that gives us the truly horsey American book—not the animal-story book such as *Tomahawk*, *The Pinto Pony*, and other, often Western, tales. The Goose Bar Ranch in *My Friend Flicka*, *Thunderhead*, and *Green Grass of Wyoming* is in the West, but the McLaughlins (stars of the trilogy) are Easterners and raise not cow ponies but Thoroughbreds for polo, hunting, and racing.

The change in actual schooling methods from "horse-breaking" to the sort of training advocated in *You and Your Pony* is reflected in fiction. Dorothy Lyons' books *Golden Sovereign*, *Silver Birch*, *Midnight Moon* illustrate the principle of training with kindness and patience from the day a foal is dropped.

With the rising level of riding ability (and of course of general sophistication) youngsters are impatient with "cute" books like Martin Gale's *One Winter* and *One Summer* and Walter Farley's early

**Unlike early storybook heroines, today's young rider is used to working without reins or stirrups—on the flat or over jumps.**

Black Stallion books, deeming them sadly amateurish and empty. (How anticlimactic the climax, the "last unbelievable feat, jumping without reins!" of *High Stepper*, written in the early 1930s, seems to the child of the 1970s, who routinely works without reins or stirrups under today's more advanced instruction! Young riders today like not only Dorothy Lyons but all the books by Lavinia R. Davis, Mary O'Hara, Janet Randall, and Patsy Gray.

## "BRING OUT MY HORSE, JAMES."

Like so much else that is admirable in "horsey" books, the trend away from the portrayal of riding as something luxurious is largely due to English influence. If you long for a horse it's much more satisfying when storybook people have to consider finances, as they do in *Stable for Jill* and *Ponies for Hire*. *Fortune's Foal*, one of the best of the earlier English stories, does have a heroine who hands her horse over to a groom after a ride, but the story is so technically good, so charmingly told, and the "Bring out my horse, James" slant so played down that this does not detract from the book as a whole. More recently, Diana Pullein-Thompson's *Three Ponies and Shannon* features a "groom-ridden" rich girl, but sympathetically, and not as a "prize prig."

You identify with Jill and Andy in *Five Proud Riders* more easily because their mother can't afford to let them ride in style; if they want to keep Fly and Jester, they've got to look after them. Major Brownlow, whose son hasn't that problem, agrees: "Of course it's worth it. They know twice as much about horses as Nigel does." In *Fly-by-Night* there is a moving scene in which a tack shop owner humiliates a girl whose meager savings won't cover the cost of the tack she chooses. *The Wednesday Pony* gets its title from the fact that the pony pulls a bakery cart, so that it is only on Wednesday that the children can ride him. If you've run errands and saved for a once-a-week ride, you feel an instant kinship with those children.

English stories are about children who not only ride but also care for their horses—tack up, groom, muck out, "cope." However exciting, they are probable—not impossible fantasies about nonriders who tame wild stallions. So are the better American books.

Of course a certain amount of fantasy is welcomed

**Children who not only ride but care for their ponies don't have to employ Tom Sawyer tactics to get help with pony chores. Robin and Pony Pal Jane consider grooming Stardust not work, but fun.**

by children. In *Norah's Ark*, Norah rescues a horse from a raging flood, repairs his wounds with an ordinary needle, takes good care of him, and eventually has him given to her as her own. "This happy ending would bother literary critics because they're so cynical but not me," one Pony Pal told me firmly.

But on the whole readers object to the tendency of authors to give an "ordinary" hero or heroine a horse by one stroke of luck. They like plausible explanations of how children can afford to be riding. (In *High Hurdles*, Debby's father is the groom on a wealthy estate; in *High Guy* the children can keep their horses because their father owns the riding academy; in *Bright Spurs* Gay shoes her own horse, to save money. "We use malleable horse shoes," she explains.) Young readers prefer the exceptional wealth of the owner of Fortune's Foal to the shipwreck which gives Alex his black stallion. The only criticism I've ever heard of *National Velvet* is that "Velvet shouldn't have had all those other horses willed to her too. It was enough to win the Piebald in a raffle." Most annoying to the Pony Pals is the luck of Connemara McGuire in the Silver Birch books: to get one horse by luck is okay, but for such extraordinary chance to bless her through three books is hard to take.

While many stories contrive to get around the financial problems of a child's acquiring a horse, even "realistic" ones don't fully suggest the work involved for a teenage rider in combining school and horses. "I don't know of any book that gives a true account of getting up before school every single day, lugging water, carrying hay, picking up stalls and paddocks, and grooming, cleaning tack and boots, let alone doing blankets—on top of emptying wastebaskets and the dishwasher and making your bed *and* your high school homework schedule," Robin points out. "Most authors just get around this by having the action take place during summer, or vacations."

Even fewer deal satisfactorily with what happens when it is time for a young rider to go on to higher education. How do you both go to college and keep your horse? (Of course young skaters, tennis players, ballerinas, musicans also face a problem; but they do not have animal care added to their program as does the horseman.) In *A Horse Called Bonnie*, Julie Jefferson gives up college to train and race her horse—but not all riders want riding *as a career* (and not all parents would choose that career

for their children). *Olympic Horseman*, by John Richard Young, is one of the few books in which the rider plans to enroll in college and the need for a good academic education is stressed. (Though the motivation is rather special: "The language of equitation is French, as the language of business is English or Spanish," the General tells Don with a steely glint in his eye; "learning French will be good discipline for you—".) But even here the true conflict of scholastic demands and riding is evaded, for the main action of the story takes place during the summer and Don becomes an Olympic horseman before the opening of term. *College on Horseback* is more realistic in several respects. Holly Daggett is a college freshman, and her involvement with horses is that of the one-of-the-millions who want to work with horses, not that of the one-in-a-million who makes the U.S. Olympic Team. I know only too well how realistic Esther Greenacre Hall's book is. When I was in college my mare Maureen was like Holly's Napoleon: "undeniably a luxury she simply couldn't afford. He'd had to be shod. And she'd bought a curry comb. And he ate so many oats." Today, many colleges offer riding with credit towards a degree, so it does not have to be extracurricular only; perhaps some student will write a book about college on horseback, new style.

## GIRLS, BOYS, PARENTS, AND PONIES

Whether the characters in today's horse stories are of college age, or little children, or somewhere in between, the plot is basically the same: Girl—and it usually is a girl—girl wants horse; girl finds horse; girl makes friends with, masters, trains, wins with horse, when no one else can; and girl gets horse. But it does not matter that the same formula is used over and over again. The appeal is to the universal (seemingly universal) wish for a horse of one's own and the dream of fulfillment.

Books for younger children may have a hero or a heroine, or a mixed group sharing honors. "Juveniles" more typically have a heroine, and boys drop out here as readers just as many of them drop out as riders. For it's mainly girls who seem to ride in this age group. And the kind of riding differs. I've found that boys over twelve or thirteen want to ride for thrills and speed (and turn to cars rather than horses to get them); girls, even if they love thrills equally, place more value on horsemanship, form, and equestrian tact.

So, except for the O'Hara trilogy and possibly *Red Horse Hill* and *Olympic Horseman*, horse stories are directed at boys under eleven—and at girls regardless of age. The older boy reader is neglected. A few books like the Black Stallion series, *Mountain Pony*, and *Wild Palomino* do have heroes but these verge on the "adventure story" rather than the horsey book. Many stories, like those of Davis, have both heroes and heroines, but here again the appeal is mainly for the younger boy.

In their preponderance of heroines, horse books contradict the usual equation of boy/doctor, girl/ nurse literature, and have always been well in advance of Women's Liberation. No need to rewrite or change the pronouns to the feminine gender. In these books, girls are given something traditionally reserved for boys—are encouraged to think and act independently (even against parental advice), to enter and master a field where athletic skill and physical ability are prerequisites, to choose an unconventional career—and even to choose a horse over a boy.

The fact that it is a girl does not lessen the prowess of the main character, of course. Velvet wins the Grand National. Connemara McGuire raises and trains a prize-winning stallion and his get. Gay and her sister make huge profits on their Hawaiian dude ranch.

But the heroine does not lose her femininity. She may be a horseman, and must be able to do all her own work, but she is never "horsey" in the awful riding-crop-thigh-whacking sense that all too many real girls, alas, become. Authors endow their heroines with the accepted "feminine" accomplishments. In *Dark Sunshine*, Blythe is presented as being musically gifted; Connemara cooks meals when her mother is ill; Margo (of *Scarlet Royal*) takes over the housekeeping in another family emergency.

In American books the heroine is always pretty, attractive, meeting the standards of the *Seventeen*-ager. She has a boy friend hovering, if not in the foreground, in the background. (In *Red Embers*, Phil Blake not only earns a place on the country's leading women's polo team but has twin boys friends.) She is always a good sport, putting the horse first. Inevitably the "baddy" (quite likely another girl) is stereotyped as someone who, like Claire in *High Hurdles*, "doesn't ride for fun, it's just cups and ribbons she wants"; she may want the heroine's boy friend as well. She is a poor sport. ("Shows are fun, when you win—sometimes, though, the judges aren't fair.") Her attitudes contrast with the more nobler ones of heroines like the girl in C.W. Anderson's *High Courage* ("'We won't get the cup, Bobcat,' she whispered, 'but we'll show them who's who.'") However unattractive this second girl, the antiheroine, may be morally and ethically, personally she is as pretty, well-dressed, and presentable as the heroine herself.

English writers are more realistic about their heroines. Vian Smith's are usually plain, simply dressed, possibly poor, and even fat. They don't always have boyfriends; they may not even have friends. In Pat Smythe's *Three Jays over the Border*, plump old Penny-weight's problems stem partly from her being "just another over-fat girl that people laugh at." Furthermore, these heroines sometimes have families and their characters are shown in their relations with those families as well as with horses.

Not until some of the younger Pony Pals pointed it out did I realize how rarely parents (or adults in any capacity) play a role in stories—not even the role of chauffeur-in-suburbia. This is particularly true in books where a could-take-place-anywhere teenage romance is laid against a horsey background. Even in some truly horsey stories parents are conveniently gone—in *A Stable for Jill*, to America to tell stories to children at summer camps (the mother) and sailing around the world (the Vicar). Perhaps one reason for the appeal of *Misty*, *Auction Pony*, *Pony in the Family* to young readers is the strong family scenes, scenes which even include grandparents.

While the more satisfying teenage books—Patsy Gray's, Dorothy Lyons'—include one parent or the other, more often than not, if present, parents are nonhorsemen. Rarely do we find horsey parents— ranchers in *Olympic Horsemen*, hunting people in *Moorland Mousie*. Perhaps the typical casting of parents as nonriders reflects a real-life situation. Many horse-crazy youngsters are unique in their families, though many, like Velvet, pray "O God, give me horses, give me horses! Let me be the best rider in England." Neither of Velvet's parents is a horseman. Her mother had been a Channel swimmer and although accepting her life of domestication ("'What's past's past,' said Mrs. Brown heavily and shut her mouth and her door") she could support Velvet's dream of glory for the Pie and her dedication to the hard work involved. But in most horse stories the dream is the heroine's only.

## FOR OLDER READERS

Once beyond the picture-book level, many young readers, while devouring every title aimed at their own age group, will also take up books designed for older groups and read them selectively for whatever they have about horses, screening out the "romance" invariably brought in from teenage onward. They may even seek out those books which can be read on one level as young people's horse stories and on another as adult fiction. (Because of the lack of good solid horse stories realistically slanted to boys over twelve, many boys, especially, make this jump.)

Horse books as such for adults (or for the youngster reading beyond the juvenile shelves) are few and far between. What few there are are good, whether one thinks of the odd exception like *Brat Farrar*, the one horsey story in all Josephine Tey's remarkable output, or of the long list of Dick Francis's thrillers. Novels by Marguerite Bayliss, Joyce Stranger, F. Ruth Howard, Jane McIlvaine McClary, and Vian Smith offer adults far more than the horsey worlds they recreate with such authenticity.

With children's books the author can create a dream world and expect of the reader a "willing

**A good book can make even a good little rider forget such rules as "Never tie your pony up by the bridle," but a good little pony stands still.**

suspension of disbelief." With adult books, and the best of the children's horse stories, the writer—unless he's a Tolkien—must be exploring, interpreting, sharing, reconstructing, peopling, a "real" known world. A children's book may be published simply because it's a horse story, regardless of literary merit. An adult book must meet other criteria than that of simply being horsey: plot, character development, setting, above all plausibility, so often stretched to breaking point in children's horse books. This is not to say that adult readers require a higher level of "good writing." Children unconsciously want and appreciate fine writing; their choice of books to reread again and again (and of ones to discard after a first reading) bears this out.

## A TOUCH OF FANTASY

Perhaps the most popular horse story ever written appeared in the late nineteenth century: Anna Sewall's *Black Beauty*. The *Uncle Tom's Cabin* of horse books, *Black Beauty* served its purpose (and is still a well-loved book), but the harsh treatment it attacks has pretty well disappeared, and with it the sentimental handling. Black Beauty, "uncomplaining and obedient, though often sore harassed and downhearted," tells her own story and is assigned human feelings and attitudes. "My mind was hurt quite as much as my poor sides," she tells us; "To be punished and abused when I was doing my very best was so bad it took the heart out of me."

Later, though the humanitarian impulse remained, the approach became more objective. In reading *Sleepy Tom*, you're just as sympathetic and indignant, but Akers lets the unembellished facts speak for themselves. Like Black Beauty, Moorland Mousie, in Golden Gorse's book by that name, tells her own tale, but without self-pity and more realistically. Moorland Mousie is always Mousie the horse, whereas Black Beauty is often Anna Sewall the woman. *Jumper* tells a similar story almost starkly but with no loss of emotional force.

*Black Beauty* was the first of a long line of books in which the horse or pony rather than the rider is the hero. *Greylight, Hamish, Misty of Chincoteague, Harum Scarum, Beyond Rope and Fence*, and many of the stallion books, belong to this anthropomorphizing category.

Related to them—though often of incomparably greater literary value—are those books which you'd

**Pony Pals agree with what the White Knight told Alice (in Through the Looking Glass): The great art of riding . . . is,—to keep your balance properly." " 'Plenty of practice!' " they quote " 'Plenty of practice!' "**

never think of describing as "about" horses but in which some horse stands out as a character: the White Knight's patient horse in *Alice in Wonderland*, the old Cart Horse in *The Wind in the Willows*, Feste the chestnut stallion in *The Children of Green Knowe*, young Arthur's white steed Canrith in *The Hollow Hills*, the horse who chatted with Doctor Doolittle about his need for spectacles, the talking horse in C.S. Lewis's Narnia books, the Houyhnhnms in *Gulliver's Travels*. Then there are the horses and ponies in the *The Hobbit* and *The Lord of the Ring*: "The Hobbits use ponies a lot," says Scott, who is a serious Tolkienist. "The Hobbits themselves are so small, the ponies are like chargers. Tom Bombadil gives the ponies names which they answer to—'Sharp Ears, Wise Nose, Swish Tail, and Bumpkin, Whitesocks my little lad, and old Fatty Lumpkin.' Bill the Pony was bought when he was half starved, and nursed back to health, and he was used as a pack horse on the journey to Mordor. Then there are the evil black horses and the silver white steed Shadowfax; Gandolph tamed him and he could ride him without saddle or bridle twelve hours at a stretch—"

## NEAR SIDE, OFF SIDE, FUNNY SIDE

The comical aspect of riding and riders has been seized upon by writers and caricaturists from the days when horses were more or less a part of everyone's "life style" right up to our own time, when the cleavage between the horsey and the nonhorsey is so sharp. Fanatical horse-lovers, speed maniacs tearing along in gigs, pretentious "authorities" on horsemanship, uncouth sporting squires, fraudulent horsecopers have all come in for ridicule gentle, caustic, or on occasion savage. Classic examples are the hunting Monk in *The Canterbury Tales*, the Dauphin of France in *Henry the Fifth*, Squire Western in *Tom Jones*, John Thorpe in *Northanger Abbey;* more recently we have the brief but hilarious account of the reluctant rider in Nancy Mitford's *Christmas Pudding*, the hunting episode in *Auntie Mame*, the whole of Dylan Thomas's *Me and My Bike*.

Sporting literature, like sporting prints, spared no one, least of all the riding gentry and the would-be riding gentleman, the best-known examples of the latter being Mr. Nathaniel Winkle in the *Pickwick Papers* and Surtees' Cockney grocer Mr. John Jorrocks, who is still widely quoted ("no foot, no 'oss," etc.) in *Handley Cross, Jorrocks' Jaunts and Jollities, Hillingdon Hall.*

Surtees was an ardent horseman; so were Somerville and Ross (two Victorian ladies), the authors of *Some Adventures of an Irish R.M.* and *Further Adventures*; and indeed the most enjoyable treatment of the foibles and follies of the horsey set has always come from shrewd observers *within* that set.

Today, John Tickner may be cited as an authority on horsemanship who is also a satirist; he combines jocular commentary and advice with cartoons, the text far outweighing the drawings, and many riders in England and America alike derive amusement from *Tickner's Show Piece*, *Tickner's Hunting Field*, and other books in his long series.

But the great contemporary humorist is Thelwell. He is without rival. His popularity, immense in England, has spread throughout the Western world until today *Thelwell* and *pony* are synonymous. Unlike Tickner, he is a draftsman of genuine distinction who delights nonriders as much as readers who have first-hand experience of the kind of life he depicts.

Thelwell pokes fun at equine and equestrian, usually pint-sized pony and pint-sized rider, with bland simplicity. Fearless pigtailed equestriennes—Fiona, Penelope, and the rest—constantly pit their skill against roly-poly ponies whose devilish eyes peek out from under bushy forelocks. Full manes and tails, well-shaped hooves and short sturdy legs, rotund bodies, all brought alive with a few telling strokes, explode into action. The moments of frustration, anger, fear, anticipa-

**A Thelwell pair.**

tion, ruthless determination, and triumph or defeat that every pony owner and pony owner's family—and pony—experience are caught in these spoofs; and tens of thousands of readers of all ages double up with a joyful and mirthful feeling of identity. Thelwell's puppy-like ponies appeal even to people who don't like horses, and even people who don't like children give a grudging, laughing admiration to his tiny riders—spunky, bratty, brashly exuberant—whose heads may be bloody but are certainly unbowed. For people who *do* like ponies, the laughter is tickle-full of conscious kinship. Each sketch brings the merry realization that "There but for the grace of God go I"—or, more often, "There *went* I also."

## PONIES AND PICTURES

Illustration of horse books is a specialized field—understandably, since the illustrator needs to have a genuine knowledge of live horses, not just of horse anatomy, in addition to artistic ability. Of course it is mostly books for younger readers that have pictures. (Teenagers lament the lack of illustration in their books, and will sometimes buy a book for the sake of the pony on the dust jacket.) But these younger readers are demanding. While they will accept fantasy in the text of horse stories, they insist on literal correctness in the drawings; they'd rather visualize for themselves the pinto pony they're

reading about than see him delineated with faulty conformation or impossible action.

Some artists are also authors, and their stories seem to have been written to accompany the picture rather than the reverse: C. W. Anderson with the *Billy and Blaze* series, *High Courage*, *Salute*; Paul Brown with *Piper's Pony* and *High Guy, the Cinderella Horse*; Wesley Dennis with *Flip*. Such books usually seem to follow the establishment of the artist as a "horsey illustrator"; the "illustrated and written by" Sam Savitt books, such as *Vicki and the Black Horse*, come within this class.

The Pony Pals are unanimous as to the first three when they rattle off their list of favorite "artists." Sam Savitt is number one, then Paul Brown (in my day he ranked first), then C. W. Anderson. Then the others: Wesley Dennis, Robert Lougheed, Anne Bullen, Jean Bowman, Lionel Edwards, Pers Crowell, Peter Biegel, Michael Lyme, Paul Durand, Henry Bishop, Susan Jeffers, Lynd Ward, Adrienne Adam, Heather St. Clare Davis, Laurian Jones—

Of course no list of horse stories in a book such as this can be up to date. Some of the favorites given here may be out of print. But you may enjoy searching for them in your library and in second-hand bookstores. You will certainly find some new titles. And—try writing a story of your own! We have found these three R's, Riding, Reading, and 'Riting, great fun in our world of ponies at High Hickory.

# APPENDIX

## FAVORITE TITLES FOR YOUNG READERS AND RIDERS

### SPECIFICALLY PONY:

• C. W. Anderson, the *Billy and Blaze* series. Lonzo Anderson, *Ponies of Mykillengi*.
• N. L. Banning, *Pit Pony*. J. M. Berrisford, *Pony in the Family*. Blair, *The Easter Pony*. Paul Brown, *High Guy, Piper's Pony, Pony Farm, Pony School*, and others.
• J. Cannan, *Hamish*. Chandler, the *Cowboy Sam* books. D. Clewes, *The Old Pony*. Primrose Cummings, *Mystery Pony, The Wednesday Pony*.
• Maureen Daly, *The Ginger Horse*. Lavinia R. Davis, *Pony Jungle*, etc. Derman, *Pony Ring*. J. S. Doty, *Summer Pony*.
• Walter Farley, *Little Black; A Pony*. R. Ferguson, *A Pony for Jill* and others in the series. Frances Frost, *Windy Foot, Windy Foot at the Country Fair, Fireworks for Windy Foot, Maple Syrup for Windy Foot, Sleigh Bells for Windy Foot*.
• Gottlieb, *Pony for Tony*. A. B. Greene, *Greylight*. V. Griffiths, *A Ride for Jenny*.
• Marguerite Henry, *Little Fellow, Misty of Chincoteague, Sea Star, Orphan of Chincoteague, Stormy, Misty's Foal*.
• M. S. Johnson, *Kelpie, a Shetland Pony*.
• Helen Kay, *A Pony for the Winter*. Kingman, *Peter's Pony*.
• Lansing, *A Pony Worth His Salt, The Pony That Kept a Secret*. Henry Larom, *Mountain Pony*.
• M. MacPherson, *Ponies for Hire*. McCully, *The Christmas Pony*. Miska Miles, *Pony in the Schoolhouse*.
• C. N. Parkinson, *Ponies Plot*. K. M. Peyton, *Fly-by-Night*.
• J. Randall, *Pony Girl, Saddles for Breakfast*.
• Linell Smith, *The Auction Pony*. Ann Stafford, *Five Proud Riders*. John Steinbeck, *The Red Pony*.
• Norman Thelwell, *Angels on Horseback, A Leg at Each Corner, Penelope, Riding Academy, Thelwell Country*.
• Walters, *Ponies for a King*. Suzanne Wilding, *Dream Pony for Robin*. Wing, *Pony Twins*.

### BOOKS YOU HATE TO FINISH—THAT SEND YOU SEARCHING FOR MORE FROM THE SAME AUTHOR:

• Enid Bagnold, *National Velvet*. Dorothy Benedict, *Bandoleer, Fabulous, Pagan the Black*.
• Betty Cavanna, *Spurs for Suzanna*.
• Elizabeth H. Friermood, *Circus Sequins*.
• Patsy Gray, *Challenger, Horse Trap, Jumping Jack, Norah's Ark, Star the Sea Horse, Star Lost, Star Bright, Show Ring Rogue*.
• Marguerite Henry, *Album of Horses, Black Gold, Dear Readers and Riders, Five O'Clock Charlie, Gaudenzia, Pride of the Palio, Justin Morgan Had a Horse, King of the Wind, Marguerite Henry's Horses, San Domingo, the Medicine Hat Stallion*.
• Bonnie Highsmith, *Kodi's Mare*.
• Pat Johnson and B. Van Tuyl, *A Horse Called Bonnie, A Sweet Running Filly*.
• Dorothy Lyons, *Blue Smoke, Golden Sovereign, Midnight Moon, Shamrock Stables, Silver Birch*.
• Marjorie Reynolds, *Dark Horse Barnaby, Keep a Silver Dollar, Ride the Wild Storm, Sire Unknown*.
• Margaret Cabell Self, *Sky Rocket*. Vian Smith, *Come Down the Mountain, The Lord Mayor's Show, Martin Rides the Moor, The Minstrel Boy, Pride of the Moor, Tall and Proud*.
• Newlin Wildes, *The Horse That Had Everything*. Suzanne Wilding, *Big Jump for Robin, Harlequin Horse*.

### LIPIZZAN STORIES:

• Bowen, *The Emperor's White Horses*.
• Marguerite Henry, *White Stallion of Lipizza*.
• Richard, *Snow King, the Lippizan White Horse*.
• Felix Salten, *Florian*.

### BOOKS ABOUT STALLIONS (*see also* Lipizzans, Westerns):

• Walter Farley, the *Black Stallion* series. Forester, *The Mountain Stallion*.
• D. Grew, *Sorrel Stallion*. H. Griffiths, *Stallion of the Sands*.

• S. Holt, *Phantom Roan, Prairie Colt, Stormy, The Whistling Stallion, Wild Palomino.*
• Les Savage, Jr., *The Phantom Stallion.* Lytle Shannon, *Golden Stallion.*
• Thompson, *Outcast, Stallion of Hawaii, Star Roan.*

## WESTERN THEME:

• Glenn Balch, *Christmas Horse, Keeping Horse, Midnight Colt, Spotted Horse.* Bowen, *Appaloosa Curse.*
• Franklin, *Pioneer Horse, Wild Horse of the Rio Grande.*
• Zane Gray: most of his books. D. Grew, *Buckskin Colt.*
• Marguerite Henry, *Mustang, Wild Spirit of the West.* T. Hinkle, *Black Storm.*
• Will James, *Sand, Scorpion, Smokey.* McGiffin, *The Domino Horse.*
• Gerald Rafftery, *Twenty Dollar Horse.* Glenn Rounds, *Blind Colt.*
• Scharmach, *White Thunder.* Eugenia Stone, *Sagebrush Filly.*
• Thomson, *Spook the Mustang.*

## OTHERS:

• Arundel, *White Cap's Song.*
• Gillian Baxter, *Horses and Heather.* Bendick, *Horse Named Summer.* Bronson, *Pinto's Journey.*
• Arthur Catherwell, *Last Horse on the Sands.* Margaret Clark, *Mystery Horse.* Coburn, *Stirrup High.* Comens, *The Jade Filly.* Olive Cooke, *Serilda's Star.* William Corbin, *The Golden Mare, Horse in the House.*
• Monica Dickens, *Cobbler's Dream.* Dillon, *Island of Horses.*
• Eames, *The Good Luck Colt.* Anne Emery, *Scarlett Royal.* Phoebe Erickson, *Black Penny.*
• H. Griffiths, *Wild Horse in the Clouds.*
• Herald, *Sabre, The Horse from the Sea.* Florence

Hightower, *Dark Horse of Woodfield.* Hoffman, *Summer at Horseshoe Ranch.* Hudnut, *A Horse of Her Own.*
• Keeping, *Shawn and the Cart Horse.*
• Norma C. Klose, *Benny. The Biography of a Horse.*
• Lang, *Strawberry Roan.* T. Lea, *The Hands of Cantii.* Leitch, *Last Summer to Ride.*
• Marcus, *Young Rider of the High Country.* McMasters, *The Gallant Heart.* Stephen Meader, *Cedar's Bay, Red Horse Hill.* Shirley Murphy, *White Ghost Summer.*
• Noble, *Nelly Bly.* Nuller, *The Golden Spur.*
• Ormsley, *The Right Hand Horse.*
• B. C. Perrin, *Born to Race.* Pomeroy, *The Mallory Barn.*
• Carl Raswan, *Drinkers of the Wind.* Pamela Reynolds, *Horse Shoe Hill.* Richard, *Double M for Morgans.* Riley, *Mystery Horse.* David Rook, *Run Wild, Run Free (The White Colt).*
• Linell Smith, *And Miles to Go.* Pat Smythe, *Flannigan, My Friend.* Don Stanford, *The Horsemasters.* Sykes, *The Stubborn Mare.*
• Judy Van der Veer, *Gray Mare's Colt, Hold the Reins Free.*
• Phyllis Whitney, *The Mystery of the Crimson Ghost.*
• J. R. Young, *Olympic Horseman.*

## FOR OLDER READERS:

• Marguerite Bayliss, *The Bolinvars, Earth Eagles.*
• Dick Francis, *Blood Sport, Flying Finish, For Kicks, Nerve, Odds Against, Rat Race, Smokescreen.*
• F. Ruth Howard, *Green Entry, View from a Window.*
• Jane McIlvaine McClary, *A Portion for Foxes*
• Mary O'Hara, *My Friend Flicka, Thunderhead, Green Grass of Wyoming.*
• Vian Smith, *Horses in the Green Valley.*
• Josephine Tey, *Brat Farrar (Come And Kill Me).* Thelwell, of course! See the previous section on "specifically pony" books. John Tickner, *Tickner's Horse Encyclopedia, Tickner's Hunting Field, Tickner's Light Horse, Tickner's Ponies.*

# BIBLIOGRAPHY

## READING LIST

(Works on care and training, rather than on equitation, are stressed in this bibliography.)

Abbey, Harlan C. *Showing Your Horse*. South Brunswick and New York: A. S. Barnes; London: Thomas Yoseloff, 1970.

Andrist, Friedrich. *Mares, Foals, and Foaling. A Handbook for the Small Breeder*. Trans. Anthony Dent. London: J. Allen, 1962.

Baker, Jennifer. *A Source Book of Horses and Ponies*. London: Ward Lock, 1973.

Baranowski, Zdzislaw. *The International Horseman's Dictionary/Lexique International du Cheval/Internationales Pferde-Lexikon*. South Brunswick and New York: A. S. Barnes. [n.d.].

Boudet, Jacques. *Man and Beast*. Trans. Anne Carter. New York: Golden Press, 1964.

Chamberlin, Harry D. *Riding and Schooling Horses*. London: Hurst and Blackett [1946 ].

————. *Training Hunters, Jumpers and Hacks*. London: Hurst and Blackett, 1938, repr. 1947.

Chenevix-Trench, Charles. *A History of Horsemanship*. Garden City: Doubleday, 1970.

Delgado, Alan. *Introducing Ponies*. London: Spring Books, [n.d. ].

D'Endrödy, A. L. *Give Your Horse a Chance. The Training of Horse and Rider for Three-Day Events, Show-Jumping, and Hunting*. London: J. Allen, 1959, new ed. 1971.

Dickerson, Jan. *Make the Most of Your Horse. The Practical Application of Collection in All Types of Riding*. Garden City: Doubleday, 1970.

Disston, Harry. *Equestionnaire. Questions and Answers for Horsemen*. New York and London: Harper, 1936.

————. *Know about Horses. A Ready Reference Guide to Horses, People, and Horse Sports*. New York: Bramhill House, 1961.

Fawcett, William. *The Young Horseman*. London: Black, 1943.

Fillis, James. *Breaking and Riding*. Trans. M. R. Hayes, rev. and ed. Geoffrey Brooke. London: Hurst and Blackett, [194-? ].

Gay, Carl W. *Productive Horse Husbandry*. Philadelphia and London: Lippincott, 3rd ed. rev., 1920.

"Golden Gorse." *The Young Rider*. London: Country Life, and New York: Scribner's, 1928; 4th ed. 1952, repr. 1966.

Goldschmidt, Sidney G. *An Eye For A Horse: A Guide to Buying and Judging*. London: Country Life, rev. ed. 1944, repr. 1947.

Goodall, Daphne Machin. *Ponies*. South Brunswick and New York: A. S. Barnes, 1963.

Hayes, M. Horace. *Riding and Hunting*. (1st ed. 1901). 6th ed., rev. by Geoffrey Brooke, London: Hurst and Blackett, 1948.

————. *Veterinary Notes for Horse Owners* (1st ed. 1877). 16th rev. ed. London, Stanley Paul, 1968, repr. 1970.

Hinton, Phyllis, ed. *The Rider's Treasury*. South Brunswick and New York: A. S. Barnes, 1963, repr. 1965.

Hitchcock, F. C. *"Saddle Up." A Guide to Equitation and Stable Management, including Hints to Instructors*. London: Hurst and Blackett, 1933, rev. ed. 1948.

Hurst, Mrs. Victor. *Ponies and Riders. A Book of Instruction for Young Riders*. London: Collins, 1948.

Isenbart, Hans-Heinrich. *The Kingdom of the Horse*. Trans. Fritz A. Bauchwitz, ed. Barbara Rey. [New York ], Time-Life, 2nd corr. ed., 1970.

Jankovich, Miklós. *They Rode into Europe. The Fruitful Exchange in the Arts of Horsemanship between East and West*. Trans. Anthony Dent. New York: Scribner's, 1971.

Jackson, Noel. *Effective Horsemanship for Dressage, Three-Day Event, Jumping and Polo*. New York: Arco, 1967.

Joyce, Patrick. *Horse and Man*. London: Odhams, 1964.

Klimke, Reimer. *Cavaletti. Schooling of Horse and Rider over Ground Rails*. Trans. Daphne Machin Goodall. London: J. Allen, 1969.

Lewis, Benjamin. *Riding*. Garden City: Doubleday, 1936, repr. 1939.

Littauer, Vladimir S. *Horseman's Progress*. New York: Van Nostrand, [196? ] (Publ. in London by J. Allen as *The Development of Modern Riding*, [197? ] or later.)

———. *Riding Forward*. New York: Morrow, 1934.

Lyon, W. E. *Youth in the Saddle*. London: Collins, 1955.

Macgregor-Morris, Pamela. *Great Show Jumpers*. London: Allen and Unwin, 1950.

———. *The World's Great Show Jumpers*. Garden City: Hanover House, 1956.

McTaggart, M. F. *The Art of Riding*. New York: Bonanza Books, 1951.

Marks, Jane, *et al. The Book of the Horse*. London: Hamlyn, 1970.

Miller, William C. *Feeding Ponies*. London: J. Allen, 1968.

Morris, George H. *Hunter Seat Equitation*. Garden City: Doubleday, 1971.

Müseler, Wilhelm. *Riding Logic*. Trans. F. W. Schiller. (1st ed. 1937). London: Methuen, repr. of 3rd ed., 1971.

O'Donoghue, Mrs. Power. *Riding for Ladies. With Hints on the Stable*. Boston: Roberts, 1887.

Osborne, Walter D., and Patricia H. Johnson. *The Treasury of Horses*, New York: Ridge Press/Golden Press, 1966.

Pearce, James J. *The Horse Rampant*. London: Hale, 1947.

Pittenger, Peggy Jett. *The Back-Yard Foal*. North Hollywood: Wilshire, 1972.

———. *The Back-Yard Horse*. North Hollywood: Wilshire, 1972.

———. *The Wonderful World of Ponies*. South Brunswick and New York: A. S. Barnes; London: Thomas Yoseloff, 1969.

Podhajsky, Alois. *The Complete Training of Horse and Rider*. Trans. Eva Podhajsky and V.D.S. Williams. London: Harrap, 1971.

Ricci, A. James. *Understanding and Training Horses*. Philadelphia and New York: Lippincott, 1964.

Romaszkan, Gregor de. *Horse and Rider in Equilibrium*. Trans. M. A. Stoneridge. Brattleboro: Stephen Greene Press, 1967.

Rooney, James R. *The Lame Horse. Causes, Symptoms, and Treatment*. South Brunswick and New York: A. S. Barnes; London: Thomas Yoseloff, 1974.

St. Clair, Jane and Melinda. *Keeping a Pony*. London: Sphere Books, 1968.

Self, Margaret Cabell. *The Horseman's Almanac and Handbook*. New York: Bonanza Books, 1965.

———. *The Horseman's Encyclopedia* (1st ed. 1946). South Brunswick and New York: A. S. Barnes, 1963.

———. *Horses. Their Selection, Care, and Handling*. New York: A. S. Barnes, 1943.

———. *Teaching the Young to Ride*. (1st ed. 1935). New York: A. S. Barnes, 1946.

Seunig, Waldemar. *Horsemanship. A Complete Book on Training the Horse and Its Rider*. Trans. Leonard Mins. Garden City: 1956.

Smythe, Pat. *Show Jumping*. South Brunswick and New York: A. S. Barnes, 1968.

Smythe, R. H. *The Mind of the Horse*. Brattleboro: Stephen Greene Press, 1965.

Steinkraus, William. *Riding and Jumping*. Garden City: Doubleday, new and rev. ed. 1961, repr. 1969.

Stoneridge, M. A. *A Horse of Your Own*. Garden City: Doubleday, rev. ed., 1968.

Summerhays, R. S. *Summerhays' Encyclopaedia for Horsemen*. London and New York: Warne, 1952.

Thelwell, Norman. *Drawing Ponies*. London: Studio Vista; New York: Watson-Guptill Drawing Books, 1966.

Thomson, Bill. *Constructing Cross-Country Obstacles*. London: J. Allen, 1972.

Uzé, Marcel. *The Horse in Nature, History, and Art*. Milan: Hyperion Press, n.d. [195-? ].

Vesey-Fitzgerald, Brian, et al. *Horses Horses Horses Horses*. London: Hamlyn, 1962, repr. 1967.

Voss, Pauline, and Carol Baker. *Horses and Ponies. A Magpie Pocket Book*. London: Lutterworth Press, 1969.

Wadsworth, William P. *Riding to Hounds in America. An Introduction for Foxhunters*. Berryville [Va. ]: *The Chronicle of the Horse*, 1962, repr. 1967.

Wentworth, Lady. *British Horses and Ponies*. London: Collins, 1944, repr. 1947.

———. *Ponies Past, Present and Future*. Lewes: Baxter, n.d. (194?).

Wheatley, George. *The Pony Rider's Book*. London: J. Allen, 1969.

Widmer, Jack. *A Practical Guide for Horse Owners*. New York: Scribner's, 1957.

Willcox, Sheila. *The Event Horse*. Philadelphia and New York: Lippincott, 1973.

Williams, Dorian. *Show Jumper*. South Brunswick and New York: A. S. Barnes, 1970.

Wright, Gordon. *Learning to Ride, Hunt, and Show*. (1st ed. 1950). Garden City: Doubleday, 1966. New and rev. ed., [n.d. ].

Wynmalen, Henry. *Dressage. A Study of the Finer Points of Riding*. South Brunswick and New York: A. S. Barnes, 1952, repr. 1971.

———. *Equitation*. (1st ed. 1938). London: Country Life;

New York: Scribner's, 1949.

Xenophon. *The Art of Horsemanship.* Trans., with chapters on the Greek riding-horse and with notes, by Morris H. Morgan. lst ed. 1894. London: J. Allen, 1962, repr. 1968.

Various organizations publish material or can provide information of interest to pony owners. A few are listed below.

The American Horse Council, Inc., 1776 K Street N.W., Washington, D.C. 20006.

The American Horse Shows Association, 527 Madison Avenue, New York, N. Y. 10022.

The United States Combined Training Association, One Winthrop Square, Boston, Massachusetts 02110.

The United States Equestrian Team, Inc., Gladstone, New Jersey 07934; and, Hamilton, Massachusetts 01936.

4-H Clubs (Horse Projects): Your County Agricultural Extension Service, or, National 4-H Service Committee, 150 N. Wacker Drive, Chicago, Illinois 60606.

Pony Clubs:

America: The United States Pony Clubs, Inc., 303 South High Street, West Chester, Pennsylvania 19380.

France: Le Poney Club de France, 15 Rue Mesnil, 75116 Paris, France.

The United Kingdom: The British Horse Society Pony Club, National Equestrian Centre, Stoneleigh, Kenilworth, Warwickshire, England.

Publications from the Agricultural or Animal Husbandry Viewpoints:

State and Federal Departments of Agriculture.

State Colleges or Universities of Agriculture and Animal Husbandry. For addresses in states other than your own, write: United States Department of Agriculture, Washington, D.C., 20006.

# INDEX

**274**